Speaking Respect

Respecting Speech

RICHARD L. ABEL

Speaking Respect

Respecting Speech

The University of Chicago Press / Chicago and London

Richard L. Abel is Connell Professor of Law at the University of California, Los Angeles. He is the author or editor of nine previous books, including *Politics by Other Means: Law in the Struggle against Apartheid, 1980–1994* and *Lawyers: A Critical Reader.*

The University of Chicago Press, Chicago 60637
The University of Chicago Press, Ltd., London
© 1998 by The University of Chicago
All rights reserved. Published 1998
Printed in the United States of America
07 06 05 04 03 02 01 00 99 98   1 2 3 4 5

ISBN 0-226-00056-7 (cloth)

Library of Congress Cataloging-in-Publication Data

Abel, Richard L.
    Speaking respect, respecting speech / Richard L. Abel.
        p.   cm.
    Includes bibliographical references and index.
    ISBN 0-226-00056-7 (alk. paper)
    1. Respect. 2. Respect for persons. 3. Hate speech. 4. Speech
perception. 5. Freedom of speech. 6. Social problems. I. Title.
BJ1533.R4A34   1998
179.7—dc21   97-30778
                                                          CIP

⊗ The paper used in this publication meets the minimum requirements of the American National Standard for Information Sciences—Permanence of Paper for Printed Library Materials, ANSI Z39.48-1992.

To my father
Reuben Abel
1911–1997
"... vitam impendere vero"

CONTENTS

PREFACE

• •

This book began with an invitation to deliver the 1992 Hamlyn Lectures in England. The charge to discuss "the Comparative Jurisprudence and Ethnology of the Chief European countries" offered an irresistible opportunity to talk about almost anything. I chose to explore how the struggle for respect is waged through speech. My interest in this topic was piqued many years earlier by Joseph Gusfield's 1963 book about the American temperance movement. Once I looked through his lenses, much of social life appeared to be a contest for respect (or dignity or status). While I was working on this book, a single day's *New York Times* featured stories about Brazilian resentment of Michael Jackson for choosing a Rio favela in which to shoot his video "They Don't Care about Us," Argentine anger at Madonna's portrayal of Eva Perón, African American dismay that Richmond's White House of the Confederacy was staging a Confederate ball, Republican efforts to force those who tested HIV-positive out of the military, and ongoing controversies concerning museum exhibits on the dropping of the atomic bomb, Freud's legacy, and depictions of slave life. This book tries to assess the scope, variation, and significance of such conflicts and to evaluate possible responses.

My style is narrative, both detailed accounts of three lengthy confrontations and numerous shorter anecdotes. I adapt William Carlos Williams—no social theories but in events. To paraphrase the Yellow Pages, I let my stories do the talking (without denying my ventriloquism). This may be a Gradgrindian obsession with "facts," a residue of childhood fascination with "Ripley's Believe It or Not." In response to such self-accusations, I would reply that the accumulation of detail can document frequency and delineate variation. One of my crucial arguments is the centrality and pervasiveness of conflict over respect; I offer my stories as Duchampian ready-mades, whose juxtaposition forms a collage. I hope readers will share some of the pleasures of discovery and interpretation I experienced in collecting and organizing these instances. My compulsion to do so may reflect my principal occupation as a law teacher who uses hypotheticals both to exemplify general ideas and to show the limits of generalization. To readers who cry "Enough!" I offer another writer's response to an editor who despairingly invoked Mies van der Rohe. "I had to fight him tooth and nail in the better restaurants to maintain excess," said Stanley Elkin, "because I don't believe that less is more. I believe that *more* is more."*

I wish to thank the Hamlyn Trustees for inviting me and—with the distance of time—for censoring what I could publish, thereby helping me make a point in chapter 5. I appreciate the hospitality of Cardiff Law School, which hosted the lectures, and Phil Thomas in particular. I am grateful for comments and conversations with friends at UCLA Law School and elsewhere, especially William Forbath, Robert Goldstein, Joel Handler, Kenneth Karst, and Gerald López. The London School of Economics Law Department gave me a place to work at the beginning of this project, and the UCLA Law School Dean's Fund provided generous support at the end. At the University of Chicago Press, editor John Tryneski has been patient and encouraging and the anonymous readers have been bluntly honest but also forbearing. Joann Hoy did a superlative job of copyediting. Had I taken the advice of my wife, Emily, this book would have been better and done sooner.

New York Times Book Review 43 (9.17.95).

CHAPTER ONE

•••

Fighting Words

This book seeks to understand the centrality of the struggle for respect in contemporary political life. Once I began attending to that issue, I could no longer read a newspaper without encountering illustrations. Everywhere I looked, collectivities were contending for dignity, fighting *with* words and *against* words. The following are a few of the examples that appeared as I was finishing the book.

In September 1995 three American servicemen were charged with raping a twelve-year-old Okinawan girl. When the commander of U.S. Forces in the Pacific disparaged the men as merely stupid—they could easily have bought a prostitute instead—he was promptly forced into retirement. The American commander in Japan immediately apologized to the Okinawa governor: "This terrible tragedy was an outrageous act toward humanity and makes all of us wearing the U.S. military uniform deeply ashamed." Ambassador Walter Mondale concurred: "It is outrageous, inexcusable. We are ashamed, and we apologize." Defense Secretary William J. Perry added: "On behalf of all members of the armed forces, I want to express my deep sorrow and anger for this terrible act." He imposed a "day of reflection" on American troops in Japan and said Marines everywhere would take up a collection for the victim. More than 4,000 Okinawans demonstrated against the American military presence, and the governor blocked a lease of land to it. A local magazine headline declared: "Japan Is Still a Colony." Four months later Japanese women took a full-page advertisement in the *New York Times* declaring themselves "shocked and infuriated" at the rape, which "took place at the time of the Fourth World Conference on Women." Decrying the large number of sexual assaults by American servicemen, they denounced the United States for "infringing the sovereignty of Japan." On advice of their Japanese lawyers, the accused (and relatives who had flown in for the trial) expressed remorse, apologized to the victim and her family, and offered compensation. But the girl's father refused the second installment when he learned the accused planned to cite it in mitigation.[1]

A few days after the rape, President Clinton berated Congress for not raising the debt ceiling: "It is basically saying you're going to be a piker and welsh on your debts." A lawyer for Twm Sion Cati Welsh-American Legal Defense, Education, and Development Fund exploded: "It's outrageous that the President of the United States would use this slur in a statement he knows would be reported and would be legitimized throughout the country." The White House promptly declared: "There was never any intention to use this as an ethnic slur, and we apologize to anyone who may be offended. The President simply used this word to point out that we must not fail deliberately to meet our obligations or debts." The Welsh-American lawyer dismissed this as a "left-handed apology" (thereby insulting the left-handed). " 'I apologize for using it, but it's O.K. because this is what it means.' The President should be ashamed." (Few today still speak of "Jewing down" a price, but many are surprised when Romany object to "gypping.")[2]

After the Simpson verdict a Los Angeles high school paper used the word "n——r" (with ellipses) in a cartoon entitled "Fuhrman 4 Mayor," accompanied by an editorial condemning Los Angeles Police Department racism. The paper, staffed by Asian Americans, had won three first-place awards. Calling the slur "most offensive to all of us," the school administration offered "our strongest public apologies." But the faculty adviser insisted "the intent is to be anti-Fuhrman, anti-racist." "I'm sympathetic to anyone who takes offense seeing [it but] I don't know how you can do anything about Mark Fuhrman without using the word." The local Council of African American Parents condemned racial insensitivity in the school district, and some members demanded the adviser's dismissal. "You do not use the word n—— in 1995. Journalistic freedom aside, no one has the right to insult a race of people." The group expressed satisfaction at his resignation.[3]

Shortly before the "Million Man March," Louis Farrakhan called Jews "bloodsuckers because they took from our community and built their community. . . . And when the Jews left, the Palestinian Arabs came, Koreans came, Vietnamese and other ethnic and racial groups came." The B'nai B'rith Anti-Defamation League (ADL) took two nearly full-page advertisements in the *New York Times* to protest the event, asking rhetorically "What if a white supremacist called for a March on Washington?" Farrakhan "not only subscribes to these hatreds, he promotes them. Aggressively. Repeatedly. Unfortunately, this will be the most mainstream event led by an anti-Semite in recent American history. And that cannot be ignored." Some African Americans condemned the exclusion of women. A gay black man warned: "There are people associated with this march who are committed to our extinction." Rev. George A. Stallings Jr., founder of the African American Catholic Congregation (unrelated to the Roman Catholic Church) dismissed such criticism: "What do you want, some milquetoast sissy faggot to lead you into the promised land?" Furious at official estimates of just 400,000, Farrakhan insisted: "There never was a demonstration or gathering in the City of Washington to equal what happened yesterday. For what reason would anyone fail to give us credit but racism?" The Nation of Islam threatened "to file suit and seek evidentiary proof that more than 1 million men came to Washington."[4]

When the San Francisco Board of Supervisors decided to rename Army Street after Cesar Chavez, some local residents qualified an initiative to restore the original. One said: "A lot of white people here feel like they don't have much they can hold on to—even if it's just the name Army Street." Another asked: "What are they going to do, change street names after everyone who comes along?" (The city recently had created Mark Twain Plaza, Dashiel Hammett Street, Isadora Duncan Lane, and Jack Kerouac Street without protest.) A Latina grocer retorted that the new name "signifies that we have a place here too." Since Chavez's death two years earlier, ten streets, twenty-one schools, four libraries, six parks, three plazas, and a bridge had been named for him. Voters defeated the measure.[5]

The pervasiveness and variety of such stories were the stimulus for this book, which attempts to understand what unites these confrontations, why they have become so prominent, and how we should respond. The rape was an insult as well as a crime, implicating dignity across the divides of nationality (American-Japanese and Japanese-Okinawan), gender, and race (the accused were African American). History strongly shaped meaning: World War II (especially the bloody invasion of Okinawa), the American occupation, Japanese disarmament and dependence on the American military, and the disproportionate burden on Okinawa. Words were both the vehicle and the object of contestation: racial, ethnic, religious, sexist, and homophobic slurs. Even street names gave whites something to "hold on to" and Latinos "a place here too." Challenge compelled response; silence signified condonation. Motive was pivotal but also obscure. And lack of evil motive might not excuse; indeed, the commander's casual acceptance of prostitution and Clinton's obliviousness to the significance of "welsh" may have aggravated their affronts. Context could invert meaning, but audiences might reach diametrically opposed interpretations. The white faculty adviser and Asian American high school students maintained that quoting Fuhrman's slur furthered the cause of antiracism; African American parents resentful of local racism resented its repetition. Critics often decontextualized: the ADL denied the difference between white supremacists and black anti-Semitism. San Francisco whites denigrated Cesar Chavez Boulevard as renaming streets after "everyone who comes along," while taking for granted place names honoring whites. Public spaces were the arenas for these struggles: official statements, the media, criminal trials, the Washington Mall, street names. Although those offended acknowledged the importance of interests like "journalistic freedom," the harms of speech also provoked restraints, both self-imposed and external. Victims often sought apologies to restore their respect at the expense of their offenders. Apologies for the Okinawa rape explicitly acknowledged America's shame. But some were undermined by qualifications or protestations of good motive. Even an unconditional apology might be insufficient: rape must be punished, African American parents forced the dismissal of the school paper's faculty adviser. Yet victims might reject reparations to preserve the offender's dishonor, as the parents of the Okinawa rape victim refused compensation.

Why another book about the culture wars, political correctness, and free speech? I offer three justifications. First, I document the pervasiveness of these phenomena instead of concentrating on the usual suspects: irresponsible academics, ambitious politicians, religious zealots, and media trendies. In place of easy digs invoking the same tired atrocity stories, I propose a sociological explanation, which seeks to find the commonalities among ostensibly disparate confrontations between widely divergent adversaries on very varied terrains and to understand why identity has overshadowed other social, political, and economic fissures. Second, I have tried to transcend the often sterile debates between civil libertarians and regulatory enthusiasts. This, finally, compels me to devise a remedy that avoids the twin pitfalls of promiscuous tolerance and statist meddling.

I begin (chapter 2) by retelling three familiar stories—the feminist campaign against pornography, the response to racial hatred in Skokie and elsewhere, and Muslim reactions to *The Satanic Verses*—all as struggles for respect. Despite differences of time, place, and characters, these narratives exhibit striking parallels, often citing each other and borrowing rhetoric, sharing an intensity and refusal to compromise, forging surprising alliances and severing old bonds. Then (chapter 3) I locate the insights derived from this juxtaposition in sociological theories about honor and social standing derived from Max Weber and later applied to postwar American social movements. Armed with this analytic apparatus, chapter 4 documents the way struggles for respect suffuse the public domain: commemorations, monuments, museums, flags and anthems, place-names, stamps and coins, ancestral remains, education, arts, the media, criminal justice, and politics. The lines of division range from the ancient hostilities of religion, language, and nation through the newer movements for racial and sexual equality to the latest contests over respect based on sexual orientation and physical difference. Since speech plays a central role in constructing hierarchies of respect, I examine the two polar responses. Chapter 5 criticizes a purist civil libertarianism, which resists all forms of regulation and demands strict neutrality from the state as speaker. The next chapter argues the arbitrariness, excesses, and perversity of state regulation. I conclude with a partisan plea for equalizing respect by amplifying silenced voices and redressing speech harms through ceremonies of apology organized by the communities of civil society.

•••

CHAPTER TWO

Pornography, Racial Hatred, and Blasphemy

Although the stories of pornography, racial hatred, and blasphemy in this chapter are familiar, this retelling may uncover new facets. I use them not to test a normative theory of free speech but to reveal their social meaning. By juxtaposing narratives that differ greatly in time, place, protagonists, and subject matter, I try to reveal their common core as contests over respect, which are conducted through the medium of speech and borrow rhetoric and precedents from each other.

PORNOGRAPHY

The prosecutions of pornography launched by Anthony Comstock's New York Society for the Suppression of Vice in 1872 ended a century later with the exoneration of Henry Miller's novels and the strong civil libertarian position of the 1970 President's Commission on Obscenity and Pornography. The subsequent explosion of pornography in movies, books, and magazines and especially the new media of video, cable television, and telephone provoked a feminist backlash.[1] In the early 1970s Gloria Steinem pronounced: "A woman who has *Playboy* in the house is like a Jew who has *Mein Kampf* on the table."[2]

Diana Russell condemned pornography as male resistance to the second wave of feminism: "[A] male fantasy-solution that inspires non-fantasy acts of punishment for uppity females. . . . As women have become stronger and more assertive, some men find it easier to feel powerful with young girls, including children."[3] Judith Bat-Ada was even more emphatic:

> Sexual fascism means that men, and in particular a few powerful men, control our behavior, attitudes, fantasies, concepts of love and caring . . . there is a triumvirate—Hugh Heffner, Bob Guccione, and Larry Flynt [publishers of *Playboy, Penthouse,* and *Hustler,* respectively]— who are every bit as dangerous as Hitler, Mussolini, and Hirohito. . . . Just as the Nazis built prisons around the Jews, and the white

man put chains on the Black women and men, so pornographers have
put women into equally constricting "genital service" structures. . . .
All the special glitter that this male society produces for women—
the makeup, the high-heeled shoes, the tight little dresses—single us
out as women as effectively as did the yellow stars on the coats of
the Jews in Nazi Germany.[4]

Feminists were far from unanimous, however. Gayle Rubin protested that "the use of S/M images in the [antiporn] movie *Not a Love
Story* was on a moral par with the use of depictions of black men raping
white women, or of drooling old Jews pawing young Aryan girls, to
incite racist or anti-Semitic frenzy."[5] At the 1979 Women Against Pornography conference a lesbian separatist called Susan Brownmiller a
"cocksucker," stinging her to retort that her attacker "even dresses like
a man."[6]

These tensions climaxed in the 1982 Barnard conference "The
Scholar and the Feminist IX: Toward a Politics of Sexuality," which
examined the "link between sexual 'political correctness' and other
forms of 'political correctness' both on the Left and the Right."[7] The
Lesbian Sex Mafia held a preemptive "Speakout on Politically Incorrect
Sex," describing themselves as

self-identified "S/M" lesbian feminists who argue that the moralism
of the radical feminists stigmatizes sexual minorities such as butch/
femme couples, sadomasochists, and man/boy lovers, thereby legitimizing "vanilla sex" lesbians and at the same time encouraging a return of a narrow, conservative, "feminine" vision of ideal sexuality.

Two days before the conference began, Barnard president Ellen Futter
seized 1,500 copies of the seventy-two-page *Diary of a Conference on
Sexuality* because it used Barnard's name, but relented under threat of
legal action.[8] The following year the Rubinstein Foundation, which had
long supported Barnard conferences, withdrew its funding; the college
provided funds but controlled the conference content.[9]

The 1980s also saw a revival of the moralistic campaign against pornography. Citizens for Decency through Law (founded in 1957) and
Morality in Media (1962) were joined by new right and fundamentalist
groups: Morality in America (1984), Rev. Donald Wildmon's National
Federation for Decency, the National Consultation on Obscenity, Pornography, and Indecency (1983), and Citizens Concerned for Community Values (1982).[10]

These disparate, and superficially antagonistic, ideologies coalesced
in two legislative battles. The Alexander family long dominated the
Minneapolis pornography industry, often defended by the Minnesota

Civil Liberties Union (MCLU), to which they were significant contributors.[11] Alleging that adult bookstores lowered property values, neighborhood groups secured passage of a 1977 zoning ordinance, but the Alexanders had it declared unconstitutional in 1982. The following summer Prof. Naomi Scheman, a feminist philosopher at the University of Minnesota, discussed the problem with the neighborhood associations. Their leaders met with women city councilors, particularly zoning commission member Charlee Hoyt, a Reagan Republican who condemned pornography as segregation. When the council asked the city attorney and City Planning Department to rewrite the zoning ordinance, Scheman put them in touch with Catharine MacKinnon and Andrea Dworkin, who were coteaching a course on pornography at the University of Minnesota Law School.

Although the written word cannot convey the instructors' (very different) charisma, it does reveal their passion. Dworkin asserted that "the eroticization of murder is the essence of pornography."[12] MacKinnon added: "[I]f you understand that pornography literally means what it says, you might conclude that sexuality has become the fascism of contemporary America and we are moving into the last days of Weimar."[13] She had recently testified before the Meese Commission:

> Women in pornography are bound, battered, tortured, humiliated, and sometimes killed. For every act you see in the visual materials . . . a woman had to be tied or cut or burned or gagged or whipped or chained, hung from a meat hook or from trees by rope, urinated on or defecated on, forced to eat excrement, penetrated by eels and rats and knives and pistols, raped deep in the throat by penises, smeared with blood, mud, feces, and ejaculate.

The MCLU and ACLU were nothing but "pornographers' mouthpieces."

During the fall zoning hearings MacKinnon and Dworkin criticized the city for worrying about property values instead of women. Dworkin was characteristically blunt: "I think that you should say that you are going to permit the exploitation of live women, the sadomasochistic use of live women, the binding and torture of real women and then have the depictions of those women used in those ways sold in this city." Pornography was a "public hanging" of women and the First Amendment "an instrument of the ruling class."

MacKinnon and Dworkin drafted an innovative "civil rights" ordinance whose preamble began: "Pornography is central in creating and maintaining the civil inequality of the sexes." It prohibited the sexually explicit subordination of women through nine specified means, while tolerating erotica premised on sexual equality, as well as sex education materials. Women coerced into producing pornography could seek civil damages and suppress publication. Assault victims who could show a causal nexus with a specific publication could seek damages from its maker and disseminator, as well as an injunction. Any woman could complain about pornography as a form of sex discrimination. The Minneapolis Civil Rights Commission was responsible for investigating, issuing cease and desist orders, and seeking judicial enforcement.

Opponents included the local gay and lesbian community and the library board. Ron Edwards, president of the Minneapolis Urban League and former head of the city Human Relations Commission, saw it as "a white folks issue," which would divert energy from the struggle for racial equality. The Civil Rights Commission felt both ignored and uncomfortable with its enforcement role. MCLU executive director Matthew Stark called the ordinance a "constitutional mockery" and an "obscenity in itself."

Pressure for passage came from a number of activists (estimates varied from 50 to 200); national women's, church, and conservative organizations kept their distance, although some local chapters were involved. MacKinnon called pornography a "Skokie-type injury," and lawyer Mary Eberts said: "[P]ornography is our Skokie." Stark's retort lived up to his name: "You can't 'properly' have people in the community tell you what's acceptable to be in their community. . . . Bookstores cannot be censored. That's all there is to it." The star witness was Linda Marchiano, the "Linda Lovelace" of *Deep Throat*, who declared: "Every time someone watches 'Deep Throat' they are watching me be raped." The local paper offered a colorful account.

> With Van White [a black city councilor] and two nationally known feminists . . . presiding, the Council chambers became part tribunal, part classroom and part confessional as a succession of battered wives, girlfriends, counselors . . . rape victims, penologists, psychologists, and former prostitutes came forward. The testimony was mawkish, moving, scholarly, dull, and at times riveting. People cried and said things they have never before made public.[14]

MacKinnon banned opposing views from the hearing: "Saying a body of research is open to interpretation to which it is not open is not professional. It is not objective. It is incompetent. Andrea Dworkin and I did not waste the city council's resources with outdated and irrelevant data and investigations." One woman described her reaction to watching a documentary about pornography: "I realized that I was any one of the women in the film, at least in the eyes of those men who have abused me. I saw myself through the abuser's eyes and I felt dirty and disgusting, like a piece of meat."

The audience "reacted to unsympathetic testimony with booing and hissing, moaning and crying." Naomi Scheman later explained: "*[T]he process was expressing that theory* by saying what we need in this discussion is to hear precisely those voices that the phenomenon we are addressing has silenced." MacKinnon discredited the motives of the editor of *GLC Voice*, who opposed the ordinance: "[T]he gay male community perceives a stake in male supremacy, that is in some ways even greater than that of straight men." Councilor Barbara Carlson, an adversary, remembered:

> We were lobbied *very hard.* Charlee [Hoyt] allowed women to really *take over* city hall. You couldn't go to the bathroom without being lobbied. And we were hearing from people in California—movie stars, Rhoda, etc. We were *just hysterical* with this whole thing. And you can see why! I mean, my God, it was just *onslaught, onslaught, onslaught!* I mean literally, they were in everyone's office. A month and a half!

Although the hearings revived her own long-repressed memory of having been raped, she insisted: "[T]his ordinance is a stronger violation of me and my rights than that rape."

After the council passed the ordinance 7-6 (half the opponents were women), the liberal mayor vetoed it and appointed a task force, which reaffirmed the old method of restricting pornography geographically. Andrea Dworkin was disgusted: "This city doesn't give a damn about women." "There's only one question before the City Council: Are they helping the pornographers or helping women?" During the spring debates on an amended bill, supporters denounced opponents as traitors to women. A member of the steering committee of the [anti-]Pornography Resource Center later wrote: "Opposing the ordinance in the name of feminism makes a mockery of the word itself. Women have fought long and hard, have even died, to make the word a verb, an action, and a movement in the sphere of existence."[15] In mid-July a woman with a history of mental illness, who had testified in December, set herself on fire at Shinder's Read-More [Adult] Bookstore, leaving a letter to city officials: "Sexism has shattered my life. Because of this I have chosen to take my life and to destroy the persons who have destroyed me." She was hospitalized in critical condition as the ordinance passed by the same vote. The police arrested twenty-four women for disrupting the council meeting. The mayor vetoed it once more. During the failed override attempt some thirty women stood in the audience

crying, wailing, moaning, or singing. Dworkin blamed the defeat on
the council's Mafia links. In the succeeding backlash women who had
revealed their sexual abuse during the hearings became pariahs. *Forum,*
published by *Penthouse,* listed some of their names, provoking threatening letters and telephone calls. The Pornography Resource Center
remained open and made several hundred presentations, but across
the street the Rialto Theatre and Bookstore added nude dancing, which
the city sued to enjoin.

Indianapolis, the campaign's next site, was a very different city, with
a small feminist community and weak civil libertarians.[16] It had been
the largest Republican city in the country since 1970 and was the American Legion's national headquarters and John Birch Society's birth-
place. The ordinance sponsor was Beulah Coughenour, a conservative
Republican city councilor who had chaired the successful Stop ERA
campaign in Indiana and opposed abortion and marital rape laws.
Neighborhood groups formed in response to the sixty-eight "adult entertainment" establishments operating in the inner city by 1983. Rev.
Greg Dixon, a fundamentalist Baptist who had been fighting pornography since the 1970s, led Citizens for a Clean Community. "The river
of smut that is flowing down our cities is . . . one of the greatest indica-
tions of a totally decadent society. . . . It's indicative that we have lost
our moral moorings . . . [and become] hedonistic, humanistic, materialistic, nihilistic." Jack Lian, who established the Indianapolis branch of
Citizens for Decency through Law in 1984 as well as the Near East Side
Community Organization, condemned "the effect [pornography] has
on our children and community in general. And it is a bit addictive
because the more you see it, the more you want." *Playboy* was worse
than hard-core porn because it was so pervasive.

Steven Goldsmith had become city prosecutor through an antipornography campaign, with the support of Mayor William Hudnut. Between 1979 and 1984 Goldsmith closed six bookstores, thirty-six mas-
sage parlors, and two adult theaters and ordered forty-five obscenity
arrests (but secured only one conviction, which was appealed). The
city increased the fees for adult bookstores and limited the size of peep-
show doors, to expose masturbation. A 1984 zoning ordinance required
that porn shops be 500 feet apart and 500 feet from residences, schools,
parks, and churches.

The mayor and city council disregarded the city attorney's opinion
that the Minneapolis ordinance was unconstitutional. MacKinnon kept
a low profile, even convincing most supporters she was conservative;
Dworkin stayed out of the city. Conservatives dominated the hearings,
totally excluding feminists. Women testified about personal experi-

ences of sexual abuse related to pornography. Police officers claimed men arrested for rape and sexual abuse often possessed pornography. For the first time the prosecutor connected a recent sensational murder to pornography. Citizens for Decency through Law declared: "We've been hollering about this problem and you can see what's happened. This girl's been murdered. *What are you guys going to do about this?*" The only opposition came from the Indiana Civil Liberties Union, a former member of the Indianapolis Human Rights Commission (which would have to enforce the ordinance), the Urban League president (who saw it as a distraction from the civil rights struggle), and a former city attorney, who also was a feminist. As in Minneapolis, activists from the Baptist Temple and Citizens for Decency through Law packed the audience, booing and hissing opponents. Yet the two conservative local papers expressed doubts about the ordinance.

It passed 24-5 (all twenty-three Republicans in favor). Most proponents had not read it; some believed it was unconstitutional but succumbed to constituent pressure. A black Democratic councilman's motion to spend no more than $200,000 defending the ordinance against the inevitable constitutional challenge was defeated 19-7. The American Booksellers Association and the ACLU promptly sought a federal injunction against enforcement. The Feminist Anti-Censorship Taskforce filed an amicus brief, signed by Betty Friedan, Kate Millett, and Adrienne Rich, among other notables.[17] Amicus briefs for the ordinance were submitted by Linda Marchiano, Andrea Dworkin, the Minneapolis Neighborhood Task Force, battered women's shelters, some chapters of the National Organization for Women (NOW), and La Raza Centro Legal. Sarah Evans Barker, a Reagan appointee in her first month on the federal bench, issued a temporary injunction a week later, ultimately making it permanent and ordering the city to pay the plaintiffs' $80,000 legal costs.[18] She agreed that "pornography and sex discrimination are harmful, offensive, and inimical to and inconsistent with enlightened approaches to equality."[19] But if government could justify prohibition on that ground, it could also prohibit "racist material," "ethnic or religious slurs," or "literary depictions which are uncomplimentary or oppressive to handicapped persons."[20] The Seventh Circuit affirmed in a strongly critical opinion by Frank Easterbrook (another Reagan appointee):[21] "[S]exually explicit speech is 'pornography' or not depending on the perspective the author adopts. . . . This is thought control. It establishes an 'approved' view of women, of how they may react to sexual encounters, of how the sexes may relate to each other." He emphasized the difference between experience and representation: "the description of women's sexual domination of men in *Lysistrata* was not real dominance."[22] The Supreme Court denied the appeal.[23] The city's legal costs were about $300,000.

The campaign did not end, however. Similar bills were defeated in a Cambridge, Massachusetts, referendum and the Suffolk County legislature. The 1992 federal Pornography Victims' Compensation Bill—nicknamed "the Bundy bill" after the serial killer who claimed to have been incited by pornography—would have allowed rape victims to sue producers and distributors of obscene videos the rapist had viewed. The Senate Judiciary Committee received many letters from women urging passage as an act of contrition for the Clarence Thomas hearings and the William Kennedy Smith acquittal. It died after 230 anticensorship feminists protested.[24] A few months later the National Coalition against Pornography took a half-page newspaper advertisement showing school yearbook photographs of preadolescent girls with the headline "1 in 3 American girls will be sexually molested by age 18. Isn't it time we got rid of the instruction manual?"[25] Eleanor Smeal, former head of the National Organization for Women and now president of the Fund for the Feminist Majority, joined the antipornography campaign. Andrea Dworkin declared: "Women won't be able to get economic equality as long as we're seen as pieces of meat. Pornography determines our economic worthlessness. It is really a form of colonialization of the woman's body."[26]

RACIAL HATRED

Chicago has a long history of hate speech.[27] In 1950 Joseph Beauharnais distributed leaflets for the White Circle League, petitioning the city council and mayor "to halt the further encroachment, harassment, and invasion of white people, their property, neighborhoods and persons, by the Negro. . . . If persuasion and the need to prevent the white race from becoming mongrelized by the negro will not unite us, then the aggressions . . . rapes, robberies, knives, guns and marijuana of the negro, surely will." Illinois convicted him under its group libel law, which proscribed speech that "portrays depravity, criminality, unchastity, or lack of virtue of a class of citizens, of any race, color, creed or religion [thereby exposing them] to contempt, derision, or obloquy which is productive of breach of the peace or riots." The U.S. Supreme Court found the law constitutional.[28]

Twelve years later the Chicago branch of the American Nazi Party, led by Malcolm Lambert, handed out leaflets in front of a theater screening a Sammy Davis Jr. movie.

Niggers! You Too Can Be a Jew . . . It's Easy; It's Fun . . . Sammy-
the-Kosher-Coon Shows You How . . . In Ten Easy Lessons . . . Be
One of The Chosen People . . . Here's some of the Things You Learn:
Jewish customs and traditions such as how to force your way into
social groups . . . How to make millions cheating widows and orphans
. . . How to Hate-Hitler and get believing he killed six million of us
even though we are all over here living it up on the dumb Christians.

The Nazis attracted an angry mob of 200, some of whom threatened
to attack. Lambert was arrested when he refused to leave and convicted
of defamatory leafleting and criminal libel.[29]

In the early 1970s Frank Collin and the ten to twenty-five members
of his National Socialist Party of America (NSPA) demonstrated in
Marquette Park on Chicago's South Side, where ethnic whites and
blacks increasingly confronted each other.[30] The Chicago Park District
tried unsuccessfully to move the demonstrations elsewhere, ultimately
requiring a $250,000 liability insurance policy. The Nazis (represented
by the ACLU) challenged that requirement and simultaneously applied
to a dozen North Shore suburbs for permission to demonstrate, saturat-
ing them with tens of thousands of leaflets picturing a swastika with
hands reaching out to choke a caricatured Jew and the caption "We
Are Coming!" Many anxious residents called the B'nai B'rith ADL. A
Chicago Sun-Times article included Collin's reply:

> We want to reach the good people—get the fierce anti-Semites who
> have to live among the Jews to come out of the woodwork and stand
> up for themselves. . . . I hope they're terrified. I hope they're shocked.
> Because we're coming to get them again. I don't care if someone's
> mother or father or brother died in the gas chambers. The unfortunate
> thing is not that there were six million Jews who died. The unfortu-
> nate thing is that there were so many survivors.

Most communities ignored the NSPA request, but Skokie responded
by demanding a $350,000 bond. Collin threatened to demonstrate on
May Day 1977 to protest the requirement, carrying signs declaring
"Free Speech for the White Man." He was still unaware that about
30,000 of the 70,000 Skokie residents were Jewish and between 800 and
1,200 were Holocaust survivors. (His father, Max, originally Cohn, was
a Dachau survivor; Frank had been expelled from the American Nazi
Party when this emerged.) Skokie decided to follow ADL advice to
ignore the NSPA. Party "lieutenant" Roger Tedor, by contrast, eagerly
sought confrontation: "We had a picket in Berwyn and got into a brawl
with the JDL [Jewish Defense League]. Later, we went to the same place

on the pretext of picketing for free speech. We got a lot of publicity." Collin later offered a similar assessment.

> We faced the alternatives of either dying or coming up with something so dramatic that we could get it up in the world's headlines. In the courts I was a mouse in a maze, so this was an end-run. . . . Skokie was traumatic. We lost many members. Many older people left us because the Jews were on television and said they'd kill us. Even hard core people left us. There's a parallel to Hitler. He had many people until the *Putsch.* Then he found himself with no movement. But when we started making publicity, we gained numbers all over the country. . . .

In April 1977 more than a dozen party members in Nazi uniforms marched toward Skokie's city hall but were turned away by police enforcing an injunction. The Nazis hurried back to their party headquarters to see themselves on television and to pose in uniform for cameramen.

On May 2 the village passed ordinances requiring a $350,000 bond for demonstrations and prohibiting racial hate speech and military uniforms. The NSPA promptly challenged them, again represented by the ACLU, whose public relations director asserted that the organization "was built on a premise that those who preach changes in constitutional law are the enemy, possessed of sinister motive and intent." He and his family received insults and death threats (he was living with a Jewish woman he subsequently married). The Illinois Civil Liberties Union lost a third of its income in 1977 and the national organization 15 percent of its members (30,000 people) and $500,000 a year. A Holocaust survivor called ACLU lawyer David Goldberger "the greatest opportunist. He is scum. . . . If I were to have a choice, Frank Collin and David Goldberger, the first to go would be David Goldberger." His own rabbi denounced him. Survivors compared their established leadership—the ADL and the Jewish Federation—to the Judenräte. The JDL occupied the ACLU national office. When the U.S. Supreme Court ordered Illinois courts on June 14 to expedite the injunction litigation, the *Chicago Tribune* headline read "OK Nazi March in Skokie" and quoted the ACLU assertion that "the Village of Skokie shredded the First Amendment."

Holocaust survivors rejected the ADL policy of ignoring neo-Nazis. One had told the Skokie Board of Trustees: "We expect to show up in front of the village hall and tear these people up if necessary." Another explained: "The minute somebody comes and tries to attack my home, I have to defend myself." A third expressed an obligation to the Nazi's victims: "I cannot forget my very dramatic and tragic departure from my mother. And one thing she mentioned was that if you ever survive, *let the world know.*" Sol Goldstein, one of the most outspoken, declared: "It was not so much Skokie, but the idea what was Skokie—the first one to stand up and to tell the Nazis." Skokie city attorney Harvey Schwartz said their argument was "How dare the government sanctify this thing by permitting this to take place on public property?" They won the support of the local Presbyterian minister, who educated himself about the Holocaust. On behalf of Goldstein and other survivors, the Chicago ADL filed another suit to enjoin the Nazi demonstration on the ground of "menticide." When Collin threatened to march on July 4 without a permit, JDL leader Meir Kahane visited Skokie to plan a counterdemonstration, telling the press "[T]he streets of Skokie will run with Nazi blood. . . . I am not predicting violence—I am promising violence." Collin gloated: "I used [the First Amendment] at Skokie. I planned the reaction of the Jews. They are hysterical." Although the Nazis did not demonstrate, thirty-one JDL members marched in military formation, wearing black helmets and carrying sticks and clubs (in apparent violation of the ordinances' ban on "markings and clothing of symbolic significance" and "military-style uniform[s]").

The Illinois Appeals Court modified the original injunction, allowing the NSPA to carry placards demanding "Free Speech for White America" but forbidding the display of swastikas, which it characterized as fighting words. "No conclusion may be drawn from the record other than a planned exercise of 'basic constitutional rights in their most pristine and classic form.'"[31] Collin remained defiant: "This [swastika] is my party identification, that is my symbol, and we will not be parted from it." The Jewish Federation's Survivors' Committee and Public Affairs Committee (PAC) lobbied Illinois legislators to reenact a group defamation ordinance like the one the Supreme Court had sustained in *Beauharnais v Illinois.*

On January 1, 1978, the Illinois Supreme Court protected the NSPA's right to display swastikas, quoting famous language from *Cohen v California:* "one man's vulgarity [a jacket bearing the slogan 'Fuck the Draft'] is another man's lyric." Collin responded by threatening to demonstrate in Skokie on April 28—Hitler's birthday. The U.S. District Court invalidated all three Skokie ordinances on February 23 but stayed its decision pending appeal. On March 7 and 8 Skokie survivors and the Jewish Federation PAC separately announced massive counterdemonstrations against the NSPA. More than a hundred organizations representing blacks, Latinos, and Ukrainians, among others, promised to mobilize 50,000 people; the JDL, Jewish War Veterans, and

Coalition against Violence threatened to attack the NSPA. Governor Thompson and Senator Percy promised to participate. Jews strengthened their alliances with Christian clergy. About this time Israeli prime minister Menachem Begin visited Skokie and offered Mayor Smith a trip to Israel, where he was given the keys to Jerusalem.

On April 6 the Seventh Circuit lifted the District Court's stay of its injunction. Five days later, Collin applied to demonstrate on June 25, and the village promptly complied. The Seventh Circuit affirmed the district court; it refused to stay the injunction pending appeal, and the Supreme Court did the same on June 12 (ultimately denying certiorari).[32] Collin feared the counterdemonstration would overwhelm and attack his own. But though he denounced his followers as "cowards" and threatened to fine them $100 for not appearing, he offered to move his protest back to Marquette Park if the bond were dropped. The previous year the U.S. District Court had invalidated the Chicago Parks Department requirement of $250,000 as excessive; when Collin applied they reduced it to $60,000, which still was more than his minuscule party could afford. On June 28 the district court prohibited the Parks Department from demanding *any* bond. At the department's insistence, Collin reduced the estimated number of demonstrators from a hundred to seventy-five.

Meanwhile the U.S. Justice Department's Community Relations Service had planted press stories that Collin had agreed to march outside Skokie. On May 26 they flattered him that he had won his battle—two court victories and no new legislation. A week later they warned about violence in Skokie and proposed an alternative site in front of the Federal Plaza courthouse in downtown Chicago. (The ACLU "took an instant dislike" to the federal mediators, whom they derided as "social workers" with "no useful role in a legal dispute.") The NSPA canceled the Skokie rally on June 22 and demonstrated at Federal Plaza three days later, protected by a massive police presence. More than 6,000 counterdemonstrators jeered and threw things, drowning out Collin's shouts that "the creatures should be gassed" and routing him within fifteen minutes. His July 9 demonstration at Marquette Park also encountered a hostile audience and deteriorated into fights.

The aftermath of these events displayed several ironies. The village hired a public relations firm, which launched a "Skokie Spirit" campaign to erase its image as a stronghold of militant Jews—earning the council a charge of anti-Semitism. The NSPA informed the police that Collin was molesting and abusing young boys, leading to his arrest and imprisonment for seven years. Two polls in Skokie and one in Illinois found that substantial majorities believed the Constitution did not protect the right of Nazis to march. A survivor was more emphatic: "It's impossible to think that the people who wrote the Constitution, that they would say that a murderer has the right to come and express his opinion and to say that we are going to murder a certain segment of people." Another called Nazi speech "obscene."

Courts continue to wrestle with the regulation of hate speech.[33] In 1990 Russell and Laura Jones and their five children fled the drugs and crime of downtown St. Paul, Minnesota, to become the only African American family in a working-class neighborhood. Within two weeks their tires were slashed and a window broken. Soon thereafter they were awakened at midnight by a cross burning in their small fenced front yard. Mrs. Jones described her terror: "If you're black and you see a cross burning, you know it's a threat, and you imagine all the church bombings and lynchings and rapes that have gone before, not so long ago. A cross burning is a way of saying 'We're going to get you.'" Like many cities, St. Paul had a hate crime ordinance, passed in 1982, to which it had recently added cross burning, swastikas, and sexual bias. Arthur Miller 3d, an eighteen-year-old who lived across the street, pleaded guilty and served thirty days in jail. In the trial of Robert A. Viktora, a seventeen-year-old high school dropout, Miller testified that they and four friends were drinking that night and talking about getting into some "skinhead trouble" and "burning some niggers." Viktora appealed his conviction to the U.S. Supreme Court, supported by the MCLU, ACLU, American Jewish Congress, Association of American Publishers, the conservative Center for Individual Rights, and the Patriots Defense Foundation (Ku Klux Klan). Ten amicus briefs for the prosecution were filed by fifty-one organizations, including the National Governors' Association, the U.S. Conference of Mayors, seventeen state attorneys general, NAACP, ADL, four Asian American organizations, the liberal People for the American Way, the conservative Criminal Justice Legal Foundation, the National Lawyers Guild, the National Coalition of Black Lesbians and Gays, and Catharine MacKinnon (for the National Black Women's Health Project). During oral argument Justice Scalia dismissed as "a political judgment" the prosecution contention that speech and conduct motivated by racial bias aggravated the injury. Some people might be more offended by a provocative speech about economics "or even philosophy." Writing for four colleagues, Scalia overturned the conviction.[34] Lest there be any "mistake about our belief that burning a cross in someone's front yard is reprehensible," he advised the city it could have prosecuted the accused for terroristic threats, arson, or criminal damage to property. But this ordinance unconstitutionally prohibited speech "solely on the basis of the subjects the speech addresses." St. Paul could not "license one side of a debate to fight freestyle, while requiring the other to follow Marquis of Queensbury Rules. . . . Selectivity of this sort creates the possibility that the city is seeking to handicap the expression of particular ideas." Although the other four Justices concurred that the statute was unconstitutionally broad, they insisted that states could regulate some categories of speech defined in terms of conduct, which included "fighting words."[35] Responding to the decision, Mrs. Jones objected that her children, between two and eleven years old, were too young to deal with these injuries. "It makes me angry that they have to be aware of racism around them, that they notice it more and more." A few months later Viktora was convicted of fighting with a white policeman, after a companion had yelled "white power." Before the year's end a man was convicted of terroristic threats for burning a cross in a black family's front yard in another Minneapolis suburb.[36]

Several hundred miles away and a short time later, a group of young African Americans left a theater in Kenosha, Wisconsin, where they had just seen *Mississippi Burning.* Angered by the depiction of a Ku Klux Klansman beating an African American boy as he prayed, twenty-year-old Todd Mitchell asked his younger friends: "Do you all feel hyped up to move on some white people?" Pointing to Gregory Reddick, a fourteen-year-old across the street, Mitchell said, "You all want to fuck somebody up? There goes a white boy; go get him" and counted to three. Nine of his friends beat the boy, leaving him unconscious for four days. Although he recovered physically, his father reported: "He had a lot of black friends before they beat him. He didn't have a prejudice in him. Now he can't stand them." Mitchell was convicted of aggravated battery; invoking a 1987 statute, the judge doubled the maximum sentence of two years because Mitchell had selected his victim on the ground of "race, religion, color, disability, sexual orientation, national origin or ancestry." Approximately half the states have such statutes. A day after the U.S. Supreme Court's decision in the Viktora case, the Wisconsin Supreme Court reversed Mitchell's conviction 5-2 as a violation of the First Amendment.[37] Defense counsel noted that two of the four sentences augmented under the law had been imposed on African Americans. All forty-nine of the other states joined an amicus brief supporting Wisconsin. In oral argument Justice Scalia seemed pleased with the state's agreement that it could increase the penalty if the attacker chose a victim on the basis of a belief that the earth was flat or round. The Court's unanimous six-page opinion allowed the state to predicate sentence on motive, as evidenced by speech.[38]

BLASPHEMY

If crime and punishment always define the moral community, that function is unusually explicit in blasphemy.[39] In 1676 an English author was convicted for declaring that Jesus Christ was a bastard and whore-master and religion a cheat.[40] A century and a half later, two booksellers were punished for distributing Shelley's poems, whose "tone and spirit is that of offence and insult and ridicule."[41] But though Lord Denning asserted in his 1949 Hamlyn Lectures that "the offence of blasphemy is a dead letter" because "denial of Christianity" could no longer "shake the fabric of society," Mary Whitehouse successfully mounted a 1977 private prosecution for a poem attributing homosexual fantasies and acts to Christ and his circle. She declared: "I simply had to protect Our Lord."[42] And the House of Lords refused to repeal the law the following year because abolition would "reduce our civilization to be-coming the 'heir of nebulosity,' where just anything goes."[43] As late as 1990, the Video Appeals Committee invoked the law to prohibit dis-semination of a short video endowing St. Teresa of Avila with lesbian fantasies and sexual feelings for Christ.[44]

This was the environment in which Salman Rushdie's *Satanic Verses* appeared in September 1988.[45] Three months before publication, Viking sent the manuscript to nine Muslim, Hindu, Christian, and Jewish ref-erees. Dr. Zahid Hussain, Peterborough City Council race relations of-ficer, said they all read the book as history rather than as fiction because it used historical figures, and they feared it would cause great offense.[46] Khushwant Singh, an Indian journalist and adviser to Penguin Books India, warned it would "cause a lot of trouble," convincing the com-pany not to publish in India.[47]

In response to several incidents in which religious insults provoked killings, the British colonial government had enacted Indian Penal Code §295(A), prohibiting the use of words "with the deliberate inten-tion of wounding the religious feelings of any person." Less than two years before the publication of Rushdie's book, a short story entitled "Mohammad the Idiot" had led to communal rioting in two Indian cities and sixteen deaths.[48] Syed Shahabuddin, an ambitious Muslim MP and member of the Janata party, saw the book as an opportunity to embarrass the ruling Congress (I) party, which was losing popularity and facing a general election within a year. Shahabuddin was already

playing a leading role in opposing Hindu access to the shrine of Ayodhya in Uttar Pradesh.[49] The Finance Ministry banned the book and
was promptly condemned for "a philistine decision" by the *Hindu* and
"thought control" by the *Indian Express.*

Shahabuddin wrote triumphantly to the *Times* of India, denouncing
Rushdie as an "overrated Eurasian writer," the product of a "fatigued
culture," a "master of literary gimmicks and . . . a provider of cultural
shock," who acted "with satanic forethought." Rushdie was a spokesman for "the West, which has not yet laid the ghost of the crusades to
rest, but given it a new cultural wrapping which explains why writers
like [him] are so wanted and pampered." Shahabuddin denounced the
"Anglicised elite," the "pukka Sahibs," the "entire 'liberal' establishment . . . all set to overawe the government of India into surrendering
its sovereign right." "Call us primitive, call us fundamentalists, call us
superstitious barbarians." He summoned "patriots and nationalists" to
defend "the dignity of all our people." And, like most critics, he admitted: "I have not read [the book], nor do I intend to. I do not have to
wade through a filthy drain to know what filth is."[50]

Shortly after publication Rushdie had boasted to an Indian journalist: "There are no subjects which are off limits and that includes God,
includes prophets."[51] Now he responded in an open letter to Prime
Minister Rajiv Gandhi, invoking the support of Indian newspapers, the
Indian association of publishers and booksellers, International PEN,
the *Index on Censorship,* and "such eminent writers" as Kingsley Amis,
Harold Pinter, Stephen Spender, and Tom Stoppard.

> The section of the book in question (and let's remember that the book
> isn't actually about Islam, but about migration, metamorphosis, di-
> vided selves, love, death, London and Bombay) deals with a prophet
> who is not called Muhammad living in a highly fantasticated city—
> made of sand, it dissolves when water falls upon it—in which he is
> surrounded by fictional followers, one of whom happens to bear my
> own first name. Moreover, this entire sequence happens in a dream,
> the fictional dream of a fictional character, an Indian movie star, and
> one who is losing his mind, at that. How much further from history
> could one get?[52]

When Gandhi failed to reply, Rushdie accused him of playing com-
munalist politics.

> Perhaps you feel that by banning my fourth novel you are taking a
> long-overdue revenge for the treatment of your mother in my second;
> but can you be sure that Indira Gandhi's reputation will endure better

and longer than *Midnight's Children?* Are you certain that the cultural
history of India will deal kindly with the enemies of *The Satanic
Verses?* You own the present, Mr Gandhi; but the centuries belong to
art.[53]

(Indira Gandhi had won a libel judgment for *Midnight's Children* but
was assassinated before the revised text appeared.)[54]

After South Africa banned the book, the antiapartheid Congress of
South African Writers met with Muslim leaders for eight hours and
canceled a long-standing invitation to Rushdie to speak at the Johannesburg *Weekly Mail*'s annual book week. J. M. Coetzee—who was to
have joined Rushdie in a panel prophetically entitled "Whenever they
burn books, they will also burn people"—attacked Nadine Gordimer
for that decision, earning a standing ovation from the audience of 500.
Prof. Fatima Meer, a prominent antiapartheid activist, appeared only
to protest Rushdie's original invitation. "In the final analysis it is the
Third World that is being attacked by Rushdie, the belief in the Third
World itself and its institutions which he besmirches." Rushdie chose
"to play the role of the coloniser." But the audience booed her off the
stage when she admitted not having read the book.[55]

British Muslims were particularly outraged. "It doesn't matter if it's
fiction, a serious book, a dream," said an editor, "the point is that the
language should be *decent.* The problem is the abusive and insulting
way the Prophet is described in the most filthy language." Rushdie
was "a self-hating Indo-Anglian, totally alienated from his culture, who
has also learnt that it is possible to make money by selling self-hate."
Because his unhappy experience at Rugby had convinced him to "show
them all," he had engaged in "a continuous striptease, from soft to
hard and even harder porn."[56] Shabbir Akhtar, who entitled his book
on the controversy *Be Careful with Muhammad!* denounced Rushdie's
"calculated attempt to vilify and slander the Prophet of Islam," which
he compared to the abortive 1970s plot by Jewish extremists to blow
up al-Aqsa mosque in Jerusalem. Rushdie was a "*literary* terrorist."
Akhtar was particularly outraged by the derogatory appellation "Mahound" for the Prophet, the suggestion that the Qur'an was not divine
revelation, insulting adjectives applied to historical personalities
("bum," "scum," "black monster," "bastard"), and the assumption by
prostitutes of the names of Mohammed's twelve wives. "Muhammad
is easily the most maligned religious personality in the whole of history. But he is also, I would argue, the most influential." "Any Muslim
who fails to be offended by Rushdie's book ceases, on account of that
fact, to be a Muslim."

Any faith which compromises its internal temper of militant wrath is destined for the dustbin of history, for it can no longer preserve its faithful heritage in the face of the corrosive influences. . . . God does not guide a people who sell his signs for a paltry price. Small wonder that the Christian clergy is failing to preserve and transmit the faithful heritage . . . one wonders whether or not there is some truth in the old Muslim accusation that there is still a Western conspiracy, in a weak sense of the term, against Islam. Whatever may be the truth on that score, the next time there are gas chambers in Europe, there is no doubt concerning who'll be inside them.[57]

Another book-length attack complained that *The Satanic Verses*

inflamed the feelings of nearly 1 billion followers of Islam. . . . Racists found a new cause in protesting against the protests of the Muslim minority; the secularists found their cause in hatred of all religion; others in anti-Islamism, if not anti-semitism, and the assimilationists against multi-culturalists.[58]

Mohamad Siddique, leader of the Muslim Youth Movement of Bradford and assistant secretary of Jamiaat Tabligh ul Islam, concurred:

The orchestrated conspiracy against Islam is a form of oppression against the Muslim community by the mass media, the political parties, and publishing and commercial empires that thrive on the allegedly free cultures. . . . [T]he time has come for all Muslims to get their acts together and to defend the honour and dignity of the Prophet of Islam and the Islamic values which are so dear to Muslims.[59]

"[F]or the average Muslim," according to Tariq Modood, "the reduction of their religion to a selfish sexual appetite, was no more a contribution to literary discourse than pissing upon the Bible is a theological argument."[60] Liaqat Hussain, general secretary of the Council of Mosques, called it "the most offensive thing written about Islam in English literature." Dr. Saki Badawi, the liberal head of the Muslim College in Ealing, said the book was "far worse to Muslims than if [Rushdie] had raped one's own daughter. . . . It's like a knife being dug into you—or being raped yourself."[61]

Ali Mazrui, a Ugandan Asian who had taught in the United States for several decades, indulged in the pervasive hyperbole. His Pakistani friends told him: "It's as if Rushdie had composed a brilliant poem about the private parts of his parents, and then gone to the market place to recite that poem to the applause of strangers . . . and he's taking money for doing it." Mazrui declaimed:

"The Satanic Verses" could be one of the most divisive books in world politics since Hitler's "Mein Kampf." Of course, Hitler's book was anti-Jewish, while "The Satanic Verses" is interpreted as anti-Muslim. Hitler had political aspirations, while Rushdie's ambitions are literary or financial. But fundamentally, the two books are works of alienation, and divisive in intent and impact. If I had been grown up at the time of the publication of "Mein Kampf" and the Jews were burning it, I would join them in the burning.[62]

Elsewhere he declared: *"The Satanic Verses* is like a rotten pig placed at the door of *Dar es Islam,* the House of Islam."[63] In an unfortunate (and presumably unconscious) reference to Ibsen's play, Rustom Bharucha called Rushdie an "enemy of his people."[64] Feroza Jussawalla, another American academic, denounced him as an Orientalist who sought acceptance from Western intellectuals by "viciously" satirizing his immigrant compatriots while seeking "to escape the responsibilities of the monstrosities he perpetrates" through "imitative Joycean wordplay and choppy stream-of-consciousness narrative." (This critique was itself censored when published in India, illustrative quotations from Rushdie being replaced by page references to the banned book!)[65]

Muslim outrage elicited ecumenical support from the archbishops of York and Canterbury and Britain's chief rabbi.[66] The leader of Israel's orthodox Degel Hatorah party speculated about the response "if someone had written that about Moses."[67] The archbishop of Lyons, who chaired the French Bishops' Conference, denounced the book without reading it: "Once again the faith of believers is insulted."[68] The Vatican condemned Rushdie for blaspheming, its newspaper *L'Osservatore Romano* explaining "[T]he novel has been found offensive by millions of believers. . . . it is not the first time that, by invoking artistic motives or the principle of free expression, people have sought to justify the improper use of sacred texts of religious elements which thereby become blasphemous."[69]

The Muslim response, of course, was not confined to literary criticism. Sher Azam, chairman of the Bradford Council of Mosques, received letters from the Hizb ul Ulama in Blackburn at the end of September 1988 urging "Wherever possible gather in crowds and force these places not to sell such rubbish pleadingly." Azam declared: "We as Muslims will never allow or ignore such rubbish words used by a person who is either mad or thinks that he is ruling the whole world in which there are Millions of Muslims." The chairman of the Islamic Society for the Promotion of Religious Tolerance in the United Kingdom wrote to Penguin questioning "the right of anyone to falsify established historical record, albeit in a novel or otherwise. . . . [W]e might

as well knight muggers and give mass murderers the Nobel prize."
The convener of the U.K. Action Committee on Islamic Affairs demanded the book's withdrawal and destruction, an undertaking not
to reprint, an "unqualified apology to the world Muslim community
for the enormous injury to the feelings and sensibilities of the Muslim
Community," and the payment of damages to Islamic charities in
Britain.

Prime Minister Thatcher rejected Muslim demands that Rushdie be
prosecuted. "It is an essential part of our democratic system that people
who act within the law should be able to express their opinions freely."
(Three days earlier the book won the Whitbread Prize for the best
novel.) Penguin was equally adamant:

> To [withdraw the book] would be wholly inconsistent with our posi-
> tion as a serious publisher who believes in freedom of expression. We
> are truly sorry for the distress the book has caused you and some of
> your fellow-Muslims, but we feel your reaction is based on a misread-
> ing of the book . . . we stand by our view that this is a fine literary
> novel, a view that has been fully endorsed by the critics.

The Union of Muslim Organisations persisted, writing the lord chancellor and the home office and retaining a London solicitor.[70] Realizing
they would receive no satisfaction from the government or publisher,
however, Bradford Muslims met in the Pakistani community hall in
November: "But nobody reported it. We weren't being heard. . . . Then
we decided to hold the meeting outside the hall because we knew that
if it was held indoors no one would take notice."[71] Shabbir Akhtar obtained

> a dispensation from the religionists that should enable me to read the
> blasphemous sections without sin or guilt. . . . Though I took great
> care to censor some of the more profane suggestions, I was physically
> prevented from reading even some of the censored materials by a
> number of outraged Muslims in the audience—one of whom fainted
> with anger. It became rapidly clear to the Bradford Council of
> Mosques that only a dramatic ritual would ease the frustration and
> vent the profound anger of the believing community. Accordingly it
> was resolved that a copy of "The Satanic Verses" be burnt publicly
> in front of the Bradford City Hall.[72]

The Council of Mosques notified the Bradford *Telegraph and Argus*
about the demonstration at Bradford police headquarters on January
13. More than 1,000 Muslims attended, some holding placards reading
"Rushdie Eat Your Words" and "Rushdie Stinks." Bradford councilor
Mohammad Ajeeb promised to have the book banned from the library.

Liaqat Hussain of the Jamiaat Tabligh ul Islam was both jubilant and outraged: "All the newspapers commented. *Times, Daily Telegraph, Guardian, Yorkshire Post.* They compared us to Hitler!"[73]

Within a few days W. H. Smith, the largest British bookseller, heeded police advice to withdraw the book from its Bradford shop. While acknowledging that Muslims were "law-abiding," devoted to "family values," and known for "hard work and personal integrity," the *Independent* warned that they "must not seek to impose their values."[74]

Rushdie responded in the *Observer* on January 22, denouncing the "contemporary Thought Police."

> "Battle lines are being drawn up in India today," one of my characters remarks. "Secular versus religious, the light versus the dark. Better you choose which side you are on." Now that the battle has spread to Britain, I can only hope it will not be lost by default. It is time for us to choose.

In a January 27 interview (broadcast, coincidentally, on the day of the fatwa) he noted that Mohammed, on taking power in Mecca, had executed several people, including writers and actresses who had performed satirical texts.

> Now there you have an image that I thought was worth exploring: at the very beginning of Islam you find a conflict between the sacred text and the profane text, between revealed literature and imagined literature. . . . It seems to me completely legitimate that there should be dissent from orthodoxy, not just about Islam, but about anything. . . . Doubt . . . is the central condition of a human being in the twentieth century.[75]

For almost six months after publication Muslims were content to bar the book from their own countries: Saudi Arabia, Pakistan, Egypt, Bangladesh, Somalia, Sudan, Malaysia, Qatar, Indonesia, Lebanon, and Brunei. Muslim minorities persuaded South Africa, New Zealand, Kenya, Tanzania, Singapore, Thailand, and Venezuela to join. Pakistan banned *Time* and *Newsweek* for reviews quoting the book. But on February 12 thousands demonstrated in Islamabad, Pakistan, screaming "American dogs" and "God is great" and trying to storm the U.S. Information Center. Police shot into the crowd, wounding dozens and killing five. The next day a Karachi riot killed another and injured more than a hundred.

Ayatollah Khomeini followed this on February 14 with his notorious fatwa:

> I inform the proud Muslim people of the world that the author of *The Satanic Verses* book which is against Islam, the Prophet and the Koran, and all involved in its publication who were aware of its content, are sentenced to death. I call on all zealous Muslims to execute them wherever they find them, so that no one will dare to insult the Islamic sanctions. Whoever is killed on this path will be regarded as a martyr, God willing.

He denounced Rushdie as *murtad* (apostate), "an agent of corruption on earth" who had "declared war on Allah." These threats could not be ignored. The Iranian education minister had been murdered several days after a 1947 edict; Khomeini had procured the death of other prominent Iranian politicians and intellectuals from exile, and thousands were killed in Iran when he ultimately seized power.[76] The day after the fatwa Hashemi Rafsanjani, speaker of the Majlis (legislature), denounced the book as a Western conspiracy, pointing to Rushdie's substantial advance and claiming that bodyguards had been appointed before publication and that Zionists were involved in publishing it. Thousands of demonstrators attacked the British embassy in Teheran, shouting death to England and America and breaking windows. The Revolutionary Guard immediately trumpeted its readiness to execute the fatwa. To encourage others, Hassan Sanei, director of the Fifth of Khordad Foundation, offered $1 million to any foreigner and $3 million to any Iranian who carried it out.[77]

Although Rushdie's first reaction was defiance, he promptly apologized, apparently led to believe by Iranian president Ali Khamenei and the chargé d'affaires at the Iranian embassy in London that he could be pardoned. Although Viking also apologized, Iran banned all its publications. The Iranian embassy in Rome asked the pope to block an Italian translation. On February 17 Khamenei joined the chorus: "As the enemy's attack on our frontiers brings us into action, the enemy's attack on our cultural frontiers should evoke a reaction from us at least to the same degree, if not more." A day later, thirty Arab, Turkish, and Iranian writers signed a petition declaring "We are all Salman Rushdies."[78] The same day, Rushdie publicly apologized.

> As author of "The Satanic Verses" I recognise that Moslems in many parts of the world are genuinely distressed by the publication of my novel. I profoundly regret the distress that publication has occasioned to the sincere followers of Islam. Living as we do in a world of many faiths this experience has served to remind us that we must all be conscious of the sensibilities of others.

But Khomeini summarily rejected the gesture: "Even if Salman Rushdie repents and becomes the most pious man of time, it is incumbent on every Muslim to employ everything he has got, his life and his wealth, to send him to hell." To which Rushdie replied: "SV is a clash of faiths . . . or more precisely it's a clash of languages. . . . It's his word [Khomeini's] against mine."[79] The same day the *Sunday Times* reprinted Rushdie's earlier statement: "[A] writer must suppress the knowledge of what effect his words will have, in order to do the writing. If I thought this whirlwind was going to be unleashed, I could not have written." And the *Observer* editorialized: "[N]either Britain nor the author has anything to apologise for. Both can, as Rushdie has done, regret the offence caused or the anger stirred, but not the act itself."

The book was published in the United States on February 22. Associations of publishers, booksellers, and libraries took a full-page advertisement in the *New York Times,* declaring "Free People Write Books, Free People Publish Books, Free People Sell Books, Free People Buy Books, Free People Read Books." PEN held readings in New York and Los Angeles. Two days later Nobel laureate Wole Soyinka called for the expulsion of Iranian diplomats, warning "If Rushdie is unnaturally and prematurely silenced, the creative world will launch its own Jihad."[80]

The impact within Britain was profound. The fatwa was the subject of at least five conferences and five books.[81] The chairman of the Islamic Society for the Promotion of Religious Tolerance accepted Rushdie's apology, which "should pave the way out of this crisis." But the Bradford Council of Mosques dismissed it as "not a sincere apology but a further insult to the Muslim community as a whole." On February 19 the *Sunday Sport* (notorious for pornography) upped Iran's ante by offering £1 million to anyone bringing Khomeini to trial in England. The *Daily Mirror* denounced the "Mad Mullah" and British Muslims who followed their imams "with sheeplike docility and wolf-like aggression." The *Independent*'s February 21 editorial announced that Britain had been "too tolerant for too long." "It is for those who lead Britain's Muslims to respond with tolerance and maturity . . . and to ensure that their zealots obey the law of the land—not the dictates of a bloodthirsty medieval bigot." Robert Maxwell grandstanded in the *Bookseller* on February 24, offering $10 million to anyone who could get Khomeini to recite the Ten Commandments. When Sayyid Abdul Quddus boasted that "members of our religion throughout the country have sworn to carry out the Ayatollah's wishes should the opportunity arise," a Conservative MP demanded his deportation (ignoring his British citizenship). The *Sun* applauded, and the *Star* fulminated:

> Isn't the world getting sick of the ranting that pours from the disgusting foam-flecked lips of the Ayatollah Khomeini? Clearly the

Muslim cleric is stark raving mad. And more dangerous than a rabid dog. Surely the tragedy is that millions of his misguided and equally potty followers believe every word of hatred he hisses through those yellow stained teeth. The terrifying thing is not that a lot of these crackpots actually live here among us in Britain, but that we are actually becoming frightened of them.

Although the Crown Prosecution Service refused *Today*'s suggestion that it prosecute Quddus for incitement to murder, the Council of Mosques forced him to retract and resign as secretary.[82]

Intellectuals joined the chorus of vituperation. Joseph Brodsky ridiculed "Khomeini himself and what he has under his turban." "I'm quite surprised that nobody thus far has put a price on that as well. . . . Mind you, it shouldn't be too big." Former Labor cabinet minister Roy Jenkins now felt "we might have been more cautious about allowing . . . substantial Muslim communities here." Peter Jenkins was "revolted by the Bradford flames . . . the offence done to our principles is at least as great as any offence caused to those who burned the book." He denounced "obscurantist Muslim fundamentalism" and "medieval intolerance" of the "geriatric prophet in Qom." Anthony Burgess condemned the fatwa as "a declaration of war on citizens of a free country. It has to be countered by an equally forthright, if less murderous, declaration of defiance." Christopher Hitchins applied Shelley's anathema of King George to Khomeini: "an old, mad, blind, despised and dying king," adding "Is it not time, as a minimal gesture of solidarity, for all of us to don the Yellow Star, and to end the hateful isolation of our friend and colleague?"

Norman Mailer, always spoiling for a fight, welcomed the

opportunity to regain our frail religion which happens to be faith in the power of words and our willingness to suffer for them. [Khomeini] awakens us to the great rage we feel when our liberty to say what we wish, wise or foolish, kind or cruel, well-advised or ill-advised, is endangered. . . . Maybe we are even willing, ultimately, to die for the idea that serious literature, in a world of dwindling certainties and choked-up ecologies, is the absolute we must defend.

Fay Weldon wallowed in religious chauvinism: "The Koran is food for no-thought. . . . It gives weapons and strength to the thought-police. . . . You can build a decent society around the Bible . . . but the Koran? No." "Muslim society looks profoundly repulsive . . . because it is repulsive," pronounced Conor Cruise O'Brien. "A Westerner who claims to admire Muslim society, while still adhering to Western values, is either a hypocrite or an ignoramus, or a bit of both. At the heart of the matter is the Muslim family, an abominable institution. . . . Arab and Muslim society is sick and has been sick for a long time."[83]

Rushdie's detractors, like his supporters, spanned the political spectrum. The Labor left regretted the book's publication. Social Democrat Roy Hattersley opposed a paperback edition. Germaine Greer called Rushdie "a megalomaniac, an Englishman with a dark skin." Paul Johnson (former *New Statesman* editor turned conservative) mocked him as a "millionaire author who is safe and sound."[84] The openly anti-Semitic Roald Dahl called Rushdie a "dangerous opportunist" who "knew exactly what he was doing and . . . cannot plead otherwise." "In a civilised world we all have a moral obligation to apply a modicum of censorship to our own work in order to reinforce this principle of free speech." Former Conservative party chair Norman Tebbit called Rushdie "an outstanding villain." Auberon Waugh proposed deporting the author (who was a British citizen). Hugh Trevor-Roper "would not shed a tear if some British Muslims, deploring his manners, should waylay him in a dark street and seek to improve them. If that should cause him thereafter to control his pen, society would benefit and literature would not suffer."[85]

British politicians also felt compelled to intervene. The home secretary warned Birmingham Muslims on February 24: "[N]o ethnic or religious minority is likely to thrive in this country if it seeks to isolate itself from the mainstream of British life." A tabloid headline distorted this into "Behave like British, or don't live here." A Tory MP agreed: "[W]hen Muslims say they cannot live in a country where Salman Rushdie is free to express his views, they should be told they have the answer in their own hands—go back from whence you came." Another tabled a Commons motion: "It [the fatwa] is a positive outrage to civilised standards throughout the world." At a February 27 press conference Prime Minister Thatcher pronounced: "We cannot have other people inciting their citizens to murder one of our citizens."

At the same time, the government sought to distance itself from Rushdie. On March 2 Foreign Minister Geoffrey Howe spoke on the BBC World Service: "The British government, the British people, don't have any affection for the book, which is extremely critical, rude about us. It compares Britain with Hitler's Germany." Thatcher added: "We have known in our own religion people doing things which are deeply offensive to some of us . . . and we have felt it very much. And that is what has happened in Islam." But a month later the home office minister of state wrote an open letter to Muslim leaders refusing to ban the book and reiterating their obligation to live harmoniously in a multicultural Britain.[86]

These attacks unified Muslims, intensifying demands for halal food in schools and single-sex education. The Bradford Council of Mosques warned politicians: "Support our anti-Rushdie campaign or lose votes." Several organizations launched a private prosecution against Rushdie and Penguin for blasphemy, which was dismissed because the law protected only Christianity. The Union of Muslim Organisations in the United Kingdom and Eire urged prosecution under the Race Relations Act of 1976 and the Public Order Act of 1986, but the attorney general declined. At the end of May Dr. Kalim Siddiqui, director of the Muslim Institute in London, defended the fatwa on television: "We hit back. We sometimes hit back first."[87]

This provoked the predictable backlash. The Bradford Council of Mosques, never previously attacked, was vandalized four times. Its president received hate mail and telephone threats and found pro-Rushdie slogans scrawled in his home. "Rushdie" became a taunt white children flung at blacks and soccer fans screamed when playing Bradford City. Graffiti appeared: "Salman Rushdie is our hero," "Rushdie rules," "Kill a Muslim for Christmas," "Gas the Muslims." Interracial friendships dissolved. Warders forced Muslim prisoners to hear passages from *The Satanic Verses*.[88]

The fatwa convulsed the Muslim world for two months. Rioting killed twelve protesters and injured fifty in Bombay on February 24; a protest against the police action left one dead and seven injured in Srinagar; another led to a further death and eighty-four injuries in Kashmir; a hundred were injured in Dhaka. In early March Dr. Tantawi—Cairo mufti, grand sheikh, and one of the most respected authorities in the Muslim world—condemned Khomeini for issuing the fatwa without trial. "The court must ask for the writer to explain his intentions and not be limited by misreadings and misunderstandings." His views were echoed by Egyptian novelist Naguib Mahfouz, the 1988 Nobel Prize winner whose books had been banned in his own country. Sheikh Umar Abdul Rahman (a leading Egyptian fundamentalist later convicted of the World Trade Center bombing) responded by accusing Mahfouz of "blasphemy, apostasy, and Freemasonry" and pronouncing a fatwa against him as well (embarrassing Rushdie's critics). The Egyptian interior minister called Khomeini a dog and a pig. The Organization of the Islamic Conference, meeting in Riyadh on March 17, told members to ban the book and boycott Rushdie's publishers but refused to back the fatwa. The Sunni-funded World Muslim League also rejected it, and the Saudi foreign minister called the book a domestic British issue. Imam Bukhari of a Delhi mosque supported the fatwa, as did the mufti of Jerusalem's al-Aqsa mosque. There were pro-Khomeini demonstrations in Beirut, and the Popular Front for the Liberation of Palestine–General Command offered to execute the fatwa.

After a Saudi imam expressed lenience toward Rushdie on television, he and his Tunisian aide were murdered.[89]

If the fatwa divided Islam, it united the West. The Dutch foreign minister canceled a visit to Iran the day after it was declared, and West Germany withdrew its chargé d'affaires two days later. Within a week the twelve European Community ministers agreed to recall their ambassadors and freeze high-level contact with Iran, and the United States, Sweden, Canada, Australia, Norway, and Brazil followed suit the next day. Iran called all diplomats home from Europe. French president François Mitterrand asserted: "All dogmatism which through violence undermines freedom of thought and the right to free expression is, in my view, absolute evil. The moral and spiritual progress of humanity is linked to the recoil of all fanaticisms." Former prime minister Valéry Giscard d'Estaing complained that the European reaction "could have been stronger and more concrete." Some 800 Dutch authors, artists, publishers, and journalists supported Rushdie, and thousands of writers and publishers declared their complicity in the book's publication.[90] By March 22, however, the European Community allowed ambassadors to return, and Britain resumed diplomatic relations on September 20, 1990.[91]

The struggle within Britain was replicated on the Continent, if less intensely.[92] A thousand Muslims demonstrated in Paris on February 26. A week later, SOS-Racisme held an equally large rally against fundamentalist extremism. The same day, then Paris mayor Jacques Chirac (now French president) denounced those threatening Rushdie and his publishers: "If they are French they need to be pursued; if they are foreigners, they should be expelled." Neofascist politician Jean-Marie Le Pen gloated: "What Khomeini has just done with revolting cynicism is exactly what I fear for France and Europe, that is the invasion of Europe by a Muslim immigration."[93]

Muslim actions and threats did curb the book's distribution (while simultaneously boosting sales—200,000 copies in the United Kingdom in the first year). The British Library put it on the "restricted" shelves. Arsonists firebombed Collets' Penguin bookshop on Charing Cross Road in London, frightening the chain into withdrawing the book, and damaged a Dillon's store. Large American chains like Barnes & Noble, B. Dalton, and Waldenbooks, as well as many independents, pulled the book immediately after the fatwa but eventually resumed selling it. Viking, Rushdie's American publisher, received 30,000 protest letters and 16 bomb threats. After the bombing of a New York magazine that defended Rushdie, Sen. Daniel Patrick Moynihan denounced such "intellectual terrorism" and sponsored a resolution: "Let it be understood in the parts of the world from whence such threats emanate: We are not intimidated and the resources of civilization against its enemies are not exhausted."[94]

Rushdie's French publisher dropped the book the day after the fatwa in the face of threats but announced that a consortium would produce it; the same happened in Germany. Mondadori published an Italian translation two days after the fatwa, but a Padua bookshop was burned three weeks later, and Muslims threatened to blow up the Ravenna monument to Dante (who had consigned Mohammed to the ninth pit of hell). In the first two weeks of July 1991, Rushdie's Italian translator was severely wounded and his Japanese translator stabbed to death. A September 1989 memorandum from the board of directors of the English publisher recommended against a paperback edition. "People often forget that common sense is more important than principles. Some principles have to be fought to the death, but I am quite clear this isn't one of them." Rushdie complained that such capitulation meant that he and the publisher "in some sense have been defeated by the campaign against the book."[95]

As the furor over the fatwa declined, England again became the storm center. In May 1989, 30,000 Muslims staged a massive march from Hyde Park to Parliament Square, carrying banners reading

> Freedom of speach, yes! Freedom to insult, no!
> Islam is not bigoted, intolerant or unjust: for proof read the writings of Shaw, Briffault, Lamartine and others
> Rousseau greatest champion of human liberty and equality deeply inspired by the Prophet Muhammad
> Jihad on agnostics!

One poster showed Rushdie hanged in effigy, his head—sprouting horns—affixed to the body of a pig and wearing a Star of David (but for the anti-Semitism the imagery could have come from the novel). The Bradford MP demanded that Penguin withdraw the book, concluding in Urdu "I know your sadness. I'm fully with you." A counter-demonstration by Women Against Fundamentalism was attacked not only by Moslem men but also by white racists. A dozen police were injured and a hundred demonstrators arrested.[96] A three-hour film showing Rushdie as an anti-Islamic, drunken, sadistic murderer protected by Israeli soldiers and glorifying efforts to kill him, which attracted record-breaking audiences in Pakistan, was banned by the British Board of Film Classification until Rushdie interceded. On Muhammad's birthday, October 21, Dr. Kalim Siddiqui reiterated the death sentence before 500 followers, asserting that every time a Muslim saw the book in a shop or library "he feels personally insulted and humiliated." The *Independent* urged that Siddiqui be prosecuted for incitement to murder. The *Sun* advised the government to tell him "to pack up and go, preferably to Iran" (although he was not Iranian). But a poll of British Muslims found strong support for suppressing the book and significant agreement with the fatwa.[97]

Just before the first anniversary of the fatwa, Rushdie published the 7,000-word article "In Good Faith" (allegedly earning £100,000).[98] He had written a novel, not "a work of bad history" or "an anti-religious pamphlet." He had been bewildered "to learn that people *do not care about art.*" "*The Satanic Verses* celebrates hybridity, impurity, intermingling . . . and fears the absolutism of the Pure." It "is the story of two painfully divided selves": one division is secular, "between East and West"; the other is spiritual, between the "immense need to believe" and the "inability to do so." When "the Prophet's companions are called 'scum' and 'bums' . . . the insults quoted are clearly not mine but those hurled at the faithful by the ungodly. How, one wonders, could a book portray persecution without allowing the persecutors to be seen persecuting?" "Decontextualization" of his choice of a name for Muhammad had "created a complete reversal of meaning." "To turn insults into strengths, whigs, tories, Blacks all chose to wear with pride the names they were given in scorn; likewise, our mountain-climbing, prophet-motivated solitary is to be the medieval baby-frightener, the devil's synonym: 'Mahound.' " Rushdie had focused on "Muhammad's doubts, uncertainties, errors, fondness for women . . . [because] they seemed to make him more vivid, more human, and therefore more interesting, even more worthy of admiration."

He rejected the charges of blasphemy and apostasy because, "to put it as simply as possible: *I am not a Muslim.*" He denied that the book "was the literary equivalent of flaunting oneself shamelessly before the eyes of aroused men." But even if it were, "is that really a justification for being, so to speak, gang banged?" He did not "conspire against Islam; or write—after years and years of anti-racist work and writing—a text of incitement to racial hatred." He identified with other victims of Islamic fundamentalism, such as "the Egyptian Nobel laureate Naguib Mahfouz, often threatened but still, happily, with us." He regretted "that such offence has been taken against my work when it was not intended—when dispute was intended, and dissent, and even, at times, satire, and criticism of intolerance, and the like, but not . . . 'filth,' not 'insult,' not 'abuse.' "

Two days after this article appeared, Harold Pinter delivered Rushdie's Herbert Read lecture "Is Nothing Sacred?"[99] It began:

> I grew up kissing books and bread. . . . [O]nce I started kissing girls, my activities with regard to bread and books lost some of their special excitement. But one never forgets one's first loves. . . . It has always been a shock to me to meet people for whom books simply do not

> matter, and people who are scornful of the act of reading, let alone
> writing. . . . We have been witnessing an attack upon a particular
> work of fiction that is also an attack upon the very ideas of the novel
> form.

Until recently he had been confident that the question "Is nothing sacred?" could only be answered No. "I would have described myself
as living in the aftermath of the death of god." But the last year and
a half had forced him to consider whether he was "prepared to set
aside as holy the idea of the absolute freedom of the imagination and
alongside it [his] own notions of the World, the Text, and the Good."
At a Herbert Read lecture more than twenty years earlier, Rushdie had
heard Arthur Koestler propound "the thesis that language, not territory, was the prime cause of aggression, because once language
reached the level of sophistication at which it could express abstract
concepts, it acquired the power of totemization; and once peoples had
erected totems, they would go to war to defend them." Rushdie agreed
with Carlos Fuentes that the novel was "a privileged *arena*," "*the stage
upon which the great debates of society can be conducted*." Literature (and art
generally) offered the possibility of "a secular definition of transcendence," "some sort of replacement for what the love of god offers in the
world of faith." Given the "rejection of totalized explanations," the novel
had become "the form created to discuss the fragmentation of truth."

Rushdie's earliest reading—mostly comic books—had taught him
that "exceptionality was the greatest and most heroic of values." This
was as true of creators as of their characters: "the greater the writer,
the greater his or her exceptionality." In the end, however, he found
himself "backing away from the idea of sacralizing literature." The
only privilege it deserved was "the privilege of being the arena of discourse, the place where the struggle of languages can be acted out."
"The reason for ensuring that that privileged arena is preserved is not
that writers want the absolute freedom to say and do whatever they
please. It is that we, all of us" need a place where "we can hear *voices
talking about everything in every possible way*."

Unmoved by this eloquence, a majority of respondents to a May
1990 poll felt he should apologize.[100] After nearly two years in hiding,
therefore, Rushdie sought reconciliation with the community of British
Asians, especially Indian Muslims, by undergoing a conversion, while
reiterating his criticisms of clerical sexism and homophobia. On Christmas Eve 1990 he declared that "there is no God but Allah and that
Muhammad is His last Prophet," denied agreeing "with any statement
in my novel *The Satanic Verses* uttered by any of the characters who
insult the Prophet Muhammad or who cast aspersions upon Islam or
upon the authenticity of the Holy Quran, or who reject the divinity of

Allah," and promised not to publish a paperback or further translations. It was "a source of happiness to say that I am now inside, and a part of, the community whose values have always been closest to my heart."[101] Six prominent Islamic scholars accepted that he had no evil intent. On December 31 the Cairo grand sheikh (who had denounced the book months before Khomeini) formally forgave and blessed Rushdie. But three months later, Iran reiterated the fatwa and doubled the price on Rushdie's head. And two of the imams who had accepted Rushdie's conversion reneged after five months of violent protest had prevented them from saying Friday prayers. A year after the conversion, a third accused Rushdie of "bad faith."[102]

Rushdie's supporters criticized the British government for not pressing Iran and planned a twenty-four-hour vigil to commemorate his 1,000th day in hiding but canceled it at his request for fear it would delay the release of Western hostages in Lebanon.[103] British Muslims were no happier with the stalemate. The same month the U.K. Action Committee on Islamic Affairs asked why "nothing is being done or said to stop the circulation of the book which continues to cause unspeakable distress and anguish to more than one billion Muslims all over the world."[104]

In December Nadine Gordimer (who had supported cancellation of Rushdie's invitation to speak in South Africa three years earlier) used her Nobel Prize lecture to deplore that

> the edict of a world religion has sentenced a writer to death. With dictatorships apparently vanquished, this murderous new dictate invoking the power of international terrorism in the name of a great and respected religion should and can be dealt with only by democratic governments and the United Nations, as an offense against humanity.[105]

A few days later Rushdie appeared unannounced at a tribute to the First Amendment and retired Supreme Court Justice William Brennan at the Columbia Graduate School of Journalism. Comparing his last three years to drifting in a balloon incapable of carrying him and his companions to safety, he asked: "[H]as it really been so long since religions persecuted people, burning them as heretics, drowning them as witches, that you can't recognize religious persecution when you see it?" "I've been put through a degree course in worthlessness." "Sometimes I think that one day, Muslims . . . [will] agree, too, that the row over 'The Satanic Verses' was at bottom an argument about who should have power over the grand narrative, the Story of Islam, and that that power must belong equally to everyone." A year earlier he had "determined to make my peace with Islam, even at the cost of my pride," saying "Admit it, Salman, the Story of Islam has a deeper meaning for you than any of the other grand narratives." He sought "to cross the threshold, go inside the room and *then* fight for [a] humanized, historicized, secularized way of being a Muslim." But his Western "friends" now called him "spineless, pathetic, debased; I had betrayed myself, my Cause; above all, I had betrayed *them*." He was equally uncomfortable with "the granite, heartless certainties of Actually Existing Islam." "Within days" of his 1990 "conversion," all but one of the six Islamic scholars "had broken their promises, and recommended to vilify me and my work, as if we had not shaken hands. I felt (most probably I had been) a great fool. The suspension of the paperback began at once to look like a surrender." " 'The Satanic Verses' must be freely available and easily affordable, if only because if it is not read and studied, then these years will have no meaning."

> "Free speech is a non-starter," says one of my Islamic extremist opponents. No, sir, it is not. Free speech is the whole thing, the whole ball game. Free speech is life itself. . . . You must decide what you think a writer is worth, what value you place on a maker of stories, and an arguer with the world.
> Ladies and gentlemen, the balloon is sinking into the abyss.[106]

A Muslim promptly wrote to the *New York Times* denouncing the author's "lack of shame." "Instead of repenting, Mr Rushdie is 'sorrowful'; instead of admitting guilt, he becomes the grand preacher of a new order in Islam."[107] Paul Theroux displayed similar intransigence on the other side. "I have made a point of asking all the Muslims I meet their views on Mr. Rushdie and his book. . . . It ought to happen everywhere: first the question—*What about Rushdie?*—and if the answer is hostile, set them straight."[108]

Thanking twenty-five well-known writers, whose letters to him were published in newspapers in more than twenty-one countries and collected in a book, Rushdie commented:

> Those mediaeval dogs of war, "blasphemy" and "heresy," have been let slip. . . . We must win because we cannot lose; what is at stake is nothing less than our minds. . . . the attempt to create shape out of the thick soup of human experience . . . cannot be surrendered to any gang of policemen, no matter how big their guns. This is—"fundamental . . ."—a battle of wills.[109]

In January 1992 an anonymous consortium of seventy-two publishers (notably omitting the two largest American companies, Simon & Schuster and Random House) announced the paperback. Iranian leaders reiterated the death sentence under the heading "A Divine Command to Stone the Devil." Rushdie withdrew his acceptance of Islam. "After three years of having my life smashed about by religion, I don't feel like associating myself with it. I'm fighting for my life against it."[110]

Rushdie visited Washington in March but was rebuffed by Bush's press secretary: "There's no reason for any special relationship with Rushdie. I mean, he's an author. He's here. He's doing interviews and book tours and things authors do. . . . We have often said that we want better relations with Iran. We have worked toward that goal." Rushdie retorted: "I'm not here doing a book tour. The purpose of the paperback is to make a point about First Amendment rights." The State Department said a meeting "could be misinterpreted by those individuals who, as you are well aware of, have an extreme dislike for Mr. Rushdie." The *New York Times* deplored "three years of official waffling" and denounced the government as "spineless . . . shamefully squeamish—especially when compared with its steady pressure on Libya to turn over the suspects in the Lockerbie bombing."[111]

Egyptian Nobel laureate Naguib Mahfouz, who initially supported Rushdie and accused Khomeini of "intellectual terrorism," reversed himself in August, calling both "equally dangerous." An author "must be ready to pay the price for his outspokenness." Although bad eyesight prevented him from reading *The Satanic Verses*, it had been explained to him, and parts were unacceptable. Rushdie had no "right to insult anything, especially a prophet or anything considered holy." Mahfouz had been head of Egyptian movie and theater censorship and had acquiesced when al-Azhar University banned publication of his 1959 novel *Children of Gebelawi* on grounds of heresy because he believed it was more important to fight "the other medieval form of Islam"—fundamentalism. Other Arab countries banned his books when he became the first major Arab writer to support the Camp David accords. In October 1994 Mahfouz was seriously wounded by Islamic militants, who had vowed to kill him on the anniversary of his Nobel prize. He denounced this "assault on liberty. I pray to God to make the police victorious over terrorism and to purify Egypt from this evil." Calling him the conscience of the Arab world, the information minister unbanned his novel. His attackers were hanged in March 1995, and he died the following year.[112]

Germany, Ireland, and Sweden renewed their public support for Rushdie, Yasir Arafat denounced the fatwa, and even Kalim Siddiqui, who had threatened to "break every bone" in Rushdie's body, said it was time "for both sides to forgive and forget," leading the British government to drop his prosecution. With the release of the Middle Eastern hostages, Rushdie decided "to make the campaign as noisy as possible." "I regret I kept my mouth shut for so long." Shortly before the fourth anniversary of the fatwa, he met the foreign minister of state, the highest British official thus far, and then in May saw Prime Minister Major.

Iran was defiant. Rushdie had tried "to downgrade the sentiments of more than a billion Muslims. He does not deserve to exist." Ayatollah Khomeini proclaimed: "The Iranian nation will no longer allow Britain, America or any other bully to intervene in Iran's internal affairs, aims, lofty aspirations and beliefs." The fatwa was irrevocable. "This system is not on speaking terms with the arrogant enemies of the revolution, and that's forever, and we'll never reconcile with them." A *Los Angeles Times* editorial responded: "You said it, Ayatollah, we won't."[113]

In July 1993 Rushdie wrote that "secularism is the fanatics' most important target . . . because secularism demands a total separation between church and state in the Muslim world."[114] Turkey offered tragic proof. In May Aziz Nesin published unauthorized translations of *The Satanic Verses* in his journal *Ajdinlik,* provoking attacks on the editorial office and Iranian death threats. In July he addressed a symposium of writers and academics in Sivas, commemorating the hanging of a sixteenth-century poet who preached rebellion against oppression. Fundamentalists bombed the building, killing thirty-five participants. During their trial the eighty accused shouted, "Sivas is the grave of the infidels," and threw furniture at the judges and journalists. Rushdie condemned the attack as a "terrorist atrocity" but called the translation a "piratical act . . . a manipulative act."[115]

In September *Midnight's Children* won the Booker Prize for the best British novel in the previous twenty-five years.[116] Less than a month later, however, Rushdie's Norwegian publisher was shot and seriously wounded.[117] When a hundred Arab and Muslim writers, artists, and intellectuals published brief essays supporting Rushdie, he expressed "great delight" that "the most gifted, the most learned, the most important voices of the Muslim and Arab world, gathered together to subject my work and the furor surrounding it to so brilliant, so many-sided, so judicious an examination."[118]

In November the Clinton administration made amends for Bush's snub twenty months earlier. Rushdie talked at length with Warren Christopher and Anthony Lake but only shook the president's hand, an event that deliberately was not photographed. The head of the Iranian judiciary excoriated Clinton.

> By accepting such an author you have brought such notoriety upon yourself in the Islamic world that I dare say you are the most hated person before all Muslims of the world. I am really surprised that a leader with such highsounding claims should ignore 1.5 billion Mus-

lims. I ask Mr. Clinton: Has not the author of *The Satanic Verses* insulted the prophet of Islam? Has he not insulted Jesus Christ and other prophets?

A senior official of the Muslim Brotherhood in Egypt asked: "Is Salman Rushdie worth all of that, to meet the president of the biggest state in the whole world? . . . If we review the statistics, the Prophet Mohammed is the most popular human being on earth." The secretary general of the secular Egyptian Wafd party agreed the meeting was "an insult to Islam . . . you cannot say you are supporting human rights while you are attacking a religion." These voices found a surprising ally in Patrick Buchanan.

> [W]here is the sensitivity toward a religious faith of 1 billion adherents?
>
> Clinton's *beau geste* clearly scored points with the New York literary crowd, but the President put at risk the safety of his own citizens and the national interests of the United States.

Rushdie was no Solzhenitsyn but "an Indian-born British subject, a man of the trendy left, who until recently was known for savage commentary on the very governments from which he now seeks support and safety." "The way in which Salman Rushdie exercised his literary freedom was irresponsible and contemptuous." Confirming Buchanan's stereotype, Cynthia Ozick declared in the *New Yorker* that Rushdie was "a little Israel" and compared him to Dreyfus and Zola. Paul Auster wrote in the *New York Times* that he thought of Rushdie every day he sat down to write. "To write a work of fiction, one must be free to say what one has to say." In the *Los Angeles Times* Robert Coover deplored that "in response to the writer Salman Rushdie's witty comic Valentine, sent to the world in love, the Ayatollah Ruholla Khomeini replied, in holy loathing, with a more traditional one of his own . . . and legions of sacred executioners were let loose upon the world, where they roam, their hearts pierced by the barbed love of death, to this day." Coover took pleasure, however, in "the birds' love-billets, dropped in their excitement on the tombs of the world's executioners."

Clinton promptly waffled, of course, claiming that the handshake with Rushdie had been a chance encounter. "I respect the religion and I respect the culture enormously, so I mean no disrespect to the people who have that religious faith. But I do think it's important that here in the United States we reaffirm our commitment to protecting the physical well-being and the right to speak of those with whom we may intensely disagree." The Iranian news agency reiterated the fatwa on its fifth anniversary, boasting that fifty-one Muslim nations had anathematized Rushdie as an apostate.[119] But it was not formally renewed in February 1995, and Iran's ambassador to Denmark protested that his government "never had sent, was not sending and would not in the future send anyone to kill Salman Rushdie." French prime minister Edouard Balladur pledged support for Rushdie but quickly qualified it: "We French want respect for human rights in all countries of the world. But at the same time we have an economic position to defend in the world."[120] In September Rushdie made a widely publicized appearance before a large London audience to promote his latest novel, *The Moor's Last Sigh.* It, too, was banned in India—because *Hindu* fundamentalists objected that a character resembled a Bombay politician.[121] (Five years earlier a British comedian had predicted that Rushdie's next work would be "You're a Big Fat Bastard, Buddha." Now an American reviewer objected to the caricature of "a kind of Jewish Professor Moriarty of subcontinental crime. . . . Maybe this piece of portraiture could have been painted less hyperbolically, in cognizance of the paranoid mythologies of secret Jewish power so widely current.")[122] The enthusiastic reception encouraged Rushdie to appear in public: with David Letterman, at a U2 concert, and at the Edinburgh Festival—where fifty Muslims carrying signs saying "Stop Rushdie's Poison" and "Rushdie Writes Filth" did not prevent him from filling the house.[123]

It is tempting, if unfair, to see the persecution of Taslima Nasrin as illustrating Marx's dictum that history repeats itself, the first time as tragedy, the second as farce. A gynecological anesthesiologist, repeatedly divorced (reports varied between two and four times), and author of sixteen books, she had won an Indian award for her best-selling study of the plight of women in Bangladeshi society. But the mullahs denounced as "pornography" her critical depiction of violent sexual subordination of women, and their followers prevented stores from stocking her books and attacked her at the Dhaka Book Fair. Her novel *Lajja* (Shame), condemning Indian Muslims for taking revenge on Hindus for destroying the sixteenth-century Babri Masjid at Ayodhya, was banned in July 1993 after selling 60,000 copies in five months (despite bad reviews). (The book's English title was the same as Rushdie's earlier novel, and it was brought out in India by his publisher.) The Hindu militants of Bharatiya Janata party distributed a pirated edition in India.

Bangladeshi fundamentalists issued a fatwa in September 1993, offering $1,200 for her death. Maulana Azizul Haque, who had led several hundred thousand followers to the Indian border a year earlier to protest the destruction of the Babri mosque, called her "worse than a prostitute. She demands 'freedom of the vagina.' She says that if a man can have four wives, a woman should have the right to four husbands.

Even within marriage, she says a woman should have the right to other men. This is against the Koran and Allah, it is blasphemy." Thousands called for her death.

On June 4, 1994, she was charged with writings "intended to outrage the religious feeling of any class by insulting its religion or religious believers" (a British colonial law) for allegedly telling the *Statesman* of Calcutta that "the Koran should be thoroughly revised." Daily demonstrations culminated in a march on Parliament by more than 4,000 demanding her execution and then in a half-day general strike. Fighting led to an estimated 200 injuries and at least one death. A cleric called her "a creature of Satan."

On July 14 Rushdie published an open letter in twenty-one newspapers stressing their differences despite facing similar adversaries.

> How sad it must be to believe in a God of blood! What an Islam they have made, these apostles of death, and how important it is to have the courage to dissent from it! . . . Great writers have agreed to lend their weight to the campaign on your behalf. . . .
>
> It is a disgrace that your Government has chosen to side with the religious extremists against their own history, their own civilization, their own values. It is the treasure-house of the intelligence, the imagination, and the word that your opponents are trying to loot.

Nasrin did not return the compliment: "I respect Rushdie as a writer— he's very powerful. But he's repented, he's become a born-again Muslim, and that I don't respect. I will never be like him. I will never repent."

Bangladeshi fundamentalists stoked the furor in order to demand an Islamic republic and penal code and the expulsion of foreign aid organizations supporting women's education and birth control. Some feminists disavowed Nasrin (who had dismissed them as housewives slavishly obeying Islamic law). Granted bail, she fled as the court clearly intended (although some continued to demand a trial in absentia). From Sweden she vowed to oppose fundamentalism, which was "spreading darkness in many parts of the world. . . . I pledge to remain steadfast in commitment to my vision of a world ruled by reason, tolerance, love and beauty." Bangladesh was "infected" by the mullahs. "Their long hair, beards and robes conceal their insatiable lust for wealth and women." A Bangladesh court subsequently affirmed that she could be charged with insulting religion.[124]

CHAPTER THREE

• •

Theorizing the Contest

NARRATIVE COMMONALITIES

Although differing greatly in time, place, characters, and content, the dramas of pornography, racial hatred, and blasphemy also display striking commonalities. The contested terrain is symbols. (Because these conflicts, like all social behavior, are overdetermined they *also* concern money, politics, and violence.) Rushdie invoked Arthur Koestler's assertion that language had been totemized, displacing territory as the catalyst of aggression. "The row over 'The Satanic Verses,' " he observed, "was at bottom an argument about who should have power over the grand narrative, the Story of Islam." Brandishing the swastika, NSPA leader Frank Collin declared: "This is my party identification, that is my symbol, and we will not be parted from it." White racists in St. Paul burned a cross, perversely appropriating Christianity's fundamental symbol. The debate over pornography concerned control over the representation of women's bodies.

Emotions screwed to fever pitch exploded in epithets, riots, murder, and suicide. Offenses so heinous could be purified only by fire: the auto-da-fé of a woman "destroyed" by sexism, cross burnings, a bonfire of *The Satanic Verses.* Rushdie's imagery was equally apocalyptic—the balloon of civilization sinking into the abyss of primitive ignorance. Like Joseph McCarthy's red scare (and Arthur Miller's dramatization in *The Crucible*) these events became moral panics.

Confrontations borrowed symbolism. For Gloria Steinem, *Playboy* was as bad as *Mein Kampf;* for Ali Mazrui, so was *The Satanic Verses.* A British Muslim condemned tolerance for Rushdie as no better than "knight[ing] muggers and giv[ing] mass murderers the Nobel prize," while Nadine Gordimer denounced the fatwa as an "offense against humanity." Rushdie emulated secular Jews, and Cynthia Ozick called him a "little Israel," while British politicians complained that Rushdie "compares Britain with Hitler's Germany." Judith Bat-Ada saw pornographers as "every bit as dangerous as Hitler, Mussolini, and Hiro-hito." Makeup and provocative clothing stigmatized women "as effectively as did the yellow stars on the coats of the Jews in Nazi Germany." "[S]exuality has become the fascism of contemporary America," warned MacKinnon, "and we are moving into the last days of Weimar." Both she and a Minneapolis feminist lawyer compared pornography to Nazis marching in Skokie.

On the other side, Gayle Rubin condemned the antipornography campaign's appropriation of S/M images as "on a moral par with the use of depictions of black men raping white women, or of drooling old Jews pawing young Aryan girls, to incite racist or anti-Semitic frenzy" (just as conservatives call women like Rubin "femonazis"). Shabbir Akhtar warned that "the next time there are gas chambers in Europe, there is no doubt concerning who'll be inside them." British racists fueled these fears with graffiti proclaiming "Gas the Muslims." A Rushdie supporter urged others to "don the Yellow Star," while Muslim critics caricatured him wearing the Star of David and labeled him Zionist.

Sexual and scatological images suffused discourse. Nazi speech was "obscene" to a concentration-camp survivor in Skokie, while the Mac-Kinnon-Dworkin ordinance was an "obscenity" to civil libertarians, a "violation" worse than rape. British blasphemy prosecutions cited "ribald" language. Muslims compared *The Satanic Verses* to pissing on the Bible, raping one's daughter, and publicly reciting a poem about one's parents' private parts. They particularly resented Rushdie's naming prostitutes after Mohammed's wives. His language was "filthy," "rubbish," not "decent"; a placard said he "stinks." He had engaged in "a continuous striptease, from soft to hard and even harder porn," ultimately "show[ing] them all." Rushdie retorted that even were his book "the literary equivalent of flaunting oneself shamelessly before the eyes of aroused men" that was no "justification for being, so to speak, gang banged." He was the victim of a "witch-hunt." Maligned as both prostitute and pornographer, Taslima Nasrin denounced the mullahs' "insatiable lust for wealth and women."

Racists spewed hatred indiscriminately. A decade before Skokie, Chicago neo-Nazis attacked Sammy Davis Jr. for being both black and Jewish. Salman Rushdie, born an Indian Muslim, was the target of anti-Semitic slurs. Critics called *The Satanic Verses* antiblack, and MacKinnon denounced pornography as slave trade in women.

The three contests sought a common prize: respect, honor, dignity. Participants often complained of public humiliation. Antipornography campaigners forced Warner Brothers to remove a billboard showing a woman enjoying a beating because such representations were "designed to dehumanize women, to reduce the female to an object of sexual access." One Minneapolis woman "saw myself through the abuser's eyes and I felt dirty and disgusting, like a piece of meat." Another immolated herself because "sexism has shattered my life." Andrea Dworkin denounced pornography for colonizing women's bodies; by condoning it, the city showed it "doesn't give a damn about women." Fatima Meer called Rushdie a "coloniser." The black youths who assaulted a white boy in Wisconsin sought revenge for the racial humiliations depicted in *Mississippi Burning*. Blasphemy laws in Britain, India, and Bangladesh protect religion from "offence and insult and ridicule." Britain's limitation to Christianity denigrated other religions. Both demagogues who led the campaigns against Rushdie and Nasrin had attained prominence by defending the Babri mosque against Hindu attacks.

Muslims protested the "insults" in *The Satanic Verses*, which rankled every time they saw the book and were reiterated by Rushdie's defenders. Khomeini proclaimed the fatwa on behalf of the "proud Muslim people." Rushdie had sought to "downgrade" Islam, whose honor must be vindicated. Tolerance of blasphemy had "totally undermined" Christianity. "God does not guide a people who sell his signs for a paltry price." Islam defiantly preserved its "internal temper of militant wrath." Two years after publication, a British Muslim declared that Rushdie's greatest sin was his lack of "shame" (the title of novels by both him and Nasrin). Rushdie, in turn, had "been put through a degree course in worthlessness." He had converted to Islam "at the cost of my pride" and later regretted his foolishness. National honor was constantly implicated. The fatwa was an offense against Britain and France. Western nations withdrew diplomatic representatives from Iran. Rushdie collected public appearances with heads of state the way he boasted of endorsements by prominent writers; his critics retorted that fifty-one Muslim nations had declared him an apostate. Clinton characteristically tried to play both sides, meeting Rushdie casually while maintaining his respect for Islam.

Advocating passage of the Pornography Victims' Compensation Bill, women pointed to William Kennedy Smith's rape acquittal and Senate confirmation of Clarence Thomas. Both the white cross-burners in St. Paul and the black assailants in Kenosha were protesting their lowly status. In the controversy over *The Satanic Verses* each side donned the mantle of civilization while labeling the other barbarian. Rushdie protested against "tyranny and vilification and murder." Embracing the fundamentalism for which they were despised, Muslims took Rushdie's book title literally, proclaiming both him and Nasrin to be the devil, satan. The Egyptian interior minister descended to gutter language, calling Khomeini a dog and a pig. All competed for victimhood. MacKinnon complained of a "witchhunt by First Amendment fundamentalists who are persecuting and blacklisting dissidents like Andrea Dworkin and myself as arts censors." Holocaust revisionists portrayed the *Nazis* as victims of historical lies. A billion Muslims maintained that Rushdie had "mugged" them and declared war on Allah. *They* were not the terrorists—it was he who was a "literary terrorist."

Each protagonist championed fundamental values. Norman Mailer hailed literature as "the absolute we must defend" in a "world of dwindling certainties." Mitterrand saw the attack on freedom of thought as "absolute evil." For Rushdie free speech was "the whole thing, the whole ball game," "life itself." He defended a tolerant, secularized Islam as "a culture, a civilization . . . *family*." Taslima Nasrin remained loyal to "reason, tolerance, love and beauty." Naguib Mahfouz prayed to God "to purify Egypt from this evil, in defense of people, freedom and Islam."

Such absolutes impelled total warfare. Muslims protested that Christian Europe was still fighting the Crusades. Iranian president Khamenei declared that "the enemy's attack on our cultural frontiers should evoke a reaction from us at least to the same degree." Anthony Burgess equated the fatwa "to a *jihad*," which had "to be countered by an equally forthright, if less murderous, declaration of defiance." Wole Soyinka threatened a jihad by the creative world if Rushdie were killed. Rushdie castigated Muslim fundamentalists for loosing "those mediaeval dogs of war, 'blasphemy' and 'heresy.' . . . We must win because we cannot lose" this "battle of wills." He suffered delusions of grandeur.

> Dead dictators are my specialty. I discovered to my horror that all the political figures most featured in my writing—Mrs. G., Sanjay Gandhi, Bhutto, Zia—have now come to sticky ends. It's the grand slam, really. This is a service I can perform, perhaps. A sort of literary contract.[1]

Others leaped into the fray. Senator Moynihan boasted that "the resources of civilization against its enemies are not exhausted." A *New York Times* advertisement invoked "Free People" five times; the shibboleth had not been uttered that often since the height of the Cold War. Freedom was threatened by the "thought police." Rushdie's plight was not individual but emblematic of universal human rights. To which Muslims replied: "[Y]ou cannot say you are supporting human rights while you are attacking a religion." "Muhammad is easily the most maligned religious personality in the whole of history."

Two polarities dominated the controversy over *The Satanic Verses*.[2] The first opposed art to religion. The response to the book mirrored its content: "a conflict between . . . revealed literature and imagined literature." Rushdie loved art the way believers loved God; he kissed books as they did sacred texts and icons. When India banned the novel, he taunted Rajiv Gandhi: "You own the present . . . but the centuries belong to art." He demanded that the uncommitted decide "what value you place on a maker of stories, and an arguer with the world." He made common cause with Nasrin: their enemies were "trying to loot" the "treasure-house of the intelligence, the imagination, and the word." He extolled the "exceptionality" of romantic artists as "the greatest and most heroic of values." Rushdie was tempted to declare that "the absolute freedom of the imagination" was "holy." But though he "back[ed] away from sacralizing literature," he continued to insist that "all of us" need a place where "we can hear *voices talking about everything in every possible way*." Doubt was "the central condition of a human being in the twentieth century." He uncompromisingly condemned the sexism and homophobia, "the granite, heartless certainties of Actually Existing Islam," with its "God of blood" and "apostles of death."

Rushdie's supporters echoed these themes. Suggesting parallels with Plato's philosopher king and Shelley's poet as unacknowledged legislator, Carlos Fuentes extolled the novel as "a privileged arena," "*the stage upon which the great debates of society can be conducted*." Paul Auster declared that a fiction writer "must be free to say what one has to say." Mocking Muslims who sought to execute the fatwa, Robert Coover imagined birds defecating "on the tombs of the world's executioners." Rushdie sought endorsements from intellectuals and politicians and urged the same tactic on Nasrin. Literary prizes confirmed his artistic worth: the Whitbread for *The Satanic Verses*, the Writers' Guild for *Haroun and the Sea of Stories*, and the Booker designation of *Midnight's Children* as the best novel in twenty-five years. (No great reader, President Bush was unimpressed; his press secretary dismissed Rushdie as just "an author . . . doing interviews and book tours.")

The insults produced various ripostes. Khomeini denounced Rushdie for having "declared war on Allah." The author thought "he is ruling the whole world in which there are Millions of Muslims." These numbers kept growing, to one and then one and a half billion, making Mohammed "the most popular human being on earth." Muslims invoked Western partisans: Rousseau, Shaw, Lamartine. Both Nadine Gordimer and Bill Clinton pointedly declared their respect for Islam (while condemning the fatwa). Muslims threatened to blow up a statue of Dante for having consigned Mohammed to hell more than six centuries earlier. Muslims found allies in Catholic, Protestant, and Jewish leaders equally reluctant to concede the transcendence of art. Muslims belittled Rushdie, who was not worth meeting "the president of the biggest state in the whole world."

The confrontation between religion and art overlapped those of East and West, black and white. The West was arrogant. The Muslim MP who had the novel banned in India condemned Western imperialists, who had "not yet laid the ghost of the Crusades to rest, but given it a new cultural wrapping." He ridiculed the "fatigued" West, whose lackeys belonged to the "Anglicised elite," the "pukka Sahibs," the "entire 'liberal' establishment . . . all set to overawe the government of India into surrendering its sovereign right." Their slurs exposed Western racism: "Call us primitive, call us fundamentalists, call us superstitious barbarians." A South African sociology professor descended from Indian Muslims declared: "[I]t is the Third World that is being attacked by Rushdie." Bangladeshi fundamentalists used their pursuit of Nasrin to assail all Western influence. Ayatollah Khomeini denounced Britain and the United States as bullies; mobs demonstrated outside their embassies in Muslim countries. British Muslims intensified their ethnic loyalties.

Rushdie was outraged at being accused of writing "a text of incitement to racial hatred" after his "years and years of antiracist work." He celebrated hybridity, mongrelization, the hotchpotch of cultural mingling in the metropolis. His supporters were less circumspect, however, their anger quickly erupting through the veneer of British civility to reveal virulent racism. Khomeini was the "Mad Mullah," "stark raving mad," a "rabid dog," the "geriatric prophet in Qom," a "bloodthirsty medieval bigot" with "foam-flecked lips" and "yellow stained teeth," an "old, mad, blind, despised and dying king." His "potty followers" were "crackpots," superstitious bigots, exhibiting "sheeplike docility and wolf-like aggression." The Koran was "food for nothought," no foundation for a decent society. Islam was "profoundly repulsive." The Muslim family was "an abominable institution." "Arab and Muslim society is sick." Where Rushdie praised hybridity, they demanded immediate assimilation: "Behave like British, or don't live here." His name became a racial taunt, which whites flung at blacks and scrawled on walls.

Because struggles for respect transcend class and other material interests, they create strange alliances and divisions. Identity politics questions authenticity—the right to represent the group. Who spoke for women: antiporn campaigners or advocates of exuberant, often lesbian, sexuality? Some lesbians denounced heterosexual women opposing censorship as "male-identified." MacKinnon and Dworkin denigrated civil libertarian women as compradors of male supremacy who aspired to "do better" under patriarchy. Jews accused Jewish civil libertarians of treachery. Rushdie painfully contained these contradictions. Shahabuddin dismissed him as a "self-hating Indo-Anglian." From the other side of the racial divide Germaine Greer called him "an Englishman with a dark skin." Others disparaged his novel as a work of "alienation." "*I am not a Muslim,*" Rushdie retorted. "I have never in my adult life affirmed any belief." Many Muslims rejected "the idea that they belong to their faith *purely by virtue of birth.*" By the year's end, however, he underwent a conversion, happy "that I am now inside, and a part of, the community whose values have always been closest to my heart." Less than a year later, finding himself "among people whose social attitudes I'd fought all my life," he repudiated that conversion. Muslims retaliated by accusing him of Anglicizing his name to Simon Rushton and selling his soul to the West, while Western supporters (and Nasrin) denounced his capitulation. A Muslim declared that anyone "who fails to be offended by Rushdie's book ceases, on account of that fact, to be a Muslim." Conor Cruise O'Brien countered that "a Westerner who claims to admire Muslim society, while still adhering to Western values, is either a hypocrite or an ignoramus, or a bit of both."

These clashes fractured old alliances. Civil rights leaders in Minneapolis and Indianapolis opposed feminists, seeing pornography as a "white folks' issue," while La Raza supported the ordinance. Gays and lesbians condemned censorship. Egypt castigated Iran; Naguib Mahfouz switched sides. Nadine Gordimer, who had defended the Congress of South African Writers' withdrawal of Rushdie's invitation in 1989, used her Nobel Prize lecture two years later to condemn the fatwa. At the same time struggles forged paradoxical bonds. S/M lesbians and heterosexual men, civil libertarians and commercial pornographers opposed regulation, while Christian conservatives and opponents of the Equal Rights Amendment joined some feminists to demand it. Blacks, Latinos, Ukrainians, and Christian clergy united with Jews to silence Nazis. Rushdie's supporters spanned the political and cultural spectrum, from the *Independent* to the *Sunday Sport*, Conservative MPs to former Labor ministers, Le Pen to Mitterrand. His critics made even stranger bedfellows: Conservatives and Social Democrats, Khomeini and English glitterati, Zionists and Sheikh Rahman, religious leaders who rarely agreed about anything. White racists joined Muslim men in attacking antifundamentalist women. An enemy's enemy became a friend—as when Hindu militants embraced the uncompromisingly secularist Nasrin, further inflaming Bangladeshi Muslims.

These struggles exposed central problems in the two dominant responses to harmful speech: civil libertarianism and regulation (discussed in chapters 5 and 6). Private constraints overshadowed governmental restrictions. Although the Nazis won the right to march in Skokie, threats deterred them from exercising it. When they finally demonstrated in downtown Chicago, thousands drowned them out. Movie producers, publishers, theaters, video shops, and bookstores exerted much greater influence than police or prosecutors over the dissemination of pornography. Viking-Penguin declined to publish *The Satanic Verses* in India and the paperback everywhere; European publishers delayed or dropped translations. Booksellers withdrew it under pressure. Rushdie withheld the paperback in the hope of reconciling with Islam; he was furious at the unauthorized translation into Turkish. Some who opposed censorship also criticized Rushdie for failing to exercise self-restraint. Legal toleration did not foster popular tolerance.

Many dissociated themselves from the clichéd metaphor of the marketplace of ideas. Critics denied that pornography expressed ideas and rejected feminist pornography as an antidote to patriarchal pornography. Jews in Skokie could not believe "that a murderer has the right to come and express his opinion" or that the government would "sanctify" the Nazi march. For Muslims, *The Satanic Verses* was "no more a contribution to literary discourse than pissing upon the Bible is a theological argument." Payment compromised rather than valorized speech. The ACLU became the "pornographers' mouthpiece." Rushdie had "learnt that it is possible to make money by selling self-hate." Paul Johnson mocked Rushdie as a "millionaire author" (a slur in England, if not in the United States). The Speaker of the Iranian Majlis pointed to Rushdie's substantial advance.

If these narratives exposed the limits of civil libertarianism, they also revealed the perversities of regulation. Prohibition, far from silencing speech, dignified it. Actors sought visibility and impact through shock. Outlawry accentuated pornography's allure. A porn movie theater responded to the Minneapolis campaign by adding live nude dancing. The Nazis invited state repression to maximize publicity. When Bradford Muslim protests were ignored, "we decided to burn the book." A leader exulted that "all the newspapers commented" and seemed thrilled that "they compared us to Hitler!" All performers know that even bad publicity is better than none. Rushdie's first reaction to the fatwa was defiance; three years later he decided "to make the campaign as noisy as possible." The affair sold far more copies of *The Satanic Verses* than all his previous works combined. Despite bad reviews, Nasrin's book sold 60,000 copies before it was banned. The attempted murder of Naguib Mahfouz led to the unbanning of *The Children of Gebelawi* and its immediate publication. Repression not only publicizes its intended targets but also has unintended consequences. More than half those convicted under the Wisconsin hate speech ordinance were African Americans (less than 4 percent of the state's population).

Regulation literalizes speech, denying metaphor and ambiguity, confusing representation with reality. Following MacKinnon and Dworkin, Canadian antipornography campaigners declared that "in, by, through, and because of pornography women are objectified, subordinated, tortured, raped, killed and silenced." Linda Marchiano testified: "Every time someone watches 'Deep Throat' they are watching me be raped." Pornography "trafficked women," MacKinnon insisted, because it "means what it says" and "is what it does." Skokie Holocaust survivors took literally Frank Collin's threat that "we're coming to get them again." "The minute somebody comes and tries to attack my home, I have to defend myself." Viking's consultants read *The Satanic Verses* as history rather than fiction. British Muslims denounced the book as a "thinly disguised . . . piece of literature" and questioned "the right of anyone to falsify established historical record, albeit in a novel or otherwise." Cairo's grand sheikh deplored that the book's "'lies and figments of the imagination' about Islam" were "passed off as facts." Rushdie's words were equated to the plot to blow up al-Aqsa mosque. His book was a rotten pig, like the actual pig British racists had thrown into a mosque several years earlier.

Many rejected this literalism, however. Rushdie reiterated the obvious: he had written a novel. "[T]o treat fiction as if it were fact, is to make a serious mistake of categories." The section causing most outrage "deals with a prophet not called Muhammad living in a highly fantasticated city. . . . Moreover, this entire sequence happens in a dream, the fictional dream of a fictional character, an Indian movie star, and one who is losing his mind, at that." How "could a book portray persecution without allowing the persecutors to be seen persecuting?" Finding the Indianapolis ordinance unconstitutional, Judge Easterbrook insisted on the difference between experience and representation—"the description of women's sexual domination of men in *Lysistrata* was not real dominance."

Meaning depends on context and motive. But though laws distinguished pornography from erotica and sex education, Bangladeshis denounced Nasrin as a pornographer for poems like "Happy Marriage," describing a husband who

> wants my body under his control
> so that if he wishes he can spit in my face,
>   slap me on the cheek,
> and pinch my rear.
> So that if he wishes he can rob me of my clothes
> and take the naked beauty in his grip.
> So that if he wishes he can pull out my eyes
> . . .
> so that I would drink, as if they were ambrosia,
> the filthy liquids of his polygynous body.
> . . .
> So that, loving him
> on some moonlit night I would commit suicide
>   in a fit of ecstasy.

The MacKinnon-Dworkin ordinance might also criminalize this, unable to distinguish it from a hard-core snuff film. Justice Scalia could not distinguish whites burning a cross in the yard of a black family from "a provocative speech about economics," a physical attack motivated by racial hatred from one directed against flat-earthers.

Context and motive profoundly affected interpretations of *The Satanic Verses*. Muslims castigated Rushdie as an apostate, but he denied embracing Islam as an adult. Muslim *critics* translated the novel into Urdu, disseminated photocopies, reproduced the most offensive passages in periodicals, and read it aloud. Yet some countries prohibited its quotation, even in hostile reviews or news reports. A Cairo mufti declared that a fatwa should never issue without inquiry into the speaker's motive. Rushdie explained that he had called the prophet "Mahound" in order to draw the sting of that medieval Christian slur, just as "whigs, tories, Blacks all chose to wear with pride the names they were given in scorn." His adversary Shahabuddin invited intellectuals to "call us primitive, call us fundamentalists, call us superstitious barbarians."

Although advocates of regulation occasionally treated symbols as performative, their usual argument was consequentialist—speech provokes undesirable behavior. The Illinois group libel law was justified as necessary to prevent riots. Feminists often quoted Robin Morgan's aphorism: "Pornography is the theory, and rape the practice."[3] Diana Russell echoed it: "Pornography is a male fantasy-solution that inspires nonfantasy acts of punishment for uppity females." The MacKinnon-Dworkin ordinance allowed women to sue the distributors of pornography that caused them harm. Citizens for Decency through Law blamed pornography for a recent Indianapolis murder. MacKinnon exaggerated the causal link between pornography and violence. A decade later she asserted that the Seventh Circuit decision invalidating the ordinance had "explicitly embraced" a "demonstrated causal connection between pornography and social harms."[4] The National Coalition against Pornography called smut the "instruction manual" for the sexual molestation of girls. The federal Pornography Victims' Compensation Bill was nicknamed the "Bundy bill" after a serial killer allegedly inspired by pornography.

There *was* a connection between symbol and violence, but not the one posited by regulatory advocates. Antipornography campaigners invaded and disrupted adult bookstores and movie theaters. A disturbed woman tried to burn herself to death. The JDL eagerly took up Collin's gauntlet, promising that "the streets of Skokie will run with Nazi blood." Protests against *The Satanic Verses* caused dozens of deaths and hundreds of injuries. White racists attacked British Muslims. Muslims bombed bookstores and publishers in Britain and the United States. The leading liberal South African newspaper withdrew its invitation to Rushdie, claiming it could not ensure his safety. A Muslim leader was murdered in Belgium for displaying leniency toward Rushdie. The author's Japanese translator was murdered, his Italian translator wounded, and his Norwegian publisher shot. He has been forced to hide for more than eight years. Muslim fundamentalists bombed a conference addressed by Rushdie's unauthorized Turkish translator, killing thirty-five. Taslima Nasrin was attacked, and many Bangladeshis died or were injured demonstrating against her book. And Naguib Mahfouz barely survived an assassination attempt. These tragic events are classic instances of what civil libertarians properly denounce as the "heckler's veto."

These controversies seemed insoluble. Each side invoked absolutes, foreclosing compromise. The MCLU executive director pronounced: "Bookstores cannot be censored. That's all there is to it." The Chicago ACLU public relations director condemned "the Village of Skokie [for having] shredded the First Amendment." Andrea Dworkin called pornography a "public hanging" of women and the First Amendment "an instrument of the ruling class." The only question for the Minneapolis City Council was "Are they helping the pornographers or helping women?" MacKinnon assailed the opposition of gay men, whose "stake in male supremacy . . . [was] in some ways even greater than that of straight men." In response to a serious but critical review she denounced Ronald Dworkin as "startlingly incompetent, inconsistent

and ignorant," guilty of "misrepresentation, shoddy scholarship, ignorance and evasion" and of pushing "recycled junk." The difference
between him and "kept writers in pornography magazines" was "increasingly measurable in millimeters and microseconds." Critics condemned *The Satanic Verses* as "the most offensive thing written about
Islam in English literature." The fatwa was irrevocable. Each controversy escalated inexorably, insult feeding insult, attack provoking retaliation. Rushdie regretted having kept his mouth shut for four years
(hardly an accurate description). Competition for leadership within
each faction encouraged extremism.

These exchanges fundamentally violated the rules of Holmes's
"marketplace of ideas" and Habermas's unconstrained conversation.
Adversaries sought to score points, not to listen. MacKinnon refused
to tolerate skepticism about the relation between pornography and violence: "Saying a body of research is open to interpretation to which it
is not open is not professional." She supported law students who shut
down a woman artist's videos of pornography and prostitutes. She refused to debate feminists about pornography because that was "the
pimps' current strategy for legitimizing a slave trade in women." When
the Nazis finally marched in Chicago, counterdemonstrators drowned
out their cries that "the creatures should be gassed." Many of Rushdie's
fiercest critics refused to read his book: Syed Shahabuddin in India,
Fatima Meer in South Africa, Ayatollah Khomeini, the French archbishop, even Naguib Mahfouz. Renewing the fatwa for the fourth year,
Ayatollah Khomeini declared: "This system is not on speaking terms
with the arrogant enemies of the revolution, and that's forever, and
we'll never reconcile with them." The *Los Angeles Times* retorted in
kind: "You said it, Ayatollah, we won't."

Adversaries in the first two controversies would accept nothing less
than total victory. MacKinnon and Dworkin wanted to proscribe pornography; civil libertarians demanded toleration. Nazis praised Hitler
and the Holocaust; antiracists obstructed hate speech. But Rushdie and
his critics did discuss a resolution, if they never agreed on terms. A
month after publication of *The Satanic Verses* a British Muslim leader
demanded the book's withdrawal and destruction, an undertaking not
to reprint, "an unqualified apology to the world Muslim community
for the enormous injury to the[ir] feelings and sensibilities," and payment of damages to Islamic charities in Britain. Muslim protesters insisted that Rushdie "eat his words." (Several years earlier Britain had
salved Saudi honor by withdrawing the television program "Death of
a Princess" and sending the home secretary to Jidda to apologize for
the documentary about the stoning of an adulteress.) Immediately after

the fatwa Rushdie did apologize, hoping to be pardoned, and Viking joined him. Two days later he publicly recognized "that Moslems in many parts of the world are genuinely distressed by the publication of my novel," and he "profoundly regret[ted] the distress that publication has occasioned to the sincere followers of Islam." Khomeini promptly rebuffed this "even if Salman Rushdie repents and becomes the most pious man of time." A second British Muslim leader accepted Rushdie's apology, but the Bradford Council of Mosques rejected it as insincere and "a further insult to the Muslim community as a whole." The *Observer* denied that "Britain [or] the author has anything to apologise for." They could "regret the offence caused or the anger stirred, but not the act itself."

On the fatwa's first anniversary Rushdie published a 7,000-word justification. He concluded by expressing "regret that such offence has been taken against my work when it was not intended—when dispute was intended and dissent, and even, at times, satire, and criticism of intolerance, and the like, but not . . . 'filth,' not 'insult,' not 'abuse.'" At his Christmas 1990 meeting with six Islamic scholars, he publicly converted, disavowed agreement with his characters' words, canceled the paperback and further translations, and promised "to work for a better understanding of Islam in the world." He considered prefacing the book with a statement that it "was not intended as an attack on Islam." The scholars accepted his lack of evil motive, and the Cairo grand sheikh formally forgave him. A few weeks later, however, Iran reiterated the fatwa and doubled the price on his head. Within a year all but one of the imams reversed themselves. A British Muslim leader added that any apology had to be accompanied by withdrawal of the book.

Rushdie bitterly condemned his "degree course in worthlessness." His conversion had turned "friends" against him. Repudiating his apology, he insisted he had "never disowned 'The Satanic Verses,' nor regretted writing it." The book "must be freely available and easily affordable." This provoked an attack on his "lack of shame." He had to repent rather than express mere "sorrow." Rushdie responded by publishing the paperback and rejecting Islam. Asked "what reparations would I be prepared to make?" he retorted: "[W]ho is injuring whom here? . . . [A] crime has been committed against the book." Dr. Kalim Siddiqui, one of his most implacable British enemies, said it was time "for both sides to forgive and forget" (thereby persuading the government to drop his incitement charge). But Iran renewed the fatwa, declaring that fifty-one Muslim nations had anathematized Rushdie as an apostate.

These exchanges illustrate the centrality and difficulty of apology in contests over respect (discussed in chapter 7). Just as the harmful speech enhanced the speaker's status at the expense of its target, so an apology lowers the offender's status while raising the victim's. Apology is a form of self-abasement. After Rushdie's public conversion his "friends" called him "spineless, pathetic, debased." Nasrin lost respect for him. Form is crucial. The apologist must express repentance, not just sorrow, regret the act, not just the offense taken. Good motives do not excuse. Indeed, excuses, explanations, and justifications undermine the apology. An inadequate apology may aggravate resentment. Only those offended can determine its adequacy, and they may not agree. Some may demand more than the apologist is prepared to give, increasing intransigence.

STATUS COMPETITION

The stories in chapters 2 and 4 exemplify what sociologists call status competition. The idea commonly is traced back to Max Weber's conception of status groups or collectivities *(Stände):* "people who successfully claim . . . a special social esteem."[5] Because he was reflecting on historical accounts of closed, often endogamous groups, usually associated with particular occupations (in India or feudal Europe), Weber's formulation appears dated when applied to contemporary experience. Such groups were defined by "a specific *style of life*" rooted in "principles of the *consumption* of goods."[6] In the face-to-face communities he studied (and inhabited), status-group membership could readily be defined by such overt indicia as dress, manners, language, accoutrements, physical appearance, even visible signs of religious affiliation.[7] (Thorstein Veblen, Weber's close contemporary, developed an analogous theory of conspicuous consumption as a marker of social status.)[8] But though the concrete manifestations of status have changed—the mass media have leveled speech differences, dress differs far less by occupation or even wealth—the core of Weber's definition is timeless: "one's conception of what is correct and proper and, above all, of what affects the individual's sense of honor and dignity." Indeed, he prefigured the now clichéd notion of "political correctness": "the conviction of the excellence of one's own customs and the inferiority of alien ones, a conviction which sustains the sense of . . . honor."[9] Bourdieu has recently elaborated a theory of class defined by lifestyle.[10]

Sharing Weber's view that status groups were anachronistic, twentieth-century commentators used either Marxist conceptions of class or liberal pluralist notions of cross-cutting interest groups to explain contemporary politics. But the rise of working-class conservatism, especially the virulent postwar anticommunism, was not amenable to either approach. Richard Hofstadter, therefore, interpreted McCarthyism and related phenomena as "projective rationalizations arising from status aspirations." He saw this as expressive behavior, either "goalless" or motivated by goals "unrelated to the discontents from which the movement had its source" and thus analogous to the medieval dancing mania provoked by the Black Death.[11] A decade later he refined his typology, distinguishing the "clash of material aims and needs" from both cultural politics, which concerned "faith and morals, tone and style, freedom and coercion," and politics that projected "interests and concerns, not only largely private but essentially pathological, into the public scene."[12] Seymour Martin Lipset came closer to both Weber's conception and subsequent usage by defining status politics as "political movements whose appeal is to the not uncommon resentments of individuals or groups who desire to maintain or improve their social status."[13] Other analysts wrote of the "ressentiment"[14] or envy[15] of dominated groups.

The most fully elaborated treatment is found in Joseph Gusfield's account of American temperance movements. He located status politics in situations where "issues of moral reform are analyzed as one way through which a cultural group acts to preserve, defend, or enhance the dominance and prestige of its own style of living within the total society."[16] "Each status group operates with an image of correct behavior which it prizes and with a contrast conception in the behavior of despised groups whose status is beneath theirs."[17] "The public support of one conception of morality at the expense of another enhances the prestige and self-esteem of the victors and degrades the culture of the losers."[18] Other writers have talked about "deviantizing" behavior and constructing the "inferiorized person."[19] Unlike interest-group politics, status competition is not instrumental: "the action is ritualistic and ceremonial in that the goal is reached *in the behavior itself* rather than in any state which it brings about."[20] Because he was analyzing efforts by rural, native-born Protestants to defend their endangered status against immigrant Catholic urban industrial workers and by local traditionalists against cosmopolitan modernists, Gusfield said little about moral crusades as a strategy of *upward* mobility.[21]

Collective status competition must be distinguished from two related forms of conflict. Individuals seek and defend status for themselves and intimate groupings (such as families, villages, and gangs).[22] This occurs not only through formal processes—precedence, stylized insults, duels, feuds, sports contests—but also through daily interac-

tion, as Erving Goffman has shown.[23] Individual and collective assertions of status often interact.[24] Social attributions of honor also have
intrapsychic consequences: inferiority complexes, delusions of grandeur.[25] Contemporary efforts to raise depressed self-esteem in deval-
ued groups (women, racial minorities, gays and lesbians, the physically
different) acknowledge the connection between these two domains.

Although Gusfield's framework illumines a wide range of social
phenomena, it also encounters certain analytic dangers. These conflicts,
like all human behavior, are overdetermined. A focus on status consequences must not deny the importance of other dimensions. I am certainly not insinuating that participants are hypocritically manipulating
norms and values for ulterior motives. Feminist critics of pornography
genuinely believe (as do I) that its dissemination objectifies and demeans women. Many Muslims were deeply wounded by Rushdie's
parody of Mohammed's life. American Nazis are convinced that Jews
and blacks are inferior. Actors in these conflicts seek normative coherence.[26] But contrary to the critique of some sociologists,[27] it is possible
to acknowledge the authenticity of a belief and still study how controversies about it affect the social standing of contestants.

Status competition is often combined with the pursuit of material
interest.[28] Indeed, they tend to reinforce each other: status both reflects
wealth and helps create it. Status fosters the solidarity a class requires
to secure material objectives.[29] Status also reinforces political power:
Jim Crow laws compelling black deference helped southern whites retain hegemony.[30] Material anxiety can outweigh status aspirations:
some attribute antifeminism among women to fear of losing male economic support.[31] But if the two objectives often interact, it is essential
to keep them analytically distinct. Some campaigns profoundly affect
status but have few material consequences. Murray Edelman offers numerous examples of legislative, executive, and judicial actions elevating the norms or standing of one group at the expense of another but
with little expected, or observable, behavioral change.[32] And certainly
much of politics is relatively unconcerned with status: matters about
which there is a strong normative consensus (national defense in wartime); questions of interest that do not significantly implicate norms
(pork-barrel legislation).

Like most sociological explanation, the theory of status competition
is not interested in motive. Actors rarely announce their intentions, and
such declarations are never conclusive. Those who reject the theory out
of respect for the actor's normative authenticity are being fundamentally unsociological.[33] In any case, innocuous motives do not preclude
adverse status consequences. A white cab driver who passes up a black

passenger constructs their relative racial status even if the cabbie is motivated by irrational fear, a plausible statistical judgment about the risk of crime, or a desire for a more lucrative fare.

Status conflict has distinctive characteristics. It tends to be emotionally intense because the dominated must extirpate internalized feelings of subordination; Patricia Williams's concept of "spirit murder" vividly captures the hurt.[34] Insults rankle most when status claims are tenuous and contested.[35] Unlike economic disputes, status conflict is zero-sum because the pie cannot be expanded; the value of position inheres in its scarcity; one group can gain status only relative to another.[36] Because the medium is norms or values, compromise is difficult: moral perfectionism long antedates the recent debate about "political correctness."[37] Because the state imprimatur constitutes a public, official affirmation of norms and values, "seemingly ceremonial or ritual acts are often of great importance" and "the legislative victory, whatever, its factual consequences, confers respect and approval."[38] But the state is not the only arena; religion used to play this role (and still does); and the media are gaining prominence. Moral crusades may use both assimilative and coercive means to champion norms.[39]

Status competition illuminates a wide variety of historical events. My first example is relatively obscure. Two 1849 productions of *Macbeth* in New York featured rival actors: the Englishman William Macready and the American Edwin Forrest. A contemporaneous account noted

> a combination of exciting causes: the feeling against England and Englishmen, handed down to us from the Revolution [more than seventy years earlier!] and kept fresh by the insults and abuse of British writers on American manners [Dickens's *Martin Chuzzlewit* had appeared five years earlier]; the injuries committed against Forrest [snubbed on a recent English tour], with Macready as the presumed cause, and this was increased by the fact of Macready playing at the aristocratic kid-glove Opera House.

Forrest's supporters filled the Opera House gallery and aborted the performance by throwing rotten eggs, pennies, even chairs, and preventing Macready from being heard. The attempt to restage it three days later was viewed as an unpardonable insult. Opponents and supporters vied within the theater as a mob gathered outside. Soldiers summoned to the scene shot into the crowd. The contemporaneous pamphlet continued:

> Macready was a subordinate personage, and he was to be put down less on his own account than to spite his aristocratic supporters. The

question became not only a national, but a social one. . . . A distinguished clergyman of this city says of Macready and his right to act: "Though he had been of the meanest of his kind, he should have been protected here in the conclusion of his announced engagement, if an army of ten thousand men had been required to wait upon his movements." A zeal for the rights of Macready and for law and order is commendable—but it must not be forgotten that other rights must have been violated, or this riot could never have taken place. Society by its unjust distribution of the avails of industry, enables a few men to become rich, and consigns a great mass to hopeless poverty, with all its deprivations and degradations.[40]

There are striking parallels with the response to *The Satanic Verses* on the other side of the ocean a century and a half later.

The second example is much more familiar: the 1925 trial of Scopes, a Tennessee schoolteacher who advanced evolutionary theory. Prosecutor William Jennings Bryan, the former presidential candidate, denounced the defendant and his counsel: "These gentlemen . . . did not come here to try this case. They came here to try revealed religion. I am here to defend it. . . . I am simply trying to protect the Word of God against the greatest atheist or agnostic in the United States." (In England a half century later, Mary Whitehouse offered a strikingly similar justification for prosecuting *Gay News* for a poem expressing homosexual fantasies about Christ: "I simply had to protect Our Lord.") With tragic prescience Bryan described the trial as "a duel to the death." (He died of a diabetic attack shortly after it ended.) His adversary, the notorious radical and freethinker Clarence Darrow, was equally uncompromising: "We have the purpose of preventing bigots and ignoramuses from controlling the education of the United States."

Radio station WGN created the first national hookup, broadcasting the trial live for two weeks, a morality play that transfixed millions (just as the army-McCarthy hearings did in the 1950s, Watergate in the 1970s, Hill-Thomas in 1991, and O. J. Simpson in 1995). Some 200 reporters, all antifundamentalist, invaded the small town. H. L. Mencken, reporting for the *Baltimore Evening Sun,* described the locals as "gaping primates, yokels, peasants, hillbillies, Babbitts, morons, mountaineers" and ridiculed Bryan's verbal excess, dress, appetite, and corpulence. Circus performers displayed two chimpanzees, representing mankind's alleged ancestors.

Testifying as an expert witness, Bryan was mercilessly grilled by Darrow.

> Bryan: The only purpose Mr. Darrow has is to slur at the Bible, but I will answer his questions. . . . I want the world to know that this man,

who does not believe in God, is trying to use a court in Tennessee . . .
to slur at it, and, while it will require time, I am willing to take it.
Darrow: I object to your statement. I am examining you on your fool
ideas that no intelligent Christian on earth believes.[41]

Gusfield has sought insights from status competition into other controversies, including civil rights, civil liberties, vivisection, and Sunday
blue laws.[42] He followed Hofstadter in attributing progressivism to
mugwumps—old wealthy well-educated families—who responded to
the threat from corporate business, machine politics, and the nouveaux
riches by championing antitrust legislation, a merit-based civil service,
and anticorruption laws.[43] Americans were still debating school curricula four decades after the Scopes trial (as they are today), although this
was eclipsed by such flashpoints as communism, human relations, and
the United Nations.[44] Support for Sen. Joseph McCarthy's attack on
the State Department was seen as expressing Midwestern agricultural,
middle-class resentment of elite Ivy League graduates: "striped-pants
diplomats," "egghead security risks" ("effete Eastern intellectuals" in
Spiro Agnew's catchphrase two decades later).[45] When Eisenhower
prefaced his inaugural address with a short prayer he had written, a
Women's Christian Temperance Union officer called it "the finest thing
we've had in years from a president's lips." When his successor, Kennedy, had Robert Frost read a poem at the inauguration, John Steinbeck
exclaimed: "[W]hat a joy . . . that literacy is no longer *prima facie* evidence of treason." E. B. White thanked Frost "for your brave words. I
promise that whenever I can manage I'll blow my little draft of air on
the beloved flame." African Americans and women welcomed Clinton's selection of Maya Angelou thirty-two years later.[46] Kennedy's
election also enhanced the status of American Catholics, just as Knute
Rockne's football victories at Notre Dame had done a decade earlier.[47]

Other writers have used the framework to interpret a wide variety
of social phenomena. Moral panics are natural candidates: alcohol,[48]
marijuana,[49] cocaine,[50] homosexuality,[51] contraception,[52] and pornography and obscenity.[53] All facets of crime have offered fertile ground:
juvenile delinquency,[54] gangs,[55] child and spousal abuse,[56] the death
penalty,[57] and the role of criminal justice in race relations.[58] Status elements have been found in 1960s counterculture (especially among students),[59] attacks on media licentiousness,[60] opposition to nuclear weapons,[61] and resentment of the "new class" of mediacrats.[62] Status is
prominent in controversies over religion, especially in public schools.[63]
Concern about toxic substances—fluoridation in the 1950s, pesticides
like alar and electromagnetic fields more recently—and environmentalism generally can express status anxieties.[64] The campaign against

tobacco has become a moral crusade, whose overtones transcend the clash between health and profit.[65] An R. J. Reynolds Tobacco Company scientist denounced federal legislation to ban smoking in public places as "politically correct." A month later, during contentious congressional hearings over accusations that the industry had manipulated nicotine levels to keep smokers addicted, a Virginia Republican declared: "I am proud to represent the thousands of honest hard-working men and women who earn their livelihood producing this product . . . and I'll be damned if they are sacrificed on the altar of political correctness."[66] Even representations of smoking are controversial. When the committee advising the Postal Service deleted a cigarette in a stamp depicting 1930s blues guitarist Robert Johnson, the publicist of the National Smokers Alliance called this "an affront to the more than 50 million Americans who choose to smoke."[67]

As chapter 4 documents, struggles for respect have become more pervasive, intense, and public in recent years. This requires explanation. The Enlightenment saw status as a feudal relic. In 1733 Voltaire wrote approvingly:

> Go into the London Exchange, a place more dignified than many a royal court. There you will find representatives of every nation quietly assembled to promote human welfare. There the Jew, the Mahomatan and the Christian deal with each other as though they were all of the same religion. They call no man Infidel unless he be bankrupt. There the Presbyterian trusts the Anabaptist, and the Anglican accepts the Quaker's bond.[68]

Marx chronicled the rise of capitalism and predicted the triumph of socialism, which would eliminate class distinctions. Although Weber devoted much energy to refuting Marx, he agreed that capitalism was incompatible with status pretensions: "[T]he market and its processes knows no personal distinctions: functional interests dominate it. It knows nothing of honor. The status order means precisely the reverse: stratification in terms of honor and styles of life peculiar to status groups as such."[69] Maine (Weber's precursor) and Tönnies (his contemporary) proclaimed the movement from status to contract, gemeinschaft to gesellschaft. Parsons restated Weber in terms of pattern variables, asserting the inevitability and desirability of a shift from particularism to universalism. Rationalists expected science to replace religious divisions with unitary truth.

Nationalism was discredited by nineteenth- and twentieth-century wars and thought to have been rendered obsolete by weapons of mass destruction. Wars of liberation overthrew colonialism, repudiating beliefs in the superiority of nations or ethnicities. Americans expected immigrant diversity to dissolve in the melting pot. If the proletariat never became Marx's universal class, bourgeois sociology saw the "middle class" doing so: all Americans claimed membership, material differences were quantitative rather than qualitative, dress and speech became indistinguishable, and individuals moved up and down the stratification system according to merit.[70] The Enlightenment commitment to equality was generalized from class and religion to race and gender.

We know, however, that history has not followed this Whiggish path. Rather than eclipsing status, class elaborated new status distinctions.[71] The classic nineteenth- and early twentieth-century European writers—Dickens, Stendahl, Zola, Strindberg, Ibsen, Tolstoi—vividly portrayed the clash between the declining aristocracy and rising bourgeoisie. A century after science prematurely claimed victory, religion is enjoying a global revival, generating increasingly bitter battles within and across denominational lines.[72] Relations between Islam and the West have not been this strained since the Crusades; the Hindu-Muslim confrontation at Ayodhya launched the careers of demagogues who led attacks on Rushdie and Nasrin; Northern Ireland has been racked by sectarian strife for decades. Nations may be ceding sovereignty to regional or even global unions, and some are experiencing separatist movements. But trade rivalries are as intense as ever—witness American resentment of OPEC and Japan and China. And national disintegration has produced bloody war and genocide in the former Soviet Union and Yugoslavia, Sri Lanka, and Rwanda. Political colonialism has been replaced by economic and cultural imperialism, with the predictable backlash. Unable to fulfill their substantive promises, revolutionary movements remain preoccupied with the symbols of the old order: matters of dress (banishing the veil in Turkey and Soviet Central Asia after World War I and mandating it in Iran, Algeria, and Afghanistan today; Mao suits in China and Tanzania, blue jeans and Western pop culture among restive communist youth) and address ("comrade" and its vernacular equivalents).

The roadblocks encountered by the civil rights and feminist movements contributed to the rise of black power and lesbian separatism; many whites contemporaneously rediscovered ethnic identities. Murray Edelman captured this acutely.

> When members of the protesting group perceive the established order as entrenched and generally supported and its own resources for superseding it manifestly inadequate, attacks on the symbols of its own degraded status are predictable, as are attacks on weak groups per-

ceived to be on the margins of the elite or benefiting from the established order without sharing in its resources for exercising power.[73]

Occupations acquire genteel euphemisms: "custodian" for janitor,
"sanitation worker" for garbage collector.[74] Alternatively, the despised
may perversely embrace their degraded status through self-destructive
or criminal behavior.

How should we understand the failure of the modernist vision? One
explanation is materialist. As the economic pie grows more slowly and
even contracts (because productivity gains decline and competition becomes global), frustrated ambitions are rechanneled into status claims,
and anxieties fuel status resentments. Witness the disproportionate
anger directed at immigrants, trade competitors, affirmative-action
beneficiaries, welfare recipients, criminals, and the homeless. Weber
saw this clearly.

> [E]pochs and countries in which the naked class situation is of pre-
> dominant significance are regularly periods of technical and economic
> transformation. And every slowing down of the change in economic
> stratification leads, in due course, to the growth of status structures
> and makes for a resuscitation of the important role of social honor.[75]

Many have interpreted white male anger as a defense of status in conditions of declining economic and political power. Confronted with the
uncertainties of the global market, some nations turn to protectionism
and others resist alien cultural influences, especially the constantly ex-
panding hegemony of American popular culture.[76]

The prominence of status politics in the United States appears to be
another manifestation of American exceptionalism.[77] As de Tocqueville
remarked more than a century and a half ago, "[E]quality of condition
is the fundamental fact from which all others seem to be derived."[78] Yet
class politics have always been poorly developed in both the American
electoral arena and workplace. The two principal parties, increasingly
indistinguishable on bread-and-butter issues whose intricacies defy lay
comprehension (e.g., Federal Reserve rates, trade policy, tax reform,
a balanced budget), seek to stake out positions on hot-button social
questions or adopt or flirt with women or minority candidates (Geraldine Ferraro, Colin Powell).

Cultural representation has become a pivotal battlefield for another
reason. It is already clichéd to observe that information increasingly
plays the central economic role that capital, natural resources, and land
occupied in previous eras. The mass media powerfully shape social
status. This helps to explain the intensity with which the demand for
equality has been extended from polity and market to the cultural do-

main. Leisure expands, displacing work as a primary source of identity (team loyalties instead of occupational uniforms). The entertainment industry provides surrogate satisfactions to the masses, contemporary circuses (in lieu of bread). Women and minorities, whose collective status aspirations are blocked, see token representatives attain fame, mass adulation, and unimaginable wealth. Celebrity status may even be convertible into political position—Ronald Reagan, for example, or Sonny Bono. Politics becomes spectacle, appealing to taste rather than opinion. The next chapter documents the centrality and diversity of status conflict.

CHAPTER FOUR

•••

The Politics of Respect

In the last two chapters I argued that the controversies over pornography, racial hatred, and blasphemy fundamentally concern the same issue—respect. Despite modernist optimism status ambitions, resentments, and anxieties still fuel bitter, often intractable, conflict. This chapter documents the pervasiveness of the politics of respect and explores its distinctive characteristics. I begin by surveying the arenas in which it is conducted before turning to the principal fault lines: religion, nation, and language; race; and the newly contested identities of gender, sexual orientation, and physical difference.

OCCASIONS FOR CONTESTING STATUS

Claims to respect suffuse contemporary political life. Many evoke the past, whose emotional power sometimes *increases* with time. Human remains evoke strong feelings: the display of an embalmed African near the Barcelona Olympics, the graves of Jews in Germany and non-Jews in Israel, American Indian and African American cemeteries in the United States.[1] Controversies erupt over commemorations of people and events: declaring holidays or naming streets for Martin Luther King and Cesar Chavez, renaming Custer Battlefield National Monument after Little Bighorn, observing the quincentenary of Columbus's landfall in America, even debating the historicity of the Alamo or William Tell.[2] Passions are inflamed by museums about Nazism, Disney theme parks on American history, stamps honoring Nixon, or Croatia's revival of its fascist Ustashe currency. Partisans seek to erect monuments—to the suffragists in the Capitol and Arthur Ashe in Richmond—or tear them down—Henrik Verwoerd statues in South Africa and Lenin's mummified body in the Kremlin.[3] They clash over the content of national anthems—the nationalism of "La Marseillaise," the Jewish exclusivity of "Hatikvah"—and the design of and respect for flags.[4]

Many of these issues emerged at the fiftieth anniversary of World War II's conclusion. After the RAF Bomber Command erected a statue to their leader, Sir Arthur Harris, whose raids killed half a million German civilians, the German foreign minister endorsed a protest by mayors of the bombed cities, and residents booed when the queen visited Dresden. Prince Philip sought to make amends by laying a wreath at the Dresden cemetery during a commemoration of the saturation bombing. But though German president Herzog maintained at the service that "no one wants to offset the atrocities committed by Germans in the Nazi state," protesters shouted "Germans were the criminals, not the victims!" Chancellor Kohl also ignited a furor by dedicating a memorial statue in Berlin with the inscription "To the Victims of War and Tyranny." The chairman of Berlin's principal Jewish organization refused to attend because the inscription "places victims and perpetrators on the same level." But when Kohl added a brass tablet naming the groups that suffered Nazi terror, Ignatz Bubis, the country's principal Jewish spokesperson, called it "a compromise we can live with."[5]

Kohl refused to attend the Normandy landing ceremony because Mitterrand had not personally invited him. An aide complained: "How long will they be celebrating this? A hundred years?" Kohl was somewhat mollified when Mitterrand invited him to review German troops marching in Paris on Bastille Day for the first time since 1944. Having persuaded the four victorious allies to attend a commemoration in Berlin, Kohl refused to invite Lech Walesa because "then you would have to ask the same about Slovakia and the Czech Republic. Then we have to consider the Netherlands, Luxembourg, Belgium or Denmark or Norway."[6]

The wounds of the Pacific war were even rawer. Although 40 percent of Americans felt Japan should apologize for Pearl Harbor and 55 percent of Japanese agreed, only 16 percent of Americans felt the United States should apologize for dropping the atomic bombs, compared to 73 percent of Japanese. George Bush expressed this in typically fractured English: "No apology is required and it will not be asked of this President, I can guarantee you that. . . . there should be no apology requested. And that, in my view, is rank revisionism." On Pearl Harbor Day he made a point of speaking next to the battleship *Missouri,* where Japan had formally surrendered. Veterans reunited in Honolulu complained about Japanese characters on street signs and declared their refusal to buy Japanese cars. The Pearl Harbor survivors association banned any meeting with Japanese pilots. A veteran of the European war burned a Japanese flag at the moment of the attack—in a Georgia town with four Japanese companies.[7] During his first state visit to the

United States three years later, Emperor Akihito considered touring the battleship *Arizona* to express sorrow for the war begun under his father. Instead he laid wreaths at Arlington National Cemetery and Punch Bowl Cemetery in Honolulu, declaring that awareness of "the lives that were lost, the wounds that were inflicted, the feelings of those who suffered anguish never disappears from my heart, however many years and months pass." But he would not say whether the attack was justified.[8]

The Smithsonian Institution created another explosive situation with its 1994 Air and Space Museum exhibit featuring the *Enola Gay* (which had dropped the bomb on Hiroshima).[9] Veterans were upset by first-hand accounts from survivors of the Nagasaki bombing; they also challenged estimates that 30,000 to 50,000 Allied soldiers would have died in a land invasion, insisting that the number would have been at least ten times higher. Twenty-four members of Congress protested to the Smithsonian secretary about the exhibit's anti-American, "historically narrow, revisionist view." The museum responded by adding an account of the war illustrated with fifty photographs. Brig. Gen. Paul W. Tibbets said this acknowledged the lack of "balance and context." But a former combat pilot was not satisfied: "No matter how you look at it, it will be a 'ban the bomb' display." "The Enola Gay is an excellent symbol" to honor America. The pilot of the Nagasaki bombing called the exhibit "a collection of distortions, half truths, and outright lies."

After consulting veterans' groups for two weeks, the Smithsonian made further concessions. It dropped the assertion that most Americans viewed the Pacific theater as "a war of vengeance," whereas most Japanese saw it as "a war to defend their unique culture against Western imperialism." It raised the casualty estimate to 200,000 in a first assault and a million had resistance persisted. It deleted documentation that Eisenhower had told the secretary of war "that Japan was already defeated and that dropping the bomb was completely unnecessary" and that the chairman of the Joint Chiefs of Staff agreed that "the Japanese were already defeated and ready to surrender." But a historian remained appalled "that the planned text gave moral equivalency to Japan's sneak attack on Pearl Harbor with our own contingency planning for an attack on Japan." The Fellowship of Reconciliation complained that the exhibition had eliminated "a watch dial with its hand frozen at the moment of the bombing" and other artifacts showing "the human face of the Japanese who died."

Historians denounced the concessions as "intellectual corruption" and "historical cleansing"; it was "the highest form of naivete" to confer "intellectual authority" on veterans simply for "being there." Although the museum claimed to be "comfortable where we are now," it revised the initial casualty estimate back down to 63,000. The American Legion national commander objected that "hundreds of thousands" of veterans were "now to be told their lives were purchased at the price of treachery and revenge." The House Government Reform and Oversight Committee announced plans to conduct hearings on the exhibit, and more than eighty members of Congress demanded the museum director's resignation. The furor affected fund-raising for the Smithsonian's sesquicentennial; although it offered corporations use of its name and logo for the first time, the only donor demanded anonymity. Newt Gingrich warned the Smithsonian against becoming "a plaything for left-wing ideologues."

Within days the Smithsonian's new secretary (a former chancellor of the University of California, Berkeley, and an ex-marine) admitted that "we made a basic error" and eliminated everything but the *Enola Gay* and a video of its flight crew's recollections. "[V]eterans and their families were expecting, and rightly so, that the nation would honor and commemorate their valor and sacrifice. They were not looking for analysis." "The aircraft speaks for itself." The American Legion commander declared that "the battle over this exhibit is a metaphor for the war's climactic last act. The winners, just as they were 50 years ago, are the American people." Gingrich applauded the Smithsonian's "very wise decision," adding that "the academicians had overreached." Clinton agreed that "some of the concerns expressed by veterans' groups and others had merit." The Smithsonian secretary acknowledged "the institution has much to learn from this experience" but was pleased that "there are some gifts we will receive that have been holding fire until this controversy can be resolved." The *New York Times* editorialized: "[T]he real betrayal of American tradition would be to insist on a single version of history or to make it the property of the state or any group." The museum director resigned several months later because of "continuing controversy and divisiveness."

At the official opening protesters poured ashes and human blood on the *Enola Gay*, shouting "We repent! We regret!" The American Legion was undisturbed when American University displayed some of the banned artifacts. "The Smithsonian is a federal agency supported by taxpayer money, and rightly or wrongly, what it portrays is seen as the United States version of history." The former Japanese ambassador to France deplored the Smithsonian exhibit: "[T]hese bombings were acts committed during a war for which both the vanquished and the victors share responsibility." Hiroshima's mayor was extremely disappointed "that the perspective of humanity has been lost from the altered Smithsonian exhibition."[10]

Showing the Postal Service had learned nothing from the experience, the stamp commemorating the fiftieth anniversary of Hiroshima and Nagasaki featured a mushroom cloud captioned "Atomic bombs hasten war's end, August 1945." The Nagasaki mayor (who had been severely wounded by an assassination attempt for intimating the emperor's war guilt) called the stamp "heartless." Japan's foreign minister cautioned that his compatriots would not have "positive feelings." Even the U.S. State Department called for reconsideration. But the Postal Service was unmoved: "Our purpose is to provide a comprehensive history of the events of World War II, and we are not making a value judgment on any of those events." A day after the White House suggested "there could be more appropriate ways to depict that event," the Postal Service capitulated, substituting a picture of Truman preparing to announce the war's end. The Japanese embassy expressed its appreciation for "the deference to Japanese sensitivities." Fearful that the phrase suggested too much influence, however, it changed the wording to "consideration" of "the sentiments of the Japanese people."[11]

Groups also compete for status by seeking a state imprimatur of their values. Education at all levels is a hotly contested terrain: texts and curricula, multiculturalism, sex, and religion. Government support for the arts (National Endowment for the Arts [NEA] and for the Humanities [NEH]) and media (Corporation for Public Broadcasting [CPB]) also has engendered bitter fights over the portrayal of sexuality (Robert Mapplethorpe, Ron Athey), race, and religion. As the narratives of pornography, racial hatred, and blasphemy revealed, the criminal law represents official recognition of group norms. A striking example is graffiti: both the act and the response express status concerns. Taggers rebel against anonymity and marginality. A twelve-year-old Los Angeleno explained:

> I bomb [tag] . . . to get known, to get up. . . . The way to get known is to get up on the big stuff, on heavens [freeways, billboards, tall buildings]. But they buff [paint over] you. You get known with landmarks [stop signs, trees, utility posts] because landmarks don't get buffed as much and people see it.

After the city council voted to increase the penalty, a member suggested the appropriate punishment would be to "chop a few fingers off." Calling graffiti a "constant assault on the psyche of Angelenos," the new mayor praised the law as an important step in "turning the city around and making it safe . . . a month in boot camp for a first offense, with tough physical training, is the kind of thing we need."[12] A state assemblyman upped the ante by introducing a bill authorizing the paddling of taggers.[13] Shortly thereafter William Masters, a white man, surprised two Chicano taggers, shooting one to death and wounding the other. Masters called his situation "what everybody lives in fear of—a couple of skinhead Mexicans robbing you at 1 A.M. with a screwdriver" and accused the deceased's mother of having "murdered her son by being an irresponsible, uncaring parent." He was inundated with offers of free legal representation, and a city councilor in nearby Simi Valley (whose jury had acquitted Los Angeles police officers of beating Rodney King) called Masters a "crime-fighting hero." The Los Angeles district attorney refused to charge homicide, despite protests by the Mexican American Bar Association, and Masters was convicted only of gun-possession misdemeanors.[14]

Well before Ronald Reagan successfully wooed white ethnic Democrats, politicians have played on voters' status anxieties. George Wallace explained his 1962 victory as Alabama governor, four years after being defeated by a virulent racist: "I started off talking about schools and highways and prisons and taxes—and I couldn't make them listen. Then I began talking about niggers—and they stomped the floor."[15] Sen. Jesse Helms (R-N.C.) built his long tenure on similar rhetoric. He voted "no against the forces who have driven God out of the classroom." America must not "allow the cultural high ground in this nation to sink slowly into an abyss of slime to placate people who clearly seek or are willing to destroy the Judaic-Christian foundations of this republic." "Are civil rights only for Negroes?" he asked. "White women in Washington who have been raped and mugged on the streets in broad daylight have experienced the most revolting sort of violation of their civil rights." "Think about it. Homosexuals and lesbians, disgusting people marching in our streets demanding all sorts of things, including the right to marry each other. How do you like them apples?" He found an AIDS prevention comic book "so obscene, so revolting, it's difficult for me to stand here and talk about it. I may throw up." He denounced Clinton's nomination of Roberta Achtenberg, "a militant-activist-mean lesbian, working her whole career to advance the homosexual agenda. . . . if you want to call me a bigot, go ahead."[16]

Patrick Buchanan sought to launch his political career by pandering to collective insecurities and fostering feelings of social superiority. In his 1992 campaign for the Republican presidential nomination, he proposed to build a high fence and deep trench along the Mexican border, to be patrolled by the National Guard. He condemned foreign aid as "routinized annual transfers of our national wealth to global bureaucrats who ship it off to regimes who pay us back in compound ingratitude." He cleverly melded economic anxieties with nationalism, racism, sexism, homophobia, ageism, sizism, and anticommunism. A Bush campaign adviser who lobbied on behalf of the president's "little friends in Japan" "ought to be wearing a kimono." Those who quit government to work for foreign powers were "the geisha girls of the New World Order." Deng Xiaoping was an "eighty-five-year-old chain-smoking communist dwarf." "Those little dinky countries can't beat us. You know, you take Germany, East and West Germany, put 'em together, that's about the size of Oregon and Washington. . . . You take Japan. It's a pile of rocks over there. You could put the whole thing in California."

He bashed gays relentlessly. AIDS was "nature's retribution" on homosexuals. "A visceral recoil from homosexuality is the natural reaction of a healthy society wishing to preserve itself." A television commercial excerpted the NEA-subsidized PBS documentary *Tongues Untied,* showing scantily clad gay black dancers. The voice-over declared: "The Bush Administration has invested our tax dollars in pornographic and blasphemous art too shocking to show. This so-called art has glorified homosexuality, exploited children and perverted the image of Jesus Christ." Calling the NEA the "upholstered playpen" of the "Eastern liberal Establishment," he demanded the director's "scalp" and promised to "shut down, padlock and fumigate" it.

Seeking the kind of mileage Bush had gained from Willie Horton in the 1988 election, Buchanan played the oldest race card: the 1987 "racial hazing of a black cadet at The Citadel is played up big . . . little mention is found, however, of the rapes of white coeds by black criminals." "There is a legitimate grievance in my view of white working-class people that every time on every issue that the black militants loud-mouth it, we come up with more money." Shortly before entering the 1992 campaign he said: "I think God made all people good. But if we had to take a million immigrants in, say, Zulus next year, or Englishmen, and put them up in Virginia, what group would be easier to assimilate and would cause less problems for the people of Virginia?" "Why are we more shocked when a dozen people are killed in Vilnius than a massacre in Burundi? Because they are white people. That's who we are. That's where America comes from." (African Americans actually outnumbered Lithuanian Americans forty to one and could trace their American ancestry back many more generations.)

His sympathy for the people of Vilnius apparently did not include the hundreds of thousands of Jews murdered by the Nazis, since he questioned how many died in the gas chambers of Treblinka. But his anti-Zionism displayed an uncharacteristic solicitude for Latinos and blacks. He opposed the Persian Gulf War because all the fighting would be done by "kids with names like McAllister, Murphy, Gonzales and Leroy Brown," while "the Israeli Defense Ministry and its amen corner in the United States" beat the drums of war.

Anticipating the white electoral backlash two years later, he denounced "a landfill called multiculturalism" and encouraged resentment of affirmative action.

> [T]he 'African-Americans' of the 90's demand racial quotas and set-asides, as Democrats eagerly assent and a pandering G.O.P. prepares to go along. Who speaks for the Euro-Americans who founded the United States? [He conveniently forgot they founded it on slavery.] . . . Quotas of any kind are wrong.

He uncompromisingly defended patriarchy. "Women are less equipped psychologically to stay the course in the brawling areas of business, commerce, industry and the professions." Reagan had been right to oppose the Equal Rights Amendment because women should be content with the "honorable" and "honored" role of wife and mother. "The momma bird builds the nest. So it was, so it ever shall be. Ronald Reagan is not responsible for this; God is." He ridiculed Anita Hill's charges against Clarence Thomas: "As the harridans of feminism unsheathe the castrator's knife on their last emasculated bulls, Republicans should revisit the Thomas battleground and review how they won, and how they almost lost it all."[17] Seeking the Republican nomination again in 1996, he condemned federal judges for protecting "criminals, atheists, homosexuals, flag burners, illegal aliens—including terrorists—convicts and pornographers."[18]

While conservatives vied for the 1992 Republican nomination, Bill Clinton was confronting the "character issue"—his rivals' thinly disguised attempt to win voters by stoking status antagonisms. His response to the marijuana charge dissatisfied both those who hated pot-heads and those who had inhaled. His avoidance of military service during the Vietnam War angered both patriots and protesters who had suffered for their principles. His marital infidelity with Gennifer Flowers inflamed those who believed in faithfulness (or at least in not getting caught). Italian Americans were furious when the press reported a phone conversation in which Clinton told Flowers that Mario Cuomo "acts like" a mafioso. Condemning the comment as "part of an ugly syndrome that strikes Italian Americans, Jewish people, blacks, women, all different groups," Cuomo told Clinton to "save himself the quarter" to telephone an apology.

Clinton's supporters also disserved him. Introducing the candidate to the Georgia Senate, the state lieutenant governor said that "when the people of the state vote, the message will go out clearly that Tsongas is not Greek for Bubba." This not only incensed Paul Tsongas and Greek Americans but also failed to endear Clinton to southerners. Humorist Ray Blount Jr. wrote: "New York columnists toss around the term 'cracker' awfully loosely, and now Bubba is taking over as an ethnic term. There's no other ethnic group that you could use such a slur about so lightly." Revealing an indecisiveness that was to become far more troubling in the White House, the Clinton team could not even choose a campaign song. The Chicago-based staff liked the Blues Brothers—but lead singer John Belushi had died of a drug overdose. Others proposed James Brown's "I Feel Good"—but he had recently been released from federal prison. Even the Doobie Brothers' "Taking It to the Streets" contained a questionable reference to Jesus.

The day after his primary victories in Michigan and Illinois, Clinton relaxed by playing golf at the all-white Little Rock Country Club. Virginia governor L. Douglas Wilder, an African American rival who had dropped out of the race after New Hampshire, exploded: "It is inconceivable to me that a sitting governor would either accept membership or recreate in a club that openly discriminates against blacks and other minorities." Although Clinton quickly promised not to return until the club integrated, the Little Rock NAACP chapter president said he was "all style and no substance" on civil rights.

Hillary Clinton was running her own symbolic obstacle course. She had earlier adopted Bill's surname because antifeminist voters resented her keeping her patronymic. After he was accused of adultery, she had to apologize to Tammy Wynette for making a disparaging reference to the country star's hit song "Stand by Your Man." Charged with conflicts of interest in law practice, she insulted millions of homemakers by retorting "I suppose I could have stayed home and baked cookies and had teas"—and then tried to repair the damage by doing just that. Perhaps believing that an attack is the best defense, she repeated gossip about Bush's extramarital affairs and then apologized (but did not retract).[19]

Basking in the Republican's 1994 congressional triumph, Newt Gingrich denounced the "profound things that went wrong starting with the Great Society and the counterculture." Clinton was "a very smart, very clever tactician whose core system of activity is a combination of counterculture and McGovern. He was McGovern's Texas director, he and his wife were counterculture at Yale." Gingrich expected a long battle between conservatives and "leftist elites" who advocated Stalinist measures. Portraying Clinton Democrats as "the enemy of normal Americans," he pretended to catch himself and substitute "middle class" for "normal" because "I was once told, to my shock, that the use of the word normal is politically incorrect." "We spent a generation in the counterculture laughing at McGuffey Readers and laughing at Parson Weem's vision of Washington." He unapologetically called for a higher moral tone.

> If, by moral tone, you mean voluntary school prayer, the bulk of Americans are for it; if, by moral tone, you mean punishing violent criminals the first time they're violent, the majority of Americans are for it; if, by moral tone, you mean teaching the truth about American history, teaching about the Founding Fathers and how this country came to be the most extraordinary civilization in history, the vast majority of Americans are for it.

Accepting the speakership, Gingrich acknowledged "the reality that this is a multiethnic society, but it's one civilization. People come here to be Americans and they want to be Americans, and that implies a civilization with a set of habits and patterns." He accused up to a fourth of the White House staff of recently using illicit drugs. When challenged, his spokesperson claimed the figure came from unnamed law enforcement officials and sought to connect the smear to Clinton's "counterculture" background. A day later Gingrich proposed cutting welfare rolls by placing children in orphanages. His mother soon got into the act by revealing on television that her son had once called Hillary a "bitch." (Barbara Bush similarly compared Geraldine Ferraro to a word that "rhymes with rich." Borrowing a leaf from her husband's malapropisms, she claimed she meant "witch.") Newt refused to comment, but a week later his mother asked: "What's all the fuss about? Because I said she is a bitch? And that's what all the pins are saying. Yes, she is."[20] After biting his tongue for months, Gingrich reverted to form following the murder of a woman and two children and the abduction of her viable fetus. This had "happened in America because for two generations we haven't had the guts to talk about right and wrong." It was

> the final culmination of a drug-addicted underclass with no sense of humanity, no sense of civilization, and no sense of the rules of life in which human beings respect each other. Let's talk about what the welfare state has created. Let's talk about the moral decay of the world the left is defending.

In fact, the churchgoing victim was trying to get off welfare; and the accused had no drug convictions.[21]

These diverse examples share common features with each other and with the narratives that began this book. Collectivities sought respect by asserting claims to public symbolic space; the wider the audience and the more official the imprimatur, the higher the stakes. Some groups insisted on the power to interpret history in order to construct a pedigree for assertions of moral superiority. Just as Rushdie fought the mullahs to control the grand narrative of Islam, so American historians criticized Disney's proposed theme park in rural Virginia as "plastic history, mechanical history," calling the company a "cultural strip miner" who would "bury our genuine past." CEO Michael Eisner retorted that he had "sat through many history classes where I read some of their stuff, and I didn't learn anything." Veterans who had "been there" challenged historians' accounts of World War II. Memories never faded: the Civil War and the Alamo were over a century old, Columbus five centuries, William Tell seven, bones in the Holy Land two millennia, those in California eight. The emotional intensity of confrontations framed as policy debates betrayed other motives. Railing against the homeless, a Santa Monica resident felt "like I'm living in Sarajevo. I'm living [under] siege." The city council's inaction was "insulting every working man and woman in this city." Another resident complained: "[I]t's insane to let the least fortunate members of society . . . dictate your lifestyle." A Los Angeles radio talk show host called the homeless a "burden" and a "waste of space," who should "be put to sleep."

The subtext of respect often became explicit. A parent of an Indiana elementary school pupil expostulated: "What kind of sense does it make when you can't pass out the Bible but you can pass out condoms and homosexual literature? . . . It's like something is wrong with the Bible." Seven decades after the Scopes trial, Christian conservatives in California wanted to put "creationism on an equal footing with evolution." A Boston suburbanite complained that his town's embrace of creationism reduced it to "just a gooberville in Arkansas."[22] Championing school prayer, a Texas school board member pronounced: "In a democracy, the majority rules. In the last 30 years, I think we have sort of turned that around so that the minority rules."[23] Locals resented cosmopolitan outsiders. The Cincinnati prosecutor of the Mapplethorpe exhibit boasted: "We're not going to let the [Contemporary Arts Center] or anyone from New York come into Hamilton County and dictate to local officials what they will or will not do." Just as Syed Shahabuddin had embraced the epithets "primitive" and "superstitious barbarian," so Jesse Helms welcomed critics to "call me a bigot."

Attacking multiculturalism, Patrick Buchanan declared: "Our culture is superior because our religion is Christianity and that is the truth that makes men free." Having gained control of a rural Florida school board, his followers required that instruction "instill in our students an appreciation of our American heritage and culture such as . . . capitalism, a free-enterprise system, patriotism, strong family values . . . and other basic values that are superior to other foreign or historic cultures." American intellectuals joined the chorus (echoing British counterparts who defended Rushdie by attacking Islam). Successfully wooing a $20 million gift, Yale College dean Donald Kagan proclaimed that "Western culture and institutions are the most powerful paradigm in the world." Cynthia Ozick (who had compared Rushdie to Dreyfus) insisted on the superiority of Homer, Austen, and Kafka to any "Aleutian Islander." Not to be outdone, Newt Gingrich called the United States "the most extraordinary civilization in history."

The same buzzwords pervaded many contests. A caricature of Simon Bolívar was pornographic and blasphemous, Disney's history theme park was sacrilege, Latvia's proposal to exhume and deport Russian bones was blasphemous. When Rev. Louis Sheldon called the work of NEA grantees hate art and Patrick Buchanan denounced it as filthy and blasphemous, NEA chair John Frohnmayer equated such critics to Nazis. Scatological phrases abounded: an opponent of AIDS education found her "entire life . . . sucked down the emotional toilet." Homelessness was associated with urine and feces. Barbara Bush and Newt Gingrich's mother called Geraldine Ferraro and Hillary Clinton "bitches"; Buchanan openly labeled feminists "castrators."

Antagonists embraced a Manichaean view of the world: the Judeo-Christian tradition versus godless atheism, "white women raped and mugged" versus "civil rights for Negroes," straights versus "homosexuals and lesbians, disgusting people," natives versus immigrants, Americans versus foreigners, families versus illegitimacy, workers versus welfare scroungers. Adversaries employed the tropes of war. The "battle" over the Smithsonian exhibit was "a metaphor for the war's climactic last act." Opponents saw school prayer as a "do-or-die issue." "Just look at a map: Beirut, Sarajevo, Belfast." The Christian Action Network issued a "Declaration of War" against Ron Athey's performance art. South African blacks toppling Verwoerd's statue were "taking the capital." Jesse Helms saw America sinking into an abyss of slime. Sounding like Muslims attacking Rushdie and Norman Mailer putting up his dukes, Patrick Buchanan warned flag burners: "When someone spits in your mother's face you don't sit them down and persuade them they are wrong. You put a fist in their face."

RELIGION, NATION, AND LANGUAGE

Although Muslims who equated *The Satanic Verses* with the Crusades were being hyperbolic, religious honor remains a powerful engine of social conflict. The Hindu-Muslim clash over Ayodhya, which touched both Rushdie and Nasrin, reflected ancient religious hostilities throughout the Indian subcontinent. If sectarianism receives more publicity in non-Western societies, the West displays its own intolerance.[24] After Denver Nuggets star Mahmoud Abdul-Rauf refused to stand for "The Star-Spangled Banner" at basketball games, shock jocks from a local radio station invaded his mosque wearing their shoes and blasted it on trumpet and bugle. The president of the Colorado Muslim Society complained that the intruders had "disrespected our sanctity, dressing like clowns and symbolically thrusting the national anthem down the throats of the Muslims."[25] Britain long banned Sikh turbans in the workplace. When a Birmingham primary school headmaster conceded Muslim demands that pupils be excused from drawing pigs or even pronouncing the name, the local Conservative MP fulminated: "The pig is a major part of British life. These children are living in Britain, not in India or Pakistan."[26] Although France allowed Jewish schoolboys to wear yarmulkes, the education minister banned the *hijab* (headscarf). "We must respect the culture and faith of Muslims, but history and the will of our people was to build a united, secular society." When Lyons Muslims omitted the traditional spire and muezzin's call from their mosque, the interior minister welcomed this "French Islam," which respected republican principles and did not view the country as "a space to conquer."[27] In Italy, by contrast, the Catholic Council of the Northern League denounced a new mosque in Rome as "a veritable foothold in a Western country, a general headquarters for the expansion of Islam."[28] Israeli police prosecute the five daily Muslim calls to prayer as violations of noise ordinances; some mosques retaliate by turning up the volume on the Jewish Sabbath, while West Bank settlers scale minarets to tear down loudspeakers.[29]

Christianity recently began to repudiate its historical anti-Semitism. The Evangelical-Lutheran Church in America disavowed the "anti-Judaic rhetoric and violent recommendations" of its founder. A year after Pope John Paul II referred to Jews as "elder brothers" in the faith, the new Catholic catechism rejected the blood libel of deicide and affirmed God's covenant with Israel, the validity of the Hebrew Bible, and Jesus' life as a Jew.[30] But the limits of tolerance are quickly reached when Jews practice their religion too publicly. Orthodox Jews asked the London borough of Barnet for permission to create an "eruv," relaxing Sabbath restrictions within its confines. Although the perimeter of nearly invisible fishing line would require just eighty-five additional utility poles in an area that already had 50,000, it provoked fury. A local newspaper headline warned "Jewish Zealots: We'll Patrol Eruv." Lord McGregor, council chair for the Hampstead Garden Suburb Trust, denounced the eruv as "a rotten idea." Jews "have affronted every other sect. . . . We've had for a century in this country a tradition of religious tolerance. It is based on the proposition that no one sect ever behaves in a manner to affront another." What was next, he asked, "totem poles on Hampstead Heath?" Greeted by cries of "Shame" and "Resign" at the trust's 1992 annual meeting, he did so on the spot. An Orthodox Jewish woman denounced opponents who "worried that they're going to be seen again as Jews. They're afraid that the whole we're-ever-so-English sense of who they are will be destroyed." But another Jew warned that the eruv would turn the area into a Jewish ghetto by attracting orthodox Jews and Hasidim from northeast London (already known as Volvo City for the large Jewish families in station wagons, some decorated with menorahs at Chanukah). A writer to a local paper said: "England is basically a Christian country and if other faiths choose to live here they should not disrupt local populations." The former head of the Methodist Conference called the eruv "a piece of impertinence." The Barnet planning committee rejected a staff recommendation to approve the eruv. The former chief rabbi testified at the Department of Environment review that "the increasingly pluralistic character of our city environment has emboldened Jews to seek facilities . . . proudly affirm[ing] their customs and beliefs where formerly they often used to be very discreet." The editor of a magazine for younger Jews said they believe that "in a multicultural society— like gay people, like black people—[Jews] have to demand their rights." The secretary for the environment approved the proposal six years later, but opponents vowed to keep fighting in the courts.[31]

Although the First Amendment purported to resolve these controversies, Americans continue to struggle over public recognition of religion.[32] Rev. Pat Robertson—sometime candidate for the Republican presidential nomination—told a Christian Broadcasting Network prayer meeting that "Jews were 'spiritually deaf' and 'spiritually blind.'"[33] At the 1992 Republican governors' conference, when Kirk Fordice of Mississippi called the United States a "Christian nation," his South Carolina colleague suggested adding "the 'Judeo' part." Fordice refused to deny the "simple facts [sic] that Christianity is the predominant religion. That can't possibly be construed as denigrating the Jewish faith."[34] Alan Dershowitz would not agree. Rejecting George Washington's concession of "toleration" to the Jewish community two centuries earlier, Dershowitz exulted when the Clintons accepted his invitation to High Holy Day services and wished the congregation

"Shana Tova," making "many Jews feel like first-class citizens, rather than tolerated guests."[35]

Controversies over abortion, contraception, and now fetal-tissue research implicate the status of Catholics and conservative Protestants. When State Department population coordinator Faith(!) Mitchell criticized Vatican opposition to the United Nations International Conference on Population and Development, which was "really calling for a new role for women, calling for girls' education," the church urged Clinton "to direct Mitchell to retract and apologize for her statement, and to recommit your administration to religious tolerance." A reply advertisement by Catholics for a Free Choice, Conference for Catholic Lesbians, National Association for a Married Priesthood, National Coalition of American Nuns, and Women's Ordination Conference quoted a twelfth-century Benedictine abbot saying "To embrace a woman is to embrace a sack of manure," and St. Thomas Aquinas's slur on women as "defective and misbegotten."[36]

Surgeon General Dr. Joycelyn Elders became a lightning rod for these clashes with her stands on Norplant, AIDS, abortion, and sex education. After Elders dismissed the antiabortion movement as the voice of "a celibate, male-dominated church," a bishop called her "bigoted." Although she apologized, she soon resumed her attacks on the "unChristian religious right" "who are selling our children out in the name of religion." Eighty-seven representatives demanded her dismissal for urging consideration of legalized narcotics, telling girls to bring condoms on dates, and accusing the Boy and Girl Scouts of discriminating against homosexuals. Clinton demanded her resignation when newspapers reported that she had "condoned the idea of teaching schoolchildren to masturbate as a way of avoiding the spread of the AIDS virus." (Asked about the prospects for "a more explicit discussion and promotion of masturbation" as a means to limit AIDS, she had called herself "a very strong advocate" of sex education "at a very early age," adding "As per your specific question in regard to masturbation, I think that is something that is part of human sexuality and . . . perhaps should be taught. But we've not even taught our children the very basics.") When Rep. Vic Fazio (D-Sacramento) criticized "the intolerant . . . religious right" for blocking Dr. Henry Foster as her replacement because he had performed thirty-nine abortions in his more than thirty years as an obstetrician, all forty-four Republican senators accused Fazio and the Democratic party of "religious bigotry." Rep. Henry J. Hyde denounced the Democrats' "calculated smear campaign," and Rep. Robert Dornan warned that McCarthyism was being replaced by Fazioism.[37]

Respect for religion also is contested in the private sphere. The Catholic League for Religious and Civil Rights denounced the film *Priest* (scheduled for release on Good Friday), which blamed "church teachings" for both a priest's affair with his housekeeper and a blasphemous gay priest. A newspaper advertisement asked how

> Jews would react if a movie called "Rabbi" portrayed five rabbis in a depraved condition? Would gays tolerate a movie that showed them to be morally destitute? What about a cruel caricature of African-Americans? . . . And just think what would happen if those movies had been scheduled to fall on Yom Kippur, Gay Pride Day or Martin Luther King Day.

Without seeing the film, John Cardinal O'Connor called it "viciously anti-Catholic," "scrawling on the walls of men's rooms." Denouncing it as a "distorted, negative and fundamentally unfair picture," the Knights of Columbus sold their $3 million of stock in Disney (which distributed the film) and canceled a trip to Disneyland. Appearing on *Meet the Press* on Easter Sunday, Robert Dole echoed Ralph Reed and Rev. Donald Wildmon by condemning the film as evidence of Hollywood's lack of family values. (It actually was made by the BBC and opened without incident in Italy and Ireland.)[38]

Although national and ethnic loyalties still inspire bloody imperial conquests, liberation struggles, and civil wars, much of the conflict is symbolic. When the former province of Macedonia sought recognition as an independent nation following the dissolution of Yugoslavia, Greece's fierce opposition persuaded the European Union and the United States to withhold recognition. Residents of *its* adjacent province of Macedonia claimed they had used the name for four millennia and promptly conferred it on the Salonika airport. They fetishized famous "Macedonians," preeminently Alexander the Great (after whom they hastily named another airport and warship) but also Democritus (the "founder of Atomic Theory") and Aristotle ("one of the greatest philosophers the world has known"). Anticipating the European Union's Edinburgh summit, more than a million Greeks demonstrated in Athens, some flying in from North America and Australia. A Greek court imprisoned a seventeen-year-old boy for a year for distributing a leaflet showing Alexander sitting on a "barbarian" with a text reading "This man was a megalomaniac. There are no clean races in the Balkans, we are all mongrels." The Thessaloniki Chamber of Commerce and Industry quoted Henry Kissinger to the European Union: "Greece is rightfully opposed to the (usurped) name. The reason is that I know history."

Although the United States, the United Kingdom, France, the World Bank, the International Monetary Fund, and the United Nations recognized the "Former Yugoslav Republic of Macedonia" (Fyrom), Greece refused any compromise containing Macedonia. Bishop Pateleimon denounced the United States for "indecent behavior in recognizing this pseudo state." After the government fell over this issue, the new Socialist prime minister protested: "Another state wants not only our name but also our flag and symbols." The foreign minister (his son) compared it to "a breakaway state in Mexico decid[ing] to use the Alamo as its flag and say[ing] Texas should be part of this new nation, and that Dallas is their future capital." Although Fyrom agreed to remove the sixteen-pointed star of Vergina from its flag and renounce territorial claims, the two countries could not agree on a name.[39]

The previous section discussed the unresolved grievances of World War II. Resentment among victims of Japanese aggression intensified in 1991, when a leading Japanese newspaper reported documentation that 60,000 to 200,000 "comfort women" had been forced into prostitution for Japanese occupying forces. Three days before Prime Minister Miyazawa's first official trip to Korea, his government offered "heartfelt apology and soul-searching to those women who had a bitter hardship beyond description." Korean prime minister Roh Tae Woo refused to accept this: "Japan must confront its past history . . . and only then will it eliminate the concerns of its Asian neighbors." A former "comfort woman" declared: "The Japanese treat their dogs better than they treated us." A leading Seoul daily ran a cartoon showing Miyazawa at the airport grabbing the arms of a twelve-year-old girl presenting flowers and leering: "You are a pretty girl. How old are you?" More than a year later, Japan formally admitted forced prostitution and offered apologies; but Philippine women demonstrated outside the Japanese embassy in Manila, demanding compensation.[40]

Japan debated its guilt throughout the fiftieth anniversary of World War II. The emperor made his first visit to Okinawa, expressing "deep sorrow" that the island "was turned into a battlefield," but some dignitaries boycotted the event because he had not formally apologized. Although Prime Minister Hosokawa spoke for the first time of "a war of aggression . . . a terrible mistake" and broke a forty-seven-year-old tradition of visiting Yasukuni Jinja, the Shinto war memorial to Japan's 2.6 million dead (including Admiral Tojo and five other class A war criminals), Shigeto Nagano, a former army chief of staff and justice minister in the next government, repudiated Hosokawa's phrase, insisting that Japan had "liberated" Asian countries from Western colonialism and denying (as an eyewitness) the Nanjing massacre. The Chinese Foreign Ministry was "shocked and indignant." Nagano equivocated.

> Japan did not have the support and understanding of other countries
> for the purpose of the war, and specific actions in the war were not
> quite matched to the purpose of the conflict. But the fact that there
> was an element of self-defense does not mean the war can be justified.

When China and Korea complained that this "explanation" aggravated
the offense, Nagano withdrew the remarks and apologized but was
fired anyhow. Three weeks later, a Japanese man angered by such revisionism attempted to shoot former prime minister Hosokawa. When
the Environmental Agency director said Japanese soldiers had been
seized by an "unusual psychological condition" at the front, which
made them "give other people a hard time," he also had to retract and
resign. But the cabinet defied Prime Minister Murayama by openly
worshipping at the Yasukuni shrine, and 212 MPs endorsed a petition
opposing any apology: "These countries had been colonized and oppressed by whites, so our purpose was to free those nations and stabi-
lize them." Some 4.5 million Japanese signed the petition, and eighteen
of forty-seven prefectural assemblies expressed gratitude to those who
had died in the war.

Although Murayama announced that Japan would commemorate
the fiftieth anniversary of the war's end by creating a "peace fund"
and publicly apologized to "comfort women" in Manila, Hanoi, Kuala
Lumpur, and Singapore, Philippine women demanded $200,000 each.
And minutes after he warned the cabinet not to express personal opinions about the war, a member asserted: "Whether Japan committed
aggression or not is a matter of how you look at things. Isn't an exchange of aggressions what war is all about? . . . it's the winner who
decides that the other party was the aggressor." Nevertheless, Murayama finally offered a formal "heartfelt apology" to the victims of Japanese aggression, substituting the unambiguous "owabi" for "hansei"
(variously translated as "reflection," "contrition," and "remorse"). A
few months later, however, the head of the Management and Coordi-
nation Agency said that Japan "did some good things" during the occupation. It "built schools in every town in Korea to raise the standard
of education and also constructed railroads and ports." Murayama reprimanded the official but was forced to fire him when Korea threatened
to recall its ambassador and cancel an impending summit meeting.[41]

Cultural imperialism has largely replaced conquest. Just as the appearance of Le Drugstore on Boulevard St. Germain upset Parisians in
the 1960s and McDonald's cannot flaunt its golden arches on the
Champs Elysées, so French anger at American hegemony congealed
around Euro Disneyland. Critics mocked the dress code governing hair
color and length, makeup, fingernails, jewelry, and "appropriate un-
dergarments." The communist Confédération Générale du Travail

struck the rail line to Paris on opening day, citing a wage dispute (although Disney's president noted: "I could fill the park with CGT requests for tickets"). French intellectuals denounced the "cultural Chernobyl" and "Imperialism of Mickey," the "horror made of cardboard, plastic and appalling colors, a construction of hardened chewing gum and idiotic folklore taken straight out of comic books written for obese Americans." Recalling the May 1968 attack on the Bourse, one writer hoped "with all my heart for a May 1992 that will set fire to Euro Disneyland." Others called it a "terrifying giant's step toward world homogenization," whose "appearance of civilization" concealed "the savage reality of barbarism." When the competing Parc Asterix (named after a Gaul whose heroic resistance to the Roman invaders in 50 B.C. inspired a French comic book character) regained the 30 percent of visitors it had lost to its competitor, the marketing director gloated: "We're proud to have won this battle. . . . Disney is based on fantasies, we are based on realities."[42]

France repelled the invader on other fronts. Resentful that America had made eighty-eight of the hundred most popular films in the world in 1993 and captured more than 60 percent of French box office revenues, the government turned protectionist, spending more than $200 million annually on the domestic film industry and requiring 60 percent of French television to be European and 40 percent of radio music to be French. When these measures were challenged at the General Agreement on Tariffs and Trade (GATT) negotiations, the French communications minister told the European Parliament: "It's a question of creativity and our cultural heritage." Gérard Depardieu condemned the Hollywood "war machine," and director Claude Berri warned that "if the GATT deal goes through as proposed, European culture is finished." Evoking sensitive memories, the minister of culture denounced the "occupation of screens" by *Jurassic Park,* which opened in 450 theaters spanning a fourth of all cities and large towns. Supporting the ban of Turner Network Television from French cable, his predecessor urged the country to "fight back against this American aggression. It is intolerable that certain North American audiovisual groups shamelessly colonize our countries and bombard our continent with exclusively American images." President Mitterrand declared it "vital to increase the influence and the circulation of works of art produced in Europe."[43] For Britain, however, *Europe* was the cultural imperialist. When the country finally went metric, a reader complained to the *Daily Express:* "Once again, one of our cherished British traditions sinks into the swamp of an integrated Europe." And the British Weights and Measures Association threatened a "massive campaign of public resistance," "another October Revolution." "They'll have to set up camps all over the country . . . [for] hundreds of thousands of small-business people."[44]

If popular culture is a particularly visible provocation, language is a more pervasive irritant. Governments champion languages to advance or repress separatist and imperial aspirations and to manifest dominance and subordination. Turkey harshly suppresses the Kurdish language in education and broadcasting, while Catalunya *requires* Catalan in schools and employment and considered a quota for dubbed movies. As Yugoslavia fragmented, so did its language. Government broadcasters in Croatia created neologisms and revived archaisms (some reminiscent of the fascist Ustashe); Croatian Serbs replaced the Latin alphabet with Cyrillic; and Bosnian Muslims revived Turkic and Arabic loanwords.[45] Fighting a losing battle against Americanization, Russia required business signs to use Cyrillic and created a "code of speech behavior" to be enforced by a Federal Language Service. Its former Baltic colonies celebrated independence by reimposing their own languages; Estonia has deployed thirteen full-time language police with the power to issue spot fines against anyone not speaking its difficult Finno-Ugric tongue.[46] China is purging Westernized commercial names because, according to a Beijing professor, "confusion and pollution in the language is harmful to national dignity." Afrikaners rightly fear that the postapartheid regime will dethrone their language as well as their monuments. Prof. Hans du Plessis—poet, author, and director of both the Afrikaanse Taal en Kultuur Vereniging and the Federasie vir Afrikaanse Kultuur—deplored the South African Broadcasting Corporation decision to reduce Afrikaans to "a mere vernacular, a mere indigenous language," demeaning "the status of the Germanic language that it is." An English-speaking white complained to a Johannesburg paper: "[L]et's hear [accents] on the street, and never over the air. What they have done is imposed their will on us . . . [making us] listen to black music and mangled black English." A black radio producer retorted: "[I]f they are going to be the guardians of English, they must pack and go back to England."[47]

France has long battled linguistic enemies, both internal and external. It threatened to veto any U.N. secretary general candidate unable to speak the language of Racine. Mitterrand promised to dismiss any official giving a speech in something other than "the world's most glorious language." More than three centuries after Cardinal Richelieu created the Académie Française to maintain linguistic purity, Prime Minister Balladur inaugurated the Higher Council of the French Language as "an act of faith in the future of our country." New legislation prohibited foreign words in commerce, broadcasts, public announcements, and advertisements whenever there was a "suitable local equivalent." Arguing that this would permit France "better [to] assume its responsibility" for former colonies, he appointed a Delegation for the French Language to prepare a dictionary, substituting "valeurs de premier ordre" for "blue chips" and "arrêt de jeu" for "time out." "The use of a foreign language is not innocent," he cautioned. Anglo-Saxon countries were making "considerable efforts" to conquer new linguistic territory, and 80 percent of high school students chose English as a second language. (A Tory backbencher responded with a bill to ban French in Britain, using traffic wardens as enforcers.) When the Constitutional Court found the law in violation of the 1787 Declaration of the Rights of Man, Balladur retorted that language was the "primary capital" of the French people, "the symbol of their dignity, the passageway to integration, the diapason of a universal culture." In his successful presidential campaign, Jacques Chirac warned that though "our language has never been spoken by so many . . . it has never been as threatened by what seems to be the irresistible rise of English, or rather of the impoverished form of it that is tending to become the language of international communication."[48]

French Canada feels even more besieged. A 1977 Quebec law required that all outdoor signs be in French and all indoor signs use larger type for French words than for English. When it was declared unconstitutional, the province invoked a provision allowing it to override Charter guarantees. Mordechai Richler harshly ridiculed the "tongue troopers," who planned to spend $552,000 replacing Montreal's eleven remaining "stop / arrêt" signs with "arrêt," send undercover agents to investigate whether retail clerks mistreated French shoppers, and require French on school playgrounds. He and his drinking buddies formed a "Twice as Much Society," which required that French be spoken twice as loudly and restaurants serve twice as much food to Francophones. MPs urged that the book be banned as hate literature. A Montreal newspaper called it "delirium," while the *Toronto Globe and Mail* compared it to *The Satanic Verses*. An undertaker fifteen miles from the U.S. border, ordered to rename his funeral parlor "salon funéraire," won a ruling by the Human Rights Committee of the U.N. General Assembly that the law violated the International Covenant on Civil and Political Rights. Over opposition by the Parti Québecois, the province repealed all but the requirement that French words on signs be twice the size of those in other languages. Although Quebec narrowly defeated a secession referendum in November 1995, 82 percent of French-speakers supported it.[49]

The U.S. language wars have been another form of immigrant bashing.[50] The Florida Constitution declares English "the official language" (although the 1990 census found that only 43 percent of the population spoke it at home, while 50 percent spoke Spanish). In 1980 Dade County (Greater Miami) prohibited employees from "utilizing" any other language or "promoting any culture other than that of the United States." After numerous court challenges and repeal efforts failed, the Spanish American League against Discrimination tried again to rescind "something that was done to hurt a people, and that is racist and discriminatory." Citizens of Dade United retorted: "These Cubans apparently don't adhere to the principle that in Rome you do as the Romans do. They have already established another Cuba inside Dade County, and now they are forcing Spanish down our throats." Calling the successful repeal "a symbolic slap in the face," U.S. English warned that the county would become a Spanish-speaking "enclave within the United States, an apartheid enclave for Cubano culture and language, like Transkei in South Africa." The son of Italian immigrants called it tantamount to "deciding that both the yen and the dollar will be the official currency." At a subsequent county commission meeting an African American woman complained that "they are taking over, and I am a victim."[51]

After the 1994 Republican congressional sweep, Newt Gingrich pronounced: "English has to be our common language. Otherwise we're not going to have a civilization." Guarding his right flank, Sen. Robert Dole parroted: "[A]ll our citizens [must be] fluent in English. . . . We must stop the practice of multilingual education as a means of instilling ethnic pride or as a therapy for low self-esteem or out of elitist guilt over a culture built on the traditions of the West." A third of representatives cosponsored a bill to make English the official language, eliminate government publications and citizenship ceremonies in other languages, and abolish the office of bilingual education. Complaining that "the demagoguing is unbelievable" and the bill was "trying to empower people," Rep. Randy "Duke" Cunningham (R-Calif.) asked rhetorically: "Have you ever been in a foreign country and you hear someone speak English and it doesn't excite you?"[52]

Many of these protagonists, like those in earlier confrontations, explicitly sought respect. A Hindu militant who called himself the "Hitler of Bombay" challenged Indian Muslims: "How strong you are, how strong we are, that we shall see." (Rushdie's caricature of him in *The Moor's Last Sigh* led India to ban the book.) A Milwaukee minister warned those opposing vouchers for religious schools: "You're picking on a giant that's bigger than you are" and advised them "to quit while they're behind." Australian prime minister Keating anticipated the queen's visit by criticizing Britain for having deserted its former colony in World War II, mocking "old fogies who doffed their lids and tugged their forelock to the British establishment." He defied protocol by putting his arm around the queen, and his wife refused to make the customary curtsy. British MPs demanded an apology, calling him "an utter buffoon" and "idiot" whose boorishness was typical of "a country of ex-convicts." Adversaries openly ridiculed each other. When critics condemned the award of the Booker Prize to James Kelman because *How Late It Was, How Late* was "not literature, just oral tradition" written in "vernacular" or "dialect," the author retorted that this was "just another work of inferiorizing the language." The mayor of Brussels, a former nightclub bouncer, ridiculed John Paul II's views on contraception. "Who is this man who doesn't know how to use a condom and puts it on the index? . . . The Pope? No, thank you." A Bavarian atheist sought to ban crucifixes from schoolrooms because he did not want his children exposed to a "bleeding, half-naked male corpse." Opposing fetal tissue research, Catholics called the federal advisory committee "the gods of science," while Southern Baptists warned against "playing God" by trying to patent genetically engineered species.

The common social dynamic driving these diverse controversies emerged in their promiscuous borrowing of metaphors. Polish antiabortionists called their adversaries Hitler and Nazi. French Canadians compared Mordechai Richler's diatribe to *The Satanic Verses.* Catholics insulted by *Priest* asked whether Jews, African Americans, or gays would tolerate such insults. The Scots novelist whose prize-winning book was derided for its profane Glaswegian dialect called his critics racist. To a Greek bishop American recognition of Fyrom was "indecent." Scatological images abounded. Refusing payment to accept sludge as fertilizer, West Texans made it clear they wouldn't take any shit from New York. Antagonists invoked history to justify status aspirations, as when the two Macedonias competed to claim descent from Alexander the Great. They fought through numbers (as Farrakhan did about his "Million Man March"): how many were killed in the Holocaust, or slaughtered at Nanjing; how many Americans would have died invading Japan? Just as Rushdie had cited intellectual supporters and Muslims invoked the enthusiasm of Shaw, Briffault, Rousseau, and Lamartine, so Greece claimed the endorsement of Henry Kissinger for its view of history. Religion and nationality overlapped when colonized peoples protested against missionary activity: Goans at St. Francis Xavier's racism, Sri Lankans at Pope John Paul II's derogatory remarks about Buddhism, Latin Americans at Catholicism's assault on indigenous religions, Russians at aggressive Protestant proselytizing after communism. One of the most pervasive symbols of national status was linguistic usage.

Although these disputes often adopted utilitarian rhetoric, this always hid a symbolic subtext. Jewish women seeking to pray at the Western Wall and Saudi women driving their own cars undoubtedly had religious and material motives, but they also were asserting equality with men—who responded predictably. Conflicts produced bizarre alliances: animal rights groups, political conservatives, and secularists joined to oppose animal sacrifice. Muslims and Catholics united against abortion, France and Islam against American cultural imperialism. Issues coalesced without regard to ideological coherence: opponents of Dr. Joycelyn Elders cited her positions on contraception, AIDS, sex education, abortion, homosexuality, drugs, and masturbation. Values inverted their meanings in different settings. Hunting is a male working-class symbol in the United States but a prerogative of upperclass men and women in Britain. American conservatives sought to compel obeisance to the flag, but Jehovah's Witnesses and Muslim and Jewish fundamentalists refused to genuflect. In Western (or Westernizing) countries, Muslim girls and women seek respect for their religion by donning the *hijab* and *niqaab;* in strict Muslim countries, they seek respect for their gender by disrobing.

Adversaries recklessly indulged in apocalyptic language. "Any [Philippine] politician who attacks the Catholic Church" was "committing suicide." If America did not halt immigration in two years, it would surrender "control of the Southwest" and no longer be "a sovereign country." "If you kill a nation's language," warned Afrikaners, "you kill its soul." War imagery abounded. The Future of the French Language Association accused compatriots patronizing American films of having "chosen to betray their language and their culture." The Independent Union of Interpretive Artists denounced French "collaborators with certain American audiovisual interests." Somehow forgetting the Norman conquest, Norman Tebbit boasted that Britain had very successfully "repelled those who wanted to come take [these islands] from us for the last 1,000 years." Exhorting his troops to extirpate Western music and videos and enforce Muslim dress regulations, the head of Iran's religious vigilantes proclaimed: "This war goes to the root of our existence . . . our young people are being felled by cultural bullets." Just as actual warfare left smoldering embers that could reignite symbolic struggles years, decades, and even centuries later, so cultural wars could turn violent, as when patriotic Japanese attacked "revisionists" or Muslim fundamentalists assailed dissenters. Actual power relations were mystified. U.S. English compared Miami's recognition of its Spanish-speaking majority with South African apartheid.

Whites in postapartheid South Africa complained that black radio announcers "have imposed their will on us."

Groups demanded symbolic action to redress their subordinate status—typically an apology. Sri Lankan Buddhists sought it from the pope, "comfort women" from the Japanese, Japan and the United States from each other. Lutherans offered it to Jews, and Yeltsin to Eastern Europe and Japan. The precise wording of the apology was as important as that of the provocation; merely regretting offense taken was clearly inadequate. After years of manipulating the ambiguity of "hansei," Japan finally accepted "sekinin" (responsibility) by offering "owabi" (heartfelt apology). But most offenders found it difficult to apologize without a qualifying explanation or justification.

RACE

Asked to identify the single greatest divide in their society, few Americans would hesitate to name race. More than four decades after the Supreme Court invalidated school segregation, antagonisms are as bitter as ever. Racial status is constructed and contested through history, public and private segregation, the criminal justice system, politics, the media, universities, and science.

Because slavery was the ultimate humiliation for African Americans, badges of servitude (explicitly proscribed by the Thirteenth Amendment) possess the same kind of symbolic power that swastikas hold for Jews. A black Alabama state assembly member waged a long fight to remove the Confederate flag from the capitol, arguing that it "represents treason, sedition, slavery and oppression toward my people." Although he won an injunction, the governor vowed to continue flying it at his official residence, the First White House of the Confederacy. The Georgia legislature refused to remove the Confederate emblem from its state flag, to which it had been added in 1956 to express continued commitment to segregation. Responding to demonstrations by Sons of Confederate Veterans, the Descendants of Enslaved Africans burned the flag on the capitol steps. Atlanta's African American mayor removed it from city hall, calling it "the fruit of a poison tree." State senator Ralph David Abernathy 3d (son of the civil rights leader) sought to banish "this Confederate swastika." Responding to black protests, South Carolina's governor proposed a compromise: moving the flag to Confederate monuments on statehouse grounds and building a civil rights monument. But the NAACP was adamant: "We're not asking for compromise. We're saying it violates our rights." The

Council of Conservative Citizens retorted: "If we can have a Martin Luther King Day, a Black History Month, why can't we have the Confederate battle flag fly above the Statehouse?" Calling the flag "a symbol of defiance, courage, bravery," Patrick Buchanan declared that if "there is room in America for the song of the civil rights movement, 'We Shall Overcome,' there's got to be room for 'Dixie.' "[53]

In May 1993 the United Daughters of the Confederacy (UDC) applied for a routine renewal of their century-old congressional design patent to a logo including the Confederate flag. But Sen. Carol Moseley-Braun (D-Ill.) convinced the Judiciary Committee (in which she was the first African American woman) to reject the application 12-3. Sponsor Strom Thurmond (R-S.C.) asked sarcastically: "Why stop here? Why don't we demolish the memorials to the Confederate soldiers at Arlington Cemetery?" Moseley-Braun replied that UDC "had every right to . . . honor their ancestors" but "those of us whose ancestors . . . were held as human chattel under the flag of the Confederacy have no choice but to honor our ancestors by asking whether such action is appropriate." "On this issue there can be no consensus. It is an insult. It is absolutely unacceptable to me and to millions of Americans, black or white, that we would put the imprimatur of the United States Senate on a symbol of this kind of idea." When Sen. Jesse Helms complained that "race should never have been introduced," Ben Nighthorse Campbell (D-Colo.), the only other senator of color, rejoined: "There are some places in this country yet where American Indians are called 'prairie niggers.' . . . I would like to point out to [Helms and others] that slavery was once a tradition, like killing Indians like animals was once a tradition."[54]

Indians have challenged the appropriation of their names and images. Although many college teams dropped Indian names and mascots in the 1970s, the visibility of the Atlanta Braves in the 1991 World Series and the Kansas City Chiefs and Washington Redskins in that year's NFL playoffs revived the issue in professional sports. A Pawnee professor at Arizona State University said: "[T]he movement is to gain a place of respect and dignity. It's to show that we are not just savages captured in the distant past and not to be made a mockery of." A Crow woman in Kansas City said: "People started coming up to me at work and going 'chop-chop' and 'woo-woo.' A white guy . . . pointed to the Chiefs' symbol on his t-shirt and said 'This is mine. You can't take it.' " When a federation of 300 tribes established the American Indian Anti-Defamation League to monitor affronts, University of Illinois alumni mobilized to keep the team name Illini and the mascot Illiniwek, who danced in an inappropriate Sioux costume while fans shouted "Chief!"

They gained the support of the state house of representatives. An Indian professor threatened to resign because "there's no such thing as honor in this." But the local Republican congressman applauded the U.S. Department of Education for rejecting the Indians' complaint, thereby affirming "our freedom to celebrate our heritage without interference."[55]

In the 130 years since the end of slavery, segregation remains the most visible manifestation of racial subordination—not just in education, housing, employment, and public accommodations but also in events like Tampa's Gasparilla parade and the far better known Mardi Gras. Even symbolic segregation can offend. In February 1990 the Food and Drug Administration recommended against Haitian and sub-Saharan African blood donations. In response, some 50,000 to 80,000 Haitians demonstrated (virtually the entire New York community), carrying signs reading "We're Proud of Our Blood," "Let's Fight AIDS, not Nationality." Mayor David Dinkins was sympathetic: "Discrimination against entire groups will do nothing to stop this disease." Speakers called AIDS "a germ created by white folks to kill black folks." The FDA reversed its position.[56] Six years later Ethiopian Jews held their first major protest when told that Israel discarded their blood donations. An estimated 10,000 participated in a demonstration in which sixty-two were injured. Unconsciously evoking Shylock's famous lament ("If you prick us, do we not bleed?"), their banners proclaimed "Our blood is as red as yours and we are just as Jewish as you are," "Apartheid in Israel," "The 2nd Holocaust! Genoceid! in the Holy-Land."[57]

The influence of verbal slurs on status relations varies with the speaker's prominence and authority. The Los Angeles Dodgers fired manager Al Campanis less than forty-eight hours after he said blacks lacked the "necessities" for management positions. The National League suspended Cincinnati Reds owner Marge Schott for a year for calling some of her players "million-dollar niggers" and complaining that "sneaky goddam Jews are all alike."[58] Political campaigns attempt to play the race card, but not too blatantly. Maine senator Edmund S. Muskie's run for the 1972 Democratic presidential nomination foundered soon after Nixon's campaign team forged a letter to a New Hampshire newspaper falsely quoting a Muskie aide saying "We don't have blacks but we have Canucks."[59] Jews will not forgive Jesse Jackson's 1988 reference to New York as "Hymietown." When Jerry Brown sought the Democratic presidential nomination four years later, New York Jews shouted "Welcome to Hymietown" (alluding to rumors that Brown would court the black vote by making Jackson his running mate). Clinton spent the same day at Jewish events, inspiring the *New York Times* headline "Yarmulke in Place, Clinton Courts Crucial Constituency."[60]

As this reveals, New York politics are unusually racialized. In his first year as mayor, David Dinkins was criticized for police inaction during the Crown Heights disturbances in which blacks, angered that a Lubavitcher motorcade had accidentally killed a black child, murdered a rabbinical student. Anticipating a 1993 rematch for the mayoralty, Republican challenger Rudolph Giuliani called Crown Heights a pogrom and claimed that Dinkins "retreats into black victimization" whenever criticized. Dinkins accused Giuliani of having "attempted to inject race into this contest." During the campaign a black minister said "fascist" elements surrounded Giuliani. When the challenger called this an ethnic slur, Dinkins declared no tolerance for "racial statements." But Rep. Charles Rangel, an African American, called race one of Giuliani's main assets. Puerto Rican leader Herman Badillo responded for Giuliani: "The Dinkins campaign is trying to make this an election about race because they want to avoid the issue of competence. We don't need these anti-Semitic and racial attacks." Rangel, he added, was "half Puerto Rican." Rangel retorted that Badillo "doesn't even know who his own parents are," while the head of the black police officers' association noted that Badillo's wife was not Hispanic. Badillo expressed outrage that a Dinkins supporter "attacked me for marrying a Jewish woman." Giuliani also noted Dinkins's refusal to reiterate his 1985 condemnation of Louis Farrakhan's anti-Semitism.[61]

Early in Giuliani's term Deputy Mayor John S. Dyson criticized the Democratic city comptroller for hiring a company owned by a black woman to market municipal bonds: "The Comptroller ought to know the difference between a bid and a watermelon." Dyson said he meant no offense: "If someone takes this as a racial comment, I'm sorry for that. . . . I think my record of 20 years in public life shows that I'm not racially motivated one way or the other." "It was a poor analogy. I should have used a difference [sic] fruit." Insisting that a watermelon "in and of itself doesn't suggest" a racial slur, Giuliani asked "people of good will to have a little tolerance." But the city comptroller said that Dyson's "irresponsible and insensitive" remark showed his "apparent compulsion to create the public impression that he is a bigot." Calling it a "clearly racist statement," Democratic council speaker Peter F. Vallone and two black councilors demanded that Dyson repudiate the remark or resign. State Comptroller H. Carl McCall (black and Democratic) told Giuliani: "Mr. Dyson's comments are not only hurtful to the African-American community, they also demean the integrity and fairness of your administration." And the *New York Times* admonished Giuliani "to inspire Mr. Dyson to admit publicly and without qualification, that he used language that most blacks and many whites would recognize instantly as racist. That should be followed by a promise to avoid both language and behavior that cast doubt on the administration's racial fairness."[62]

By officially proclaiming transgression of our weightiest norms, criminal accusations and convictions can profoundly influence racial status: Tawana Brawley's claim to have been beaten and raped by white cops, Bernard Goetz's shooting of black alleged muggers in a New York subway, white gang attacks on blacks in Howard Beach and Bensonhurst, the black gang rape and near-fatal beating of a white woman jogger in Central Park, Charles Stuart's allegation that the wife *he* murdered was killed by a black man, the police beating of Rodney King, and of course the O. J. Simpson trials.[63] In November 1991, when tensions between Korean merchants and black customers were high, Los Angeles Superior Court judge Joyce A. Karlin gave a Korean grocer a $500 fine and 400 hours of community service (plus probation) for shooting to death a fifteen-year-old African American girl suspected of shoplifting a $1.79 bottle of orange juice. The Committee for Justice quickly gathered 20,000 signatures on a petition urging the state to appeal the sentence. Its chair declaimed: "If you beat a puppy in Glendale, you go to jail. You kill a black child who lives in South-Central Los Angeles and you get probation. . . . It reminds me of a Jim Crow kind of justice that we thought had disappeared." Black community activists demonstrated at Karlin's courthouse every week until the presiding judge transferred her to juvenile court. A black activist welcomed this evidence "that the community is not powerless." Seeking reelection, City Attorney Ira Reiner appealed the sentence, comparing himself to President Kennedy criticizing the 1960 jailing of Martin Luther King. Reiner's principal challenger accused him of inciting the black community to storm Karlin's courthouse. Organizers collected 280,000 signatures on a petition to recall Karlin. One called the affirmation of the sentence "the incentive that will cause citizens to finish it up and send a message loud and clear to the justice system." A black Compton councilwoman sought "to keep the issue alive until the election" in order to ensure "more notoriety and more publicity" than her opponent. When a twelve-year-old African American girl complained of being assaulted in a Korean grocery soon thereafter, activists picketed with signs demanding "Respect, Respect, Respect" and boasted of closing down two other Korean shops.[64]

Even without an official imprimatur, racial representations in art and mass media possess great emotional power and often enjoy broad dissemination.[65] Murals may become flashpoints: minority groups were furious that two Russian Jewish immigrant artists chose twelfth-century European angels to represent "La Reina de Los Angeles"; when an artist of Mexican and Indian ancestry included Mayan symbols in the design of a San Fernando Valley subway station, a local real estate developer whose ancestors had settled the area complained that "the Mayans had zip to do with the Valley"; in response to parental complaints, a suburban Chicago elementary school removed a 1936 WPA mural of "People of the World" showing Africans in loincloths carrying spears, "yellow" Asians with slit eyes, "red" Indians attacking a wagon train, and black sharecroppers picking cotton.[66] Advertisements also can offend: Quaker Oats replaced Aunt Jemima with Gladys Knight on their pancake boxes; AT&T apologized to the NAACP for a map showing phone calls between people on four continents—and monkeys in Africa; Italian Americans pressured G. Heileman Brewing Company to remove billboards declaring that "in 1929 Al Capone persuaded all his friends to try Old Style" beer—and to substitute Enrico Fermi.[67]

Lyrics can make music controversial. A *New York Times* columnist condemned the performance of a fifteenth-century Latin work whose English translation read "More trust is to be put in the honest Mary alone than in the lying crowd of Jews." The critic maintained that one reason "for the persistence of anti-Semitism in our culture . . . must be the reinforcement [it] receives in so much art that is a product of Christian doctrine." In "They Don't Care about Us," Michael Jackson sang: "Jew me, sue me, everybody do me / Kick me, kike me, don't you black or white me." When the ADL regional director called the words "hateful and hurtful," Jackson promised to include an apology in all future copies of the album. Music can offend even without lyrics. A November 1938 performance of Wagner in Palestine was canceled following Kristallnacht, and he has not been programmed in Israel since. An unscheduled Wagner encore in 1981 provoked shouting matches and fistfights in the audience, and several musicians walked out. Protests halted a repetition several nights later. When the Israel Philharmonic decided to perform Wagner a decade later, the Knesset speaker, who had been interned at Dachau, dissented.

> A woman phoned me about Wagner on an earlier occasion. She doesn't go to hear the Philharmonic. But just knowing that Wagner is being played in Israel brings back the picture at night of the girl who was removed from her arms forcefully and screams of this girl. Even if it is only because of the suffering of this one woman—why do we need this?

The orchestra submitted the issue to its 30,000 subscribers and bowed to their opposition.[68]

Because of its communicative power and wide audience, film generates intense feelings. The NAACP greatly increased its membership by picketing the 1915 opening of *Birth of a Nation*, and the Klan also used it to recruit. The NAACP protested its certification as a classic eighty years later, although the Library of Congress insisted that inclusion in the National Film Registry was intended only to preserve the prints and did not imply "some kind of national honor." When *Falling Down* appeared shortly after the 1992 Los Angeles riots, local audiences often applauded Michael Douglas beating up a Korean merchant and vandalizing his store and shooting a Mexican American gang member. The Korean American Coalition protested to Warner Brothers, and the *Los Angeles Times* published seven critical articles about the film. The Japanese American Citizens League called *Rising Sun* "another twist on the Japanese Invaders / Yellow Peril genre," and the Media Action Network for Asian Americans complained that it depicted Japanese as "ruthless, aggressive people intent on getting their way in business through blackmail, extortion and even murder."[69]

Disney has been an equal opportunity offender. *Three Little Pigs*, which appeared just months after the Nazis took power, made the Big Bad Wolf a peddler with a heavy Jewish accent. The contemporaneous *Mickey's Mellerdrama* used extensive blackface. Disney gave the villain Stromboli an Italian accent in the 1940 *Pinocchio* and the black crows African American accents in *Dumbo* the following year. It stereotyped Mexicans in *The Three Caballeros* (1945), Uncle Remus in *Song of the South* (1946), and Indians in *Peter Pan* (1953), and was still using a black stereotype for King Louis of the Apes in the 1967 *Jungle Book*. By the 1990s Disney was becoming self-conscious. The 1991 reissue of *Fantasia* (1940) edited out Sunflower, a black centaurette shoeshine girl in the "Pastorale Symphony." The American-Arab Anti-discrimination League secured a change in the opening lyrics of *Aladdin*. The faraway place "Where they cut off your ear / If they don't like your face" became "Where it's flat and immense / And the heat is intense" (although it remained "barbaric"). The league still objected to the film's lesson "that anyone with a foreign accent is bad." Michael Eisner's refusal to meet or even communicate suggested that "we are not worthy of his time or attention. Certainly I think it would be different if the situation involved African-Americans or Jewish Americans." Perhaps not the former. As late as 1994 *The Lion King* gave the evil Scar a black mane and his sidekick hyenas inner-city accents. Having learned its lesson, Disney involved prominent American Indians in *Pocahontas*. But the principal of the American Indian Heritage School in Seattle protested that the film promoted "racism, rape and child molestation." "It's like trying to teach about the Holocaust and putting in a nice story about Anne Frank falling in love with a German officer."[70]

Even scientific discourse can implicate racial pride. Dr. Frederick K. Goodwin, director of the NIMH Alcohol, Drug Abuse and Mental Health Administration, described "hyperaggressive," "hypersexual" male monkeys who "reproduce more to offset the fact that half of them are dying" violently, commenting that

> if some of the loss of social structure in this society, and particularly within the high impact inner-city areas, has removed some of the civi-lizing evolutionary things that we have built up . . . maybe it isn't just the careless use of the word when people call certain areas of certain cities jungles.

Although he apologized for these "insensitive and careless" remarks, the Congressional Black Caucus accused him of "ignorance about the use of behavioral sciences." The secretary of health and human services, himself African American, appointed a Blue Ribbon Panel on Violence Prevention, chaired by the president of Howard University, to investigate allegations that department research sought to establish a genetic correlation between race and violent behavior. Although it exonerated Goodwin, he was reassigned and left government. When he appeared as lead speaker at the "Conference on Psychopathology, Psychopharmacology, Substance Abuse, and Ethnicity," a black activist protested: "This is a person who has spoken against our inner-city youth, and to invite him to kickoff a conference in our community is an insult to us." The National Institutes of Health (NIH) contemporane-ously defunded a University of Maryland conference called "Genetic Factors in Crime" after protests by the Congressional Black Caucus. The president of the Association of Black Psychologists denounced the topic as "a blatant form of stereotyping and racism." Dr. Peter Breggin concurred: "It's like if you go into the concentration camps and see how bad the Jews are doing to look for genetic factors for it." When the university finally held the conference three years later, Goodwin complained: "In every fact sheet we have ever sent out, we have said that [NIMH] determined years ago that race and crime don't correlate. But that information has never been effectively conveyed, because it takes the punch out of the controversy."[71]

Universities may be unusually prone to such conflict because they combine cognitive and normative authority with a racial diversity that is unusual in our profoundly segregated society. Student insults rein-force minority feelings that they are there on sufferance: the notorious "water buffalo" shouted at black women at the University of Pennsylvania, a mock mug shot of a black assault suspect captioned "Dartmouth's Newest Quota," and Southern California fraternity parties mocking "Mexican whores."[72] Faculty speech can be even more inflammatory. City University of New York (CUNY) philosophy professor Michael Levin published articles asserting that blacks were "significantly less intelligent" than whites and "exhibit disproportionally high rates of illiteracy, dropping out, absence from the more prestigious disciplines, and other forms of academic failure." The faculty senate rebuked him, and the university president launched an investigation, declaring that Levin's views had "no place here at City College." On the senate's recommendation the administration took the unprecedented step of creating an alternative section in Levin's introductory philosophy course in order to "protect" students from "harm," finding that "utterances by faculty, even outside of class," that denigrate "the intellectual capability of groups by virtue of race, ethnicity or gender have the clear potential to undermine the learning environment and to place students in academic jeopardy." Levin obtained an injunction against the alternative section and disruption by the International Committee against Racism Club, who had picketed his class with bullhorns, shouting "We know where you live, you Jewish bastard; your time is going to come."[73]

CUNY black studies chair Leonard Jeffries Jr. expressed his views in class as well as outside. Europeans were "ice people," materialistic and intent on domination; those of African descent were humanistic "sun people," whose abundant melanin conferred intellectual and physical advantages. He denounced "rich Jews who financed the development of Europe [and] also financed the slave trade," objected that "the Jewish Holocaust is raised as the only holocaust," and blamed Jews and the Mafia for movies aimed at the "destruction of black people." Students demonstrated at his home with signs calling him "Racist Pig." When the president terminated his chairmanship, after nearly two decades, a *New York Times* editorial condemned "his penchant for bigoted remarks and behavior." Jeffries allegedly told the dean of social sciences that massive community resistance would make Crown Heights "pale in comparison." When a federal court ordered his reinstatement and awarded $360,000 damages, an Orthodox Jewish city councilor warned that if CUNY did not appeal he would seek to cut its funding. "I am not going to fund anti-Semites and hatemongers." At Jeffries's next class a large young man wearing a gold, black, and red dashiki stood in front of the room facing the class, claiming to be an "assistant." Jeffries discussed "enuro melanin" and "epidermal melanin," to which he attributed internal and external development, claiming that "the interaction" of RNA, DNA, and melanin "represents cell development in the human." While the appeal was pending, Jeffries gave a speech representing white nationalities as animals: the English as elephants, the Dutch as squirrels, and the Jews as "skunks" who "stunk up everything." When the federal courts finally upheld Jeffries's removal, he claimed that the Nigerian political scientist who succeeded him as chair was "our candidate . . . not their candidate."[74]

The most inflammatory incidents were campus speeches by Khallid Abdul Muhammad, a Nation of Islam minister and aide to Louis Farrakhan. Using the NOI's "Secret Relationship between Blacks and Jews" as his text, he spoke at Kean College in New Jersey, affecting a Jewish accent and effeminate mannerisms and frequently referring to "Columbia Jewniversity" and "Jew York City." He drew laughter and applause by urging South African blacks to give whites twenty-four hours to leave after the overthrow of apartheid and then kill all who remained.

> We kill the women. We kill the babies, we kill the blind. We kill the cripples. We kill them all. We kill the faggot. We kill the lesbian. . . . When you get through killing them all, go to the goddamn graveyard and dig up the grave and kill them a-goddamn-gain because they didn't die hard enough.

State chancellor Edward D. Goldberg criticized Kean president Elsa Gomez for failing to create a "moral framework" in which to criticize such "patently racist ideas and opinions." When the Jewish Faculty and Staff Association complained that Kean "has become a hotbed of anti-Semitism in recent years," the Africana Studies Program assistant director retorted that Jewish faculty "will punish anyone who has a valid criticism of Jews." After the ADL excerpted the speech in a full-page advertisement in the *New York Times*, African American community leaders, elected officials, ministers, and academics condemned Muhammad. A unanimous Senate and 361 members of the House passed critical resolutions.

Although Farrakhan dismissed Muhammad, condemning his "manner," he "stood by the truths" Muhammad spoke. A few months later NOI was selling tapes of Muhammad's latest diatribe against

> the old no-good Jew, that old imposter Jew, that old hooknose, bagel-eating, lox-eating, Johnny-come-lately perpetrating a fraud, just crawled out of the caves and hills of Europe, so-called damn Jew. . . . I will never apologize to this bastard—never. I want to see my enemy on his back, whining, crying on his back begging for mercy.

When Trenton State College (also in New Jersey) invited Muhammad to speak at African-American History Month, Jewish War Veterans and the JDL promised to picket. Although his rhetoric was more subdued, Gov. Christine Todd Whitman and Sen. Bill Bradley denounced him. At the NOI annual conference, Farrakhan called Muhammad "a warrior, a fighter for his people." Muhammad spoke at Howard University, praising the African American who had killed six white Long Island commuters: "God spoke to Colin Ferguson and said, 'Catch the train, Colin, catch the train.'" After defending Howard's "tradition of honoring free speech," President Franklyn G. Jenifer resigned under threat of being fired. His replacement strengthened the guidelines for outside speakers and vetoed the next invitation to Muhammad.[75]

The power of the Holocaust for Jews resembles that of slavery for African Americans.[76] Debate about accountability elevates the moral standing of victims and degrades that of culprits. When the German chancellor invited Austrian president Kurt Waldheim (accused of Nazi collaboration), Jews said Kohl "brought dishonor to Germany." He retorted:

> I don't need any advice. . . . I ask the gentlemen at the World Jewish Congress for a reply to a request for information about an occurrence in November 1989, when they sent an emissary to East Berlin, where he polemicized in an outrageous manner against German reunification, and thereby against Germany's right to self-determination.

The acting speaker of the Israeli Knesset said Kohl's comment "brings to mind the Nazi Holocaust and the crimes that Germany committed against all humanity."[77]

Several countries recently acknowledged complicity. The Lithuanian prime minister declared that "hundreds of Lithuanians took part in this genocide. This obliges us to repent and ask the Jewish people for forgiveness." But the head of the Simon Wiesenthal Center office in Jerusalem insisted that "thousands of Lithuanians were involved in the murder of Jews, not hundreds." Soon thereafter the new Austrian president visited Israel for the first time, admitting that his country produced "many of the worst henchmen in the Nazi dictatorship." "I bow my head with deep respect and profound emotion in front of the victims. No word of apology can ever expunge the agony of the Holocaust." Israel sent an ambassador to Vienna, which it had withdrawn during Waldheim's term. Early in his presidency, Jacques Chirac commemorated the fifty-third anniversary of the roundup of 13,000 French Jews for deportation.

> Those dark hours forever sully our history and are an insult to our past and our traditions. . . . Yes, the criminal folly of the occupiers was seconded by the French, by the French state. . . . Breaking its

word, it handed those who were under its protection over to their executions. . . . We owe [the victims] an everlasting debt.

The chief rabbi of Paris was "fully satisfied" with the statement. Israel's establishment of diplomatic ties with the Vatican provoked a rash of protest. The country's largest newspaper called the church

one of the most conservative, oppressive and corrupt organizations in all human history. Israel has no reason to court the Vatican. The reconciliation can be done only if the Catholic Church and the one who heads it fall on their knees and ask for forgiveness from the souls of millions of tortured who went to Heaven in black smoke, under the blessing of the Holy See.[78]

If verdicts and sentences for all racialized crimes implicate racial honor, the trials of those accused of the Holocaust are even more potent (e.g., Eichmann in Israel, Barbie in France, Priebke in Italy). When John Demjanjuk was finally acquitted in Israel sixteen years after being accused, the daughter of inmates killed at Treblinka (where he allegedly worked) shouted: "My God, my God, my God. How in the name of justice, how in the name of the Almighty, can this man be set free?" A Treblinka survivor who testified at the trial said: "It's very painful. You have no idea how painful. I never imagined. I am not an expert on all these things. Only I, I, Czarny Josef. Am I not authentic? Am I not authentic? Am I not authentic? I am authentic." Another protested that the supreme court gave "a certificate of honesty to the many Nazi criminals who are to be found in Germany, America and Canada. Now they can come out in the open, hold their heads up and say, 'I murdered people now do something to me.' "[79]

Memorials, commemorations, and narratives reaffirm the suffering of Jews and the guilt of Nazis and collaborators. At the dedication of Washington's Holocaust Museum, Jews strongly criticized the presence of Croatian president Franjo Tudjman, whose 1988 book *Wasteland: Historical Truth* declared that only 900,000 Jews had died in concentration camps. The estimate "of six million dead is based to the greatest extent on exaggerated data, on post-war calculations of war crimes, and on the settling of accounts with the defeated perpetrators of war crimes." Six months later (courting Jewish support against Serbs and Muslims), Tudjman formally apologized to the ADL. The Holocaust has become the standard by which to judge all other crimes against humanity. "Faces of Sorrow: Agony in the Former Yugoslavia"—the Washington museum's first account of events outside the Third Reich—managed to anger all sides. Jews objected to the depiction of Croats as victims, while Serbian Americans were unhappy that the permanent exhibit contained little about the 300,000 to 400,000

Serbs killed by Nazis, the Croatian Ustashe, and Muslims. The museum chairman replied that World War II "does not give the Serbs of today a license to kill and maim women and children." The director of SerbNet retorted that Croats and Muslims should not "be permitted to use the Holocaust as a political forum to advance their cause."[80] Israeli officials have forbidden the use of Yad Vashem to commemorate homosexual victims of the Nazis. After the Egyptian foreign minister refused to visit its Hall of Remembrance, where he would have had to don a yarmulke, Israel removed the memorial from the mandatory tour for most foreign dignitaries. The Knesset speaker, a concentration-camp survivor, protested that decision, calling the Holocaust memorial "an identity card and gateway to Israel."[81]

The fiftieth anniversary of the liberation of the concentration camps reopened questions of moral standing. Although Polish president Lech Walesa pacified the American Jewish Committee by adding a Jewish service to the official ceremony, Polish Jews found the event too ecumenical. "We have the right to weep alone. We decided that in Auschwitz and especially in Birkenau there should be special ceremonies as Birkenau is the tomb of one and a half million Jews." At Cracow, Walesa emphasized Polish suffering and did not mention the Jews. The next day he changed his Auschwitz speech at the last minute: "The distance we have walked from the sign that says 'labor liberates' to this death house is a symbolic journey . . . down the road that stands for the suffering of many nations, especially the Jewish nation." But he undercut this by adding "Whole nations, the Jews and the Gypsies, were supposed to be exterminated here together with others—above all, us Poles." Elie Wiesel, Clinton's emissary, reasserted Jewish claims: "The Jewish people—singled out for destruction during the Holocaust—have shouldered history's heaviest burden."[82]

Steven Spielberg's film *Schindler's List* generated extreme reactions. The director met President Mitterrand, and presidents von Wiezsaecker and Walesa attended the German and Polish premiers. It was the most popular film for months in Germany, Austria, Italy, Japan, and Latin America; but Malaysia banned it as "propaganda with the purpose of asking for sympathy as well as to tarnish the other race." "The story of the film reflects the privilege of virtues of a certain race only." And Jordan banned it following the Hebron massacre because Hollywood did not depict Palestinian suffering. But though it won Oscars in virtually every category, not all Americans were enthusiastic. Students from a predominately African American high school in Oakland, on a Martin Luther King's birthday field trip, jeered at Nazi atrocities and laughed when a guard shot a woman to death. Outraged patrons—some Holocaust survivors—stormed the lobby to complain, forcing the theater to stop the movie and expel the students, to loud applause. One student explained: "We don't know about those concentration camps, but I do hear a lot of Jew jokes." Eerily echoing Neville Chamberlain, she added that the war "was long ago and far away, and about people we never met." Although Spielberg got standing ovations at the school several months later and emphasized parallels between the Holocaust and slavery, Black Muslim protesters asked "how a Zionist Jew could teach them about racism and oppression." A social studies teacher complained: "We haven't dealt with our own African American holocaust; now we're getting the Jewish Holocaust up to our eyeballs." When New Jersey governor Whitman announced five free screenings of the movie in response to Khallid Abdul Muhammad's Kean College speech, African Americans objected that it should be balanced with *Eyes on the Prize* or *Roots*. Louis Farrakhan concurred: "Why is it that we have so many stories about a Jewish Holocaust . . . but there is nothing that is said of the holocaust to black people, which was 100 times worse?"[83]

These controversies resemble those in earlier sections. Race overlaps with nation—explicitly when equated with ethnicity. The combination intensifies resentments—for instance, when a Japanese justice minister compared foreign prostitutes in Tokyo to American blacks who "ruin the atmosphere" by moving into white neighborhoods. Anti-Semites confuse religion and race, just as many Americans confuse Islam with Arabs (another Semitic people). Oppressed groups borrow from each other's experience: Jews recall their enslavement in Egypt, while African Americans call slavery their Holocaust; the Confederate flag is a swastika; Indians are "prairie niggers"; Israel's rejection of Ethiopian blood was "apartheid in the Holy Land." Racial hatred, sexual exploitation, and blasphemy are conflated. The NOI's anti-Semitic diatribe was "gangsta history." Jews denounced the proposal to re-create an Auschwitz gas chamber as "voyeuristic" and a "profanity." Malaysia demanded twenty-five cuts in *Schindler's List* for "sex, cruelty, horror, and obscene dialogue."

Racial confrontations explicitly contest respect. Seeking to "honor" her ancestors, Senator Moseley-Braun opposed the UDC congressional patent as an "insult," which placed "the imprimatur of the United States Senate on a symbol" of slavery. In suburban New York, Mount Vernon's black mayor saw the closure of a footbridge to the predominately white Pelham as "a slap in the face." Attacking segregated Mardi Gras *krewes*, the black chair of the New Orleans School Board said: "[N]o tradition or economic loss is worth more than my dignity." Those protesting athletic teams' appropriation of their name and likeness held up signs declaring "Indians before football." The Kean College president justified tolerating Khallid Muhammad's speech as a means of "empower[ing] students who often come from a disadvantaged background." Challenging stereotypes and invisibility, a black mother demanded a black Santa Claus at Selma's shopping mall: "I'll be damned if I'll let my children believe some fat white man brought their presents."

Subordinated groups compete in victimhood. Jealous of the sympathy garnered by Spielberg's film, Louis Farrakhan insisted that slavery "was 100 times worse than the Holocaust of the Jews." But Jews claim sole ownership of the Holocaust, excluding Romanies and homosexuals and rejecting analogies to other persecutions. At the fiftieth anniversary of the liberation of Auschwitz, Polish Jews insisted: "[W]e have the right to weep alone." A German making a film about Nazi crimes encountered Jews "sitting at a gate . . . that opened onto the zone of the Holocaust. And they were the ones who decided who could enter." The Knesset speaker (a Holocaust survivor) called Yad Vashem the "gateway to Israel." Revisionism is intolerable because it questions victims' moral superiority. *Die Welt* declared: "He who belies Auschwitz . . . attacks Jews' human dignity." The German Constitutional Court called denial "an insult to those Jews living in Germany today." When the Israel Supreme Court overturned Demjanjuk's conviction, a Treblinka survivor shouted three times "Am I not authentic?" Acquittals and lenient sentences for racial crimes have similar effects.

Dominant groups view these confrontations from the opposite side, dismissing accusers as hypersensitive whiners responsible for their own degradation. Japan rejected as racist American charges of anti-black racism. "In Japan, there is no discrimination against any races." A contemporary American songwriter disparaged Indian complaints about his lyrics—"You can find me in my wigwam / I'll be beating on my tom-tom"—as just "a way to be heard." The Chippewa president of the National Coalition on Racism in Sports and the Media retorted that "the ones who are doing the offending try to dictate to us what should be acceptable. That's boorish arrogance." Disregarding substantive inequality, the dominant champion formal equality. Why should Selma's Santa Claus be black rather than green, purple, or orange? If African Americans can have a black history month, celebrate Martin Luther King's birthday, and display African flags, why cannot whites fly the Confederate flag? A Los Angeles sheriff seeking recognition for an organization of white officers resisted being "punished or penalized for any real or purported transgressions of our forbears. . . . no member of this organization ever bought, owned, sold or traded a slave. None of us worked at Treblinka or Manzanar nor sailed under Pizarro. None rode to Wounded Knee."

These struggles for respect were waged through ambiguous sym-

bols whose meaning varied with context and motive, speaker and audience. Critics of Zionism disavowed anti-Semitism (if often disingenu-
ously). Some African Americans saw all genetic research on crime as
racist. Both Jews and gays took offense at a Benetton model tattooed
"HIV Positive." Jews saw a reference to gas chambers in a roller coaster
named Zyklon. The NAACP first denounced and then applauded a
Colonial Williamsburg reenactment of a slave auction, directed and
acted by African Americans. The ADL reproduced some of Khallid Muhammad's most offensive language in a *New York Times* advertisement.
A highly qualified candidate was dropped from consideration as Michigan State University president for once having said "a black athlete
can actually outjump a white athlete on average." But Hollywood
could make a successful film entitled *White Men Can't Jump*. Whoopi
Goldberg could not confer on her white partner Ted Danson the exclusive black privilege of self-mockery. Eden Jacobowitz claimed to see
no difference between pupils at an all-Jewish primary school calling
each other "behameh" and himself calling black women students at
the University of Pennsylvania "water buffalo" and suggesting they
belonged in the zoo.

Racial disrespect provokes passionate responses. The Wedowee
high school principal reduced a student to tears by calling her a "mistake" of miscegenation. Actors and spectators at the Colonial Williamsburg slave auction burst into tears. Combatants resorted to hyperbole. Canadian blacks denounced *Show Boat* as "hate literature."
Giuliani called the Crown Heights attack a "pogrom." The National
Congress of American Indians issued a "declaration of war" against
"non-Indian 'wanabees' " who appropriated their rituals. Conservative
faculty equated the University of Pennsylvania with Beirut and Yugoslavia.

Both sides see the conflict as a zero-sum game. Superiors dread suffering the degradation they inflict on inferiors. The dominant practice
exclusion, fearing that contact with subordinates will contaminate
them. Any concession endangers the precarious status hierarchy. A
white New Orleans city councilor expressed his horror at black demands to integrate Mardi Gras *krewes:* "The blacks stood up and said
'This city is ours.' " The Sons of Confederate Veterans saw the campaign against the Confederate flag as a "national attack on everything
related to the Old South," which threatened "oppression and censorship of our people." Once aroused, resentment was hard to allay. A
celebration of black-Jewish cooperation reawakened mutual recrimina-
tions that Jewish trade unions had discriminated against blacks and the
black campaign for school decentralization was anti-Semitic. Remedies,
even if represented as "educational," also were degradation ceremo-

nies: Greenwich high school students who had smuggled racist slurs into the yearbook spending 100 hours learning how blacks lived, compulsory courses on genocide following anti-Semitic incidents, "sensitivity training" for Marge Schott.

Apology was the only way to equalize status. The pope wanted the Catholic Church to enter the third millennium since the birth of Christ cleansed of sin. But some Israelis demanded that Catholics "fall on their knees and ask forgiveness" for the church's complicity in the Holocaust. Opening the records of his country's protection of Nazis, President Menem said: "This is a debt Argentina is paying to the world." The German Bishops' Conference in consultation with the Polish Bishops' Conference declared that the church "confesses that she bears coresponsibility for the Shoah." But most offenders undercut their apologies with protestations of good motive: "I generally love people," it was a slip of the tongue, just a joke, I am not a racist—even "some of my best friends are Jews." Forgiveness is an act of grace by the offended; some African Americans refused to accept any apology by Rutgers's president for what he claimed was a misstatement, demanding his resignation. The most heinous offenders cannot even request forgiveness; on the fiftieth anniversary of the end of World War II Germans pointedly refrained from seeking absolution, and an Israeli author explicitly withheld it. Yet an unjust refusal to accept an apology can invert the moral standing of victim and offender.

GENDER, SEXUAL ORIENTATION, AND PHYSICAL DIFFERENCE

Although feminism has a long pedigree, the third wave has been particularly concerned with respect; and though the newer identities of sexual orientation and physical difference have refought the old battles against de facto (and even de jure) discrimination, they also seek respect.

Women still confront forms of segregation that have become unacceptable against ethnic, religious, and racial groups. Private clubs ban them, and strip joints demean them. The National Federation of Business and Professional Women's Clubs called the latter "a very shrewd way of excluding women." "How can you be taken seriously when there is some woman up on stage taking off her clothes?" Writing in *Playboy*, D. Keith Mano agreed: "[M]en have come to cherish a venue . . . where they can exert control: For $20 I can make any woman in this room take off her clothing. . . . And if I admire her body, in look or in language, she will accept my male response and won't call a lawyer."[84]

Resistance to women seeking admission to military academies is clearly motivated by status anxiety. The Citadel admitted Shannon Faulkner under court order but excluded her from the extracurricular activities that are the core of student life and housed her in the infirmary—which her lawyer characterized as saying "[Y]ou're akin to a virus." Cadets called her Mrs. Doubtgender and Shrew Shannon and wore "Save the Males" buttons and T-shirts emblazoned "1,952 Bulldogs and 1 Bitch"; the student paper speculated about the "Divine Bovine's" sexual partners. Boys hissed her in the halls and shouted obscenities from the safety of their windows. The court approved a school order that she receive the same "knob" haircut as men, rejecting Attorney General Reno's argument that male nurses did not wear dresses. When Faulkner resigned just days after beginning her first term in residence, citing the emotional toll, cadets erupted in ecstasy.[85]

Responses to sexual offenses—like those to racial crimes—implicate the honor of both victim and culprit. Mike Tyson thought it "incredible" that Desiree Washington could visit his hotel room and not expect sex. At his sentencing for rape, he was unrepentant to the judge: "I don't come here begging for mercy, ma'am. . . . I've been crucified, humiliated worldwide." He apologized to his fans for letting them down but not to his victim. Film director Spike Lee and rap singer Queen Latifah condemned the conviction in a paper entitled "The Rape of Mike Tyson." Women were outraged when Harlem ministers and politicians celebrated Tyson's release, asking what the event "says about who our heros are" and urging Tyson to "issue a statement apologizing to black women."[86] During the Senate Judiciary Committee hearings on the Clarence Thomas nomination, Rep. Patricia Schroeder (D-Colo.) led a delegation of congresswomen to the Democratic caucus room, cheered by secretaries, receptionists, and female aides. Schroeder commented: "We cringe when we hear our colleagues, who are our friends, talk about 'This couldn't be sexual harassment because da-da-da-da.' And you say: 'Oh my goodness, they just don't get it.' " The NOW vice president called this "one of the issues that makes our stomachs hurt." When a group of feminists proposed to endow a chair for Anita Hill at the University of Oklahoma Law School, a Republican state representative called the idea "totally disgraceful" and her supporters "leftist loonies."[87]

Verbal and visual representations of women proclaim and reproduce their subordination. Efforts to make religion less patriarchal have been highly controversial. In England a Conservative MP urged that £1 be withheld from a vicar's stipend each time he used *Including Women: A Non-Sexist Prayer Book.* "These prayers refer to God as 'Our Mother and Father.' Curates who are themselves confused about bisexuality should not try to confuse the congregation as to whether Jesus was a hermaphrodite."[88] At a conference called "Re-Imagining," 2,000 Protestant women prayed: "Our Maker Sophia, we are women in your image; with the hot blood of our wombs we give form to new life." The audience laughed and cheered when one woman minister boasted that they had not "name[d] the name of Jesus. Nor have we done anything in the name of the Father and of the Son and of the Holy Spirit." Another declared no need for "folks hanging on crosses and blood dripping and weird stuff." The Presbyterian Church responded with a 96 percent vote reaffirming basic convictions that had been "criticized and ridiculed at the conference" and repudiating references to Sophia "that imply worship of a divine manifestation distinctly different from the Trinity."[89]

Politicians are slowly learning the costs of insulting half the electorate. Republican Clayton Williams enjoyed a comfortable lead in the 1990 Texas gubernatorial race until he compared a cattle roundup at his ranch that had been spoiled by cold foggy weather to a rape, telling ranch hands, campaign workers, and reporters "If it's inevitable, just relax and enjoy it." Although he apologized "if anyone's offended," he added: "That's not a Republican women's club that we were having this morning. It's a working cow camp, a tough world where you can get kicked in the testicles if you're not careful." Ann Richards, his Democratic opponent, said Williams's statements raised doubts about his "ability to understand the kinds of problems faced by the people of Texas. Rape is a crime of violence." She won.[90]

It is media depictions of women, however, that generate the fiercest controversy (as we saw in chapter 2). Pornography clearly demeans the women who make it. The first black Miss America was stripped of the title when nude *Playboy* photos of her were disseminated. Even *Playboy* will not publish photographs of porn-flick stars. Actresses often demand "body doubles" for nude scenes. Although Virginia Madsen had appeared nude in earlier films, she insisted on one in *The Hot Spot*, perhaps to demonstrate her improved status. Julie Strain, double-in-waiting for Geena Davis in *Thelma and Louise*, described the selection process.

> They brought a bunch of girls out to the director's trailer one by one, and we had to strip down and spin in a circle. If you had kept your underwear on, I'm sure he wouldn't have said anything. But it's just easier to show the whole thing, because if they're going to shoot a love scene they need to see there are no scars or marks.

Shelley Michele (who had doubled Kim Basinger and Julia Roberts), explained why she stood in for Catherine Oxenberg, daughter of Princess Elizabeth of Yugoslavia, in *Overexposed* (to ensure that the actress wasn't). "She's royalty. It's not really moral for her to be doing nudity."[91]

If visual representations have been the principal target of feminist criticism, gangsta rap has gained considerable notoriety for treating women as "bitches," "hos," and "trix" (whores and tricks).[92] Some of the most offensive lyrics were in "The Buck" on 2 Live Crew's *As Nasty as They Wanna Be*.

> That's the only way to give her more than she wants,
> Like a doggie-style, you get all that cunt.
> Cause all men try real hard to do it,
> To have her walking funny so we try to abuse it.
> Bitches think a pussy can do it all,
> So we try real hard just to bust the wall.
> . . .
> I'll break you down and dick you long.
> Bust your pussy and break your backbone.
> . . .
> I'm gonna slay you, rough and painful,
> You innocent bitch! Don't be shameful!
> . . .
> That dick will make a bitch act cute,
> Suck my dick until you make it puke
> . . .
> Lick my ass up and down,
> Lick it till your tongue turns doodoo brown.

Henry Louis Gates Jr., an African American literature professor, initially defended the group. But after African American law professor Kimberlé Crenshaw insisted that the lyrics were profoundly misogynist, Gates conceded that we "must not ignore the traditions of racism and sexism that inform [vernacular forms]; nor can we allow ourselves to sentimentalize 'street culture.' "[93]

The gay and lesbian struggle for respect resembles the early stages of the civil rights and feminist movements in possessing only tenuous legitimacy and suffering virulent backlash.[94] In response to Bruce Bawer's call for full equality in *A Place at the Table*, the *New York Times* book reviewer would extend only tolerance. When Newt Gingrich's lesbian half-sister Candace lobbied Congress to outlaw employment discrimination, the new speaker compared homosexuality to alcoholism, declaring that "our position should be toleration. It should not be promotion." He feared "recruitment" in schools and ridiculed the proposed bill, asking if "a transvestite should automatically have the right to work as a transvestite?"[95] Many African Americans rejected the analogy to the civil rights movement. Columnist William Raspberry stressed the difference between the valid claim that "my sexual orientation and behavior are none of your business" and the illegitimate "demand that you acknowledge my sexual choices as the exact equivalent of yours." Louis Farrakhan was uncompromising: "We must change homosexual behavior . . . [which] offends the standards of moral behavior set by God."[96]

The intense resistance to legal equality for homosexuals reflects status, not material, concerns. When Congress reviewed a District of Columbia ordinance extending employment benefits to unmarried couples, Rep. William E. Dannemeyer (R-Calif.) condemned it as "a direct effort to redefine the American family." After the Republican sweep in November 1994, the New York legislature denied health care benefits to unmarried partners because, according to Rep. Joseph L. Bruno, it did not want to subsidize an "abnormal life style." When an Austin, Texas, suburb learned that Apple Computer gave health care benefits to unmarried partners, it canceled the tax abatement that had induced the company to plan an $80 million office complex (which would add $300 million to the local economy over several years). A county commissioner explained: "I would have had to walk into my church with people saying, 'There is the man who brought homosexuality to Williamson County.' " When Alaska responded to Hawaii's probable recognition of same-sex unions by declaring marriage "a civil contract entered into by one man and one woman," the Family Research Council explained that a same-sex union

> might be called a partnership, but if it's called marriage, it's a counterfeit version. And counterfeit versions drive out the real thing. I don't see these movements as an expression of bigotry but as a long-overdue recognition that gay rights enacted into law become tyranny for those who favor traditional sexual morality.[97]

Anticipating a Hawaii Supreme Court decision upholding same-sex marriages, the states and Congress passed legislation refusing them recognition and denigrating them as an "assault on our culture," which would "degrade" and "trivialize" and "make a mockery" of heterosexual marriage.[98]

Making homophobia a call to arms, Christian conservatives launched voter initiatives to repeal and outlaw civil rights for homosexuals. Oregon organizer Lon Mabon exulted: "We are in a mode of full-scale cultural war now." The National Gay and Lesbian Task Force agreed that the electoral campaigns were "an unofficial national referendum on homosexuality in America." When the Colorado Supreme Court invalidated a successful statewide initiative, its sponsor said the court "cast aside the freedoms of those who hold politically incorrect beliefs." The founder of Colorado for Family Values condemned any attempt "to legitimize homosexual behavior as the moral, legal and ethical equivalent of the traditional nuclear family" and (forgetting the Greeks) warned that loss of the law "will annihilate the basis of our Western civilization." When the U.S. Supreme Court agreed the initiative was unconstitutional, Focus on the Family condemned it for "disparag[ing] the moral views of the people of Colorado." Cincinnati appealed a federal court's invalidation of its withdrawal of civil rights protection from homosexuals.

> What the gays are asking here is a government seal of approval on this life style. . . . We don't give [special rights] to smokers or adulterers, for example. . . . There is no constitutional requirement for local government to intervene on behalf of one segment of a community in a way that offends another segment of the community.[99]

National battles were equally intense. In an early challenge to the military's exclusion of homosexuals, Joseph C. Steffan contested his dismissal six weeks before graduating from the U.S. Naval Academy, where he had been one of the top ten students. Ruling on a discovery motion, U.S. District Judge Oliver Gasch observed that Steffan had been discharged because "he's a homo and knows other homos." Accused of bias, he refused to recuse himself and ultimately justified the exclusion by reference to the danger of AIDS. The District of Columbia Court of Appeals affirmed en banc, finding the ban no different from height and eyesight requirements.[100] Clinton quickly hedged his campaign promise to overturn the ban. The outgoing deputy assistant secretary of the navy for manpower warned that the entry of "notoriously promiscuous" gays would "really devastate military readiness [and] bring great tension into the military." Retired general Norman "Stormin'" Schwarzkopf agreed that the military would become a "second-class force, like many of the Iraqi troops who sat in the deserts of Kuwait, forced to execute orders they didn't believe in." The Family Research Council declared homosexuality "unhealthy, immoral, addictive and dangerous to others." Antiabortion activist Randall Terry gloated: "This is going to help us mobilize people to take action for the next four years." Civil rights groups distanced themselves, the NAACP taking no stand and the Leadership Conference on Civil Rights declining to lobby.[101] After four months of controversy, Clinton proposed his "don't ask, don't tell" compromise. "We are trying to work this out so that our country does not . . . appear to be endorsing a gay life style." The Campaign for Military Service promptly denounced such compulsory closeting: "soldiers can continue to serve if they're gay so long as they pretend not to be gay." Service members could go to gay bars or march in a gay rights parade occasionally but not hold hands or kiss.[102]

Political language and acts exerted great symbolic power. Soon after taking office, Clinton became the first president to meet gay groups in the White House prior to a major rally. But though he recorded a speech to be broadcast at the march, he would not attend and allow himself to be photographed there. Two years later Secret Service officers donned rubber gloves to greet fifty activists invited to the White House by Clinton's liaison on gay and lesbian issues. The *New York Times* said the affair displayed either "deplorable ignorance" or a "malicious determination to denigrate" and urged Clinton to apologize personally. Vice President Gore spent much of the evening trying to shake everyone's hand.[103]

If Clinton equivocated, Republicans shamelessly stoked homophobia. When Clinton nominated former San Francisco county supervisor Roberta Achtenberg as assistant secretary of housing, Sen. Jesse Helms (R-N.C.) attacked her "not because she is a lesbian, but because she is a militant activist who demands that Americans accept as normal a lifestyle that most of the world finds immoral." Two years later he denounced the administration for seeking "to extend to the homosexuals special rights in the Federal workplace" and introduced a bill to withhold federal money from any program that "persuade[d] employees or officials to embrace, accept, condone or celebrate homosexuality as a legitimate or normal life style." Soon thereafter he opposed funding for AIDS treatment because the disease was caused by "deliberate, disgusting, revolting conduct." "We've got to have some common sense about a disease transmitted by people deliberately engaging in unnatural acts."[104] At a Virginia Republican fund-raiser former national party chairman Charles Black joked that Clinton had wanted to change the Marine Corps hymn to "Now we don our gay apparel." Oliver North said he had tried to call Clinton but could not get through until he lisped. And a state senator condemned Clinton's "fags-in-the-foxhole" policy.[105]

As soon as the new Republican-dominated Congress convened in January 1995, House Majority Leader Dick Armey (R-Tex.) expostulated: "I don't have to listen to Barney-Fag—Barney Frank—haranguing in my ear." Insisting that the remark reflected "a climate of meanness and intolerance," Frank rejected Armey's excuse that his tongue had slipped. "There are a lot of ways to mispronounce my name. That is the least common." "I'm representative of a lot of gay people and lesbians who are a lot more vulnerable than I am to prejudice and so I have an obligation not to just shrug my shoulders and laugh it off." In an editorial titled "Hate Speech Comes to Congress," the *New York Times* said it "would have to go back to the days of Earl Butz to find a parallel example of such common behavior by a high federal official." Armey was hurt: "Implicit in your blast is the belief that a Southern conservative Republican uses such words in private. That is a stereotype, and it is wrong."[106] In a debate on water pollution a few months later, Rep. Randy "Duke" Cunningham (R-Calif.) lumped those who wanted to regulate military pollution with those who "want to put homos in the military." Frank rose "to express my contempt for the effort to introduce such unwarranted and gratuitous slurs on decent human beings on the floor of the House."[107] Defending Dole's right flank in the race for the Republican presidential nomination, his campaign returned a contribution from the homosexual Log Cabin Republicans because they had "a specific political agenda that's fundamentally at odds with Senator Dole's record and views." About the same time Dole wrote the conservative *Washington Times* opposing "the special interest gay agenda that runs from gays in the military and reaches as far as to suggest special status for the sexual orientation under federal civil rights statutes."[108]

Parades fall in the gray area between public and private activity. Although they occupy streets, consume public funds, and require official permission, many are organized by private groups, which claim the right to control participation. St. Patrick's Day parades have become flashpoints. The Ancient Order of Hibernians refused to admit the Irish Lesbian and Gay Organization (ILGO) to the 1991 New York parade, although Mayor Dinkins offered to extend the length of the march. Spectators yelled "AIDS! AIDS! AIDS!" at ILGO members who marched in another contingent. When Dinkins appeared in the parade (having declined to march at its head), he was greeted with taunts, epithets, angry signs, and beer cans, and several dignitaries turned their backs as he passed the reviewing stand. "It was like marching in Birmingham, Alabama," he said. The Hibernians reaffirmed the ban the following year, boasting "We've run the St. Patrick's Day Parade for 230 years without an administrative judge to tell us who could march." They denounced the city Human Rights Commission's finding of discrimination as "an attempt to destroy the parade." The *New York Times* condemned the exclusion as "A Sad Day for the Irish," and an op-ed called the Hibernians "a profoundly undemocratic, sectarian organization," which excluded women from full membership and non-

Catholics entirely, although they were half of all Irish Americans. The president and eight members of the city council boycotted the parade, while two state assembly members, a congressman, former mayor Edward Koch and Sen. Alphonse D'Amato prominently participated. Another congressman said exclusion of gays was justified "for the same reason I wouldn't want the Ku Klux Klan in the Martin Luther King Day Parade." Protesters chanted from the sidelines "We're here! We're Queer! We're Irish! Get Used to It!" and attendance fell from 2,000,000 to 385,000.[109]

In 1993 the police commissioner (the highest ranking Irish American in the Dinkins administration) issued a permit to the St. Patrick's Day Parade Committee, which had pledged to admit homosexuals. Hibernian parade committee chair Francis Beirne objected that Dinkins "said he was the Mayor of all the people of New York City, but he's certainly not the Mayor of the Irish or the Catholic communities." When a boycott threat forced the St. Patrick's Day Parade Committee to relinquish the permit, Beirne said Dinkins "should apologize to the Irish." Dinkins shunned the event, but his rival Rudolph Giuliani participated. John Cardinal O'Connor was triumphant: "Neither respectability nor political correctness is worth one comma in the Apostles' Creed." More than 200 protesters were arrested for sitting down on Fifth Avenue. The following year Mayor Giuliani rejected ILGO's request that he boycott the parade: "People had to be tolerant on both sides of this question." To honor O'Connor's support, parade organizers made him marshal in 1995. This time a thousand protesters were arrested. Soon thereafter the Catholic League for Religious and Civil Rights urged the city to reroute the gay and lesbian pride parade away from Fifth Avenue. "The whole purpose of the march is to insult Catholics." Some participants stripped naked as they passed St. Patrick's Cathedral; others shouted obscenities or chanted "Confess, confess, the cardinal wears a dress." The league president warned that, if Giuliani failed to act, "I'm going to make this his Crown Heights." The gay pride paraders themselves confronted skinheads sporting swastikas.[110]

Representations of sexual orientation can dignify or degrade, especially if publicly subsidized or widely disseminated. Angered by the depiction of homosexuality at a theater that derived 5 percent of its budget from local government, the Cobb County Commission (outside Atlanta) voted to condemn homosexuality and declare that "life styles advocated by the gay community are incompatible with the standards to which this community subscribe." A local politician called this "a way to say we want to live by the standards set by the parents, not some of the things they allow in big cities." The Atlanta Shakespeare

Company director condemned this "voice of pride, prejudice, bigotry and tyranny." Two weeks later the commission terminated all arts funding (0.09 percent of its annual expenditures); one commissioner charged that "art can be used as a weapon to open the door to gay lifestyles." Homosexuals were "using this to get their foot in the door and to demand greater, bigger things that are anti–traditional moral standards." Another said: "People are fed up with having the gay agenda crammed down their throat and told that they can't articulate their position because it's not politically correct." A television news personality declared: "In the span of three decades, we've become the most permissive society in the world." "It is time to draw a line in the sand and take a stand." A year later the Atlanta Committee for the Olympic Games threatened to withdraw the volleyball event unless the county repealed its resolution. The commission chair retorted: "There's no one person or group that could bring or justify enough intimidation, pressure or threats that would convince us to rescind the resolution we adopted last August." And Newt Gingrich, who represented Cobb County in the House, called the threat "grotesque."[111]

If homophobes object to sympathetic portrayals, gays and lesbians condemn stereotypes. When activists disrupted the filming of *Basic Instinct* in San Francisco, the Gay and Lesbian Alliance against Defamation (GLAAD) denounced the "gratuitously defamatory" opening—in which a bisexual woman made love to a man and then killed him with an ice pick—and the trivialization of lesbianism as a hobby when men were unavailable. GLAAD also criticized *JFK* for the sinister portrayal of Clay Shaw's homosexuality and "an unlikely and gratuitous scene depicting gay characters dressed in elaborate costumes and involved in some kind of sado-masochistic activity"; *Silence of the Lambs* for making the murderer a cross-dressing, disco-dancing, poodle-owning, misogynistic woman trapped in a man's body; the gay neighbor in *Prince of Tides* for making jaded wisecracks about sex and shopping in Bloomingdales; the gay hustlers and narcoleptics in *My Own Private Idaho;* and *Fried Green Tomatoes* for transforming the novel's strong female lovers into platonic friends.[112] Rap music often is blatantly homophobic. Public Enemy's highly successful album *Fear of Black Planet* not only was misogynistic and anti-Semitic but also proclaimed: "Man to man / I don't know if they can / From what I know / The parts don't fit."[113]

Homosexuals have sought dignity by reclaiming historical figures (and, more controversially, "outing" contemporary celebrities).[114] Lesbians have long claimed Eleanor Roosevelt; gays recently noted that Abraham Lincoln shared a bed with a man during his early years in Washington.[115] Championing equality for homosexuals in the Israeli military, Labor party MP Yael Dayan (Moshe's daughter) invoked King David, who called his grandson killed in battle with the Philistines "most dear to me" and declared: "Your love for me was wonderful, surpassing the love of women." A National Religious party member shouted: "All of you are sick. All of you should be hospitalized." His colleague screamed: "Chutzpah! Chutzpah! Scandal! Get her down from there!" The deputy education minister from the religious Shas party called her "a foul and dirty creature." "They are simply raping all of the people we Israelis hold to be holy." He quoted the Bible: "A man who lies with a man as if a woman will be cursed and cut off from the people of Israel." The Shas leader declared: "We will blow up this leftist coalition. What is being asked of this Knesset today? To remove completely all semblance of this sin and to [falsify] the Torah of Israel." Her own party leader asked her to "show some tolerance on this issue and take back your words."[116]

Scientific controversies can implicate the social standing of homosexuals (like that of racial minorities). Twenty years after the American Psychiatric Association ceased calling homosexuality a mental disorder, it denied "that any treatment can change a homosexual person's deep-seated sexual feelings." The next year the American Medical Association (AMA) stopped encouraging programs to inform gay patients of "the possibility of sex preference reversal" and urged "nonjudgmental recognition of sexual orientation." The 1,600-member Gay and Lesbian Medical Association praised the change as "admirable," but the National Association for the Research and Therapy of Homosexuality, which sought to change sexual behavior, denounced the AMA for "politically imposing a treatment modality."[117] While homophobes characterized sexual orientation as a "lifestyle choice," most homosexual activists welcomed evidence that it was genetic. Lambda Legal Defense and Education Fund hoped it would "lessen the stigma," the Gay and Lesbian Task Force said it "supports our belief that nature created us just the way we are and that there is no reason to fix anything because nothing is broken," and the Human Rights Campaign fund believed it would "increase public support for lesbian and gay rights."[118]

Even numbers carry political weight (as they do in racial censuses). When contemporary research suggested the fifty-year-old Kinsey Report estimate that 10 percent of white males were homosexual was at least three times too high, Rev. Louis Sheldon of the Traditional Values Coalition was triumphant. "Homosexuality is a behavioral oddity. . . . What Stonewall was to gay bashing, this shall be for so-called special protected status." Soon thereafter gay rights groups seized on a new Harvard study finding that about a fifth of adults acknowledged homosexual attraction. But when the University of Chicago survey of sexuality found that only 2 percent of men had engaged in homosexual relations within the preceding decade, Sheldon said this spoke "very decisively" against antidiscrimination laws. The Family Research Council concurred: "[T]he numbers show that Americans don't have to succumb to the idea that any and all forms of sexual expression are desirable."[119]

The most recent collectivities to challenge stigmatization are the physically and mentally different. When a fast-food chain plastered Los Angeles with billboards reading "THE BEST BREASTS IN L.A. WITHOUT PLASTIC SURGERY. POPEYES. new orleans style chicken," breast cancer survivors protested that the ads cheapened women. Popeyes removed the signs and offered the prepaid space to National Breast Cancer Month.[120] A reader wrote the *New York Times Book Review*, objecting to the facile use of labels like crazy, loony bin, and imbecile. A psychiatry professor objected to the Golden Globe Award to Brad Pitt in *12 Monkeys* because it ridicules the mentally ill. The National Stigma Clearinghouse, which systematically monitors such usage by advertisers, persuaded John Deere to withdraw an ad for "the world's first schizophrenic lawn mower" and Clarion Car Audio to stop warning "A Lot of Good an Airbag Will Do You If You Go Insane."[121] Just as homosexuals claim famous precursors, so the autistic have invoked Bartok, Wittgenstein, even Einstein. At a White House fund-raising dinner for the FDR memorial, the chair of the National Organization on Disability, confined to a wheelchair, urged that a statue depict Roosevelt in a wheelchair; another guest who, like Roosevelt, had polio, complained: "[T]hey are trying to steal our hero from us." The hearing-impaired took pride in the play and movie *Children of a Lesser God*, whose lead was a deaf actress, and in the selection of a deaf woman as the first Miss America with a disability. Student demonstrations forced the appointment of the first deaf presidents at Gallaudet University in Washington, D.C., and Lexington School for the Deaf in New York. The National Association of the Deaf has opposed inner-ear or cochlear transplants as an assault on deaf culture. When the mayor of Toledo, Ohio, suggested that the city deal with airport noise by moving deaf people into the landing path, the chair of a local disabled rights group called it the equivalent of saying "[L]et the blind work at night."[122] Some of the obese, who routinely are shunned and ridiculed, have joined the National Association to Advance Fat Acceptance.[123]

The disabled are understandably ambivalent toward benevolence (just as women are toward protective legislation and racial minorities toward affirmative action). Levi Strauss ran the first television ad featuring a disabled person and was soon followed by McDonald's. When Spray'N Wash showed the mother of an eight-year-old Down syndrome child saying "We use Stain Stick because the last place we need challenge is in the laundry room," *Advertising Age* called it "the most crassly contrived slice of life in advertising history." But the National Association for Down Syndrome praised it: "The more often that people with Down syndrome appear in ads, the fewer stares that other people with Down syndrome get when they go to the supermarket."[124] In 1993 Jerry Lewis's decades-old Muscular Dystrophy Telethon was the target of protesters carrying signs declaring "Power, Not Pity" and "Exploitation Is Not Entertaining." A 1970 poster boy explained: "They wrote on my poster: 'If I grow up, I want to be a fireman.' I never wanted to be a fireman. And I always knew I had a natural life expectancy." A disabled actor who refused disabled roles said work was harder to find after the telethon: "How are you going to employ somebody if you have just cried about them?"[125]

Participants in these struggles for respect by women, homosexuals, and the physically different often drew explicit analogies to those discussed earlier. A Jewish woman who refused to surrender her bus seat so Hasidic men could exclude her from prayers was compared to Rosa Parks. Religious Jews denounced as blasphemy and rape Yael Dayan's insinuation that King David was gay. A woman saw her battle against a topless club as "synonymous with the Civil War. It was fought over racial merchandising of people for profit, and this is the merchandising of flesh for profit." Catholics warned that continued insults to St. Patrick's Cathedral during the gay pride parade would be Giuliani's Crown Heights, while Dinkins (who had coped with Crown Heights) was reminded of "marching in Birmingham" by the fury of Irish Catholics toward his support for gay participation in the St. Patrick's Day parade. Homosexual activists analogized South Dakota's refusal to recognize Hawaiian same-sex marriages to southern antimiscegenation laws, while rural Mississippians compared a lesbian camp to a whore house, strip joint, and neo-Nazis, and real neo-Nazis attacked the gay pride parade.

The utilitarian arguments of those resisting equality—military morale, the difficulty of accommodating the disabled—were just as factitious as the cost arguments against multilingualism. Ostensibly material controversies became potent symbols—for instance, a homosexual couple's request to be buried in a common grave. But many clashes implicated status alone: using female pronouns for God, calling homosexual unions marriage, or replacing "disabled" with "differently abled." Fights over parades resembled those over commemorations and street names. Like racial segregation, the exclusion of women from clubs, homosexuals from the clergy and military, and the disabled from buildings and events also signified inferiority. Sexual objectification in pornography, beauty contests, strip clubs, advertising, rap, and jokes demeaned women. Media depictions and politicians' tirades perpetuated the inferiority of homosexuals. John Cardinal O'Connor boasted that "political correctness is [not] worth one comma in the Apostles' Creed." Just as Hibernians resented "an administrative judge [telling] us who could march in the [St. Patrick's Day] parade," so Cobb County resisted "intimidation, pressure or threats that would convince us to rescind the resolution" condemning homosexuality.

Subordinated groups demanded the same full acceptance Alan Dershowitz sought for Jews; but most dominant groups extended only grudging tolerance, resisting equality (which threatened their assertion of superiority) as a form of "special rights." California Republicans attacked a bill recognizing same-sex partnerships because it "legitimat[ed] the homosexual lifestyle." Defending the repeal of its antidiscrimination law, Cincinnati condemned gays for seeking "a government seal of approval on this life style" (just as Senator Moseley-Braun opposed a congressional patent for the UDC's use of the Confederate flag because "it is absolutely unacceptable to . . . put the imprimatur of the United States Senate on a symbol of this kind of idea"). Jesse Helms opposed spending federal money to "condone" homosexuality as a "normal life style." Judicial invalidation of Cincinnati's repeal of its antidiscrimination ordinance was "a very strong endorsement of homosexual behavior." Clinton carefully drafted his military policy so that "our country does not . . . appear to be endorsing a gay life style." The director of the International Foundation for Gender Education said: "[A]ll of a sudden a lot of [transgendered] people feel, 'hey, I am proud,'" provoking the Family Research Council to call this "yet another . . . deviant behavior that seeks legitimization in the social, legal and political realms."[126]

Despairing of securing respect, some subordinated groups returned insult for insult. One clergywoman refused to name the Trinity; another ridiculed "folks hanging on crosses and blood dripping and weird stuff"; a third (echoing Rhett) frankly didn't give a damn whether her faith was Christian. The Boston St. Patrick's Day parade marshal claimed that homosexuals "got into this for one reason and one reason only: to stick it in the face of South Boston, which is trying to have a family day." New York Gay Pride marchers stripped, shouted profanities, and made obscene gestures as they passed St. Patrick's Cathedral.

The conflicts in this section also possessed distinctive characteristics, however. The dominant feared contamination. Boys at Rugby School in England protested the selection of a girl as head: "Girls don't play rugby, boys don't play netball. Please don't confuse us."[127] Citadel cadets would not tolerate a single woman. Just as both incidents revealed adolescent anxieties about sexual identity, so straights are terrified of their homosexual feelings, and all of us know we are only temporarily able-bodied. Such primal fears help explain why sexism, homophobia, and bias against the disabled are so open and vituperative. Gangsta rappers routinely call women "hos," "bitches," and "trix." American officials shamelessly refer to "homos." Strangers casually insult the obese. Stereotypes are reproduced (gays are "notoriously promiscuous") and apocryphal atrocity stories recounted (Ron Athey dripped HIV-positive blood on his audience). Whereas religion played a vital role in the civil rights movement, churches have led the opposition to feminist and homosexual struggles. Just as Jews were unwilling to share the Holocaust with other victims, so some African American leaders refused to extend the civil rights movement to gays and lesbians. Women, homosexuals, and the disabled have had to relitigate the case against separate but equal, which *Brown* conclusively resolved for race more than forty years ago.

The dominant disregarded context and mystified power relations. Cincinnati equated homosexuals with smokers and adulterers. A congressman analogized the St. Patrick's Day parade's exclusion of ILGO to a Martin Luther King Day celebration banning the Ku Klux Klan. Offenders claimed victimhood. Clarence Thomas said he was lynched by the Senate hearings. Mike Tyson declared he was crucified by his prosecution; Spike Lee and Queen Latifah said he was raped. Just as Miami residents saw the repeal of their English-only ordinance as Cubans' "forcing Spanish down our throats," so a Cobb County commissioner complained that "people are fed up with having the gay agenda crammed down their throat." (The metaphor was equally, if differently, inappropriate.) *Anti*discrimination laws were condemned as "cast[ing] aside the freedoms of those who hold politically incorrect beliefs," "tyranny," and "trampling under foot the religious rights of the individual to make choices of conscience." The New York City Human Rights Commission was the "thought police."

Victims of prejudice were admonished to accept their subordination or be labeled intolerant themselves. Instead of requiring the Israeli military to tolerate homosexuals, the Labor party asked Yael Dayan "to show some tolerance on this issue." Sen. Trent Lott (R-Miss.) accused Roberta Achtenberg of "intolerance [and] discrimination" for opposing bias against homosexuals. The St. Patrick's Day parade organizer demanded that Mayor Dinkins "apologize to the Hibernians for all the problems he caused . . . apologize to the Irish." Supporting ILGO's exclusion from the St. Patrick's Day parade, Mayor Giuliani said: "[P]eople have to be tolerant on both sides of the issue"—that is, homosexuals must tolerate Catholic homophobia. A Jewish woman who resisted segregation by Hasidic men on a commuter bus had "behaved impolitely." Clayton Williams told women to "relax and enjoy" rape.

Because struggles for respect are a zero-sum game, the dominant saw any concession to the subordinate as endangering their own superiority. At a rally in opposition to gays in the military, a twenty-six-year navy veteran trumpeted: "We despise gays and all these people usurping the country." Colorado for Family Values warned that invalidation of their initiative abolishing laws protecting homosexuals against discrimination "will annihilate the basis of our Western civilization." A rally "to protect marriage" asked Republican presidential candidates to pledge opposition to same-sex marriage. "If left unchallenged, gays will dictate to the rest of us exactly what constitutes the most fundamental underpinning of our society. The implications are of catastrophic proportions." America would "be the first country in the world that throws the concept of marriage out of the window."[128] The millennium approached, Armageddon was here, apocalypse now.

CHAPTER FIVE

••

The Poverty of Civil Libertarianism

The previous chapter documented the pervasiveness and intractability of struggles for respect waged through symbols, words, images, and events. The response to such confrontations oscillates between the poles of civil libertarianism and state regulation. This chapter criticizes the former; the next details the inevitable excesses of the latter.

I call my target civil libertarianism to distinguish it from civil liberties, whose indispensability I fully acknowledge. Civil libertarianism takes the absolutist position that the state should never constrain speech and must observe strict neutrality as a speaker; it believes that these constraints on state action suffice to "free" speech. Although few scholars embrace such oversimplifications, partisans in the culture wars constantly invoke the shibboleth of "free speech," as shown by my three opening narratives. Opposing the MacKinnon-Dworkin ordinance in Minneapolis, the MCLU executive director declared: "Bookstores cannot be censored. That's all there is to it." Challenging Skokie's anti-Nazi ordinances, the Chicago ACLU public relations director said his organization "was built on a premise that those who preach changes in constitutional law are the enemy." Rushdie invoked Carlos Fuentes's assertion that the novel is "a privileged *arena . . . the stage upon which the great debates of society can be conducted.*" "All of us," Rushdie insisted, need a place where "we can hear *voices talking about every thing in every possible way.*" Free speech, he proclaimed, "is the whole thing, the whole ball game. Free speech is life itself."[1]

I seek to show the untenability of civil libertarianism in order to maintain the necessity for choice. Speech serves many fundamental values: testing scientific truth, clarifying moral judgment, processing political choices, facilitating social interaction, and permitting individual expression. But the implications of these values are ambiguous, one may conflict with the others, and they are not the only values. This chapter illustrates the necessity of balancing speech values against others through discrete contextualized prudential judgments. I begin by demonstrating the inevitability of state regulation, then argue the impossibility of state neutrality, and conclude by exposing the illusion of private freedom. If a purist civil libertarianism is chimerical, then equalizing respect has a claim to be weighed against the values of speech (the task I attempt in chapter 7).

THE IMPERATIVE OF STATE REGULATION

RAISON D'ÉTAT

All governments regulate speech they feel endangers their very existence. The more insecure are prompt to prohibit. When Mao's personal physician declared on the BBC that "women felt honoured to have sex" with the Great Helmsman because he "was God and the Supreme Ruler," China made Rupert Murdoch drop the network from his Hong Kong–based Star TV as the price of access. It has required Reuters and Dow Jones to obtain New China News Agency approval of all financial news.[2] Capitalist Singapore is just as repressive. It used the Official Secrets Act to prosecute a leading business newspaper for publishing the government's early economic estimates. Police interrogated an American economist who criticized "intolerant regimes" in Asia for being "ingenious at suppressing dissent" and relying "on a compliant judiciary to bankrupt opposition politicians." He fled the country, and the *International Herald Tribune* apologized "unreservedly" to the prime minister and judiciary. The paper did not contest civil liability and was ordered to pay $678,000 to the government and $214,000 to former prime minister Lee Kuan Yew.[3]

Even societies that extol free speech often restrain it under threat.[4] In 1835 the House of Representatives decided to stop receiving anti-slavery petitions.[5] Britain has been particularly repressive in response to the Northern Ireland crisis. It persuaded the BBC not to repeat six programs in 1959, jailed a reporter for failing to name an informant in 1971, tried to suppress the three-hour "Question of Ulster" in 1972, convinced the BBC not to interview the IRA after the assassination of Lord Mountbatten, forced it to sack an editor for filming an IRA roadblock, and banned IRA members from speaking on television.[6] During the Gulf War, the foreign secretary expressed "a good deal of concern" about reporting from Baghdad and voiced the "strong feeling in the country" that television had favored Iraq in describing the American bomb that killed 400 civilians in a shelter. The House of Commons leader said the government had made representations to the networks.[7] Because the war inspired American patriots to display the flag inappropriately, newspapers reprinted a federal statute (of dubious constitutionality) prohibiting its use in wearing apparel, bedding, or drapery, as a receptacle, or for advertising purposes, and commanding that it never touch the ground, floor, water, or merchandise.[8] California even recalled the vanity license plate "4-Jihad," relenting only when the owner produced a birth certificate showing that was his son's name.[9]

Civil libertarians might take these examples as evidence of the necessity for eternal vigilance (although the frequency of state abridgment suggests that the task is Sisyphean). To challenge the laissez-faire position, therefore, it is essential to adduce instances of state interference that principled libertarians accept.

LESS PROTECTED SPEECH

SPEECH AS CRIME

Criminal law forbids many kinds of speech: extortion, blackmail, breach of the peace, conspiracy, attempt, espionage, disclosure of official and trade secrets, threats, and harassment. The antiabortion campaign highlights the difficulty of drawing bright lines. When a doctor criticized Operation Rescue tactics, leader Randall Terry declared: "I hope someday he is tried for crimes against humanity, and I hope he is executed." A few days after a Catholic priest tried to buy a newspaper ad that portrayed killing abortion doctors as "justifiable homicide," one was murdered. Rev. Paul Hill responded that "the killing has stopped, and so [the murder] had the desired result." After Dr. John B. Britton replaced the murdered Dr. David Gunn in a Florida abortion clinic, the magazine *Life Advocate* published Britton's name and hometown, accusing him of responsibility for "the deaths of thousands of babies." Soon thereafter Hill murdered Britton. The magazine's next issue carried the headline: "Hill Shoots! 'Now is the Time . . . ' he says." John C. Salvi 3d, who killed three people at Massachusetts abortion clinics, was arrested outside a Virginia clinic named in *Life Advocate.* The director of Pro-Life Virginia shouted to Salvi in jail: "Thank you for what you did in saving innocent babies from being put to death" and called the act "justified," "moral," and "righteous."[10]

DEFAMATION

Civil libertarian fears about the chilling effect of defamation liability are amply supported. Jacqueline Kennedy Onassis forced Harper & Row to modify William Manchester's *Death of a President.* Peter Matthiessen's *In the Spirit of Crazy Horse* was out of print for eight years because of lawsuits by those he accused of framing Leonard Peltier for

killing two FBI agents. The District of Columbia Court of Appeals upheld a complaint against a *New York Times* review accusing a book of
"sloppy journalism" (but reversed itself on rehearing).[11]

Jeffrey Masson increased his notoriety by suing Janet Malcolm and
the *New Yorker* for $10 million for five quotations in a 48,500-word pro-
file: members of the Freudian establishment viewed him "like an intellectual gigolo"; he planned to turn Anna Freud's house into a place of
"sex, women, fun"; when his own theories were published, others
would consider him "after Freud, the greatest analyst that ever lived";
he did not know why he had called psychoanalysis sterile; and the
Freud Archives "had the wrong man" if they expected him to accept
dismissal without protest.[12]

PRIVACY

Concepts of privacy vary by place and time. Italian paparazzi are notorious. The Japanese Imperial Household Agency forced the dismissal of
a photographer who took informal wedding pictures of the emperor's
younger son. Two years later the Japan Newspaper Association "voluntarily" observed a three-month ban on speculation about Crown
Prince Naruhito's romantic liaisons.[13] French media refrained from
writing about President Mitterrand's illegitimate daughter until she
began appearing at official events in her twenties; even then it hid her
last name and mother's identity. Mitterrand forced his private physician to conceal his prostate cancer for fifteen years.[14] The owner of London's L A Fitness Club used a hidden camera to take photos of Princess
Diana working out on her back in tight-fitting shorts and half leotard
and sold them for $150,000. The *Mirror* papers ran them for two days
before being enjoined. The next day the *New York Times* showed Lord
McGregor, the Press Complaints Commission chair, looking at the *Mirror* photograph. Claiming this "shows how she could have been a sitting target for an I.R.A. terrorist," the *Mirror* defended publication as
a demonstration of poor security. Although compliance with commission rulings was voluntary, the *Daily Mirror* withdrew its membership,
calling Lord McGregor an "arch buffoon." He responded by urging
advertisers to boycott the Mirror Group. The latter immediately capitulated and rejoined the commission (which declined to hear the complaint because it was sub judice).[15] *Penthouse* successfully invoked a
similar argument to justify publishing photographs of Paula C. Jones
wearing only a G-string. After she accused Bill Clinton of having sexually harassed her when he was governor, she told a press conference
that she had posed for the photos wearing a bathing suit or negligee.

Claiming the photos showed she lied, *Penthouse* asked: "[W]hat does that say about the credibility of the charges she has made against the President?" A federal judge ruled that "the pictures in question have a relationship to the accompanying article and that the matter is in the public interest."[16]

Throughout a century of drawing the line between privacy and publicity, American courts have experienced particular difficulty deciding when art can justify harm—Rushdie's central defense. A New York court dismissed David Hampton's claim that John Guare had appropriated his life in the highly successful play (and subsequent movie) *Six Degrees of Separation.*[17] The Kennedy family was outraged by *Marilyn and Bobby: Her Final Affair,* a television film showing the couple making love and putting Robert Kennedy in the dying actress's bedroom. But the former director of acting at Yale Drama School called such fictionalization "a way for a writer to be able to embody issues, explore ideas and to sometimes create insights into historical events that couldn't be achieved any other way."[18] England strikes the balance differently. When David Leavitt wrote *While England Sleeps,* his publisher sent the novel to its obvious subject, Stephen Spender, and made the only change he requested. Spender also deposited a forty-page rebuttal in the British Library. Two months later, however, he sought an injunction, claiming the novel violated the copyright of his memoir *World within World* and his "moral right" under British law not to have creative work altered without consent. It was "disgusting" that Leavitt "uses my autobiography as a medium for his pornography." After three months of negotiation, Viking agreed to pulp all unsold American copies and make seventeen changes before issuing the paperback and the British edition. In an essay entitled "My Life Is Mine, It Is Not David Leavitt's," Spender asserted that "knowledge of what people do when they are in bed together may be true, but it is not true to what we know or wish to know about them." If Leavitt "wanted to write about his sexual fantasies, he should write about them being his, not mine."[19]

Subjects often seek to limit access to papers or acquaintances. The Women Writing Women's Lives Seminar of the New York Institute for the Humanities urged Doris Lessing's friends to disregard her plea for silence.[20] J. D. Salinger successfully prevented Ian Hamilton from quoting letters and papers in a biography.[21] The Kennedy family told biographer Nigel Hamilton to "alter [his] attitude," objected to his characterization of JFK's parents, denied access to hundreds of letters in the Kennedy Library, had his mail opened while he was working there, and prevented him from speaking at a conference called "JFK and Europe."[22] Former Alabama governor and presidential aspirant George Wallace conditioned Stephen Lesher's interviews on the biographer's promise to "treat him fairly and respectfully."[23] Although Random House called Ron Powers's biography of Jim Henson "a tremendous piece of work," his heirs did not "believe the book represents an accurate portrayal of their father." When Powers refused to reinterview people and revise his conclusions, the publisher canceled the contract, and the family claimed rights to the notes, interviews, and manuscript.[24] Yet determined biographers can turn these obstacles into advantages: Mark Harris made a story out of his frustrated efforts to meet Saul Bellow; and Janet Malcolm took revenge on Ted Hughes for refusing to talk about Sylvia Plath and himself.[25]

Those who consistently avoid the spotlight make a more compelling case for privacy. For twenty-five years Massachusetts prevented the screening of Frederick Wiseman's exposé of a state hospital for the criminally insane because some inmates were filmed naked.[26] When the *New York Times Magazine* revealed that Ivy League and Seven Sisters colleges had taken decades of nude photographs of entering students to test crackpot theories about body shape and personality, the Smithsonian shredded them within weeks.[27] Countries differ in protecting the identities of those who visit Web sites.[28] When the $28 million winner of Britain's first state lottery in 170 years insisted on anonymity, the *Sun* and the *Daily Telegraph* promptly offered £10,000 for his identity. The latter quickly narrowed the field to an Asian Muslim in his forties, who emigrated from East Africa in the 1970s, worked in a Blackburn factory, had been married fourteen years to a former machinist, and had three children, six to thirteen years old. The winner obtained an injunction against disclosure, which the High Court overturned, ruling that his identity was "substantially in the public domain." Although the defendants withdrew their reward and promised to respect the agreement protecting his privacy, three other papers named him within a week. He fled to India with his family, pleading for privacy.[29]

PROFANITY, SEX, AND VIOLENCE

The Supreme Court long has denied constitutional protection to profanity and obscenity. The Federal Communications Commission (FCC) recently cracked down on radio talk show hosts, fining Infinity Broadcasting Corporation $1.5 million for Howard Stern's discussion of masturbation, castration, rectal bleeding, bowel movements, and sexual behavior and fantasies. But with Stern's audience growing rapidly,

Infinity could afford to disregard the fines, especially since the FCC reluctantly approved its purchase of additional stations.[30]

Violence is the new regulatory frontier, constantly redrawn in response to atrocities. After the murder of two-year-old Jamie Bulgar, which eerily resembled *Child's Play 3*, critics warned that 181,000 British children had seen the horror film on television. A multiparty campaign of 300 MPs backed a bill classifying films as unsuitable for television or video if they "present an inappropriate model for children or are likely to cause psychological harm to children." The BBC issued stringent guidelines for news broadcasts, proscribing "regurgitating" lurid crime stories on early-morning news, requiring extra care with crime-scene shots of blood and close-ups of weapons, discouraging emotive adjectives, and banning dramatic music and speculative detail or dialogue in crime reconstructions and the use of camera angles to illustrate the criminal's alleged perspective.[31] After an eleven-year-old Quebec girl was raped and murdered, her teenage sister obtained more than a million signatures—including the prime minister's—on a petition for government control. Soon thereafter Canada banned shows with "gratuitous violence" and restricted until after 9 P.M. those with violence "suitable for adults only." Violence could not be the "central theme" in children's shows or "be shown as a preferred way of solving problems," and its consequences had to be demonstrated. Canada promptly banned *Teenage Mutant Ninja Turtles* and was joined by New Zealand in excluding *Mighty Morphin Power Rangers*. A Norwegian report that a five-year-old had been kicked to death by playmates who had watched the latter program led to its prohibition throughout Scandinavia, but this was rescinded when the story proved false.[32]

The United States has felt increasing pressure to restrict violence on television, despite the First Amendment. At 1993 Senate hearings chaired by Paul Simon (D-Ill.), the president of CBS said: "We are guests in the living rooms of America, so our personal values should be the most useful litmus test of taste." To avoid a mandatory chip, parents could use to block shows, the four networks agreed to develop standards indicating levels of sex and violence, and fifteen cable channels agreed to offer the same warnings, issue annual reports on violence, and develop technology allowing parents to block violent programs. This did not satisfy Simon, who gave the industry sixty days to show improvement before seeking legislation creating government standards. After a child burned to death in a fire that allegedly imitated a *Beavis and Butthead* episode, MTV promised to eliminate fires in future programs and reschedule them from 7 P.M. to 10:30 P.M.

Several months later Attorney General Janet Reno warned that government regulation would be "imperative" if the industry did not act. Legislators introduced bills to restrict violence to late evening, require the FCC to list violent programs and their sponsors, mandate warnings in television guides and on-screen, and discourage advertising of violent programs during family shows. Reno called these provisions "constitutionally sound" and urged parents to "bring pressure to bear on companies who sponsor violent programming." First Lady Hillary Clinton criticized news coverage of violent events, declaring that "children can't cope with much of what they see" on television.[33] As the 1996 campaign approached, presidential candidates saw the entertainment industry as an easy target. Dole attacked Hollywood for producing nightmares of depravity with "casual violence and even more casual sex." (Although he declined to return Time Warner's $21,000 donation, his wife promised to sell her Walt Disney stock—presumably at a profit.) Pete Wilson pontificated: "There is little doubt that they have done much to corrupt our culture. It's wrong, simply wrong, to profit from selling this trash to children." Clinton chimed in: "[I]f we're going to change the American culture, we have to somehow change the media culture." He approved an FCC regulation requiring networks to broadcast three hours of children's educational programs a week. Soon afterward one studio postponed the video release of Oliver Stone's unrated director's cut of *Natural Born Killers,* and another cut a rap song from the soundtrack of *White Man's Burden.* A bipartisan group of seventy-four members of Congress called on the six major networks to cleanse the 8 P.M. hour of "promiscuity and obscene language," objecting to the fact that incidents of premarital sex outnumbered marital sex 8 to 1 and characters used words like "ass," "bitch," and "bastard."[34]

Critics also condemned violence in the video-game industry, whose earnings rose from $2.7 billion in 1991 to $6 billion in 1993. Sega's Night Trap, in which hooded vampires suck the blood of scantily dressed women students, was castigated by the British Parliament and banned by Toys "R" Us (Canada) and then by the American parent after the Long Island Railroad murders. Although Sega was "very disappointed" because the game "is actually very benign and is designed as a parody of a vampire movie," it agreed to help develop a rating system, reedited Night Trap, and delayed distribution until the system was in place. Nintendo, its leading competitor, planned to eliminate "fatality moves," in which characters are decapitated and beating hearts pulled from living bodies. Wal-Mart, Toys "R" Us, and Babbage's refused to sell unrated games starting with the 1994 Christmas season.[35] Jurisdictions even seek to regulate violence in print media: a Long Island county banned sales to children of trading cards depicting "heinous crimes and criminals."[36]

To forestall or minimize state control, the media long have practiced self-regulation. Outside the United States, newspaper trade associations promulgate and enforce codes of behavior.[37] After a 1954 critique, the comic-book industry created the Comics Code Authority to police itself.[38] The Hollywood Movie Production Code, issued in 1930, contained such admonitions as "The courts of the land should not be presented as unjust"; films must not "make criminals seem heroic and justified"; "impure love must never be presented as attractive and beautiful"; "the use of firearms should be restricted to essentials"; "revenge in modern times shall not be justified"; "passion should so be treated that these scenes do not stimulate the lower and baser element." This forced Elia Kazan to cut four minutes from *A Streetcar Named Desire*. The code office originally wanted him to cut Stanley Kowalski's rape of Blanche DuBois, relenting only when Tennessee Williams insisted the rape was "a pivotal, integral truth," whose meaning was "the ravishment of the tender, the sensitive, the delicate, by savage and brutal forces in modern society."[39]

Under the Motion Picture Association of America (MPAA) rating system, which replaced the code in 1958, an NC-17 or no rating discourages theaters and video outlets (including Blockbuster, Kmart, and Wal-Mart) from distributing films. *Wide Sargasso Sea* was rated NC-17 for a distant shot of male frontal nudity, and *Boxing Helena* for two sex scenes. John Schlesinger cut *Midnight Cowboy* after it won three Academy Awards (including best picture) to improve its rating from X to R. New Line Cinema made Louis Malle reedit *Damage*, despite good foreign reviews, so it could qualify for an R. *Body of Evidence* secured an R by changing a scene in which Madonna masturbated and made love with Willem Dafoe on the hood of a car. Walt Disney Company distributed Cinergi's *Color of Night* only after it was recut to obtain an R. Paul Verhoeven cut 35–40 seconds from *Basic Instinct* to avoid an NC-17. Joe Eszterhas, who wrote it, made fifteen changes the following year to avoid an NC-17 for *Sliver*. *Clerks*, which won a Sundance Festival prize, was initially rated NC-17 for dialogue. MPAA president Jack Valenti explained: "There are millions of Americans who become hysterical about the kind of bad language that may be de rigueur around dinner tables in the East Side of Manhattan." The MPAA forced Grammercy Pictures to pull television and newspaper ads for *Dazed and Confused*, which boasted: "Finally! A Movie for Everyone Who DID

Inhale." Valenti explained: "They can't use quotes that glorify or glamorize something parents would think of as anti-social behavior." Marketing directors for 20th Century–Fox and TriStar agreed.[40]

Gangsta rap lyrics have been condemned as violent, obscene, racist, misogynist, homophobic, antipolice, and prodrugs. After numerous protests, some at shareholder meetings, Warner Brothers terminated its seven-year relationship with Ice-T. Oliver North was triumphant: "Everybody knows that there isn't room in American society for the kind of hatred and advocacy of violence expressed in Ice-T's music." When William Bennett and DeLores Tucker resumed the campaign two years later, Time Warner agreed that "there must be a balance struck between the creative process and our collective responsibilities as the world's leading communications company" and promised to develop warnings about offensive lyrics. A month later it fired the Warner Music Group chairman and two months after that sold its 50 percent stake in the rap subsidiary Interscope. Taking credit, Robert Dole proclaimed that "shame is a powerful weapon," and Bennett called the action "a warning to all the other big entertainment companies." Tucker declared: "Whoever picks up Interscope is going to be our next target." (MCA, the purchaser, was not obligated to distribute products that were "too controversial.")[41]

HATE SPEECH

European nations, which have suffered fascism and are unconstrained by First Amendment jurisprudence, have no qualms about regulating racial hatred. On the sixteenth anniversary of Franco's death, Spain prevented neofascists from paying tribute to Nazi aviators who had bombed a Basque city during the civil war. Munich's Deutsches Museum canceled a booking for "an international multi-media show" when it discovered that the "Leuchter Congress" was actually Holocaust revisionism. The British Football (Offences) Act of 1991 prohibits racist chants at matches. Lyons barred speeches by former SS member and German fascist leader Franz Schönhuber, and a Norwegian city banned the People's Movement against Immigration. Even American polities try to control hate speech. A New York City school board withdrew a permit to the "Lost-Found Nation of Islam" after learning that the lecture topic was "Are Jews hiding the truth?" Minister Abu Koss was incredulous: "You mean to ask a question is inflammatory?" The school board replied: "We cannot have hate or propaganda of any kind emanating from our schools." The group "did not tell the truth" when they claimed to be holding a "self-help" gathering, "and that is grounds for denying a permit."[42]

COMMERCIAL SPEECH

Both the definition of commercial speech and the protection it enjoys are uncertain and fluctuating. Government extensively regulates the advertising of dangerous products. Under threat of a ban, tobacco manufacturers withdrew radio and television advertising in the early 1970s. R. J. Reynolds pulled its new Uptown brand, targeted at African Americans, after protests by groups and Secretary of Health Dr. Louis W. Sullivan. Similar criticisms forced a small distributor to withdraw Menthol X, whose packaging resembled the black nationalist flag and whose large white X recalled advertising for Spike Lee's film *Malcolm X*.[43] Camels's "Old Joe" campaign elicited particular fury. Surgeon General Antonia Novello joined with the AMA to "invite Old Joe Camel himself to take a hike," urging retailers to remove the signs and print media to refuse advertising. Although the R. J. Reynolds chairman and CEO warned against depriving "the tobacco industry, or any industry, of its right to commercial free speech," twenty-seven state attorneys general asked the FTC to ban the cartoon character, and five representatives introduced a bill to prohibit ads in sports stadiums, movies, music videos, and video arcades and within 2,000 feet of schools and to require health warnings at sponsored sports events and on clothes and sports equipment displaying cigarette logos. Novello's successor, Dr. Joycelyn Elders, proposed banning all tobacco ads aimed at the young. Clinton's Food and Drug Administration (FDA) finally prohibited brand-name ads at sports events and on items unrelated to tobacco, within 1,000 feet of schools and playgrounds, and containing photos or drawings in youth-oriented magazines.[44] Boston, San Francisco, New York, and Cincinnati have outlawed tobacco advertising in public transportation. But when advocates sought to extend the ban to billboards, the Tobacco Institute threatened to sue: "On private property that is a potentially volatile constitutional issue." Under pressure from the Interfaith Center on Corporate Responsibility, however, 3M—the third largest billboard company—stopped advertising tobacco.[45]

Similar campaigns have been waged against alcohol advertising. The Distilled Spirits Council had an informal understanding not to broadcast on radio (since 1936) and television (since 1948); it was terminated six months after Seagram defied it. G. Heileman Brewing Company was forced to withdraw Power Master malt liquor, directed at blacks, because it illegally used a brand name to promote its alcohol content (each forty-ounce bottle equaled a six-pack of beer, five glasses of wine, or five shots of liquor). But though federal courts invalidated both a ban on Original Crazy Horse Malt Liquor (attacked as an "offensive exploitation" of an Indian name) and a sixty-year-old law prohibiting ads from stating the alcohol content of beer, numerous other regulations persist. New York State banned ads relating social or financial success to alcohol consumption, advertising in movies, daytime radio, electric signs, bus stops, newsstands, airports, railroad stations, service stations, and outdoor cafes and restaurants; it limited the size of billboards, banned them in cities, and prohibited posters within 100 feet of schools.[46]

Courts constantly revise the scope of regulation. After two decades of rewriting the line between permissible advertising and forbidden solicitation by professionals, the Supreme Court upheld a Florida statute requiring lawyers to wait thirty days after an accident before contacting victims. Although a federal court invalidated a New York law against blockbusting, local officials continued to issue cease and desist orders against real estate agents who used racial fears to scare homeowners into selling cheaply. Courts have wavered over restrictions on telephone solicitation, especially by computerized dialing and recorded messages. When Space Marketing proposed a satellite whose billboard would appear half as large as a full moon, several members of Congress pledged to block the launch, leading the company to add ozone sensors to disguise the enterprise as a scientific venture.[47]

The definition of commercial speech is inherently political. There is sharp disagreement whether begging is a business or free speech. Expressing the southern Californian belief in a constitutional right to drive, Anaheim prohibits beggars from approaching cars; New York bars panhandlers from the subways; and Memphis outlaws abusive language.[48] Courts have protected vending machines for newspapers (whose cost is largely defrayed by advertising) but not for free magazines advertising adult education and housing.[49] How would judges classify Whittle's "free" books, whose costs were defrayed by some twenty pages of advertising by the pharmaceutical industry (for medical professionals) and by Cessna Aircraft Company and Federal Express (for executives)?[50] Are advertising posters sold to decorate college dorm rooms still "art" if advertisers pay to be included in the Posters Preferred catalogue and get the names and addresses of student consumers?[51] Spanish intellectuals and artists successfully defended the four-ton Osborne bulls used to advertise Beterano brandy from a ban on advertising visible from the highway. The cultural association España Abierta called them "part of the popular culture of our country, transcending commerce to enter the realm of the universal."[52]

Such ambiguities invite evasion. Children find it particularly difficult to identify commercial speech. Inspired by the success of "Yo! It's the Chester Cheetah Show!" in pushing Cheetos, Fox planned a cartoon series starring Cheesasaurus Rex, who advertised Kraft's macaroni and cheese dinner. Under pressure from public-interest groups and the FCC, the network abandoned both programs, while insisting that Chester Cheetah was "one of the best characters since Bugs Bunny, and the fact that he is associated with a product was irrelevant to us."[53] Schools are ideal sites for sowing such confusion. "Free" curricula encourage pupils to learn about the environment by taking photographs with Kodak film and cameras, pursue home economics by listing the Revlon products they would need on a desert island, and study forestry by reciting the "innovative practices Weyerhauser has introduced in recent years." Whittle Communications' Channel One offers ten-minute newscasts on "free" television monitors to schools that require pupils to watch the two-minute commercials. When its desirability was debated in the California Assembly, a Democrat (later state superintendent of public instruction) said such advertisements "compromise the integrity of the classroom. . . . Christ drove the money-changers from the temple." One Republican called this "the moral equivalent of book burning," and another asked: "Should the Los Angeles Times be barred from our classrooms simply because it contains advertising for things such as lingerie and guns?"[54]

Adults, though more sophisticated, also are targets of manipulation. Criticized for using the House floor to announce the 900 number to order his audio- and videotapes, Newt Gingrich maintained he "didn't sell them. I just told members how they could get a copy if they wanted them."[55] Tobacco companies (among others) buy "product placement" in films: Marlboro in *Superman II*, Camels in *Roger Rabbit*, Kents in *Beverly Hills Cop*, Lark in a James Bond movie.[56] "Advertorials" and "infomercials" deliberately blur the line. Upjohn Company produced the first program-length commercial for its Rogaine hair restorer, using a talk-show format hosted by *Laverne and Shirley* star Cindy Williams.[57] CNN and CNBC screen two-minute commercials in which former reporters and anchors "interview" sponsors' executives about new products.[58] Following a tradition in which John Cameron Swayze pushed Timex watches and Linda Ellerbee promoted Maxwell House coffee, Mary Alice Williams left twenty-five years in television news to do barely distinguishable commercials: "NYNEX will be the name for a lot of new things that'll make your life more manageable. My job is to stay on top of what they're doing and keep you posted." Kathleen Sullivan, the first female Olympics anchor and former coanchor of CBS's *This Morning*, testified that the SuperStart "diet is working for me, and I believe that I am helpful to other women." The manufacturer said: "[H]er work as a newscaster gives her both celebrity and credibility."[59]

REGULATION

In addition to subjecting particular kinds of speech to greater control, states regulate all speech in many ways. Time, place, and manner restrictions have justified limits on the lung power of street preachers and antiabortion protests outside clinics and doctors' homes; zoning regulates filmmaking (Hermosa Beach refused to allow the shooting of *Beverly Hills 90210*) and the distribution of pornography.[60] States place immigration and trade restrictions on foreign speakers and media. Britain banned a Danish director who wanted to make a film portraying Jesus as bisexual, deported both an American Holocaust revisionist and an Operation Rescue leader, and sought to deport a leader of the Saudi opposition. The United States excluded many world-famous authors under the McCarran-Walter Immigration Act, including Graham Greene and Gabriel García Márquez.[61] The European Union requires that half of television movies be domestic; Hungary planned to demand that 70 percent be European and half Hungarian; France and Belgium banned Turner Network Television and Turner Cartoon Network. Canada replaced Nashville's Country Music Television with a local imitator, 30 percent of whose performers are Canadian. It prevented Borders from opening a 50,000-square-foot bookstore in Toronto in order to ensure that "Canadian stories, Canadian books, Canadian authors are going to get the kind of exposure that they need within Canadian retailers." American magazines pay an 80 percent excise tax on Canadian advertising revenue. Actors Equity prevented the British cast of *The Rise and Fall of Little Voice* from performing on Broadway and required the British cast of *Dancing at Lughnasa* to be replaced by Americans after four months. Congress recently tightened restrictions on ownership of American radio and television stations by nationals of countries that deny "effective market access" to American firms.[62]

States control even the most personal speech acts, such as naming oneself. France long required that "Christian" names be those of biblical figures and saints, relaxing the rule only under pressure from the growing immigrant population. A Japanese family register refused to accept "devil" as a given name but allowed the father to substitute "god." The Nazis named all Jewish babies Israel or Sarah; contemporary Germany prohibits Jesus and Hemingway.[63] American states limit vanity license plates. Claiming he wanted to "create discourse" about government intrusion, a Virginia driver sued over the recall of "GOVT SUX." A court overturned a ban on "GODZGUD" because the "no deity" policy was impermissible viewpoint discrimination but permitted restrictions on offensive language and references to drugs. A urologist convinced the state to reverse its denial of "PPDR," and a pickup truck with oversized wheels retained "IMSOHI." Washington was persuaded to restore "MENOPOZ." One state reluctantly allowed the surname "LUST," and another permitted the initials "JEW." Although California has rejected over 50,000 requests, it allowed "PUSSY" (which the *New York Times* coyly called "a feline nickname") when the owner sent a photo of her Mercury Lynx with cat decals and stuffed cats in the rear window. But it rejected "HIV NEG" and "HIV POS," declaring "the California license plate is not the place to fight our culture's rhetorical battles."[64]

Government regulates much more than appellations. Ever since the "Son of Sam" mass murderer tried to finance his defense by writing a book, states have prohibited criminals from profiting from accounts of their crimes. New York applied its law to famous convicts such as Jean Harris (who murdered Scarsdale diet book author Dr. Herman Tarnower), Sidney Biddle Barrows (the "Mayflower Madam"), and Jack Henry Adam (the recidivist murderer championed by Norman Mailer). Although the U.S. Supreme Court invalidated it in a case brought by Henry Hill (paid $96,000 for the Mafia tales that became Nicholas Pileggi's book *Wiseguy* and Martin Scorsese's movie), the state promptly reenacted a modified version, under which Mary Jo Buttafuoco sought to seize the $60,000 that KLM Productions paid high school student Amy Fisher for telling about her affair with Buttafuoco's thirty-nine-year-old husband and attempted murder of Mary Jo. When Katherine Ann Power surrendered after several decades in hiding for an antiwar bombing in which a police officer died, the Massachusetts judge reduced her life sentence to eight to twelve years plus twenty years probation on condition that she not sell her story. California invoked its law to seize proceeds from the 900 number of the "Billionaire Boys Club" leader convicted of murder and the $110,000 a filmmaker paid a woman who murdered her son's killer during his trial; but it declined to act against Stacey Koon, who earned at least $80,000 for his account of beating Rodney King. The O. J. Simpson prosecution prompted laws giving victims the right to income earned from books and movies by criminals convicted of serious crimes and prohibiting witnesses and jurors from selling their stories until after trial.[65]

Taxation affects the profitability of speech even more profoundly.[66] California sought to impose its 7.25 percent sales tax on camera-ready cartoons, which could be "felt, weighed, measured or smelled," but not on those transmitted electronically.[67] States tax adult video rentals and purchases, using the proceeds for sex-crime victims.[68] Commercial enterprises, but not nonprofits, can deduct speech expenses in calculating taxes. Congress allowed a deduction for lobbying costs in 1982 but drastically curtailed it a decade later.[69] The limitation on political speech by nonprofits has forced churches to curtail antiabortion campaigns. The Church of Scientology litigated forty years to win tax-exempt status in the United States; but Germany taxed the church and sought to ban it.[70] A Colorado initiative proposed to eliminate the tax-exempt status of religious institutions, partly to curb the growing influence of evangelical Christian organizations.[71]

Government control of the means of communication may affect price, access, and content. Postal rates can have momentous consequences for periodicals—and turn on details like the use of staples.[72] Until its 1987 repeal, the fairness doctrine required radio and television stations broadcasting controversial views to give opponents equal time. For twenty-five years the FCC limited the amount of network programming on prime time. Cable channels must devote a third of their capacity to local broadcasts and observe a schedule of prices. After years of heated debate, the FCC required television stations to carry three hours of children's educational programming a week.[73] Phone companies must service all areas at the same rate, subsidizing higher costs in dispersed rural communities by overcharging urban businesses (an estimated $20 billion annually).[74] Television manufacturers and stations must provide captions for the hearing impaired on every set and program.[75] Antitrust laws, which foster the diversity of voices by limiting horizontal and vertical concentration, frustrated mergers between Bell Atlantic Corporation and Tele-Communications Inc. and between Southwestern Bell Corporation and Xoc Enterprises Inc. Westinghouse Broadcasting promised more educational programming for children to secure approval for its acquisition of CBS.[76]

Government not only regulates who speaks, what they say, and what speech costs but also compels speech. Manufacturers must warn about the dangers of hazardous chemicals, cigarettes, and alcohol. Meat and poultry must carry cooking instructions. Processed food must specify the ingredients, total calories, and proportion of daily recommended consumption of fats, cholesterol, sodium, carbohydrates, protein, and vitamins per serving. Producers who claim their milk is free of BST must add that "no significant difference has been shown" with BST-produced milk. The FDA delayed and then regulated the American Heart Association award of its torch-and-heart logo to healthful food. Dietary supplements that make health claims must state that these have not been evaluated by the FDA and the product is not intended to diagnose, treat, or cure disease.[77] Child abuse must be reported by health care workers, educators, and others and child pornography by film processors. Convicted sex offenders may have to disclose their whereabouts after discharge from prison. California has required the Center for Unplanned Pregnancy to inform every caller that it takes "a Biblical anti-abortion perspective" and provides neither abortions nor abortion referrals. Airlines and car-rental agencies must provide extensive detail about cost and availability; municipal bond dealers and concert-ticket vendors may have to disclose profits. Over vociferous objections, defense lawyers have been compelled to report cash payments and airlines have secured routine access to black-box recordings to monitor pilot performance.[78]

STATE ARENAS

Every theory of free speech emphasizes its importance in public arenas, where values are clarified, conflicting interests compromised, decisions made, and officials held accountable. Paradoxically, however, speech is *more* constrained when uttered by public employees, during governmental processes, or within state institutions.

JUDICIARY

Although judges are insulated from electoral and other political pressures, even they must curb their tongues, and not only in obedience to procedural rules. When two Ninth Circuit judges condemned the death penalty in off-the-bench remarks, complaining that they had to "commit treason to the Constitution" in passing such sentences because the Supreme Court "has made it plain that the Bill of Rights is no longer its primary concern," a colleague accused them of "threatening . . . the independence of the judiciary" and urged they be reprimanded by the bar and disciplined by the judiciary.[79] Supreme Court justice Clarence Thomas, already criticized for attending a conservative fund-raiser whose participants paid $250 to meet him privately, was forced to cancel a speech billed as a "challenging message from his heart" to Concerned Women for America, which lobbies for school prayer and against abortion.[80]

Even so, judges can speak far more freely than other actors in the legal system. Ethical rules greatly restrict what lawyers can say to clients, prospective clients, adversaries, opposing counsel, judges, and juries. Judges use contempt powers, sanctions, and disciplinary threats to control lawyers in and out of the courtroom: Judge Ito compelled Marcia Clark and F. Lee Bailey to apologize to each other during the O. J. Simpson trial; a New York judge fined a male lawyer for patronizing a woman adversary during a deposition.[81] Procedural and evidentiary rules drastically constrain questions by lawyers and testimony by witnesses and parties. Just as statements by judicial nominees can torpedo their appointment, so speech by potential jurors can obstruct their impanelment. Misstatements during jury deliberations can invalidate verdicts. The Florida Supreme Court ordered a new trial following allegations that jurors had made racist comments while awarding an African American tort victim only $10,500 of his $235,000 claim.[82] Judges strictly control the information reaching jurors. Judge Ito ordered *prospective* jurors not to read newspapers or magazines, watch television, listen to radio, or enter bookstores. He removed two from the pool for briefly hearing radio music and two more for seeing Spanish soap operas and cartoons, a financial news station, and a Barbara Stanwyck film. Impanelled jurors could not watch television news (or even "teasers"), talk shows, or entertainment magazines. They received a special *Los Angeles Times* purged of all trial news.[83]

The legal system is almost as restrictive about what information gets *out* of trials as what gets in. Most jurisdictions have rigid rules about sub judice cases. The Supreme Court has upheld a double standard for gag orders: judges may silence the defense if there is a "reasonable likelihood" that speech would prejudice a fair trial but the prosecution only if there is a "substantial likelihood."[84] The federal judge trying those accused of bombing the World Trade Center threatened both sides with a $200 fine for a first offense and geometric multiples for recidivism ($40,000, $1.6 billion, etc.). In a related trial another judge warned that if leaks did not stop

> I am going to start asking . . . every agency and office involved in this prosecution, to start submitting statements under oath by people with authority and knowledge about who is doing what, who knows about what, who has authority to stop what. . . . It may be that the only power I have to stop is the power of embarrassment, but I'm going to use it.[85]

Judge Ito repeatedly clashed with both lawyers and media about Simpson trial publicity. He ordered all pretrial motions filed under seal and released only when argued in court. After television reported that the blood DNA on the sock found in Simpson's house matched Nicole's, he angrily warned: "I am contemplating terminating media's coverage in this case." He briefly barred a newspaper from the courtroom for publishing the jury questionnaire a day early. When Faye D. Resnick wrote a biography of her friend Nicole, which the defense called "a drive-by shooting of a trial in progress," Ito told television stations that interviewing the author "will serve only to fan the already raging fires of adverse publicity" and hoped the media "will find it in your conscience . . . to cooperate with this request and delay this program's broadcast until after the jury in this case has been selected and sequestered." CBS refused, but CNN complied. He barred the media from part of the jury selection, dismissed one juror for allegedly contemplating a book about the case, and prohibited all dismissed jurors from discussing the reasons for their discharge. Lawyers restrain their own clients. After O. J. Simpson proclaimed his innocence and denied he was fleeing during the "slow chase," Robert Shapiro announced: "Mr. Simpson, I am telling you that I will not allow you to speak and that I will resign as your lawyer if you continue to do so." A chastened O. J. complied. Prosecutor Marcia Clark claimed to have urged family members not to talk to reporters even though they had had a "bellyful" of defense gamesmanship. The legislature responded to the trial's excesses by urging the state bar to prohibit lawyers from making out-of-court comments that could prejudice trials.[86]

Judges can muzzle the media in other ways. The *Metropolitan News-Enterprise* had a long-standing feud with Los Angeles Superior Court presiding judge Richard A. Torres, whom it called a "despotic twit." He retaliated by telling the nearly 300 judges and commissioners that the county would pay for only one legal journal, leading most to choose the larger *Los Angeles Daily Journal* and costing the *News-Enterprise* a significant portion of its 2,000 circulation. The latter responded with a fake memorandum on Torres's letterhead, in which he described himself as "a judicial officer with august status" who was suspending "the election of my successor until such time as I determine it to be appropriate." Torres had bailiffs seize those distributing the memo and held them in contempt. When they sued, he responded with a suit for libel, fraud, deceit, and false imprisonment.[87]

Judges also regulate media coverage *in* the courtroom. Although forty-seven American states permit television, most other countries forbid it. After a three-year experiment with televising civil trials, the U.S. Judicial Conference banned cameras from all federal courtrooms, worried about judicial dignity and resentful of being used as backdrops while reporters talked; it later entrusted each circuit with this decision. Judge Ito temporarily barred a network for inadvertently showing the jury, and a federal judge withdrew a reporter's press credentials for airing a tape with the judge's voice in the background.[88] The U.S. Supreme Court long has allowed the public to hear tape recordings of oral argument. When Peter Irons and Stephanie Guitton sold edited annotated versions of twenty-three landmark cases, however, the Court threatened legal action. Irons acknowledged violating his agreement not to reproduce the tapes but countered that they were not copyrighted and the Court lacked authority to restrict them. It retaliated by instructing the National Archives to deny him further access without its permission. Such repression had the predictable result of pushing sales to an unprecedented 60,000 copies. A month later the Court capitulated.[89]

Legislature

Although courts restrict speech to insulate law from politics, the two explicitly political branches also curb debate. Congress accredits journalists: it barred women until World War II and African Americans until 1947 and now awards accreditation to just 2,000 out of 10,000 Washington reporters.[90] All legislatures impose rules of etiquette. Alberta (but not Manitoba) prohibits "scumbag"; an Indian state bans "insincere"; and New South Wales forbids "he is the biggest nong in the place" but not "it takes a dickhead to know a dickhead."[91] A South African MP can call a statement an untruth but not a lie, say another is "crawling on his knees" but not call him a "hensopper" (quitter) or "skelm" (rascal), and must refer to members by their constituencies rather than by surnames.[92] Told he could not call half the cabinet asses, Benjamin Disraeli substituted "half the Cabinet are not asses." A century later the parliamentary speaker urged members to "make use of the richness of the English language to select elegant phrases that express their meaning" instead of reviling each other as dimwit and nitwit, liar, hypocrite and drunk, guttersnipe, blasphemer, and pharisee.[93]

American legislatures also demand civility. California forced a new assembly member to apologize for speaking of contractors "Jewing down" subcontractors. The Pasadena City Council disciplined a member for calling others "racists on a coon hunt." New York mayor Rudolph Giuliani threatened to censure a councilor for comparing him to Mussolini.[94] When Newt Gingrich accused a quarter of Clinton's staff of drug use, the White House chief of staff retorted that he was not "the editor of a cheap tabloid . . . an out-of-control radio talk show host." "He's got to learn to behave as the Speaker of the House" or Clinton would not do business with him. Gingrich appeared to acknowledge the strictures of his new role: "Either I have to close down that part of my personality or I've got to learn to be more careful, more specific, about what I say . . . I have answered questions that I'd have been better off sidestepping. I don't think you should ever pick a fight, if it's avoidable." He regretted calling the Clintons "counterculture types," admitting "I was still too much the assistant professor."[95] Other Republicans were unrepentant. Shortly before announcing his presidential candidacy, Rep. Robert Dornan (R-Calif.) accused Clinton of having given "aid and comfort to the enemy" during the Vietnam War and having "avoided the draft three times and put teen-agers in his place." When Democrats demanded an apology, Dornan retorted, "Hell no," and promised to "be back tomorrow with the same one-minute speech." But he was banished from the floor for a day, and his remarks were stricken from the *Congressional Record*.[96]

EXECUTIVE

Because high officials are elected or appointed for their views, these can also disqualify. We have seen Dr. Joycelyn Elders forced to resign. Reagan fired Interior Secretary James G. Watt for boasting that an advisory panel on coal sales had "every kind of mixture. I have a black, I have a woman, two Jews and a cripple."[97] When Clinton nominated Lani Guinier as assistant attorney general for civil rights, Sen. Joseph Biden (D-Del.) was blunt:

> If she can come up here and . . . convince people that what she wrote was just a lot of academic musing . . . it's conceivable that she can be confirmed. If she comes up here and says she believes in the theories that she sets out in her articles and is going to pursue them, not a shot.

Within two days Clinton withdrew the nomination because her publications (which he claimed not to have read) "clearly lend themselves to interpretations that do not represent the views I expressed on civil rights during the campaign." The *New York Times* agreed that her "writings suggest that, despite her obvious talents as a civil rights attorney, she was not the right person to be Washington's civil rights enforcement chief."[98]

Civil servants, by contrast, are not supposed to express *any* political views publicly. The 1939 federal Hatch Act, for instance, allowed them to display election posters at home but not to carry them in rallies. More than forty years later this was relaxed to allow all but FBI, Secret Service, and CIA employees to hold office in political parties and participate in nominating conventions and campaigns but not to run for office in partisan elections, solicit contributions from the public, or wear buttons at work. A 1989 amendment to the Ethics in Government Act prohibited them from accepting payment for articles and speeches unrelated to their work—such as a Department of Health and Human Services (DHHS) employee reviewing plays, a Nuclear Regulatory Commission (NRC) lawyer writing Russian history, or a mail handler describing Quakerism. The regulations allowed fees "for performing a comedy routine at a dinner theater" but not for speech that includes jokes "or otherwise amuses an audience," for a series of articles or speeches but not for an individual speech. The Supreme Court invalidated the act while intimating that a better drafted law might survive scrutiny.[99] Roles like the police carry much tighter restrictions, such as those regulating interrogation and entrapment; Iowa instructs law-enforcement officials how to inform next of kin about the death of a loved one.[100]

ELECTIONS

Although elections might be viewed as the quintessential libertarian environment, they also have rules. Bush had to withdraw his first 1992 campaign ad because it illegally used the presidential seal. After Rep. Cass Ballenger (R-N.C.) accused Clinton of lies about the draft and involvement in antiwar protests, the House Speaker extended to presidential and vice-presidential candidates the rule of courtesy forbidding "derogatory, demeaning or insulting" references to the president, vice president, and members of Congress. Although the United States could not ban television ads (as South Africa did during its first democratic election), Americans as prominent as the Democratic candidate for California governor, two *New York Times* columnists, a leading advertising agency, and the Time Inc. chairman urged limitations of the thirty-second spot. The Supreme Court has upheld bans on electioneering near the polls. California candidates can call themselves "taxpayer advocate" and "acting secretary of state" but not "mother" or "gun-control" or "anti-abortion" advocate.[101]

GOVERNMENT AUTHORITY

The state restricts speech that challenges its authority. The military is an extreme example (as Clinton's "don't ask, don't tell" policy con-

firms). A reporter who broke a condition of pool participation by releasing the news of Germany's 1945 surrender a few hours early lost
his accreditation for two years and was fired by Associated Press.[102] A
major general who claimed to be merely "ice-breaking" by calling Clinton "draft-dodging, pot-smoking, womanizing, gay-loving" was summarily fined $7,000 and retired with an official reprimand. A few weeks
later the navy prohibited sailors from making sexual and other offensive comments about Rep. Patricia Schroeder.[103] Prisons limit what inmates can read, hear, and see, monitoring all telephone calls not to lawyers. They retaliate against prisoners who publish newspapers. During
the 1992 election the U.S. Bureau of Prisons director instructed federal
officials to throw Brett C. Kimberlin into solitary to keep him from telling
reporters he had sold marijuana to Republican vice-presidential candidate Dan Quayle when they were in college; both Quayle and James A.
Baker 3d (Bush's campaign director) knew of this directive. Prisoners
cannot speak even after their deaths. A federal judge ordered the destruction of the videotape of California's first execution in a quarter century,
which Robert Alton Harris wanted used for a posthumous challenge to
the gas chamber as cruel and unusual punishment.[104]

Schools are only slightly less authoritarian. For inarticulate youths
obsessed with consumption, appearance, and peer culture, dress may
be the core of self-expression. The Oakland, California, school board
banned clothing and jewelry denoting gang identification, expensive
jogging suits, hats, anything designating membership in nonschool organizations, and T-shirt slogans using profanity, approving drug use,
or denigrating race, ethnicity, religion, sex, or sexual preference. Long
Beach imposed uniforms on all K–8 pupils. A Los Angeles middle
school suspended a fourteen-year-old girl for pinning condoms on her
clothes to warn friends about pregnancy and AIDS, because the messages were inconsistent with the school's policy of sexual abstinence.
A federal judge upheld the suspension: "Educators—not children—
should be given the right to choose which values to emphasize and
the means by which those values will be instilled in their students."[105]
Schools also regulate student speech. One Los Angeles high school suspended three students for making a video purporting to show classmates smoking marijuana on campus (they claimed it was oregano).
A teacher in another fined students for every obscenity or insult. An
Irvine, California, school banned the traditional homecoming spoof,
in which boys donned miniskirts and balloon-filled bikini tops. The
Martha's Vineyard Regional High School graduation prohibited the sa-
lutatorian from describing her rape three years earlier by a senior football star. Nearly 40 percent of principals censor their school newspapers—a practice condoned by the Supreme Court.[106]

Teachers are almost as constrained as students. Schools have disciplined them for showing *Zoot Suit* in response to anti-Mexican racism among eleventh graders, helping seventh graders with a report on witchcraft, teaching Latin with suggestive phrases like "braccae tuae aperiuntur" (your fly is open), inviting a gay man to answer second graders' questions about homosexuality, lending students E. M. Foster's *Maurice* and May Sarton's *Education of Harriet Hatfield*, and holding office in the North American Man-Boy Love Association.[107] Parents have forced schools to ban a wide variety of books from classrooms and libraries: *Snow White*, J. D. Salinger's *Catcher in the Rye*, John Steinbeck's *Of Mice and Men*, Toni Morrison's *Song of Solomon*, Richard Wright's *Black Boy*, Ernest Gaines's *Autobiography of Miss Jane Pittman*, Shel Silverstein's humor, and Nikki Giovanni's poetry. A Nevada school even banned Merriam-Webster's college dictionary for defining "inappropriate" words.[108] The Traditional Values Coalition made California eliminate from its new Learning Assessment test Alice Walker's "Roselily" (for references to "the wrong God") and Annie Dillard's *American Childhood* (for descriptions of a snowball fight and vegetarianism).[109] It got the state to reconsider a school health curriculum that acknowledged the existence of "families headed by grandparents, siblings, relatives, friends, foster parents and parents of the same sex."[110] It also forced deletion of textbook passages, asserting "There is no scientific dispute that evolution has occurred and continues to occur. . . . These sequences show that life has continually diversified through time, as older species have been replaced by newer ones."[111] Alabama required textbooks to say "No one was present when life first appeared on earth. Therefore, any statement about life's origins should be considered as theory, not fact." And a Colorado high school dropped a PBS film it had shown for ten years after a sophomore objected to the phrase "from these one-celled organisms evolved all life on Earth."[112]

GOVERNMENT PROPERTY

The state as landowner constrains what may be said on its property. The Defense Department decides whether to make equipment available to film projects, cooperating with *Top Gun*, *The Hunt for Red October*, and *True Lies* after they made requested changes but not with *Apocalypse Now*, *The Deer Hunter*, *Platoon*, *Born on the Fourth of July*, and *Crimson Tide*. It refused equipment to *Courage under Fire* because it showed officials covering up a friendly fire incident and Denzel Washington was drunk in uniform and Meg Ryan too "butch."[113] New York's (Republican) mayor Giuliani stopped the city's (Democratic) public advocate from criticizing the Contract with America at a senior citizens' center.[114] The Veteran's Administration prevented a UCLA extension class on its premises from showing the film *Article 99*, which criticized the VA.[115] An African American Los Angeles city councilor forced the Los Angeles Police Revolver and Athletic Club, which leased space from the city, to cancel a fund-raising dinner for Laurence Powell, one of the officers convicted of beating Rodney King.[116] In response to a doctor's complaint, Ellis Island removed a book on alternative medicine from a display on immigrant health traditions and from its gift shop.[117] Governments use permits for location filming to shape content. Displeased by its depiction as a high-crime area in *Grand Canyon*, Inglewood (Los Angeles) threatened to require that all future projects not disparage the city. "Hollywood has artistic license," said a councilor, "but Hollywood also has social responsibility." Several years earlier the chief justice of New Jersey had prohibited Warner Brothers from filming *The Bonfire of the Vanities* inside the Essex County courthouse because it would undermine blacks' faith in justice. The New York City Transit Authority opened the subways to *The Taking of Pelham One Two Three* only after it cut profanity by TA employees. "We don't want to create this image that the subways are not safe." It rejected a film about a mob chief headquartered underground, which "suggests we don't know what's going on in the subway system." It prohibited shots of graffiti and required changes in *The Money Train*. Croton-on-Hudson considered revoking a permit for a film premiering Amy Fisher's lover. A village trustee said: "I would not invite Joey Buttafuoco into my home. I don't necessarily think he should be invited into our village." The secretary of state of Washington, running for reelection, sought to prevent *Body of Evidence* from shooting in the capitol: "the character played by Madonna seduces a man to death. . . . Why should we condone or cater to anything of this kind?"[118]

CONSTITUTING THE MARKETPLACE OF IDEAS

Despite continual criticism, Holmes's metaphor continues to inspire civil libertarians. But even they must acknowledge that markets do not arise spontaneously; states create them by defining and protecting ownership interests. State action is particularly essential for intellectual property, which is relatively new, constantly changing, and rarely susceptible to physical control. The markets for speech, and thus the worth of messages, are constructed by laws concerning copyright, trade names and marks, patents, new technology, property, contract, and tort.[119]

COPYRIGHT

Parodies require courts to balance the interests of creator and critic. 2 Live Crew's 1989 album *As Clean as They Wanna Be* (which mocked their own *As Nasty as They Wanna Be*) included "Big Hairy Woman," parodying "Oh Pretty Woman" over the objections of Roy Orbison and William Dees. The trial judge accepted their expert testimony that the parody "ridiculed the white-bread original," exposing it as "bland and banal," but the Sixth Circuit rejected the claim of fair use because the album was commercial. *Mad Magazine,* the *Harvard Lampoon* and the Capitol Steps backed the satirists' appeal, while the Songwriters Guild, Michael Jackson, and the estates of Leonard Bernstein and the Gershwins supported the publisher. The Supreme Court ordered a trial on the fair use issue.[120] The Second Circuit found that Jeff Koons's sculpture *String of Puppies* infringed Art Rogers's kitsch postcard of a couple with eight German shepherds, condemning the defendants' arrogant belief that they were immune because "they were significant players in the art business, and the copies they produced bettered the price of the copied work by a thousand to one." Koons responded contemptuously: "[S]ince when did judges qualify as art critics. . . . The ruling not only hurts me but every other artist. It was only a postcard photo and I gave it spirituality, animation and took it to another vocabulary."[121] Scott French spent ten years programming a computer to imitate Jacqueline Susann's prose, opening with the sentence "Silent vibrations of power emanated from the four men who occupied the plush velvet chairs surrounding the antique cherry wood table supposed to have once been owned by Napoleon." Susann's estate allowed French to publish his parody—but not to describe their agreement.[122]

What constitutes infringement can be a highly subjective judgment, as in the dispute between MCA's King Kong and Nintendo's Donkey King video games, Apple's claim that Microsoft Windows had the "overall look and feel" of Macintosh visual display software, or Philip Glass's allegation that an Acura commercial appropriated his musical style.[123] Edgar Rice Burroughs Inc. asserts ownership of any "character in a loincloth with a knife in a jungle setting."[124] Although Nancy Sinatra lost her suit against Goodyear for hiring a blonde in a miniskirt and go-go boots to advertise a tire called the Boot, Bette Midler won $400,000 from Young & Rubicam for using her former backup singer to imitate her voice in a Lincoln-Mercury commercial, Tom Waits was awarded $2.5 million against Frito-Lay and its ad agency for copying his voice in a Doritos jingle, and Infiniti settled with Chris Isaak for using a guitar riff resembling his hit song "Wicked Game."[125]

Stephen B. Oates's 1978 biography of Lincoln quickly became the standard account, selling 100,000 copies; twelve years later another history professor exposed similarities with a 1952 predecessor by Benjamin P. Thomas.

> Herndon was something of a dandy . . . affecting a tall silk hat, kid gloves and patent-leather shoes. Five feet nine inches in height, thin . . . with raven hair, he had sharp black eyes. . . . (Thomas)

> Herndon stepped about in fancy clothes, a big silk hat, kid gloves, and patent leather shoes. He was thin, stood about five feet nine, and had raven hair and black eyes. (Oates)

The American Historical Association called the latter "derivative to a degree requiring greater acknowledgement" but did not conclude plagiarism. An NIH computer program, however, found 175 such instances in the book and 340 in Oates's biographies of Martin Luther King and William Faulkner.[126] The Church of Scientology invoked rights in its "sacred religious scriptures" to discourage criticism on the Internet site alt.religion.scientology.[127]

The perquisites of ownership vary across genre, jurisdiction, and time. Choreography gained protection only in the 1950s, when dance notation allowed recording.[128] Landmark preservation laws restrict the alteration or destruction of buildings.[129] British libraries—but not American—pay royalties every time an author's work is borrowed. California gives artists 5 percent royalties each time their works are resold. In response to an Australian entrepreneur who cut up a Picasso print to market "original Picasso pieces," the 1990 federal Visual Artists' Rights Act gave American artists moral rights to prevent destruction or alteration of their works (something Europeans and Latin Americans have long enjoyed). Three New York artists invoked it to prevent Helmsley-Spear from dismantling an 18,000-square-foot sculptural installation, which took 2.5 years to create. But the Second Circuit rejected their claim, finding them to be employees.[130] Directors unsuccessfully opposed colorization of their films.[131] Universities have sought to prevent professional note-takers from marketing lecture notes.[132] The National Basketball Association (NBA) is seeking to prevent Stats Inc. and Motorola from disseminating basketball scores via a Sports Trax pager; the *New York Times,* Associated Press, and America Online are supporting the defendant, while NBC backs the plaintiff.[133] American music, videos, and computer programs are widely pirated abroad, especially in Russia and China.[134]

TRADE NAMES AND MARKS

Controversies over commercial insignia also require the state to balance interests in property and free speech. The more famous the symbol, the more possessive its owner. The Academy of Motion Picture Arts and Sciences has sued a carpet company promoting its "Academy Award" style and a Mississippi disco incorporating the trophy in its decor; it made a manufacturer destroy 300 chocolate Oscars prepared for a preaward party.[135] In anticipation of the 1996 summer Olympics, the International Olympic Committee (IOC) planned to challenge the hundreds of Atlanta enterprises using the word in a name or advertisement; it sold NBC exclusive rights to film the Olympic flame and the *exterior* of any venue.[136] McDonald's Dutch subsidiary settled a $2.7 million claim by Paul Bocuse for picturing the famous French chef preparing chicken and thinking "Big Mac." The American fast-food giant is no less protective of its carefully cultivated image. Claiming to have created a "McLanguage" for more than seventy-five products, it sued La Capoterie for selling McCondoms, using its stylized yellow M.[137]

Conflicts may be dignitary as well as commercial. We saw earlier that Senator Moseley-Braun blocked the reissue of a ninety-five-year-old congressional patent including the Confederate flag.[138] The U.S. Office of Patent and Trade Mark refused Old Glory Condom Corporation's application to register a logo of red, white, and blue condoms waving from a pole decorated with stars and stripes because it would "scandalize or shock the conscience of a substantial composite of the general public." But the decision was reversed because other trademarks incorporated the flag, and many condom companies had scandalous names or logos.[139] When the German makers of Toljstoj vodka put the author's portrait and dates on the bottle label and sold it at the gate of his estate, a great nephew threatened to sue: "[T]his is neither trivial nor funny. It is blasphemy."[140] A California dairy had clothed its Clo the Cow mascot as Vincent Van Clo (sans ear), Moona Lisa (with an enigmatic smile), and Supreme Quart (in judicial robes). But when she appeared as Cowsteau, in wet suit, weight belt, and flippers, the oceanographer sued for $1.2 million. "He felt his personal integrity was attacked here. It doesn't make any difference that Clo is funny. Clo sells milk. Jacques Cousteau does not."[141] World Youth Day, which brought 160,000 Roman Catholics to Denver, obtained an injunction against unauthorized souvenirs and ordered security guards to seize $5 styrofoam papal miters, calling them "a little like blasphemy." Its merchandising arm harangued sellers that profits "should burn in your hand. Anyone wishing to get legal should call us. It's never too late to get right with God."[142] When an African American judge created a civil rights museum at the Loraine Motel, where Martin Luther King had been assassinated, the family prevented him from calling it the Martin Luther King Jr. Memphis Memorial Foundation, denouncing the idea as "morbid."[143]

Parody again blurs the line between free expression and infringement. The Gap stopped Paramount Pictures from advertising *The Coneheads* by dressing Beldar and Pryamaat in Gap garb over the caption "Scarnblad. For that subtle, conventional, yet unconventional look. Classic MEB. It's French for when you want to blend in."[144] But Virginia Slims (wisely) did not object to a New York subway ad showing a woman's gray, sunken face and the caption "You've Come the Wrong Way, Baby! In 1984, lung cancer surpassed breast cancer as the #1 cancer killer of women."[145] When Adbusters Media Foundation published an "Absolut Nonsense" spoof of Absolut vodka, the company demanded retraction, apology, and destruction of the remaining copies but dropped its lawsuit when Adbusters offered to debate alcohol advertising. Adbusters then organized a competition of Absolut parodies, publishing four in its Culture Jammer's 1995 Calendar, including a coffin labeled "Absolut Silence" (about drunk-driving fatalities), a hangman's noose shaped like their bottle and labeled "Absolut Hangover," and a corpse, tagged Johnny Doe, age eighteen, labeled "Absolut on Ice."[146]

PATENTS

Federal courts constantly make difficult judgments in deciding what is patentable and when a patent has been infringed.[147] Both the Patent Office and the courts have vacillated on the protection of software.[148] In 1991 the National Institutes of Health sought to patent some of the approximately three billion genetic sequences; but after being rejected by the office, it decided to seek protection only for entire genes.[149] Doctors and universities increasingly seek to patent medical procedures, such as a method for determining whether breast-cancer tumors are developing resistance to Tamoxifen. An ophthalmic surgeon outraged many colleagues by seeking the first patent on a procedure unrelated to instrumentation.[150]

TECHNOLOGICAL INNOVATION

Technological change constantly forces government to rewrite intellectual property laws and media regulations.[151] Stephen Dunifer operates two pirate radio stations in the Bay Area, sells kits, publishes a "microcasting" newsletter *Reclaiming the Airwaves*, and conducts workshops. "For me this is a free-speech issue." His lawyer added: "Radio is the leaflet of the 90s. In a lot of areas, kids don't read and write, and radio provides the ability to communicate orally." Although such low-wattage stations do not interfere with others, the FCC fined him $20,000. "There is a reason for these regulations," said its enforcement head. "It's the same reason we have a white line down the center of the highway." But a federal judge refused to enjoin Dunifer.[152] The federal government decides how to allocate and price new frequencies for cellular telephones and high-definition television and access to the Internet.[153] Government is constantly changing the regulatory framework for older media: competition among local and long-distance phone companies and between them and cable, the price of cable, antitrust limitations on ownership of newspapers and radio and television stations, and minority preferences for new licenses.[154] Government has to decide whether to protect the public from automated prerecorded telephone, fax, and E-mail solicitations;[155] allow telephone callers and E-mailers to preserve anonymity or receivers to block anonymous calls; permit E-mailers to protect themselves from eavesdropping through encryption or mandate a computer "Clipper chip" giving law-enforcement agencies a backdoor. The Church of Scientology's successful lawsuit compelling a Finnish remailer to reveal his sources led him to close his service, which handled 7,500 messages a day.[156] Just as the invention of photocopying created bitter disputes over fair use, so digitalization encourages piracy by permitting perfect virtually costless copies of computer programs, words, music, and soon video.[157] The introduction of both the VCR and digital audiotape (DAT) were delayed and complicated by fears of uncontrolled reproduction. Commercial publication on the Internet presupposes a way to charge for downloading and subsequent reproduction.[158] Should government prevent computer manipulation of photographs, allowing movies to resurrect the dead or Benetton to give Arnold Schwarzenegger African features?[159]

Because the much-ballyhooed information superhighway bears a disconcerting resemblance to 42d Street, Congress passed the Communications Decency Act, imposing more stringent controls on "indecency" in cyberspace than in any other medium.[160] Government has had to redefine what constitutes harassment in virtual reality.[161] It charged a fifty-one-year-old man with endangering the welfare of a minor by E-mailing a fourteen-year-old girl and then flying across the country to meet her. A University of Michigan graduate student wrote stories about the torture rape of a woman classmate and posted them on Usenet's alt.sex.stories bulletin board, labeling them "sick stuff." Contemporaneously, he E-mailed a Canadian acquaintance, describing his "desire to commit acts of abduction, bondage, torture, mutilation, sodomy, rape and murder of young women." "Just thinking about it anymore doesn't do the trick. I need to do it." Although he never named or addressed the woman, who remained oblivious, he was charged with interstate transmission of a threat. A California woman responded with a story in the *Detroit Free Press*, in which she tortured and shot him; she was not charged.[162]

The new media raise difficult questions about transmitter liability for message content. Should on-line services enjoy the immunity of bookstores and telephone companies or be liable as publishers? The New York investment firm Stratton Oakmont and its president sued Prodigy Services Company and a subscriber, whose message accused the firm of crimes. Prodigy screens its 75,000 daily messages but also warns that it "does not verify, endorse or otherwise vouch for the contents of any note and cannot be held responsible in any way for information contained in any such note." The subscriber was able to prove his account had been manipulated by another. After the judge found that Prodigy's editorial activities exposed it to liability, the company settled by agreeing to remove any reference to the firm, screen all messages to its "Money Talk" bulletin board for three months, and find the culprit.[163] Other carriers have been more interventionist. German prosecutors forced American on-line services to block access to Internet sites offering pornography and racial hatred.[164] The U.S. Department of Education's Office of Civil Rights ruled that sexual statements about women on a California community college men-only bulletin board constituted sexual harassment and urged a ban on comments that harassed, denigrated, or showed hostility based on sex, race, or color. The college paid each woman $15,000.[165] A federal judge dismissed wire fraud charges against an MIT undergraduate who used the university computer for two months to operate a secret bulletin board on which others anonymously posted software for illegal copying.[166]

Some networks engage in extensive censorship. Flaming, abusive language, and threats led Santa Monica's Public Electronic Network to limit the length of messages about controversial topics like homelessness.[167] America Online has closed feminist discussion groups with the word "girl" in their names, fearing they would attract children "looking for information about their Barbies." It terminated a subscriber whose eleven-year-old daughter typed nonsense in a children's chat room and responded to Guide EOR's chastisement of another by writing "Everyone who thinks Guide EOR is a good-goody, type 1." Prodigy declares that it

> is for people of all ages and backgrounds. Notes containing obscene, profane or sexually explicit language (. . . whether or not masked with '*'s and the like) are not allowed. A good test is whether the language in your note would be acceptable at a public meeting.

The network uses George Carlin software to locate offending language and threaten senders with censorship. America Online has denied access to junk E-mailers.[168]

In addition to regulation by government and commercial carriers, every communicative system develops its own rules.[169] Like all outlaws even hackers have ethics. One explained: "[T]he golden rule of hacking is that it's about exploring, it's not about breaking. If a hacker trashes a system . . . we'd say he's not a hacker, he's a jerk." The San Diego Supercomputer Center security expert said of those who stole numerous programs: "Somebody should teach them some manners. Gentlemen are not supposed to read each other's mail." An Intel employee who broke into his former division claimed to be testing its security: "As long as I'm not trying to hurt you, I can poke at your system a little bit, because you don't have time to do it." But he was convicted and severely punished.[170] All language relies on conventions, such as those governing turn-taking. Electronic mail has begun to devise ways of simulating inflections (such as ;-) for a knowing wink). President Clinton exposed his inexperience by using capitals to write the Swedish prime minister. The moderator of the Echo network in New York complained that men "Yo" to women strangers.[171] Even addresses can create conflicts. An arbitrator made the *Princeton Review* relinquish kaplan.com, which it had taken to annoy its chief competitor Stanley H. Kaplan Education Centers Ltd. Some felt that the book *E-Mail Addresses of the Rich and Famous* violated privacy.[172]

Although the Internet has quickly become commercialized, as companies create Web sites and cable shopping programs proliferate, there is a tacit ban on E-mailing advertisements—the electronic equivalent of junk mail and faxes and telephone solicitation. Laurence A. Canter and Marsha S. Siegel, law partners and spouses, had been suspended by the Florida and Tennessee bars before settling in Phoenix. Charging individuals $95 and couples $145, they offered to help immigrants enter the green-card lottery (a free procedure requiring no legal skills). In less than two hours they posted their ad on 5,000 to 6,000 bulletin boards, reaching most of the twenty million Internet users. Outraged surfers "flamed" them with 30,000 messages, some containing their home address. Internet Direct Inc. suspended them: "They crashed our computer about 15 times . . . because of the volume of incoming complaints." They also received death threats, obscene telephone calls, and anti-Semitic hate mail. Digitized "Wanted" photos appeared on electronic bulletin boards. One vigilante programmed a robot to call their office voice-mail forty times a night. Others threatened to post their credit card numbers and reports and suggested forging threats to President Clinton in their name. A Norwegian created a "cancelbot," which responded to each ad with a message ordering its interception and destruction. Some talked of "site kill files," which would allow bulletin boards to exclude future messages from particular sources. Although Canter was thrown off Pipeline in New York and NetCom Inc. in San

Jose, he claimed to have received 20,000 replies and to be getting 500 to 1,000 a day. He and Siegel formed Cybersell, whose first product was a health drink of "super-oxygenated water." They also threatened to sue their flamers. Siegel warned: "If anything is going to bring down the net, it'll be things like robot cancelers and self-styled censors." Less than six months later HarperReference announced publication of their book *How to Make a Fortune on the Information Superhighway*. Within days the editorial director's name, address, and telephone and fax numbers appeared on America Online, with the exhortation that no one flame her. But though she received a stream of requests to withhold the book, publicity convinced the publisher to increase the first printing from 25,000 to 100,000.[173]

OTHER LEGAL CONSTRAINTS

Private law doctrines of property, contract, and tort also constrain speech. Can "free" newspapers be stolen? When the *Dartmouth Review* reported that a man accused of assaulting a woman in the Afro-American Society House had just won a minority scholarship and said his arrest "adds much to the diversity of this pool of scholars," the Black Freshman Forum seized most of the copies. The university called it "a distribution issue, not a free-speech issue." The dean of students said: "[W]e treat it as abandoned property." The *Washington Post* and the *Baltimore Sun* supported students who destroyed an offensive paper at the University of Maryland, but the state legislature made it a misdemeanor to take "one or more newspapers with the intent to destroy the newspapers or prevent others from reading the newspapers."[174]

For two decades after being forced to resign, Nixon fought the release of his presidential papers and tapes. In response to a lawsuit he filed two months after leaving office, Congress ordered the National Archives to "provide the public the full truth, at the earliest reasonable date." But this only involved the 63 hours of tapes provided the federal grand jury—not the other 200 of Watergate tapes or the 3,000 of White House tapes. Even so, Nixon managed to suppress twenty-eight of seventy particularly damning passages. Just days before his death, he sued to prevent the archives from releasing additional tapes; his heirs vowed to keep resisting disclosure. Although a 1978 law sought to prevent a recurrence of this controversy by giving the government rights to presidential papers, Bush used his last night in office to persuade the national archivist to give him control of his administration's computerized records, transferred them to the George Bush Center—and hired the archivist to head it![175]

Contract law allows people to sell not only speech but also silence (within the limits of antitrust law). Members of the British royal household take a vow never to speak. Arista and BMG record company managers could not reveal that Rob Pilatus and Fab Morvan lip-synched "Girl You Know It's True." Rev. Donald Wildmon sued to enjoin American release of an Emmy-award-winning British documentary about cultural censorship on the ground that he had agreed to be interviewed only for a British audience. After Edward J. Rollins quit as Ross Perot's 1992 campaign manager and ridiculed the candidate, Perot required his successor to agree to "refrain from making any disparaging remarks or negative comments, either publicly or privately" and then fired him. A New York court upheld Ivana Trump's agreement never to discuss her marriage in return for a $22 million divorce settlement. "The judges are saying that this is not a freedom of speech case," declared Donald Trump's lawyer. "Mrs. Trump, for a price, waived her right." When she published a thinly disguised novel about a Czech skier married to an American tycoon whose affair with a younger actress leads to a messy divorce, Donald threatened to sue for breach of contract. Settlements of disputes over the estates of Doris Duke and Averell Harriman pledged the contestants to secrecy. Fearing liability for tortious interference with contract, CBS pulled an interview with a former tobacco executive whom Brown & Williamson claimed was bound to silence.[176]

In addition to defamation and invasion of privacy, the torts of fraud, misrepresentation, and disparagement also constrain speech.[177] Personal injury settlements often buy victim silence. The risks of silicon-gel breast implants, for instance, were documented in a 1984 lawsuit whose record was sealed; millions of women retained or received implants in the eight years before the FDA acted. Heart-valve recipients accepted settlements preventing them from disclosing defects. Manufacturers and distributors may be liable for injuries caused by inadequate product warnings. When Planned Parenthood won more than $1 million for disruptions of its Dallas clinics during the 1992 Republican convention, a local Operation Rescue leader objected: "Our breath has been taken away . . . because we preached the Gospel on a public sidewalk across the street from an abortion mill."[178] Doctors, lawyers, accountants, architects, and other professionals may be liable for misinformation causing economic, physical, or emotional injury. *Soldier of Fortune* magazine has been held liable for a murder committed by a hit man hired through its classified ads.[179] A man won a $500,000 verdict against a social worker and a psychotherapist who used hypnotic drugs to convince his daughter, falsely, that he had sexually molested her, leading to his divorce, alienation from all three daughters, and loss of employment.[180] A California radio station was held liable for a contest encouraging teenagers to race around the San Fernando Valley, killing another driver.[181] Speakers can be liable for assault or intentional infliction of emotional distress. Cult victims (and their parents) have sued for conversion.[182] Fraternities have curtailed offensive language for fear of liability.[183]

THE IMPOSSIBILITY OF STATE NEUTRALITY

Because civil libertarians are especially critical of content-specific regulation of speech, some insist on strict viewpoint neutrality when the state speaks. Recent attacks on school curricula and government support for the arts and humanities employ similar rhetoric. Yet neutrality is neither possible nor desirable.[184]

OFFICIAL ACTS

Chapter 4 offered numerous examples of the passion with which groups seek a public imprimatur for their symbols. The Smithsonian's difficulties in commemorating the end of World War II were not unique. The Library of Congress closed "Back of the Big House: The Cultural Landscape of the Plantation" when African American employees objected, and it postponed "Sigmund Freud: Conflict and Culture" after Gloria Steinem asserted that Freud "was likely abused" and had "suppressed criticism of his work."[185] The U.S. Postal Service deleted a cigarette from the portrait of 1930s blues guitarist Robert Johnson, while the village of Hyde Park could not decide whether its town seal should include the famous profile of FDR with his jaunty cigarette holder.[186]

The government is unabashed about taking strongly partisan positions toward foreign "enemies." It attacked communism through the Voice of America, Radio Free Europe, Radio Liberty, and Radio and TV Marti (which many criticized as the mouthpiece of anti-Castro multimillionaire Jorge Mas Canosa, who chaired its advisory board). Although *Problems of Communism* claimed complete independence, the United States Information Agency initially refused to allow it to mention Marx, Engels, Lenin, or Stalin! When the Agency for International Development bought Russian television commercials promoting privatization, the slogan "Your Voucher, Your Choice" somehow became "Your Voucher, Russia's Choice"—the name of the party supporting Yeltsin. With false naiveté, the Russian government agency that placed the ad said: "[I]t's just a good play on words."[187] Until protests by the

American-Arab Anti-discrimination League and an American Muslim sergeant, the Marines regularly screened Jack Anderson's virulently anti-Arab film *American Expose: Target USA*.[188]

The flap over Newt Gingrich's choice for the House of Representatives historian nicely illustrates both the inevitability and limits of partisanship. The new Speaker appointed Dr. Christina Jeffrey, a forty-seven-year-old Kennesaw State University assistant professor of political science (who had supported Gingrich's controversial "course" "Renewing American Civilization"). She would be "chronicling the Speaker and doing for the Republicans what academics did for F.D.R." "It has never been done on a day-to-day basis for a Speaker, and Newt is very interested in that." He fired her a day later, however, after disclosure of an evaluation she had written for the Department of Education eight years earlier opposing a proposed curriculum on the Holocaust that

> gives no evidence of balance or objectivity. The Nazi point of view, however unpopular, is still a point of view and it is not presented. Nor is that of the Ku Klux Klan. . . . It is a paradoxical and strange aspect of this program and [sic] the methods used to change the thinking of students is [sic] the same that Hitler and Goebbels used to propagandize the German people. This re-education method was perfected by Chairman Mao and is now being foisted on American children under the guise of "understanding history."

The Simon Wiesenthal Center said that "calling for equal time to present Hitler's point of view is outrageous and bizarre." Gingrich's spokesperson insisted the Speaker "still has tremendous admiration" for Jeffrey, but she had gone too far. "This is the historian for the House of the whole United States of America. . . . this is a matter of great sensitivity and many Americans would be offended."[189]

GOVERNMENT EMPLOYEES

Government exercises extraordinary control over what it tells the public. World War I files are still classified; it took the Pentagon fifty years to acknowledge exposing some 60,000 servicemen to poison-gas tests during World War II and even to release war photographs. A history professor battled for years to obtain the twenty-year-old FBI file on John Lennon, which Richard Nixon began in 1971 in an effort to deport the Beatle. Clinton reversed Reagan's 1981 executive order instructing officials to err on the side of secrecy and released 44 million pages. His Department of Energy reviewed 32 million more concerning clandestine nuclear tests, radiation experiments on human subjects, and the government's reserve of weapon-grade plutonium. Government still classifies 7 million new documents a year; at the same time, courts recently extended to electronic messages the 1950 law requiring preservation of records.[190] Officials routinely condition their disclosures on anonymity and limit what can be disseminated. Although cable has been televising Congress for over a decade, controversy continues over what the camera shows and whether coverage extends to committees. The House recently ruled that changes in the *Congressional Record* (other than grammatical and typographical errors) be printed in different typeface.[191]

Subordinates must support government policy. An assistant secretary for health who told an international conference on tobacco and health that it was "unconscionable for the mighty transnational tobacco companies—and three of them are in the United States—to be peddling their poison abroad" was barred from testifying before the House Subcommittee on Health and the Environment because tobacco exports were only "a trade issue," not a health issue.[192] The Census Bureau fired Beth Osborne Daponte for estimating Iraqi civilian deaths in the Persian Gulf War at more than twice the official figure. The bureau claimed she had disseminated the information without peer review, although she consulted three superiors and released it only when the agency refused to do so. Later that year the bureau required the screening of all reports by the assistant director for communications. "I don't edit reports," the political appointee said, but "I do ask a lot of questions about press releases." Before the 1992 election the bureau withheld evidence that the proportion of full-time workers earning less than $12,195 (in constant dollars) declined in the 1960s, remained constant in the 1970s, and then grew from 12.1 to 18 percent in the 1980s. When the report finally appeared, a press release minimized its significance.[193]

Government also controls private critics. During J. Edgar Hoover's long directorship, the FBI discouraged stores from stocking critical books and planted unattributed derogatory reviews of them. Expert witnesses who challenge DNA identification suffer FBI retaliation. A British scientist was interrogated about his visa status, charged with fraudulent billing practices, and ordered to produce all his research; an American professor was threatened with a night in the Oakland jail for lacking a California driver's license. After *Science* accepted an article criticizing DNA evidence, the editor forced the authors to qualify their conclusions and took the highly unusual step of delaying publication until a rebuttal was prepared. While the manuscript was being reviewed, the Department of Justice Criminal Division Strike Force urged the authors to withdraw it.[194]

Soon after the Persian Gulf War Theodore A. Postol, MIT professor of national security policy and former Pentagon science adviser, published an article in the Harvard peer-reviewed journal *International Security*, asserting that the Patriot missile had been "almost a total failure." Although Postol claimed to rely entirely on unclassified data, the Defense Investigative Services told him: "I could not speak about any part of my article in public without being in violation of my secrecy agreement." A dozen years earlier Postol has been an expert witness for the *Progressive*, which was resisting government suppression of an article demonstrating that laypeople could assemble virtually all the information necessary to make a hydrogen bomb. Hans Bethe, who testified for the government in that case, himself had been prevented from publishing an article on thermonuclear weapons in *Scientific American* in 1950. While conceding that it contained no secret information, the Atomic Energy Commission forced the magazine to destroy the entire print run and melt down the type.[195]

GOVERNMENT FUNDS

Government always has attached strings to support for the arts, humanities, and media. When Paul Cadmus painted *The Fleet's In!* for the Public Works Art Project, a retired naval officer denounced it as "a most disgraceful, sordid, disreputable, drunken brawl," which "originated in the sordid, depraved imagination of someone who has no conception of actual conditions in our service." The secretary of the navy banned it from the 1934 Corcoran Gallery show, and the assistant secretary appropriated it, until a lawsuit forced its public display fifty-eight years after completion.[196] The Federal Theater Project closed Marc Blitzstein's *Cradle Will Rock* on its opening night in 1937. When the Dies Committee investigated (and defunded) the project the following year, Sen. Everett Dirksen (R-Ill.) condemned its recent productions: "If you want that kind of salacious tripe, very well, but . . . if anyone has an interest in real cultural value, you will not find it in this kind of junk."[197] La Guardia Airport painted over the mural *Flight* in 1952 in the belief it was socialist (the offending figure actually was religious). The JFK International Arrivals Building eliminated the phrase "the wretched refuse of your teeming shores" in a mural reproducing Emma Lazarus's famous poem "The New Colossus"—although the full text was inscribed on the base of the Statue of Liberty![198]

The National Endowment for the Arts intensified such controversies.[199] The word "bullshit" in an NEA-funded Living Stage improvisation for Baltimore schoolchildren created a three-week furor in 1969.

About the same time the White House "persuaded" the American Film
Institute to cancel a benefit premiere of Costa-Gavras's *State of Siege*
because "a film at the Kennedy Center praising assassins was not appropriate."[200] Soon after Bush appointed him director, John Frohnmayer suspended a grant to "Witnesses: Against Our Vanishing," an
exhibit about AIDS, because the catalogue criticized Rep. William E.
Dannemeyer (R-Calif.) and Sen. Jesse Helms (R-N.C.). Frohnmayer's
justification revealed the incoherence of any aspiration to neutrality.

> I think it's essential that we remove politics from grants and must do
> so if the endowment is to remain credible to the American people and
> to Congress. Obviously, there are lots of great works of art that are
> political. . . . The endowment supports some works which have a com-
> ponent of politics in them [like Larry Gelbart's Watergate parody
> "Mastergate"], but what it comes down to is what is the primary in-
> tent of the piece. . . . The catalogue to this show is a very angry protest
> against the specific events and individuals involved over the last eight
> months in the most recent arts legislation in Congress [which prohib-
> ited NEA from funding "materials considered obscene, including sa-
> domasochism, homoeroticism, the sexual exploitation of children, or
> individuals engaged in sex acts"].

A spokesperson said Helms was "much more pleased by this than he
was by the N.E.A.'s reaction under the former acting chairman to the
Mapplethorpe exhibition." Dannemeyer commended Frohnmayer "for
doing what I think Congress told him to do."[201]

But Frohnmayer could not please everyone. His defunding of four
artists was overturned by a federal judge. Congress responded by ordering the NEA to take into consideration "general standards of decency." When five San Diego artists used a $12,000 grant for billboards,
performances, a book, and a gallery show criticizing police failure to
investigate the murders of forty-five women, NEA instructed the gallery to withdraw the NEA's name. The artists issued a response entitled
"The NEA Is Dead," contending it had "finally succumbed to the attack
of a 'sound-bite polemicist.'" But the local Republican congressman
was triumphant: "You don't use advertising space for advocacy art
and charge it to the American public." Bush finally fired Frohnmayer,
fearing that Patrick Buchanan was gaining too much political mileage
by attacking the NEA. The director's valedictory called the Republican
challenger a "Frankenstein monster" whose "shameless" attacks resembled the Nazi "Entartete Kunst" exhibit. "A sign on the wall of that
show said: 'Your tax money goes to support this filth.' That could come
from the Congressional Record, my friends." His memoir complained

of pressure from John Sununu, Irving Kristol, and Dan Quayle and revealed that Bush had told him to appear "a little right of center" and refuse grants to "flash points."[202]

His successor, Anne-Imelda Radice, promptly vetoed two grants recommended by her advisory committee (one unanimously, the other with one dissent) and planned to bypass it in allocating $750,000 in fellowships. While denying instructions from the White House, she acknowledged: "[I]t wouldn't be necessary because those people know me and my work."[203] The following year the House cut NEA's budget 5 percent to retaliate against a Whitney Museum exhibit, which Rep. Dan Burton (R-Ind.) accused of including a three-foot mound of excrement and two women having oral sex. When three San Diego artists used a grant to give undocumented workers $10 bills for their contribution "in an economy indifferent to national borders," Rep. Randy "Duke" Cunningham (R-Calif.) could not "imagine a more contemptuous use of taxpayers' hard-earned dollars." "Americans will not long support government funding for the arts if those funds are . . . handed out to illegal aliens." NEA disallowed the $4,500 charged to the grant because currency was neither "supplies" nor "materials," although it had no definition of either. A spokesperson insisted: "[T]his decision was made outside of the political climate and does not have anything to do with the controversial nature of the project."[204]

Ron Athey's Minneapolis performance about AIDS provoked Senators Robert C. Byrd (D-W.Va.) and Don Nickles (R-Okla.) to warn Clinton's new NEA chair: "Without the benefit of your response that safeguards will be instituted immediately to insure that such grossly improper activities are not undertaken in the future N.E.A. funding for FY 1995 is in serious jeopardy." A week later Byrd proposed a 5 percent cut "directed at those grant programs which have been at the center of recent controversies." The NEA responded by prohibiting institutional recipients from redistributing grants to individual artists and rejecting peer-recommended grants to Andres Serrano, Barbara de Genevieve (on aging women's bodies), and Merry Alpern (photographs of a strip-club bathroom). Senator Helms added an amendment forbidding support for "materials or performances that depict or describe in a patently offensive way, sexual or excretory activities or organs" or "denigrate religion."[205] Relishing the November 1994 victory, House Speaker Gingrich declared his opposition to "self-selected elites using your tax money . . . to pay off their friends." House majority leader Dick Armey said that the NEA "offends the Constitution of the United States . . . there is no constitutional authority for this agency to exist." Former NEH director Lynne V. Cheney excoriated both endowments for making political statements "rather than revealing truth or revealing beauty." Former education secretary William J. Bennett said government had no business putting "its official stamp of approval, its imprimatur, upon any particular work of art or scholarship." Rep. Barbara F. Vucanovich (R-Nev.) denounced the endowments for funding works that were "corrupt, immoral and very offensive to the people in my district." Sen. Larry Pressler (R-S.D.), chair of the committee overseeing the Corporation for Public Broadcasting (CPB), even condemned the Ken Burns series on baseball: "[E]very night I'd have to listen to Mario Cuomo tell about his boyhood."[206]

Government funding constrained other forms of expression. Bush packed the NEH advisory committee with conservatives. Although Clinton's director, former University of Pennsylvania president Sheldon Hackney, was attacked as too liberal, he refused $30,000 to plan a commemoration of the twenty-fifth anniversary of the Stonewall riots because the proposal was "too celebratory," although peer reviews were "laudatory in the extreme" and the resulting exhibit at the New York Public Library was highly praised.[207] Several Republican senators placed a hold on funding for CPB, charging "liberal bias." Then Senate minority leader Robert Dole (R-Kans.) said he had "never been more turned off and more fed up with the increasing lack of balance and unrelenting liberal cheerleading I see and hear on the public airwaves." Sen. Conrad Burns (R-Mont.), who had sponsored the hold, condemned a PBS program criticizing grazing on public lands: "[W]hen that particular program ran, my constituency, which is a lot of cattlemen and sheepmen, absolutely went through the roof." Jesse Helms declared that the Point of View program *Tongues Untied* "blatantly promoted homosexuality as an acceptable life style." Sen. John McCain (R-Ariz.) criticized "Maria's Story" for "glorifying the life of a F.M.L.N. guerrilla in El Salvador."[208]

Yet public broadcasting actually sought to avoid controversy. Under police pressure, National Public Radio's *All Things Considered* canceled a commentary on prison conditions by Mumia Abu-Jamal, on death row for killing Daniel Faulkner, a Philadelphia policeman. The managing editor of news expressed "serious misgivings about the appropriateness of using as a commentator a convicted murderer seeking a new trial." The Fraternal Order of Police was triumphant: "Officer Faulkner doesn't have the freedom of speech he once had. Neither should [Abu-Jamal]."[209] PBS rejected the 1990 Oscar documentary nominee *Building Bombs* and the 1991 and 1992 winners: *Deadly Deception: General Electric, Nuclear Weapons, and Our Environment* and *The Panama Deception*. The executive vice president for national programming explained that the

Academy Awards honored "artistic merit," while PBS had its own editorial standards. After entertainment industry protests, PBS found time
for a greatly revised version of *Building Bombs*, which eliminated "a
substantial earlier portion about the Cold War and the buildup of nuclear arms [and] some allegations that seem quite dated in light of the
end of the Cold War." These included a physicist's estimate that
America had 30,000 hydrogen bombs, a retired Du Pont engineer declaring "better dead than Red," and Reagan's energy secretary asking
"[I]f . . . the Soviet Union had pressed the button, wouldn't it be nice
to know we had some to press the button back?"[210] PBS put boxer shorts
on the nude gay men in the British-made *The Lost Language of Cranes*
and cut a scene in which Violet Trefusis, dressed as a man, climbed
into bed with a fully clothed Vita Sackville-West in the BBC's *Portrait
of a Marriage.* It modified the BBC production of Armistead Maupin's
Tales of the City and reneged on a sequel after Rev. Donald Wildmon
sent all members of Congress a twelve-minute excerpt featuring four-
letter words, momentary nudity, pot smoking, and the one gay kiss.
The PBS president (whom Bush had earlier appointed to the FCC with
support from the National Association of Evangelicals) claimed that
"sequels often fail to match the quality of the original, and open any
programmer to the danger of formulaic repetition"—as confirmed by
PBS's screening of the *third* sequel of *Prime Suspect.*[211]

Ideology even infects government support for science. In 1991 the
DHHS secretary "temporarily" blocked and then canceled a National
Institute of Child Health and Human Development grant for the American Teenage Study after Rep. William Dannemeyer (R-Calif.) objected
to questions about oral and anal sex, which decent parents would not
allow their children to answer. Although the NIH director called it "a
wonderful study," the secretary was "concerned by the possible inad-
vertent message this survey could send." Dannemeyer followed up his
victory by introducing a bill prohibiting DHHS from conducting or
supporting "any national survey of human sexual behavior." Although
this failed, federal funding was withdrawn from the University of Chicago study of sexuality, which Dannemeyer and Jesse Helms had opposed. The Senate transferred $10 million from the Survey of Health
and AIDS Risk Prevalence to the Adolescent Family Life Program,
which Helms (its sponsor) extolled as "the only federally funded
sex-education program that counsels our children to abstain from
having sexual relations until they are married." He denounced the defunded study's questions as prurient; their real purpose was "not to
stop the spread of AIDS . . . [but] to compile supposedly scientific and

Government-sanctioned statistics supporting ultra-liberal arguments that homosexuality is normal behavior."[212]

THE ILLUSION OF PRIVATE FREEDOM

By highlighting state action as the principal, even the exclusive, threat to free expression, civil libertarianism reflects liberalism's fundamental dichotomy between the public as a realm of constraint and the private as the domain of liberty. End government regulation and speech will be liberated. Curtail government partisanship and private voices will flourish. The previous sections argued that state regulation and partisanship are inevitable and sometimes desirable. The following contend that private freedom is a mystification. Holmes's much-touted "marketplace of ideas" imposes constraints far more pervasive than those emanating from the state.

THE COMMODIFICATION OF SPEECH

In all markets value *is* price. Yet we are deeply ambivalent about the commodification of speech. We mistrust all mouthpieces: lawyers, actors, public relations firms, advertising agencies, press officers, lobbyists, ghostwriters, official biographers, diplomats, court flatterers. The First Amendment is far more protective of noncommercial speech. Those who market their names often incur contempt (if they also excite envy): Earl Spencer selling his to a Japanese golf club; the World Wide Fund for Nature leasing its panda logo to Procter & Gamble's paper diapers and soap powder; the Duchess of York pushing her children's book *Budgie, the Little Helicopter*, complete with spinoff merchandise; Prince Charles promoting an Oaten Biscuit and a Gingered Biscuit, made to his own recipe, under his Duchy Originals brand.[213] Eyebrows were raised when former president Reagan accepted $2 million for a week's visit to Fujisankei Communications Group and former president Bush $100,000 to address Amway distributors.[214]

REPRESENTATION

Although their professional status increases with income, lawyers gain public honor by appearing pro bono. The contingent fee, which gives plaintiffs' personal-injury lawyers a stake in recovery, is anathema outside North America. Money may be the mother's milk of politics, but it poisons as well as nurtures. Although the Supreme Court has had enormous difficulty defining when the state can regulate campaign contributions and lobbying, the increasing dominance of politics by money has greatly increased public cynicism.[215] After Christine Todd Whitman won the New Jersey governorship, her campaign manager Edward J. Rollins revealed that Republicans had distributed $500,000 in "walking around" money.

> We played the game the way the game is played in New Jersey. . . . We went into the black churches and basically said to ministers who had endorsed Florio: "Do you have a special project? . . . don't get up in the Sunday pulpit . . . and say it's your moral obligation to vote on Tuesday, to vote for Jim Florio."

They asked Democrats hired to get out the vote: "How much have they paid you to do your normal duty? We'll match it, go home [and] sit and watch television." Other Whitman campaign officials corroborated these revelations. When the winner was harshly criticized, William Safire reminisced about Kennedy's massive payments and Carter's donations to black churches, while Daniel Bell noted that Tammany Hall required precinct captains to collect blank ballots.[216]

Slate mailers instructing California voters how to complete their long complicated ballots sell endorsements; "Voter Guide" earned $3.6 million in 1990. The Peace Officers Research Association of California paid the *Republican* Vote by Mail Project $20,000 to support the *Democratic* candidate for attorney general. The beneficiary rationalized: "It's known as a free press." The victorious Democratic candidate for State Board of Equalization (which administers property taxes) paid $20,000 to get on the Howard Jarvis Taxpayers Association mailer, although he had not supported Jarvis's Proposition 13 and his opponent had. The 1994 California Democratic Alliance "Voters Guide" included a conservative Republican candidate for state superintendent of public instruction and a judicial candidate who characterized himself as "just to the right of Genghis Khan." Playing it safe, a Republican seeking reelection as Los Angeles County supervisor bought places on both Republican and Democratic versions of "Your Ballot Guide." Some guides feature highly visible candidates at the top without their permission; others threaten to include an opponent unless the candidate coughs up.[217]

Cognizant that their sponsorship can discredit advocacy, paymasters strive hard for invisibility. When the pharmaceutical industry lobbied for inclusion of its products in the Medicaid formulary, it hid behind the Coalition for Equal Access to Medicines, which included victims of disease (depression, multiple sclerosis, lupus), ethnic minorities, and the elderly. When Pfizer sought to have its antidepressant

Zoloft added to Tennessee's Medicaid formulary (which already included its competitor Prozac), it spent $67,000 for a conference called "TennCare: An African-American Perspective," ostensibly sponsored by a conservative think tank and a black physicians' association, and paid the African American former secretary of health and human services Louis Sullivan to deliver the keynote. Children and Adults with Attention Deficit Disorder, calling itself a "non-profit, tax-exempt organization directed by the volunteer efforts of parents of children with attention deficit disorder," petitioned the Drug Enforcement Administration to allow refills of Ritalin prescriptions without physician examination. It did not mention that $800,000 from Ciba-Geigy, the drug's manufacturer, had helped the group grow from a few hundred members in 1988 to 35,000 in 1995, as the number of children taking the drug rose from 500,000 to 2 million.[218]

The tobacco industry is even more bashful. A California ballot initiative that would have eliminated local antismoking ordinances was sponsored by the Hospitality Coalition, purporting to represent restaurateurs. Its lawyer declared: "The vast majority of the contributions came from Southern California businessmen who will be affected by this ordinance." But sixty-two of the eighty-two local contributions totaled only $4,000, and tobacco companies contributed $211,355 of the $216,000. R. J. Reynolds hid behind Citizens for a Sound Economy while bankrolling its campaign to limit tort litigation in California. A letter to the *New York Times* championing smokers' rights identified the author as president of the National Smokers Alliance rather than vice president of Philip Morris's public relations firm. When it was revealed to have paid for smokers' rights advertisements in that paper, Philip Morris pulled the ads. Tobacco companies, like pornographers, are masters at disguising their commercial interests as solicitude for free speech and the arts. Between 1987 and 1992 Philip Morris gave $500,000 to the ACLU, which testified against congressional proposals to regulate cigarette advertising. The manufacturer also supported the Alvin Ailey Dance Troupe, which criticized Surgeon General C. Everett Koop's campaign against smoking: "A nation has a cultural health as well as a physical health."[219]

Although the most successful politicians tend to be the best fundraisers, venality can become too brazen (as illustrated by revelations of foreign donations to the Democrats in November 1996). A Republican California assembly member wrote thirty prospective donors "specifically in the utilities and commerce arena," boasting of his recent appointment as chair of the Utilities and Commerce Committee and inviting them to contribute $2,500 to attend a basketball game and gain "access (3+ hours to discuss your utilities and commerce issues with [Republican assembly] Leader Brulte and me)." He conceded he should not have put the word "access" in writing. Triumphant after the 1994 election, Newt Gingrich urged business to withdraw advertising from newspapers that opposed Republicans, and the president of the Business-Industry Political Action Committee said "some committee chairmen are reportedly denying access to lobbyists who support the other side." Although Clinton's 1992 campaign promised to end "cliques of $100,000 donors," a 1995 fund-raiser offered the title of "managing trustee" of the Democratic party, two meals with Clinton and two with Gore, honored guest status at the 1996 convention, a place on annual foreign trade missions, and a Democratic National Committee contact to help handle "personal requests." When this hit the press, the White House press secretary conceded Clinton was not "very happy with the tone of the specific brochure" and would "make any changes that are necessary."[220]

TRUTH

Because science enjoys a far higher reputation for candor than does politics, lucre's taint is more damaging. The Princeton Dental Resource Center sends its newsletter to hundreds of dentists without mentioning that 90 percent of its costs are paid by a $1 million annual subsidy from M&M / Mars. A recent issue cited "scientific" evidence that chocolate is as good for teeth as apples: "So the next time you snack on your favorite chocolate bar or bowl of peanuts, remember—if enjoyed in moderation they can be good-tasting and might even inhibit cavities." The Wm. Wrigley Jr. Company financed studies showing that sugared gums are good for teeth because they produce saliva. The Chocolate Manufacturers of the United States sponsored a conference at the University of Texas Medical Center, which announced that a chocolate ingredient (stearic acid) promoted health. Food producers provide about 15 percent of the budget of the American Dietetic Association, which asserts that "there are no good or bad foods." Disregarding inconsistent findings, it cooperated with producers of Chinese food and margarine to disseminate statements that MSG caused no discomfort and "there is little scientific evidence to suggest that current consumption levels of transfatty acids need to be changed."[221]

Perhaps because its own research is so thoroughly compromised, the tobacco industry founded the Council for Tobacco Research in 1954, directed by a board of eminent scientists who claimed total autonomy. Over the next forty years it spent $220 million on some 1,400 studies.

But in 1994 a House subcommittee obtained 1953 memos by the Hill & Knowlton public relations firm defining the council's purpose as "a public relations campaign" to persuade consumers of "the existence of weighty scientific views which hold there is no proof that cigarette smoking is a cause of lung cancer." During the early years it spent half its budget sending every American doctor booklets declaring smoking safe, finding and promoting scientists who agreed with that view, and placing favorable articles in the media. Tobacco company lawyers suggested research projects. At the 1994 hearings the urologist who had chaired the council for four years denied that smoking caused cancer or was addictive.[222]

The size and rapid growth of the health care industry create great temptations to sway medical judgment. Fearful that government might regulate the $165 million its members spent on physicians in 1989, the Pharmaceutical Manufacturers Association adopted "voluntary" guidelines banning gifts of "substantial value," cash payments, and travel expenses. The medical profession has fiercely debated limitations on physician referrals to their own laboratories, x-ray and imaging centers, physical-therapy facilities, home therapy devices, hospitals, nursing homes, and pharmacies. A physician who prescribed Genentech's and Caremark's human growth hormone received more than $1 million from them in "research grants," although he produced no useful findings and published no research. Genentech also paid a nonpracticing pediatric nurse $10,000 to identify short children in schools and refer them to the local pediatric endocrinologist—who happened to be her husband! Both companies ended school screenings. The FDA requires pharmaceutical companies to disclose the financial interest of physicians performing clinical trials; some medical journals make authors detail this in articles. *Arthritis and Rheumatism* acknowledged the impropriety of an editor's accepting $300 an hour to consult and testify for breast-implant manufacturers. Yet Edelman Medical Communications offered a Harvard Public Health School professor $2,500 to write about potential liability for prescribing drugs with sedative side effects and enclosed an editorial it had commissioned the previous year, published in *JAMA* without editorial knowledge of its involvement. Manufacturers seeking product endorsements pay a $9,000 enrollment fee and $1,500 annually to the American Dental Association, $750 per test and a donation of $2,500 to $10,000 per endorsement to the American Podiatric Medical Association, and $10,000 a year to the Skin Cancer Foundation. A Johnson & Johnson subsidiary paid the Arthritis Foundation $1 million.[223]

As their mottoes frequently declare ("veritas," "lux," "scientia"), universities dedicate themselves to the disinterested pursuit of knowledge, toward which end they hire and reward faculty according to strict meritocratic criteria and promise them academic freedom. Money is always an embarrassment: even after they became secular, professors retained the monk's hood so they could appear oblivious while pupils placed donations in it. When the University of Bridgeport honored Rev. Sun Myung Moon, whose $98 million gift had saved it from closure, the president—Moon's friend for twenty years—said: "If you have somebody who's that much of a benefactor, you don't just shake his hand and say thank you." The president insisted Bridgeport was "a normal American university with a unique funding source," neglecting to mention that Moon's World Peace Academy chooses a majority of the trustees, who had appointed him.[224] Lee M. Bass gave Yale $20 million to develop and staff a year-long undergraduate course on Western civilization because the field "for more than a decade has been under attack while many colleges and universities increased their emphasis on the study of people and cultures outside the Western tradition." But Yale felt compelled to return the grant when Bass insisted on approving the five endowed chairholders and the eleven faculty who would teach the course. This so angered the Class of '37 (to which Bass's father belonged) that it threatened to withhold all donations. Yale responded by increasing enrollment in directed studies and the humanities major. The Class of '37 still demanded a say in selecting a committee to monitor Yale's commitment to teaching Western civilization.[225] When Theodore Postol criticized the Patriot missile's performance during the Gulf War (discussed above), MIT's president sent him two alumni letters threatening to withhold support because of the university's "anti-defense posture," and the provost said the school was losing money because of him.[226]

After Michael Milken completed his securities fraud sentence, UCLA Graduate School of Management made him an unpaid visiting lecturer, allowing him to market videotapes of his course, using UCLA's name, for only 5 percent of the profits. When it emerged that Milken recently had given the university $3.3 million, $40,000 just before signing this contract, the university was shamed into renegotiating it.[227] Newt Gingrich brazenly sold donors favorable coverage in his Reinhardt College course, which was beamed by satellite to 132 sites in thirty-one states. Those contributing $50,000 to his Progress and Freedom Foundation (which paid 30–40 percent of the course's cost) got to enroll three students and "work directly with the leadership of the . . . project in the course development process"; $25,000 bought donors an invitation "to participate in the course development."

Golden Rule Insurance's promotional video was shown after it paid $117,000; textile magnate Roger Milliken got twenty minutes of class time for a $300,000 donation. After the GOPAC finance director noted "a very real possibility here of $20,000 to $25,000 if the course can incorporate" the Employment Policy Foundation position that restaurant and fast-food jobs were not necessarily dead ends, Gingrich told students: "The welfare state, they say, well, you're just going to worry about getting a hamburger flipping job. Well, it's a first step. It's not the last step."[228]

JOURNALISM

Although reporting may have lesser pretensions to advance fundamental knowledge, it also claims disinterest. A South African cabinet minister was dismissed in the 1970s for secretly trying to purchase foreign newspapers to secure more favorable coverage of apartheid.[229] Richard Gott was forced to resign as literary editor of the *Guardian* in 1995 when the *Spectator* revealed he had accepted "Moscow gold" decades earlier.[230] PBS was criticized for two programs about the intifada: "Days of Rage," allegedly supported by Arab and Palestinian donations, and "The Search for Solid Ground: The Intifada through Israeli Eyes," funded partly by a $382,000 donation procured by the Israeli consul general in New York.[231] Perhaps angered by limitations on congressional speaking fees, the Senate required disclosure by all accredited reporters. Alan Simpson (R-Wyo.) asked rhetorically: "If you take 20 grand for a speech to the National Insurance Association, in your next nationally syndicated newspaper column do you rip them?" ABC news anchor Sam Donaldson earned $30,000 from an insurance group and $25,000 from an electronics group. Ted Koppel, by contrast, stopped giving talks in 1989, and Tom Brokaw donated his fees to a foundation. The *Wall Street Journal* prohibits news employees from accepting fees from "profit-making entities," and the *New York Times* forbids reporters to take them from "interests they cover."[232]

These tensions transcend news reporting. A freelance "editor at large" for *Smart Money* recommended three small companies in which his money-management firm had substantial investments, causing their value to soar. The magazine responded by prohibiting nonstaff contributors from writing about smaller companies in which they held more than 1 percent of the shares—but they could still buy into such companies during the three to four weeks between submitting the article and publication! *Money* magazine first suspended and then dismissed columnist Dan Dorfman when the U.S. Attorney's office began investigating his relationship with a stock promoter.[233] The 1950s "pay-ola" scandal exposed record-company payments to disk jockeys for spin time. Companies still spend an estimated $50 million annually on "consultants," who give some of it to stations and sponsor "contests" in which disk jockeys enjoy excellent odds of winning large prizes.[234] The game-show scandals of the 1960s—acutely captured by the film *Quiz Show*—led the FCC to require disclosure of any consideration given to contestants.[235] The impresario Sol Hurok aggressively courted reviewers with lavish birthday and anniversary gifts.[236] Howard Aibel, a prize-winning pianist and music professor, sells coverage in his *New York Concert Review* for $285. A freelance contributor (who regularly reviewed for other reputable publications) said Aibel "told me that I was under no obligation to write anything other than what I honestly feel. . . . I have the feeling that if I write a strongly negative review, as I'm apt to do, I won't be asked to contribute many more."[237] When *TV Guide* featured Fox's *Party of Five* in a front-page story, "The Best Show You're Not Watching," competitors complained that Rupert Murdoch's News Corporation owned both the network and the magazine, and NBC threatened to withdraw advertising.[238] Film critics rewrite screenplays they later review, advise studios and producers on market-ing, may have a "treatment" sitting on the desk of a producer whose film they are reviewing, and even sign studio-written blurbs to get their names in advertisements.[239]

THE FALL OF COMMUNISM

If state regulation simply oppressed speech, the fall of communism would have been an unalloyed boon. But writers and readers freed from Big Brother have learned that the invisible hand also constrains. With the end of state subsidies, Russian newspaper production costs quadrupled in the first two months of 1992, and the price of newsprint increased a hundredfold by July of that year. *Novy Mir*, which had published *Doctor Zhivago*, *The Gulag Archipelago*, and *1984*, sought $190,000 from Western donors as its costs soared to twice its income. After the initial enthusiasm for liberalization, the circulation of *Nezavi-samaya Gazeta* (Independent newspaper) plummeted from 96 million to 8 million. The only newspapers showing circulation gains in 1993 were a free weekly and the pornographic *SPID-Inform* (AIDS-inform). The next year Russian versions of *Penthouse*, *Soldier of Fortune*, and *Cosmo* were thriving. The best-sellers in mid-1994 included *The Road to Tara (Return to Scarlett)*, *The Fall and the Greatness of Beautiful Amber*, *The 30th To Be Killed: Return of the Crazy One* (about a mass murderer), and the Mexican soap opera *Wild Rose*. The writers' group Aprel complained: "The market threatens to become the grave of culture. Privatization of culture is above all privatization of the soul." *Pravda* finally closed in 1996, after its circulation had declined from 11 million to 200,000. When the Bolshoi went on tour to Las Vegas and Los Angeles, the houses were more than three-fourths empty. Moscow offered to lease Red Square during the spring festival that replaced May Day, including billboards on three sides and two dirigibles stationed above, but no one came up with the $1 million rent. The former Berlin Wall, by contrast, quickly became what one ad man called "quality high-contact," displaying ads for Camels and photos of women who were "Game for Anything." Hungary sold one of its most influential dailies, *Magyar Nemzet,* to a conservative French newspaper magnate rather than to the liberal Swedish *Dagens Nyheter* because the latter "has a 'leftist-liberal' ideology and does not stand on the national-liberal base that is so popular in Hungary. . . . this paper regularly publishes disparaging articles not only about the issue of Hungarians living in Romania, on which it shares the views of the Ceausescu-era propaganda." The print run for Gyorgy Konrád, one of the country's leading novelists, shrank from 70,000 to 10,000. After being silenced for twenty years, Ivan Klíma immediately sold out a 100,000 first printing of short stories, and his obscure Czech publisher ran off another 50,000. But though his next four books sold out quickly, readers bought only two-thirds of the 15,000 copies of his important novel *Judge on Trial* and just 5,000 of his next one, published for the Christmas 1993 season. "People in theater . . . dreamed all their lives about putting Ionesco on stage," he said, "and now that they could, no one came."[240]

THE UNFREE MARKET

Adapting Milton Friedman's aphorism, Stanley Fish declares provocatively "There's No Such Thing as Free Speech and It's a Good Thing, Too."[241] The only sites where speech is free—Hyde Park speakers' corner and its soapbox equivalents elsewhere—marginalize and trivialize speakers, exposing them to audience scorn and tourist cameras. The commodification described above not only devalues speech but also shapes and rations it, allowing those with superior material resources to drown out or silence opponents. The trials of Patty Hearst, John Z. De Lorean, and of course O. J. Simpson evoke the lawyer's cynical question to a client: how much justice can you afford? Wealthy political novices like Ross Perot, Michael Huffington, Morry Taylor, and Steve Forbes can mount highly visible campaigns. Industry spent nearly five times as much on California initiatives in 1990 as public interest groups ($57 to $12 million); the liquor industry alone spent $28 million opposing a tax to finance health research and education; two years earlier the insurance industry had spent $75 million opposing lower premiums. In the 1990 congressional race 96 percent of House incumbents were reelected (outspending challengers 9 to 1) and all but one Senate incumbent (outspending challengers 3 to 1).[242]

Civil libertarianism jealously guards individual autonomy against external pressure. But speech is a social activity; all except the hopelessly solipsistic require at least one auditor. Furthermore, the very technology that allows speakers to enlarge their audiences also increases the social cooperation necessary for communication. Cyberspace is a perfect example. Although the Internet allows rapid, low-cost global communication, intermediaries increasingly influence content. On-line access services scrutinize messages and back their censorship with the power to terminate subscribers. AT&T bans "personal matters"; America Online prohibits "harmful, threatening, abusive, harassing, defamatory, vulgar, obscene, hateful, racially ethnically or otherwise objectionable content"; CompuServe forbids speech "that would be abusive, profane or offensive to an average person." Schools and universities impose filtering software. Microsoft, Netscape, and Progressive Networks formed the Information Highway Parental Empowerment Group to develop a voluntary rating system for Internet sites and programs, allowing parents to block access. Under pressure from German prosecutors, CompuServe obstructed 200 Internet sites allegedly distributing sexual material; several were bulletin boards for sexual abuse victims.[243] The markets that organize interaction among speakers, intermediaries, and audiences exert a powerful influence on who says what to whom. This section documents those influences in book publishing, scholarship, periodicals, radio and television, film, advertising, and other environments.

BOOKS

Publishers decide who speaks and what they say. Edward Garnett cut 10 percent of *Sons and Lovers* without consulting D. H. Lawrence before Duckworth would publish it. Viking deleted obscene dialogue from *The Grapes of Wrath,* although John Steinbeck protested: "My whole system recoiled." William Morrow, Mary Renault's regular publisher, rejected *The Charioteer* for its depiction of homosexual love. Webster's president overruled its editor's inclusion of "fuck" in the *Third New International Dictionary.*[244] Calvin Klein's friends persuaded G. P. Putnam's Sons to drop a critical biography and allow the authors to keep their $400,000 advance.[245] More than two dozen publishers rejected *The Cigarette Papers,* based on documents in a lawsuit against Brown & Williamson. Dutton/Signet and Viking-Penguin claimed it would not sell, although the author appeared on *60 Minutes* and the *Peter Jennings Report* and was interviewed by *Newsweek.* Others were more candid: Basic Books said the legal department did not want to take a chance, and Oxford University Press was "reluctant to go to battle with the tobacco industry."[246] All fifteen contributors to a volume commemorating the United Nations' fiftieth anniversary removed their names when the editor deleted the list of countries that abstained from the 1948 Universal Declaration of Human Rights or had been monitored for violations. The secretary general's spokesperson explained: "[I]t was not deemed appropriate to have the book contain criticism of member states in it."[247] Feminist attacks and boycott threats persuaded Simon & Schuster to cancel Bret Easton Ellis's *American Psycho* a month before it was to appear. HarperSan Francisco's women authors convinced it to require changes in Barbara Graham's *Women Who Run with the Poodles* (a parody of *Women Who Run with the Wolves*).[248] St. Martin's Press canceled its contract to publish David Irving's biography of Goebbels because it was "inescapably anti-Semitic." The outraged author complained: "Because I write history, which runs across the track of political correctness, there has been for the last five years a determined effort to silence me globally."[249]

My own experience with the 1992 Hamlyn Lectures, from which this book derives, offers a cautionary tale.[250] Sweet & Maxwell, which had published the lectures for more than forty years, was particularly concerned by the "coarser expressions" in 2 Live Crew's "The Buck," which I used to exemplify misogynist speech (see chapter 4). They also objected to my calling Moses and Jesus "notorious blasphemers," describing the fatwa against Salman Rushdie as "a terrible blot on the reputation of Islam," quoting feminists comparing pornographers to Hitler and criticizing civil liberties organizations as "pornographers' mouthpieces," repeating Clinton's slur of Mario Cuomo, calling Patrick Buchanan conservative, or even writing that "Anita Hill testified before hundreds of millions of viewers about her sexual harassment by Clarence Thomas." Although I modified many phrases to their satisfaction, they refused my proposal to move the rap lyrics to an endnote with a textual warning to readers. While conceding that the quotations "are used in context as part of a forceful argument" and insisting that it was "by no means seeking to inhibit academic freedom to use material to illustrate an argument," Sweet & Maxwell remained "convinced that [publication] cannot be an acceptable risk" because of its "liability under UK law for producing libellous and offensive material." I reluctantly acquiesced in that decision, replacing the lyrics with an account of this exchange, noting their tolerance of other racist, sexist, homophobic, and anti-Semitic language, and noting that the lyrics were not libelous and there was no liability for offensiveness. They rejected this account as well, insisting on the single sentence that they had deleted the lyrics because "a number of readers would be likely to find" them "unduly offensive." When I declined to accept this, they canceled publication, declared the entire correspondence "personal and confidential," and threatened that if I even described it "we will ensure that the materials are reviewed by those advising our organisation based in the US, the Thomson Corporation." Other publishers took this threat seriously and lost interest in the manuscript when I sought to include an account of the controversy.

Sweet & Maxwell ultimately capitulated, publishing the lyrics in an appendix, and the *Journal of Law and Society* printed my narrative of the clash. The incident clearly reveals the principal constraints on my speech as private rather than public. The laws of defamation, privacy, and obscenity were largely irrelevant, the tastes of Sweet & Maxwell and the Hamlyn Trustees paramount. Had I been more vulnerable and the *Journal of Law and Society* and the University of Chicago Press more timid, none of this might ever have appeared.

Booksellers constitute a further impediment to distribution. The second largest English chain would not carry Jeremy Pascall's *God: The Ultimate Autobiography;* Gays the Word in London rejected the Marquis de Sade's *Juliette,* while mainstream stores (and the Royal National Institute for the Blind) barred gay and lesbian literature. Some feminist stores ban men from women's erotica and lesbian pornography.[251] Earvin "Magic" Johnson's book on AIDS sold 500,000 copies and was translated into twelve languages. The AMA declared that "[e]verybody—especially teenagers and parents—needs to read this book," which "could help save lives." But Wal-Mart's 1,747 stores refused to stock it because "we found some of the material inappropriate." Kmart, the next largest discount chain, also decided the book "doesn't fit the family orientation of a Kmart shopper," although it sold Jackie Collins's *Hollywood Wives* and a *Cosmopolitan* issue on the etiquette of oral sex.[252] (Wal-Mart also banned Grammy-winner Sheryl Crow because of criticism of the chain's gun sales.)[253] The Free Press complained that trendy stores in Cambridge and Manhattan's Upper West Side would not display its conservative books. Some chains refused to stock Howard Stern's *Private Parts* (which Simon & Schuster would not let him entitle "Penis"), and Caldor's deleted the book from first place on its display of the *New York Times* best seller list.[254] Booksellers can even influence publication; after fourteen publishers rejected a *Washington Post* reporter's proposal for an exposé of Crown Books, one confessed to fear that the chain would retaliate by not stocking its other titles.[255]

Reviews and prizes catapult a few books to instant fame, while most quickly sink into obscurity. The Caldecott Medal virtually assures at least 100,000 in initial sales and a long life on the backlist; the National Book Awards and Pulitzer and Booker Prizes increase sales severalfold. Such influence is particularly disturbing given the casual nature of the judgment. Robert Heilbroner, chair of the National Book Awards nonfiction panel, did not read most of the 190 submissions and eliminated 75 in one day on the basis of first and last pages, index, table of contents, and blurbs. When the American Booksellers Association awarded its first Book of the Year (Abby) award to *The Education of Little Tree,* that purported memoir of an Indian orphan remained a best-seller even after being unmasked as the fictional work of a white racist. The *New York Times* best-seller list may be vulnerable to manipulation. *The Discipline of Market Leaders* reached fifth place and remained on the list for fifteen weeks, allegedly because its authors bought 10,000 copies and persuaded corporate clients to buy another 30,000 to 40,000.[256]

Scholarship

Although scholarly journals purport to be guided by objective criteria of excellence, ideological considerations intrude. When Forrest M. Mims 3d applied for *Scientific American*'s "Amateur Scientist" column, after twenty years of writing for more than sixty scientific periodicals, the managing editor called him a strong candidate, who wrote good trial columns and offered impressive proposals. But the journal rejected Mims when he expressed disbelief in evolution and opposition to abortion, fearing that "*Scientific American* might inadvertently put an imprimatur on 'creation science.'" Mims protested he had never "written about creationism." "I'm a conservative. I'm willing to dialogue. But I'm not going to deny my faith. . . . I even told them I could be their token Christian, but they didn't smile at that."[257] *Reconstruction* proclaims the goal of fostering "robust, wide-open debate." But after accepting a contribution to a symposium on the Clarence Thomas nomination, Harvard law professor Randall Kennedy rejected it because of "references to the infamous Coke can and the matter involving pornography." Kennedy explained: "I press for candor, but I also press for a certain degree of intellectual discipline. I thought there was a hint of smarminess in his piece."[258] When the new *American Bar Association Journal* editor published articles to which ABA officers objected, the editorial board told the ABA director of communications "to make sure that he understands both sides of the issue."[259] The Los Angeles Mensa chapter newsletter published articles asserting that "people who are so mentally defective that they cannot live in society should, as soon as they are identified as defective, be humanely dispatched" and homeless who "are too stupid, too lazy, too crazy, or too anti-social to earn a living . . . should be humanely done away with like abandoned kittens." Other chapters received thousands of angry phone calls and letters, and the New York office suffered two bomb threats. Although the chapter unanimously expressed confidence in the editor after the issue appeared, the national organization required publications to be in "good taste" and avoid "material that reflects negatively on Mensa." The editor was fired.[260]

Scholarly institutions also constrain research. After three years as general editor of the Dead Sea Scrolls, Harvard Divinity professor John Strugnell was removed for "ill health" when an Israeli newspaper published an interview in which he said Israel was "founded on a lie" and described Judaism as "horrible," "originally racist" and "not a higher religion," "a Christian heresy . . . that we haven't managed to convert."[261] Harvard Medical School was deeply embarrassed when Professor John Mack published *Abduction: Human Encounters with Aliens,* uncritically reporting patient accounts of coerced sex with large-eyed gray creatures aboard space ships, and publicized the book on Oprah, Larry King, and other talk shows. Although his lawyer invoked "academic freedom" to protest the school's investigation into whether Mack had complied with standards of research and human experimentation, the university warned Mack not to let enthusiasm divert him from professionalism.[262] The conservative John M. Olin Foundation supports more than fifty university programs. "We don't tell them who [sic] to hire. We start with a professor who is already in place and wants to do what we want to do. If all goes well, we renew the grant." Olin also financed the American Enterprise Institute, which gave Dinesh D'Souza a $50,000 fellowship, and it bought and distributed a thousand copies of his book *Illiberal Education.*[263]

PERIODICALS

Although the British press is more openly partisan than the American—five tabloids, the *Daily Telegraph,* the *Times,* and the *Sunday Times* support the Conservatives, while one tabloid, the *Guardian,* and the

Observer support Labor—American publishers also exercise editorial control.[264] Henry Luce appointed the strongly anticommunist Whittaker Chambers as chief foreign editor and drove Theodore White to resign rather than write a celebratory story about Chiang Kai-shek.[265] Although the Unification Church claims to have "nothing to do" with the *Washington Times,* on which it lost $1 billion over twelve years, it also said Rev. Sun Myung Moon wanted to make the paper "an instrument to save America and the world."[266] After buying the *New York Post,* "Garage King" Abraham Hirschfeld fired the editor-in-chief and seventy-two editorial staff and put his own plan for international peace on the second page and his wife's poetry on the third. When employees took revenge with the headline: "Post staff to Abe Hirschfeld: GET LOST," he canceled the issue.[267] The editor in chief and executive editor of *Outdoor Life* resigned when its Times Mirror parent pulled an article criticizing bear baiting, presumably because the company saw it as antihunter.[268] Even after newspapers are printed, dealers can block distribution. In return for political support, the dominant Mexican party PRI gives a union exclusive rights to sell papers on the street and forbids vending machines and sales in small shops. The union, in return, refused to sell the antigovernment *Reforma* and obstructs sales of other papers when it dislikes the headline.[269]

Every paper imposes ethical standards. Some suppressed reports of the twenty-day kidnapping of an Associated Press reporter in Somalia to protect the victim's life. The *New York Times* declined to publish the American Coalition of Life Activists' hit list of a dozen abortion doctors.[270] Papers follow different standards of veracity and verification. *USA Today* printed a full-page apology and suspended a reporter who misled gang members into posing with their guns by claiming to write about a program in which they exchanged guns for jobs.[271] Well before Jeffrey Masson sued Janet Malcolm, the *New Yorker* told staff: "We do not permit composites. We do not rearrange events. We do not create conversations." The *Atlantic Monthly* fact-checks poetry![272] Respect for privacy often exceeds legal requirements. Although British tabloids are notorious for exposing the private lives of the royals and politicians, the *Sunday Times* Continental edition deleted the name of Mitterrand's illegitimate child's mother, and French papers first printed the daughter's given name eighteen months later when she began to appear with him on state occasions.[273] When *Advertising Age* outed *Rolling Stone* publisher Jann Wenner, the *Wall Street Journal* justified its coverage by the disclosure's effect on the value of Wenner Media Inc., but the *Village Voice* denounced the action, and the *New York Times* does not "reveal private aspects of a person's life unless it's relevant to the story."[274] When the *National Enquirer* alleged that O. J. Simpson told Roosevelt Grier "I did it!" the Associated Press did not carry it as news and the *Chicago Tribune* qualified its story by noting the *Enquirer's* reputation for sensationalism, but the *New York Times* covered it as an example of courtroom maneuvers and then repeated it in a story about the ethics of printing that first article.[275]

Some newspapers refuse advertisements for cigarettes, guns, escort services, and pornography.[276] Many will not print offensive words. The *New York Times* published a substantial article about a criminal defense lawyer charged with disorderly conduct for shouting "#L*!" when her wire-rimmed nursing bra set off the metal detector in a Texas courthouse. Yet the *Times* prints slurs like "faggot." *Los Angeles Times* reporters must obtain permission to use babe, bra-burner, Dutch treat, mailman, mankind, and deaf-mute. A lengthy article about Simpson's lawyers' attempt to impeach the credibility of LAPD detective Mark Fuhrman by showing that he lied about never having said "nigger" in ten years omitted the word (although it appeared in other *Los Angeles Times* articles).[277] Papers even restrict employee off-hours political activity. AP staff cannot participate in "a gay-rights parade, anti-abortion or pro-abortion protest, anti-war demonstration." The *Washington Post* and ABC News forbade reporters from joining a gay rights parade, and the *New York Times,* the *Los Angeles Times,* and NBC News allowed only those not covering gay issues. The *News Tribune* of Tacoma removed a reporter from covering education because she was a gay rights activist.[278]

Periodicals attribute a variety of editorial decisions to reader preferences. A number of papers refused the cartoon "For Better or for Worse," which had run in 1,400 papers for fourteen years, when a episode showed a family banishing a teenage son who came out gay. A small-town editor claimed: "[O]ur readers would not appreciate this rather striking reference to homosexuality." The *Las Vegas Review-Journal* called it "condoning homosexuality almost to the point of advocacy."[279] Many refused to run a "Doonesbury" strip in which the gay character Mark told a fundamentalist Christian married man he tried to pick up that a Yale professor had written that "for 1,000 years the church sanctioned rituals for homosexual marriage." Several months later Garry Trudeau rewrote the strip for the first time, after a paper complained about his description of Jeb Bush.[280]

Such decisions shape reader preferences as well as reflect them. The nineteenth-century *Flag of Our Nation* rejected a novel it had commissioned in which Louisa May Alcott portrayed an older man obsessively pursuing the young wife who had abandoned him. In the mid–

twentieth century a leading women's magazine rejected chapters from African American novelist Dorothy West's first book for fear of losing white subscribers.[281] Several decades ago many daily and weekly magazines each published up to 300 short stories a year. Now only six mainstream monthlies publish serious fiction. The new editor of the *New Yorker*, which rejects thousands of stories for each it accepts, declared that "one piece of fiction a week is right for the reading rhythms of our times."[282]

Radio and Television

As literacy and reading decline, politics is increasingly dependent on sound bites. But some stations refuse to carry political advertisements rather than sell the time at their lowest commercial rate, as the FCC requires. Others are influenced by content. The Buffalo CBS affiliate rejected a National Abortion Rights Action League spot displaying the Statue of Liberty and flag while urging viewers to make "abortion less necessary" by encouraging sex education and birth control. The station explained: "Even if Operation Rescue had not been in town, I'd question the ad. It's a sensitive issue, and we elected not to get involved."[283] In the hope of raising ratings (and thus advertising revenue) more than a sixth of radio stations ended local news gathering during the 1980s. Network television coverage of domestic policy issues declined 37 percent between 1975 and 1986. The networks allotted only four hours to the four-*day* 1992 Democratic National Convention. Two declined to broadcast Clinton's first news conference, and the third aired only thirty minutes. None of the eighty Los Angeles radio stations would carry his weekly five-minute talk live. Cable operators serving more than four million subscribers replaced C-Span's uninterrupted coverage of Washington politics with soap opera reruns and home shopping.[284]

Many content decisions are driven by ratings. KABC-TV in Los Angeles decided not to report Gulf War protests because they coincided with ratings sweeps and viewers had complained about antiwar coverage.[285] Commentators split about CBS's decision to transmit Kathleen Gingrich's "off camera" whisper to Connie Chung that Newt had called Hillary "a bitch." But some noted that Chung was under great pressure to help the network recapture its front-runner position and was fired a few months later.[286] WNCN-FM in New York replaced classical music with "a power rotation" of "well-known, listenable, hummable pieces" in 1987, eliminating "organ music, avant-garde, atonal, aleatoric music, waltzes, virtually all vocal music, [and] all monaural and historical recordings"; seven years later it switched to rock. Some stations have rejected gangsta rap, although cynics claimed that one was just resigning itself to its older female audience.[287]

Principle sometimes triumphs over greed. After screening a surveillance tape showing a convenience-store murder, KNBC in Los Angeles decided that it "violated any imaginable standard of good taste or good journalism." "We use the tape to identify suspects. We do not use the tape as the news equivalent of a snuff film."[288] Some radio stations dropped Watergate burglar G. Gordon Liddy's talk show when he advised listeners how to wound federal agents wearing bullet-proof clothing.[289] After a man shot at the White House, a radio station in the gunman's Colorado Springs hometown pulled the talk show by Don Baker, who had encouraged listeners to take their guns to the capital to protest the proposed assault-weapon ban. When it let Baker back on the air six months later, it prohibited advocacy of violence.[290] Two major pay-per-view cable distributors refused to buy O. J. Simpson's postacquittal interview. Request Television called it "exploitative" and "inappropriate" to make "a brutal double murder . . . into entertainment." Time Warner's New York City cable service said: "[I]t would offend our relationship with customers." Even Larry King found "it's beneath everything I've built my career on." After NBC agreed to interview Simpson, sponsors pulled commercials and feminist picketers convinced the studio to back out at the last moment.[291] But three networks screened movies about Amy Fisher, and two made films about parricides Lyle and Erik Menendez.[292]

External power can influence content. When Bush met Latin American leaders to discuss drug enforcement, a reporter for the NBC-TV affiliate cornered the president, calling the conference a "joke." The station fired him for his "insistent and persistent and aggressive" manner of asking questions.[293] A San Joaquin Valley radio station dismissed its weather forecaster for (accurately) predicting rain at the Dittohead Barbecue and Politically Incorrect Picnic and tried to have a local news photographer discharged for recording the sparse turnout. More than 20 percent of valley listeners tune in to Rush Limbaugh.[294] A year after losing his legs to a car bomb, Cuban American program director Emilio Milian was fired by a radio station for his incendiary views. A decade later, when the station he owned mocked Carlos Arboleya, a trustee of the Cuban American National Foundation, the bank of which Arboleya was vice-chairman withdrew all advertising and called its loans, forcing the station into bankruptcy. The only bidder at the sale included three foundation members.[295] Eleven Miami hotels blacked out crime reports by the local Fox affiliate because of the "continuous barrage of the body bags on the street and the blood coming out of them."

"It's certainly bad for tourism, it's certainly bad for the local economy and certainly bad for the general atmosphere."[296]

While radio flaunts its shock jocks, television networks are in thrall to their standards departments. The CBS head explained: "We look a lot to the views of our affiliates. We look to our audience mail, our daily ratings, what the critics are saying, what the advertisers are saying." His NBC counterpart agreed: "[W]e're really trying to help do what everyone wants to do: attract the most, offend the least." Scrutiny starts with words. Lucille Ball could not say "pregnant" even when obviously expecting. Seinfeld's notorious episode on masturbation never uttered the word. (Even NPR's *All Things Considered* warned listeners before attributing Dr. Joycelyn Elders's forced resignation to her discussion of masturbation; a Minneapolis station substituted "self-pleasuring.") *Thirtysomething* had to cut a reference to oral sex. "Virtually every word was looked at" in a *Law and Order* episode about abortion to ensure equal numbers of remarks on both sides. Although the occasional "bastard" is permitted, four-letter words are not. Despite the success of his *St. Elsewhere,* CBS rejected Bruce Paltrow's 1991 "Word of Mouth" pilot about a president who habitually trips over his tongue. "You can't see the president screwing up after the Gulf War." Steve Bochco was allowed to have Doogie Howser lose his virginity, but only offscreen. It took Bochco a year to negotiate an agreement with ABC specifying which profanities could be uttered on *NYPD Blue* and how often, how much flesh could be shown and from what angle. Even so, 57 of the 225 affiliates refused the premiere.[297]

Television exercises more stringent control over the depiction of homosexuality. It did not screen a single homosexual kiss between 1972 and 1992. A *Picket Fences* episode showing two sixteen-year-old girls in nightclothes sitting on two mattresses and kissing twice was rewritten to cloak them in almost total darkness, accompanied by a brief kissing sound and the line "Well, that was interesting." Even so, some stations preempted it. *L.A. Law* quickly made a lesbian character bisexual. Roseanne Barr had to negotiate at length over kissing Sharon in a gay bar. Although the camera angle obscured lip contact, ABC initially barred the scene; after capitulating it vetoed a second kiss between Roseanne's sister and Sharon's lover. It took Armistead Maupin eleven years to make *Tales of the City* (which contained a single kiss). HBO's film of Randy Shilts's award-winning book about the AIDS epidemic, *As the Band Played On,* engendered several confrontations. According to Sir Ian McKellen,

> when B. D. Wong and I kissed, it was too much for HBO, so they cut it. An executive on the set said . . . it was his responsibility to see to

it that his viewers—and this is a direct quote—not be grossed out. I reminded him that this film begins with a shot of dead and dying Ebola fever victims, one of whom spews blood almost directly into the camera.

The cable channel eliminated drag queens from the gay Halloween parade, shortened the bathhouse scene, and cut an explanation of poppers (amyl nitrate). The HBO editor objected that director Roger Spottiswoode "had shot it in a very darkly personal way. It had this documentary, realistic feel to it. HBO thought it was too dark." When Spottiswoode threw the HBO "supervisor" out of the editing room, the company excluded the director from postproduction meetings, had police seize the film, and recut it, adding documentary footage of government officials and increasing the heroic role of the heterosexual Don Francis at the expense of the dying gay activist.[298]

FILM

Artists and entertainers have always sought to please patrons and audiences.[299] Rodin repeatedly recast his *Homage to Victor Hugo* until the author accepted it.[300] Generations of London theatergoers applauded happy endings of *King Lear* and *Hamlet*. Rossini gave one to *Othello*, and after Verdi's death Rigoletto's daughter was allowed to survive kidnapping. Lerner and Loewe turned Shaw's bitter *Pygmalion* into the saccharine *My Fair Lady*.[301] Before Robertson Davies achieved fame, he adapted an early novel for Broadway. After opening night the star told Davies "he had to have 10 more sure laughs by tomorrow morning or he was going to walk out."[302] In *Bullets over Broadway*, Woody Allen lampooned the ways in which actors, "angels," and even the backer's moll's bodyguard rewrote the play.

As organizational structures grow larger and more complex, capital investment rises, and the audience necessary to show a profit increases, these influences intensify. Studios are the gatekeepers for cinema, just as publishers are for print media and networks for radio and television. They decide which books to option, which treatments to turn into screenplays, who will write, direct, and act, and how much to spend on production and promotion. Best-selling authors lose all control: Tom Clancy over *Patriot Games*, Stephen King over *The Lawnmower Man*, Dean R. Koontz over *Hideaway*. Even Orson Welles could not prevent drastic revisions of his films. The Artists Rights Association, formed to resist colorization, championed creative interests generally. A trustee complained that vesting all rights in the studio was "the same as saying that the Pope painted the Sistine Chapel." MPAA president Jack Valenti retorted: "[I]f you inject into this another area of uncertainty, the money will be diminished. The only way you can survive in the marketplace is to move briskly through videotape, pay-per-view, cable [and television]." Michael Corrente reluctantly allowed Trimark to colorize *Federal Hill* because some video rental outlets would not stock black-and-white films (including *Schindler's List*).[303]

Since studios invested an average of $38 million per film in the early 1990s, it is not surprising that Hollywood tests audience reaction before releasing at least 75 percent of the top 200 movies each year. The Columbia Pictures marketing director explained: "It's the same thing you do with a product. You sample it: Is it too sweet? Is it too hot?" Ron Howard, who directed the highly successful *Parenthood* and *Cocoon,* starts with a three-to-four-hour rough cut and chops it in half on the basis of audience reaction to as many as sixteen test screenings. *Fatal Attraction,* one of the most profitable films ever made, changed its ending after negative responses. The eponymous hero of *Guarding Tess* was miraculously cured when test audiences objected to her death from a brain tumor. James L. Brooks, who directed *Terms of Endearment* and *Broadcast News,* changed the opening of *I'll Do Anything* after the previews and reconsidered the original songs by Prince, Sínead O'Connor, and Carole King. A friend said the director's "roots—and he's proud of it—are on television . . . [where] you learn to listen to the audience." Although Joe Eszterhas strongly objected to MPAA demands that he revise *Basic Instinct,* he wrote three endings for his next film, *Sliver,* and dropped the original one. "What we discovered was, we were asking the audience to make an endorsement of an action [by Sharon Stone] that they felt to be immoral." The director of *Striptease* saw that preview "audiences loved Burt [Reynolds] so much . . . they couldn't accept him as a rapist. They were really into this movie and then we hit this point where he turned evil and I could just smell that I lost them right there. So we changed it to a more fun ending." The book's author had no objections: "I'm under no illusion that people are going to be lining up that first weekend to see what's happened to the Carl Hiaasen book. I have a really good suspicion they will be standing there because they want to see Demi [Moore] with her clothes off." The next logical step is to involve *each* audience in shaping what it sees. PacBell was experimenting with distributing films to theaters over fiber-optic lines. The company creating the switching technology explained: "Let's say in some towns you'd get five more Baptists coming into the theater if you took out the swear words. Boom, they're gone." Noneconomic considerations can shape film content. After Sony bought Columbia Pictures, it canceled a movie about sumo wrestlers directed by Milos Forman, claiming it could not get the Sumo Association's cooperation. When Matsushita bought Universal Pictures, it rewrote *Mr. Baseball,* civilizing the boorish American player on a Japanese team by having him fall in love with the coach's daughter.[304]

Just as bookstores reject titles and local affiliates decline network television, so theaters refuse films. Universal City would not screen John Singleton's *Poetic Justice* because five people were wounded when his last movie, *Boyz N the Hood,* opened there. When African Americans denounced this as racism, Los Angeles mayor Richard Riordan replied: "Let business do [its] thing." Cineplex said it was just "ensuring that the theater is programmed with an upscale demographic to make sure that CityWalk's environment is kept safe." The local NAACP director could reach "only one conclusion: that as an African-American, I'm not allowed at the Cineplex Odeon." She noted that "often times [business's] 'thing' is exclusion." The theater also refused the African American western *Posse.* And Snoop Doggy Dogg could find *no* commercial theater to screen *Murder Was the Case,* directed by Dr. Dre and based on the number-one hit song. Airlines edit films for sex and religion—and of course plane crashes. World Airline Entertainment Association said: "[B]asically, you're looking for films that are not going to offend." United Airlines did not want the "heavier" movies, which "you have to think your way through."[305]

ADVERTISING

We saw earlier that the mass media's organizational and technological requirements make it financially imperative to reach a large audience. Advertising, of course, is a crucial intermediary, generating the sales to pay these huge costs.[306] Most sponsors seek to avoid all controversy. NBC canceled Nat King Cole's variety show after its initial 1957 season for lack of sponsorship and fear of a boycott by racist affiliates. Withdrawals from a 1989 *Thirtysomething* episode showing two gay men in bed cost ABC $1.5 million. Advertisers pulled $500,000 out of a *Law and Order* episode about an abortion clinic bombing and $350,000 from one showing an AIDS victim's assisted suicide. The networks responded to these losses by demanding the power to cancel a show after three appearances (just as most theaters have a contractual right to close a play that fails to sell enough seats two weeks running). In 1973, when CBS reran an episode about the first abortion by a leading television character, not one national sponsor bought time, and thirty-nine affiliates refused the show. When Murphy Brown disclosed her pregnancy nearly two decades later, an advertiser withdrew just because abortion was mentioned. Executive producer Diane English said, "[I]t would have been lights out," had Murphy had an abortion. Although *Quantum Leap,* under pressure from Los Angeles Gay and Lesbian Alliance against Defamation and the NBC standards department, rewrote a January 1992 episode about a gay teenage naval cadet driven to suicide by student vigilantes, sponsor withdrawals cost the network $150,000. The serial offered future sponsors a plot synopsis beforehand and their money back if they did not like it. Most prestigious advertisers shunned the *NYPD Blue* premiere, although it reached nearly 15 million households and 33 percent of 18-to-34-year-old viewers. ABC also provided advertisers and agencies with a copy of each episode a week before screening.[307]

Saatchi & Saatchi's Betsy Frank spoke openly about advertiser influence.

> The creative community has a legitimate gripe, but they have to adhere to certain limits. When we use TV, we're not using it to support First Amendment rights or artistic freedom, we're using it because it's a good business decision for our client, and nobody wants the result of a business decision to be loss of customers rather than gains.

Each June advertising agencies spend about $4 billion buying up to three-quarters of the next season's heavily discounted air time. Producers and actors seek Frank's input on their scripts and videotapes. The president of NBC Entertainment admitted he was "more and more receptive every year to what the advertisers have to say." His CBS counterpart agreed: "Our direct consumer is the advertising community, and we must maintain an open dialogue with them."[308] Public television may be learning that lesson as government funding shrinks. Perhaps because it limits the amount of promotion, it pleases sponsors in other ways. PBS showcased the Pittsburgh Symphony while funded by Gulf Oil (headquartered there) and substituted the Philadelphia Orchestra for the Boston Symphony when Atlantic Richfield (of Philadelphia) replaced Raytheon (of Boston). And was it just an accident that Unisys Corporation, which donated $600,000 to *The Machine That Changed the World,* was mentioned in the first episode?[309] Blatant influence can be embarrassing, however. The History Channel, one of the fastest growing on cable, canceled its planned "spirit of enterprise" series, which intended to use corporate archives, rely on corporate subsidies, and give the subjects control.[310]

Advertisers do not just avoid controversy. The television film *Judgment at Nuremberg* could not mention gas chambers because it was sponsored by the American Gas Company. *Leave It to Beaver* never showed the boys drinking milk in case a soft-drink company became interested in sponsorship.[311] Periodicals refusing cigarette ads (the eighth-largest spender in 1990) were 40 percent more likely to publish reports about the dangers of smoking; among women's journals the difference was 100 percent. The *Saturday Evening Post* stopped accepting such ads in the mid-1970s after learning that tobacco companies would not advertise in issues containing articles on smoking and health.[312] When New York City proposed a tough antismoking ordinance, Philip Morris, a major arts patron, warned beneficiaries it might end support. The Brooklyn Academy of Music made "discreet telephone calls" to the city council. Another grantee told "the City Council that it was in the best interests of the arts in New York City that Philip Morris money stay in New York City." A councilor reported "a lot of pressure on Council members from cultural groups."[313]

Financial leverage can persuade the media to deny a competitor visibility. The 45,000-member American Academy of Pediatrics journal does not accept baby-formula ads. When the AAP denounced Nestlé's 1988 decision to begin advertising elsewhere, the manufacturer's market share dropped 30 percent. Nestlé charged the AAP with conspiring with three major competitors, whose prices doubled during the 1980s to about twice Nestlé's (which remained constant). Abbott Labs (with 52 percent of the market) settled for $140 million. Trial discovery revealed that the three competitors donated more than $8.3 million to the AAP between 1983 and 1992 and spent more on advertising other products and throwing parties. The AAP executive board minuted in 1986: "If there is a marketing war . . . the A.A.P. may have to cut back on anticipated income from industry." The year Nestlé began to advertise, a memo within Bristol-Myers Squibb (another accused, with a 32 percent market share) acknowledged it "is probably in our best interests to forestall any form of consumer advertising. The inability to advertise presents a significant entry barrier to new competitors." A year later the AAP executive director wrote the manufacturer of the Abbott product: "We're together on our opposition to direct advertising of formula to the public, and we'll continue to do what we can (within legal and ethical limits) to deal with the problem."[314]

Other advertisers are no more tolerant of criticism. After four months *Financial World* terminated University of California, Berkeley, professor Graef S. Crystal's column on executive remuneration, noting that advertising pages had dropped 30 percent. The editor acknowledged that the columnist was "the foremost authority in that field, but you know it's just pretty incendiary stuff. If you're a C.E.O. and it's your picture featured in that column, though half the time it was upbeat, you don't always like it. Some of them have spoken to their lawyers." Crystal complained: "I can't find a niche in any American magazine that has advertising pages because my enemies are going to be out there threatening to pull their advertising." He had a similar column at *Fortune* until he sought to expose the overpayment of executives at

Time Warner, the magazine's parent.[315] When *Premiere* panned *Aliens 3*, 20th Century–Fox pulled its ads for the movie. Warner Brothers barred the *Los Angeles Magazine* critic from future screenings after he criticized *Batman Returns*. Paramount indefinitely withdrew all *Variety* ads following a critical review of *Patriot Games*. The studio declared: "[T]he trade [papers] are there to assess the commercial viability of a film and give exhibitors and industry people an enlightened interpretation of what the film can do. It's not like a review for The New York Times . . . that would be assessing the merits of the film." *Variety*'s editor apologized and promised that the reviewer, who had almost twenty years of experience, would never handle another Paramount film. He warned the reviewer not to let "political opinions . . . (a) color the review emotionally . . . [or] (b) negatively critique the work done by artisans such as the composer, cinematographer, etc."[316]

When the editor of *Automobile* used the annual Automotive Press Association dinner to attack General Motors for closing twenty-one plants and eliminating 74,000 jobs and called management "piano players in the whorehouse," the carmaker withdrew Oldsmobile and Buick ads for three months. Toyota pulled ads from *Road and Track* when it failed to make the 1991 "10 Best List," and GM did the same when *Car and Driver* photographed an Opel Kadett in a junkyard, calling it "the worst car in the world." Mercedes-Benz of North America told thirty magazines not to run its ads in issues that criticized the company or *anything* German. Most magazines capitulated to its demand for the right to pull ads at the last minute if they appeared near an "inappropriate editorial." When the *San Jose Mercury News* advised readers how to negotiate car prices, the forty-seven-member Santa Clara Dealers Association organized an ad boycott, costing the paper about $1 million. It responded with a twenty-three-paragraph letter about "working to improve our relationship" and ran its own ad urging readers to buy from dealers. When GM sued NBC for its *Dateline* episode accusing pickups of fire danger from side-mounted gas tanks, the network settled the same day, publicly apologizing for using incendiary devices to stage the fires. The next day GM suspended all advertising on NBC News programs (it bought $90 million worth of advertising from the network in the first three quarters of 1992), rescinding the ban a day later. A media-buying company executive called this "a slap on NBC's hand to say, You can't just do this and get away scot free."[317]

OTHER PRIVATE CONSTRAINTS

Although the mass media may exercise the most visible private influence on speech, numerous other environments also constrain. North-west Orient Airlines ordered a couple off a flight for cursing—and were promptly sued by the passengers, who had Tourette's syndrome.[318] Downtown hotels, which give guests complimentary copies of *Philadelphia* magazine, refused to distribute it to the 6,300 delegates of the American Society of Travel Agents because the cover story was "The Issue Is Race." The Ritz-Carlton manager did not "think of it as censorship; it was an issue of economics."[319] If book prizes increase sales, Oscars and Grammys have even greater effect on audience size. Milli Vanilli lost their Grammy for *Girl You Know It's True* after admitting they had lip-synched the album. Recent changes in nominating procedures and voting rules will significantly affect outcomes.[320]

Organized sports limit the speech of athletes, owners, even spectators. The medal winners who gave the black power salute on the podium of the 1968 Olympics were summarily suspended and expelled from Mexico. The NBA fines players for taunting. The National League suspended Cincinnati Reds owner Marge Schott for racial abuse. Her Riverfront Stadium expelled an evangelical minister for violating its "good taste–bad taste policy" by displaying a sign saying "John 3:16." After a federal judge invalidated the policy, the ballpark outlawed all signs unrelated to baseball. When the minister returned with a sign saying "Go Reds John 3:16," the stadium prohibited all *non*commercial signs "to protect the family-oriented atmosphere of Riverfront Stadium from detrimental signage," although it continued to advertise cigarettes and beer.[321]

Churches enforce orthodoxy and silence criticism. The Reform Jewish Union of American Hebrew Congregations refused to accept Congregation Beth Adam because it did not explicitly acknowledge God. Church newspapers in nine major Catholic dioceses rejected ads for Andrew Greeley's novel about pedophile priests and battered women. Roger Cardinal Mahony of Los Angeles revoked an invitation to a prochoice university professor and former priest to address the largest Catholic religious education conference. "I will not abide the presence of any speaker at our congress who teaches anything contrary to the full teachings of our Catholic Church." The Vatican has even urged churches to ban secular music.[322] Although courts have invalidated speech codes at public universities, religious universities drastically limit speech. Brigham Young University has a dress code and requires students to salute the American flag whenever it is raised or lowered. It prohibits students and faculty from engaging in speech that "contradicts or opposes, rather than analyzes or discusses" Mormon doctrine. It denied tenure to a psychology professor who spoke at an off-campus abortion rally and an anthropology professor who studied anti-Mormon terrorism in Latin America, and it reprimanded a botany professor for discussing population control. Nyack College in New York fined an English professor for wearing a gay rights button. The New York Catholic Diocese has required schoolteachers to pledge not to "engage in any actions or statements which challenge, protest or interfere with the Mass" or with John Cardinal O'Connor's "rights and obligations as Archbishop of New York."[323]

Although some question whether laws can protect employees against harmful speech in the workplace, no one doubts that *employers* can restrain employee speech. Contracts protect trade secrets by limiting the speech and future employment of present and former employees.[324] Employers retaliate for any disloyalty. During one of the periodic Japan-bashing panics, a suburban Detroit car salesman said on national television: "If America makes a good product, I buy it. If they don't I buy what's good for my money." After denunciations by United Auto Workers members and the Detroit Auto Dealers Association, the dealership fired him, declaring "Truth is not an issue." Ford discharged a test-driver who told a newspaper that his recently purchased Chrysler Ram was "the Cadillac of trucks."[325] The American Israel Political Action Committee fired three top officials: the executive director, who proudly declared he had not been to Brooklyn for nine years and referred to the ultra-Orthodox as "smelly," "Hasids and New York diamond dealers"; the president for boasting about influence in Clinton's cabinet; and the vice president, who condemned Rabin for trading land for peace with Syria and called the Israeli deputy foreign minister a "little slime-ball."[326] Laws protecting whistle-blowers seek to neutralize such private constraints. When a Philip Morris scientist proved the addictiveness of nicotine five years before the surgeon general's report, he was forced to withdraw his article (already accepted for publication), fired, and told to turn off his instruments, kill all lab rats, and turn in his badge the next day. After an American Eagle plane crashed, killing sixty-eight people, the airline suspended an employee who questioned the plane's safety.[327] HMOs restrict what doctors may tell patients about treatment options and financial incentives.[328]

Speakers limit the circulation of their words: who may repeat what to whom and when. New York mayor Rudolph Giuliani and his press secretary allegedly calibrated access and information to the friendliness of journalists. A deputy police commissioner confirmed that "the department was ordered not to cooperate, even on matters of legitimate public interest, with news organizations that had carried unfavorable stories."[329] Gossip, the mother's milk of the entertainment industry, is merciless to those who break the rules of kiss and tell. Hollywood promptly fulfilled the prediction of Julia Phillips's exposé *You'll Never Eat Lunch in This Town Again.* "I've had some occasions where I'm in a club and somebody sees I'm there and leaves. Look, I don't go to Morton's anymore. I don't go to Le Dôme. That's not my life style now." Indeed, Morton's maître d'hôtel would not give her a table for fear of upsetting other patrons.[330] The *Los Angeles Times* reported that a preview audience's negative reaction to the very expensive *Last Action Hero* (reputedly costing $60–$80 million) produced a "heated dispute" at Columbia Pictures—as well as the studio's denial that there had been any screening. A week later it wrote the *Times:* "Columbia Pictures will be out of business with the entire Los Angeles Times editorial staff . . . unless you guarantee that your paper will never again run a story written [by the freelancer] . . . about (or even mentioning) this studio, its executive or its movies." It also threatened to pull all advertising from the *Times* (worth $5 million the previous year) and *New York Newsday* (owned by the parent Times Mirror). "We feel strongly that neither an apology nor a printed letter to the editor nor even a prominently placed retraction will suffice." When the paper refused to capitulate, Columbia backed down.[331]

As chapter 2 described, offended audiences take direct action: feminists against pornography, minorities against racial hatred, Muslims against Rushdie. Protesting sex, profanity, and violence, Rev. Donald Wildmon's American Family Association bought full-page ads in national newspapers declaring "This time TV has gone too far! We are FED UP!" "SHAME! SHAME! SHAME! on These Advertisers," many of which it named. It quoted the *Washington Post, Kansas City Star,* and Ann Landers endorsing pressure on advertisers to change program content. Two years later it used the same strategy against talk shows; Procter & Gamble (the largest daytime television advertiser), Unilever, Sears Roebuck, Kraft, and M&M / Mars stopped buying time. Gov. Mario Cuomo endorsed this as the "purest kind of legitimate commercial persuasion."[332] A decade after a boycott convinced the Florida Citrus Commission to fire spokesperson Anita Bryant for attacking homosexuals, another was launched when the commission hired Rush Limbaugh as publicist.[333] Angered by the stereotyped portrayal of the African American chauffeur in *Driving Miss Daisy,* the Media Image Coalition of Minorities and Women urged advertisers to boycott a 1992 / 93 CBS serial spawned by the highly successful play and movie.[334] When a Cuban American television commentator criticized the "thousands of single [Puerto Rican] mothers, very young, who try to escape poverty through welfare or through new partners who then leave, and leave behind other children to worsen the problem," Puerto Rican groups persuaded the influential Goya Foods to boycott the channel and *El Diario/La Prensa* to end the commentator's column.[335] When Howard Stern said that fans mourning Selena "live in refrigerator boxes . . . like to make love to a goat and . . . dance with velvet paintings and eat beans," the National Hispanic Media Coalition, the Mexican American Legal Defense and Education Fund, and the League of United Latin American Citizens called for a boycott, Acapulco Restaurants and Pizza Hut pulled commercials, and the Houston City Council asked Warner Cable to drop Stern's E! network.[336] American Jews and Israelis have shunned Vanessa Redgrave for supporting Palestinians; Europeans have boycotted Benetton outlets for exploiting AIDS for commercial purposes; advertisers in a South Carolina resort boycotted the local newspaper for exposing beach erosion. When Sínead O'Connor tore up the pope's picture on *Saturday Night Live*, the Notre Dame student union implicitly threatened to pull the football team's games off the network. NBC quickly declared: "[I]t goes without saying that [the network] does not condone something like that."[337]

Unlike economic pressure, violence and threats are illegal; but they can be very effective—as we saw with respect to Salman Rushdie. Reporters are attacked and killed throughout the world, even in the United States.[338] Violence can compel speech as well as silence. The Unabomber convinced the *New York Times* and the *Washington Post* to print his 35,000-word manifesto.[339] Although courts have rejected the "heckler's veto," the antiabortion movement has used it extensively. The landlord of the only abortion clinic on Manhattan's Upper West Side offered to renew its lease only if it promised not to advertise without consent, disclose its address, or engage in any practices "which result in picketing or public demonstrations."[340] The Ohio transportation department refused to allow the Ku Klux Klan to adopt a highway for fear its billboards would "attract vandalism, including people dumping trash to make the klan pick it up."[341]

THE NECESSITY FOR CHOICE

That phrase encapsulates the message of this chapter. Although speech has profound value, it can never be *free*. Expression is always subject to constraints, public and private. The numerous examples above document the inevitability of prudential judgments weighing the value of speech in a particular context against the multitude of countervailing considerations. Proof that constraint was justified in a single instance, however, would refute the civil libertarian position. If *any* control is necessary or desirable, then *each* restriction must be evaluated individually. I certainly do not endorse all the constraints enumerated above. Yet that is the point: the balance is difficult to strike; judgments vary among people and across time and place; they must be concrete. But they cannot be avoided.

Government regulates speech in myriad ways while constantly re-drawing the lines between protected political opinion and criminal threat, legitimate criticism or gossip and unacceptable harm to reputation and privacy. American exceptionalism notwithstanding, countries without a First Amendment are differently free, not unfree. I can repeat the most damaging statements, for instance, in discussing whether they should be permitted. Judgments about the acceptability of hate speech and sexually explicit or violent representations are culturally specific and highly mutable. The broad consensus that commercial speech can be regulated more extensively than noncommercial conceals the am-biguous, mutable, and ultimately arbitrary distinctions between them. All agree on the need for time, place, and manner restrictions, but these merge imperceptibly into suppression. Taxation, rate setting, and anti-trust law affect cost and availability. Government compels more speech than it prohibits. Speakers modify or curtail statements in anticipation of government regulation and civil liability; the media develop and enforce rating systems that facilitate censorship by others. Speech is particularly constrained, paradoxically, in the very arenas where free-dom might be thought most essential: courts, legislatures, and the exec-utive. Such restraints are justified in the name of truth, justice, democ-racy, authority, and simple courtesy. Politicians may have an absolute freedom to defame private individuals on the floor of the legislature—but they cannot insult each other. Even those who assail "political cor-rectness" observe compulsory standards of civility. Although resis-tance to state abuse is a core element of First Amendment theory, its protection is least available where such abuse is most likely—in schools, prisons, and the military. Free speech enthusiasts who seek to minimize these regulations still must decide which ones are acceptable. Much state action that might not survive judicial scrutiny remains un-challenged because of ignorance, apathy, uncertainty, or cost.

Even a civil libertarian who took a principled (if untenable) stance against all such regulation would confront the paradox that govern-ment action is necessary to facilitate speech. The state creates Holmes's "marketplace of ideas," as it does all markets. Even more than tangi-bles, which can be physically possessed, intellectual property is con-structed and protected by law. Every detail of copyright, patent, and trademark reflects political compromise. Technological innovation con-stantly forces government to revise these judgments. The laws of prop-erty, contract, and tort allow private individuals to mobilize state power over speech.

Some civil libertarians extend the proscription against viewpoint discrimination from state action constraining private speech to the state as speaker. Former education secretary William Bennett declared that government had no business putting "its official stamp of approval, its imprimatur, on any particular work of art or scholarship." House Speaker Newt Gingrich proclaimed: "There is no place in the constitution that says taxpayers must subsidize the weirdest things you can imagine." House majority leader Dick Armey asserted: "[T]here is no constitutional authority" for the NEA. But insistence on pure viewpoint neutrality would require destroying every government building and public statue, abolishing every holiday and parade, eliminating the inauguration, recalling all stamps and coins, and defunding all museums, universities, and research. What critics presumably mean is that greater public investment (emotional as well as material) and more visible action require broader consensus in the values affirmed. Exactly: but that means difficult, nuanced judgments, not a retreat into absolutes. Former NEH chair Lynne V. Cheney said government should support "truth" and "beauty" rather than politics. But it is impossible to speak without expressing particular values; even scientific research provokes partisan response. Those who work for or are supported by government must speak within a complex web of laws and mores. (Gingrich appeared to acknowledge this when he withdrew his appointment of the House historian, who appeared to place Nazis and Jewish Holocaust victims on the same footing.)

The obverse of the civil libertarian insistence on government abstention as regulator and speaker is the promise of freedom in the private sphere. But private action shapes speech far more pervasively and powerfully than public regulation. Indeed, state intervention may be necessary to restrain or counterbalance private influence. Our ambivalence toward lawyers and lobbyists, campaign contributions, notables who sell their names or likenesses, advertising agencies, even actors reflects the conviction that speech, like love, should be authentic, unpaid. A Cyrano de Bergerac who woos on behalf of another is both comic and tragic. Judas's betrayal was far worse for having been bought with thirty pieces of silver. We feel so strongly that market incentives contaminate speech that we regulate payments to lawyers, politicians, doctors, researchers, and journalists. The fall of communism has replaced Big Brother with the market's invisible hand, which a Russian writers' group called "the grave of culture . . . privatization of the soul."

Fiercely defending personal autonomy, civil libertarians conceptualize speech as the action of an atomistic individual. But only the most narcissistic speak just to hear their own voices. The price of absolute freedom here, as in all social life, is marginality. Speakers accept far greater restraints as employees than as political subjects. The size of the audience reached varies directly with the degree of social cooperation necessary. Every participant in the collective process of creation, production, and dissemination pursues divergent goals; all feel implicated by the message conveyed and thus entitled to shape its content. The studio mogul obsessed with the bottom line is no caricature; the capital investment required to reach a mass audience makes such financial considerations paramount. Sponsors wish to avoid offense. Bookstores, computer networks, universities, and foundations impose ideological tests; journals pander to advertisers and donors. Newspapers enforce ethical rules. Despite idealizations of starving romantic artists authentically baring their souls—*ars gratia artis,* and the public be damned— everyone wants to be heard, and preferably appreciated. Myriad environments impose their own orthodoxy: churches obviously, but also transportation, hotels, universities, sports teams, and employers. Speakers may deny access; audiences may refuse to attend; opponents may organize economic sanctions and seek to escalate the price of speech through a heckler's veto.

Context constrains, but solipsistic speech is oxymoronic. Communication requires conventions and cooperation. Regulation is pervasive, indeed constitutive, not exceptional and suspect. Because each constraint raises unique moral issues, there can be no general theory of free speech, least of all a blanket anathema against state influence. The value of speech must be weighed against all others—including the harms to collective status exemplified by pornography, racial hatred, and blasphemy. I return to that weighing in the final chapter.

CHAPTER SIX

••

The Excesses of State Regulation

There is growing enthusiasm for state regulation of pornography, hate speech, blasphemy, media violence, and advertising of harmful products. Although I see these as real and serious evils, I believe government intervention is often misguided: always costly, usually ineffective, and sometimes counterproductive.[1] Law inescapably dichotomizes reality, rupturing subtleties of meaning with arbitrary boundaries that are always over- and underinclusive. By forcing complex, nuanced events into pigeonholes, law strips them of context and history. Law cannot deal with the irreducible ambiguity of symbolic expression. Art plays with ambiguity; yet art's distinctive qualities elude legal definition. The harmfulness and moral content of speech vary with speaker identity and motive, audience response, and relationship between them; yet law inadequately accounts for such variables. The liberal state can exercise power only through formal law, which is costly and slow and fetishizes procedure. The severity of state sanctions can only be justified by consequentialist claims—punishing speech for actions it allegedly provokes. Yet consequentialism rarely is empirically substantiated, and if we really were concerned with the purported consequences, we would have to address other, more powerful causes. State regulation, finally, is often perverse: encouraging evasion, constructing deviance, valorizing evil, attracting attention, generating sympathy, even conferring martyrdom.

AN UNHAPPY HISTORY OF REGULATION

The British experience of regulating racial hatred is deeply discouraging.[2] In 1947 James Caunt wrote in his newspaper rejoicing

> that only a handful of Jews bespoil the population of the Borough!
> . . . If British Jewry is suffering today from the righteous wrath of
> British citizens, then they have only themselves to blame for their pas-

sive inactivity. Violence may be the only way to bring them to the sense of their responsibility to the country in which they live.

A jury took just thirteen minutes to acquit him of seditious libel.

Opening debate on what became the 1965 Race Relations Act, the Labor home secretary exposed the fundamental obstacle to state regulation.

> [C]riticism should be allowed, however jaundiced and one-sided it may be. . . . Nobody can be prevented from arguing, for example, that particular groups should be returned to their country of origin because their presence in this country causes an excessive strain on our social services. What is prohibited . . . is the intentional fomentation of hatred of that group, as a group, because of the origin of its members by public abuse, however camouflaged as motivated by a sincere intention dishonestly simulated, to promote discussion of the public interest.[3]

Fascists immediately exploited a statutory loophole by establishing a book club "for the study of literature dealing with the Jewish Question and other racial problems."

The first prosecution was directed at a seventeen-year-old who stuck a "Blacks not wanted here" leaflet on an MP's door and threw another through his window wrapped in a beer bottle. A court held this was not "publication or distribution." An appellate court reversed the conviction of Colin Jordan after a jury rejected his claim that a pamphlet entitled "The Coloured Invasion" was just informing the public about a grave national problem.[4] There were almost as many convictions of black-power advocates as white racists, while the more sophisticated among the latter evaded punishment. When the Racial Preservation Society was acquitted after denouncing the "dangers of race mixing," speculating about genetic differences, and urging repatriation as a "humane solution" to immigration, it celebrated by reprinting a "Souvenir Edition" of its *Southern News*, defiantly captioned "The Paper the Government Tried to Suppress."

British National Party chairman John Kingsley Read harangued a crowd of 300: "Fellow racialists . . . I have been told I cannot refer to coloured immigrants. So you can forgive me if I refer to niggers, wogs and coons. Last week in Southall, one nigger stabbed another nigger [to death]. One down and a million to go." On retrial after a hung jury, Read insisted his epithets were a "jocular aside" and the numbers referred to immigration, not murder. Judge McKinon told the jury his public school nickname had been "Nigger"; another old boy, a maharajah, had greeted him by that endearment during a chance encounter years later. He told the jury that the law

> does not contemplate reasoned argument directed to stemming the flow of immigration, or even advocating the repatriation of people who have come here from abroad. . . . It is claimed that jobs will be lost, that, goodness knows, we have a million and a half or more un-employed already and that all the immigrants are going to do is to occupy the jobs that are needed by our local population. These are matters upon which people are entitled to hold and to declare strong views expressed in moderate terms. . . . Were these words threaten-ing? abusive? insulting? . . . There is no charge known to the law of insulting the dead. . . . Is there anything that is pointed to that indi-cates that he was urging action activated by hatred? . . . He is obvi-ously a man who has had the guts to come forward in the past and stand up in public for the things that he believes in.

After the compliant jury took just ten minutes to return a not guilty verdict, McKinon told Read: "You have been rightly acquitted but in these days and in these times it would be well if you were careful to use moderate language. By all means propagate the views you may have but try to avoid involving the sort of action which has been taken against you. I wish you well."

Troubled that racists had learned to evade the act by "disclaim[ing] any intention of stirring up racial hatred, and . . . purport[ing] to make contribution to public education and debate," the government amended it to eliminate specific intent.[5] The next prosecution should have been easy even under the old law. Two British Movement mem-bers had ranted in public about "wogs, coons, niggers, black bastards." "It was shocking that white nurses should have to shave the lice ridden hair of these people . . . wiping froth off a coon's mouth and, as a result, dying of rabies. That is what these black bastards are doing to us." The defense chose the desperate tactic of arguing that these views were so extreme that "what was stirred up more than anything was sympathy for the coloured people." An all-white jury acquitted under the act, though it convicted one accused of breach of the peace. Imposing a six-month suspended sentence, the judge cautioned: "You have got to learn to curb what you say. It is not a question of preventing people from expressing their proper opinions but there is a way in which it can be properly expressed."[6]

Although juries convicted fifteen of the first twenty-one prosecuted under the amended law, the sentences were small fines and short prison terms, usually suspended. Attorney General Samuel Silkin QC declined to prosecute when "enforcement will lead inevitably to law breaking on a scale out of all proportion to that which is being penalised or to consequences so unfair or so harmful as heavily to outweigh the harm done by the breach itself."[7] He refused to charge the British Resistance Movement for a leaflet entitled "Jews Bomb Themselves," mocking the 1980 terrorist attack on a Paris synagogue: "It is an old trick of the Jews to blow up their own synagogue, machine gun their school buildings and desecrate their cemeteries and daub them with swastikas." Nor would he proceed against a National Front member who published a book of photographs with captions like "Asian thugs," "Black Savages," "Ape-Rape—the wrong one is behind bars," "I'm a death camp survivor. I was nearly exterminated 5, no six million times in my life." Even when the language clearly met statutory requirements, he would not act if the only audience was the victims themselves.

The Home Affairs Committee rejected a proposal to forbid words exposing any racial group to "hatred, ridicule or contempt" for fear that "an increase in the rate of successful prosecutions . . . might create the impression among the public that the sensibilities of ethnic minorities were being protected in a manner not extended to other groups in society."[8] A contemporaneous government policy paper agreed that punishing opinions "would be totally inconsistent with a democratic society in which—provided the manner of expression, and the circumstances, do not provoke unacceptable consequences—political proposals, however odious and undesirable, can be freely advocated."[9]

This dismal record illustrates many of the problems inherent in state regulation. It focused on extremes, implicitly condoning the myriad harms of quotidian discourse. Style was more important than content. Legal formalism equated black resistance with white racism. The law took account of audience only to exculpate hate speech directed at unsympathetic listeners or targets. The ambiguity of speech facilitated evasion. The boundary between legitimate political debate and forbidden vituperation was arbitrary. Although motive can be decisive, difficulties of proof led the government to dispense with intent. Juries and judges felt penalties were excessive. Prosecution further disseminated hate speech, generated sympathy for the accused and resentment of their victims, and left racists unrepentant.

DICHOTOMIZING CONTINUA

REGULATORY WRONGS

From the perspective of hindsight, censorship is almost always embarrassing.[10] The Salon banned Manet's *Execution of Maximilian* as too political and his *Déjeuner sur l'Herbe* as pornographic. Théophile Gautier said Manet's *Olympia* "can be understood from no point of view, even if you take it for what it is, a puny model, stretched on a sheet. . . . Here there is nothing, we are sorry to say, but the desire to attract attention at any price." The Salon des Refusés, which Napoleon created for Manet, Pissarro, Whistler, Fantin-Latour, and Cézanne, quickly attracted far greater interest.[11] Italians booed off stage the 1904 premiere of Puccini's *Madama Butterfly*, objecting to the Japanese folk elements and the clash between East and West. Nijinsky was barred from dancing *Giselle* in 1911 for refusing to wear floppy shorts over his tights. Reviling expressionism, the Nazis launched their own House of German Art. The 1937 "Entartete Kunst" exhibit in Munich labeled paintings "Insults to German Womanhood" and "Nature as Seen by Sick Minds." Hitler, who prided himself on his painting, called for the imprisonment of artists who continued the "practice of prehistoric art stutterings." Stalin criticized music, terrorizing composers like Shostakovich.[12] New York banned Sholem Asch's play *God of Vengeance* in 1923 and others for sexual "degeneracy" or "perversion" in 1927. Joseph Moncure March's novel *The Wild Party*, banned in Boston in 1928, was not published fully until 1995; Ernest Hemingway's novel *The Garden of Eden* appeared only in 1986.[13] Edward Kienholz's *Back Seat Dodge '38* disclosed a sculpted couple necking in the back seat. When the Los Angeles County Museum of Art displayed it in 1966, county supervisors denounced it as "revolting," "blasphemous," "dastardly," and "way beyond the limits of public decency," threatening to terminate support until the museum closed the car door, opening it only to patrons who asked. Thirty years later Union Station briefly covered a mural on "human locomotion" reproducing Eadweard Muybridge's photographs of a nude man running.[14]

There is no need to look to other times or places, however. Contemporary America offers ample instances of regulatory absurdity. The immediate provocation for the 1968 MPAA film-rating system was the word "screw" in *Who's Afraid of Virginia Woolf?* and brief shots of breasts in *Blow-Up*.[15] Television critics tabulate violent acts per hour—including thirty-eight in *The Three Stooges*, twenty-two on *World News Tonight*, and untold numbers in reruns of Alec Guinness's *Kind Hearts and Coronets* and *The Ladykillers*. The 1994 annual Day of TV Violence survey found a 41 percent increase in incidents—but included news reports.[16] Like several Muslim nations, schools in West Virginia and Wisconsin banned *Schindler's List* for its R rating; a California school fired a teacher for showing *Dead Poets Society* (about a teacher fired for introducing students to literature). Although *Six Degrees of Separation* won drama awards in New York and London, Dallas police charged a theater production with operating a sexually oriented business without a license because the protagonist is found in bed with another man. Two weeks later the MPAA forced MGM to edit its trailer for the PG-13 rated film version because a reproduction of Michelangelo's *Creation of Adam* showed the first man's genitals. MPAA president Jack Valenti was chagrined: "I would have overturned this in a New York minute. I know St. Peter's and the Sistine Chapel [which is not in St Peter's]." "Some of our people are going by the book. It says 'no nudity.' Michelangelo must not be in the book." Unfortunately, he was in the church's: most of the nude figures had been painted over by the papacy centuries earlier.[17]

The mass media are not the only target. Commissioned by Brookline, Massachusetts, an artist designed crosswalk signals showing a mother protecting a child; although both were nude, the mother's genitals were not visible, and the child's sex was indeterminate. Challenged to explain it, the artist replied facetiously: "Hang on to your kid and take your clothes off." A nearby liquor-store owner pontificated: "There's a time and place for everything." After eighty complaints the village removed the work, while denying it had succumbed to pressure. Holocaust survivors protested what they saw as swastikas on a wrought-iron fence, two of which were vandalized; but the Buddhist temple noted that this had been their symbol of peace for millennia. A rural Illinois town prohibited the Star of David (which allegedly honored a dead gang leader), and the local jeweler stopped selling infant earrings when a teenager said the crucifix resembled a gang symbol.[18]

BOUNDING THE AMORPHOUS

Every attempt to trap speech within legal categories is fatally flawed.[19] Gloria Steinem, whom we earlier encountered equating *Playboy* with *Mein Kampf*, sought to echo Holmes by declaring a "clear and present difference" between pornography and erotica.

> [A]ny photo or film of people making love; really making love . . . [displays] a sensuality and touch and warmth, an acceptance of bodies and nerve endings. There is always a spontaneous sense of people who are there because they want to be, out of shared pleasure. Now look at any depiction of sex in which there is clear force, or an unequal power that spells coercion. It may be very blatant, with weapons of torture or bondage, wounds and bruises, some clear humiliation, or an adult's sexual power being used over a child. It may be much more

subtle: a physical attitude of conqueror and victim, the use of race or class to imply the same thing, perhaps a very unequal nudity, with one person exposed and vulnerable while the other is clothed.[20]

Would these criteria differentiate instructional or safe-sex videos from porn? Male porn from porn for couples (like the films of Candida Royale) or women (the film *Erotique* or magazines like *Ludus, Bite, For Women, Women on Top,* and *Women Only,* some of which address an S/M audience)? Porn from *Naked Killer,* which spoofs Hong Kong action films by showing sexy lesbian avengers using Kung Fu to castrate, mutilate, and kill?[21] How would Steinem categorize Giovanni Bologna's statue *The Rape of the Sabines,* Bernini's sculpture *Apollo and Daphne,* or the innumerable other representations of Greek and Roman myths? Hieronymus Bosch's fantasies? Shakespeare's *Taming of the Shrew* or its musical version *Kiss Me Kate?* Would she agree with the Salon in banning Manet's *Déjeuner sur l'Herbe?* What about Cézanne's *Battle of Love,* Delacroix's *Massacre at Chios* or *Death of Sardanapalus,* René Magritte's *Menaced Assassin* (the suspect stands listening to a record next to a murdered naked woman), Balthus's *The Street* (implying sexual harassment of a white girl by a black boy), or André Derain's *Balthus* (an old man in a bathrobe watching a partly dressed young girl)? How would she view Picasso's paintings in light of his numerous sexual conquests? Would she see *Les Demoiselles d'Avignon* differently, knowing he painted it after his mistress, Fernande Olivier, had left with the thirteen-year-old girl they had adopted, to whom Picasso was sexually attracted?[22]

Catharine MacKinnon would prohibit expression depicting the sexually explicit subordination of women. This, too, disregards both creative intent and audience response. It would seem to sweep up Hamlet's treatment of Ophelia and Othello's of Desdemona, Bizet's *Carmen,* Tolstoi's *Anna Karenina,* Hardy's *Tess of the d'Urbervilles* and *Jude the Obscure,* and Bergman's *Virgin Spring.* It might cover Philip Carey's pursuit of Mildred Rodgers in *Of Human Bondage* but not Emma Bovary's of Rudolphe. Bruno Bettelheim argued that fairy tales fascinate and satisfy children precisely because they express the profound ambivalence of human emotions.[23] An amicus curiae brief for the plaintiffs in the Indianapolis case argued the ordinance would proscribe *Last Tango in Paris,* John Updike's *Witches of Eastwick,* and Anaïs Nin's *Other Side of Midnight.*[24] After the Canadian Supreme Court adopted MacKinnon's approach, the government successfully prosecuted a Toronto gay and lesbian bookstore for stocking the S/M magazine *Bad Attitude* but tolerated Madonna's *Sex.* Her publisher's lawyer explained: "[Y]ou can't show 'double penetration' and you can't show ejaculation on the face of a woman. Apparently, it's O.K. to show it on her neck." A photograph of Madonna bound and kneeling in a see-through leotard while a woman pressed a switchblade to her crotch showed "no penetration . . . so we say it's not obscene because there's no sex." Another, where she was dressed as a schoolgirl, held by one thug while another pushed up her skirt and pulled down her underpants, was "sort of a rape scene. . . . But since there was no penetration we could say it was just violence, no sex." The largest pornography chain in North America (and perhaps the world) was acquitted of selling five titles with spanking but convicted for another three in which the judge found "the spanking went beyond playfulness and there was a reddening of the buttocks."[25]

MacKinnon's ordinance might have banned Newt Gingrich's novel *1945*, in which the "beautiful and so very exotic mistress" panted, purred, and hissed while he "stirred at the movement of her fingers, which were no longer on his chest." Jennifer Montgomery's film *Art for Teachers of Children* recounts her affair at fourteen with a married teacher, who took nude photographs of her. (Had the teacher read *The Prime of Miss Jean Brodie*? If so, would MacKinnon's ordinance have given Montgomery a civil claim against Muriel Spark?) The film combines criticism of the seduction with Montgomery's growing awareness of her sexual power. Would MacKinnon accept *New York Times* reviewer Janet Maslin's conclusion that the writer-director's "feminist vantage point allows her to film near-pornographic scenes with careful detachment." How would MacKinnon deal with a recent Paris exhibition of sexuality in twentieth-century art, including Robert Morris's textiles folded to resemble vaginas, Kiki Smith's *Uro-Genital System*, Zoe Leonard's photograph of a naked bearded transsexual, Man Ray's close-ups of sexual intercourse, Hans Bellmer's of a naked woman tightly wrapped in string, and Sue Williams's sculpture of a battered woman covered with denunciations of domestic violence? What about *National Geographic*'s partly nude women, whose photos have titillated generations of boys?[26]

Attempts to circumscribe hate speech are less satisfactory, if anything. Mari Matsuda would punish a speaker who directs a persecutorial, hateful, and degrading message of racial inferiority against a historically oppressed group.[27] But her loopholes virtually give away the game. The exception for scientific arguments would condone the racism of Carleton S. Coon, H. J. Eysenck, A. R. Jensen, Richard Herrnstein, William B. Shockley, Seymour Itzkoff, Philippe Rushton, both CUNY professors (see chapter 4), and Michael Bradley's *Iceman*

Inheritance, which attributes the viciousness of whites (of whom Jews are the "purest" example) to their direct descent from brutish Neanderthals.[28] Her tolerance for satire could protect the deliberate nastiness of Andrew Dice Clay, Jackie Mason, or shock jocks like Rush Limbaugh and Howard Stern.[29] Her exception for museums might permit a neo-Nazi display of Hitler memorabilia or the KKK trophies that Long Island firehouses showcased as late as 1992. How would she deal with *Mein Kampf?* Schocken Books refused a Hebrew translation: "[W]e suffered too much as a result of this man and this book, and should not perpetuate his ideas." Yad Vashem also found it "still emotionally difficult." But the translator, an Austrian Jew whose parents were murdered by the Nazis, persisted: "It's a sad episode but a historical fact, and the younger generations must know what really happened and why."[30]

EXEMPTING ART

Rushdie idolizes art; Matsuda excepts it; but MacKinnon resists art's claims. So did black critics of William Styron's *Confessions of Nat Turner* and feminists incensed by Bret Easton Ellis's *American Psycho.* Does the greatness of *Huckleberry Finn* outweigh the offense many African Americans take at the portrayal of "Nigger Jim"? What about lesser works, which reflect but do not transcend contemporary prejudice, like Booth Tarkington's Penrod stories? When National Political Congress of Black Women head DeLores Tucker attacked rap for propagating "derogatory negative stereotypical images," Rep. Maxine Waters (D-Calif.), also African American, called it their children's "new art form to describe their pains, fears and frustrations with us adults. . . . These songs merely mimic and exaggerate what the artists have learned about who we are." African American cultural critics have pointed to ironic black traditions of bathos, signifying, and lewdness. But *New York Times* columnist Brent Staples has condemned rap as an "uncritical mirror," which "'plays' at rape and murder in a way that celebrates them."[31]

The publisher of *Juliette* claimed that the Marquis de Sade's "works are considered by many academics and students of history, literature and philosophy to address serious issues of personal liberty and freedom of expression."[32] Such tautology justifies all transgression. Filmmakers decorate pornography with the trappings of art by hiring reputable scriptwriters and directors, adding plot and character, attending to "production values," and seeking historical verisimilitude. "The Naughty Nude" at a SoHo gallery offered "some helpful hints" to photographers. "[S]oft focus is probably art. . . . Abstract design is one good clue; solemn expression is another. Anonymity is a useful indicator; headless torsos qualify by staking a claim to Greek classicism and even averted faces will do."[33]

Art defies definition. When a sculptor commissioned by Hartford, Connecticut, dumped boulders in the town square, the mayor and citizens protested it was not art. Los Angeles bans signs visible from freeways unless they are art. But though the Cultural Affairs Department excepted a fifty-foot Jeep Wrangler mural, the Department of Buildings and Safety decided it was commercial. How would Matsuda classify performances by the Art Guys of Houston: walking through town with leaf blowers, working twenty-four hours at a Stop 'n' Go convenience store, celebrating the summer solstice by spending twenty-four hours at Denny's, or "Driving Two Cars to Galveston" by jointly driving each one a few hundred feet and then going back for the other?[34]

Art's essential ambiguity renders meaning indeterminate. Leonard Freed declared: "The more ambiguous the photograph is, the better it is. Otherwise it would be propaganda." John Gardner agreed: "Morality is infinitely complex, too complex to be *knowable*, and far too complex to be reduced to any code, which is why it is suitable matter for fiction, which deals in understanding, not knowledge." David Levinthal's *Mein Kampf* amply met this criterion: unfocused photographs of dolls showing two guards in swastikas before a row of naked women. So did Thomas Eakins's nude photographs of himself and his male and female students and Diane Arbus's of freaks and the mentally retarded.[35] Intolerance of ambiguity is agitprop in producers and philistinism in critics. The American Life League demanded that Walt Disney recall *Lion King* videos when a four-year-old claimed to have seen sexual activity in the clouds. A Stasi officer berated East German writer Lutz Rathenow: "I forbid you to write poems with double meanings! Also poems with triple meanings! We have experts who can decipher everything!"[36]

Sally Mann's photographs appear to show her children poor and abused. But the seven-, ten- and twelve-year-olds claim to enjoy posing nude, vetoing poses selectively. "They don't want to be geeks or dweebs," their mother said, but "nudity doesn't bother them." "I don't think of my children, and I don't think anyone else should think of them, with any sexual thoughts." And a legal expert insisted: "[T]here isn't the slightest question that what she's doing is art." But religious conservatives have sought to close her shows, and a federal prosecutor urged her not to exhibit some of the photos. *New Yorker* writer Janet Malcolm described a photo cropped at chest and knees showing the

twelve-year-old in tight shorts and T-shirt. "Its transfixing feature—
you could almost call it its 'face'—is the girl's vulva, which plumply
strains against the soft stretch fabric of the shorts." Malcolm concluded,
however, that the collection's "ambiguity . . . allows the family to escape with its secrets." "To look at Sally Mann's photographs of her
children as unfeeling or immoral is simply not to be looking at them
. . . and demanding a cliche." But the *New York Times* critic warned
that "many people regard photographs of naked children as inherently
exploitative and even pornographic . . . and will object to her using
children to act out the fantasies, some of them sexual, that are central"
to her vision of childhood.[37]

Less famous photographers have greater difficulty clothing their
work in art's mantle. In fulfillment of an International Center of Pho-
tography assignment to take photos "as you have never seen yourself
before," Ijlat Feuer, a forty-five-year-old father of three, married eighteen years, took nude pictures on a glass-topped table, first of himself
and then, while his wife watched, of his daughter. He was sufficiently
unconcerned to have them developed commercially and show them
to his classmates, many of whom had taken similar pictures. But the
processor informed the police because "they were not normal . . . not
typical pictures of a young child with bubbles around them." Feuer
was jailed and released on condition that he have no further contact
with his daughter. The court-ordered therapist said he had showed
poor judgment "in today's cultural climate." Although Feuer's expert
called the photos "hasty, affectionate, amused, playful," the prosecutor
said they were "graphically explicit; spread-eagle comes to mind," and
the judge found that "the focal point of the visual depiction is on the
child's genitalia." Michigan police investigated two college professors
who, eighteen years after taking it, enlarged a photograph of their five-
year-old son getting out of a bath. The U.S. Postal Inspection Service
asked: "[I]s the purpose to incite lust in the viewer? Is the focal point
of the picture on the genitals?" The president of the National Law Center for Children and Families, which assists pornography prosecutions,
declared: "I wouldn't take a picture of my child naked. If I did, I would
not take a picture of the kid's genitals. You can take pictures of the
face, arms, legs, buttocks."[38]

Although sexuality poses unique problems for art, even common-
place objects can resist interpretation. J. S. G. Boggs, a fellow in art and
ethics at Carnegie Mellon University, paints paper money, replacing
"Washington, D.C." with "Pittsburgh, Pa," substituting his signature
for the treasurer's, and labeling the product "The Unit of State of Bohe-
mia." He earned about $250,000 in eight years by "spending" these

bills in performance art and selling the receipts to collectors, who buy back the "originals." After an English jury acquitted him of counterfeiting, he paid his lawyer in his own currency. The U.S. Secret Service seized some of his work after he publicly announced a project of printing a million dollars; they also confiscated a thousand pairs of underwear silk-screened with images of $100 bills by another artist. The U.S. Postal Service decided not to take action against anarchists who printed stamps commemorating Abbie Hoffman, Amy Fisher, Tonya Harding, and Charles Bukowski but planned to charge postage due if they were used for mailing.[39]

Political protesters manipulate ambiguity to provoke while escaping punishment. After the riots following the acquittal of police who had beaten Rodney King, Robbie Conal plastered Los Angeles with a poster showing a burning police baton and the caption "DisARM." Michael Antonovich, a conservative county supervisor, condemned it for "glorifying violence." Conal retorted that the poster did "exactly the opposite . . . it was a call for peace and humane law enforcement." Necessity made communist dissidents masters of double entendre. Beijing Experimental Drama Troupe actors repeated "wo ai [I love] Tian An Men," accelerating so that "wo ai" became "why." A Chinese Performance Company production of Goethe's classic clearly made Faust refer to Deng Xiaoping.[40]

Art not only demands ambiguity; it also startles, shocks, and offends, seeking novelty and heightened effect "pour épater les bourgeois."[41] Pornography was revolutionary in ancien régime France. John Gardner acutely captured this impulse.

> The man who blows up grand pianos is howled at from every side "Fraud! Not art!" but what counts is that the crowd is there to howl. . . . They experience a shock of terrible metaphor—"Grand pianos are in my way, the whole tradition is in my way, and *you* are in my way: I can say nothing, do nothing, affirm nothing because of the piano's intolerable high-tone creamy plinking, which you fools adore; I will therefore destroy them, I will destroy you all!"

Resisting the moral panic about child pornography, Marjorie Garber noted that

> the high and pop culture of the 1990's flirts with the most forbidden of all topics, the borderline between adult and child. Transgression and erotic borderlines have long been powerful motives for fantasy in literature and art, as they are in advertising. Museums are filled with images of naked cherubs and mischievous putti.[42]

There is no shortage of examples, from the Salon des Refusés through Dada to the latest performance artist. In 1961 the Italian artist Piero Manzoni produced twenty-nine small cans labeled "the artist's shit"; three decades later Gilbert and George photographed themselves naked with their bodily wastes. In 1971 a British court found the *Oz* School Kids Issue obscene for featuring a naked Rupert Bear having sex with a gigantic Gypsy Granny. Two decades after that, Karen Finley invited viewers to drink red wine and spit on the American and British flags at the Newcastle festival, and former prostitute Annie Sprinkle performed *Sluts and Goddesses* by stripping, douching, displaying her vagina, and gagging on a row of rubber phalluses. Commissioned to produce a centerpiece for the new National Museum of Catalan Art, the region's greatest artist sculpted a sixty-foot sock with a hole in the heel. Antoni Tapies refused to explain his creation: "I have always felt that works of art are like delicate flowers; the more you handle them, the more they are harmed. . . . I wonder how far I would have gone if I had submitted each one [of my 7,000 works] to a referendum." Robert Mapplethorpe's photographs show a man urinating into another's mouth, a man up to his elbow in another's anus, Mr. 10½ displaying his penis on a table, a man grabbing the testicles of another suspended upside down, and *Man in a Polyester Suit* with his penis hanging out of his fly. Andres Serrano painted *Piss Christ* (a crucifix submerged in the artist's urine), *Stigmata* (a nude female with white leather cuffs and bloodied hands), *Cabeza de Vaca* (a calf's head on a pedestal and pun on the name of a fifteenth-century conquistador), and *Heaven and Hell* (a cardinal turned away from a bloody nude woman with bound hands and head flung back). "You can't have the sacred without the profane," he insisted (sounding like Rushdie). "I wouldn't be so obsessed with Christianity if I didn't have a feeling for it, and I find it strange when people call me an anti-Christian bigot." He photographed *Ejaculate in Trajectory*, the *Red River* series (close-ups of used sanitary napkins), and *Morgue*. "Pathological clinical studies are far more gruesome than what I was doing." The physician F. Gonzalez-Crussi substantiated that with his photographs of skulls, bottled fetuses, and skeletons. In the United States, Bruce Nauman displays butchered coyote and deer reassembled; in Britain, Damien Hirst suspends a shark, a bisected cow, and a lamb in formaldehyde.[43]

Other arts exhibit similar motives and success. The literary tradition that includes Rabelais, the Marquis de Sade, Baudelaire, Céline, Joyce, Lawrence, and Henry Miller has numerous contemporary imitators, like Nicholson Baker on phone sex and sexual harassment, or Bret Easton Ellis, who defended his obsession with violence by claiming that "the theme of my fiction is the abuse of . . . freedom." Robert Baker, whose kamikaze hero's motto is "If I get AIDS, I'm going to take some-one with me," describes beheading Barbara Bush with a chainsaw, gut-ting Catholic bishops, and burning conservatives. "Even the most radi-cal ideas in art aren't enough," said the author, because "the wrong people are dying." Howard Stern's *Private Parts* was the fastest-selling book in Simon & Schuster's history—225,000 in hours, a million in two weeks, at the top of *Publisher's Weekly* and the *New York Times* best-seller lists.[44]

Elvis was not the first pop musician to exploit outrage, and rap will not be the last. At an AIDS benefit after he died of the disease, the leader of the pop group Queen appeared in a video dressed in royal crown and cape, singing "God Save the Queen." The lead of Porno for Pyros sings about masturbating while watching the Los Angeles riots on television. Mexican soap opera actress Gloria Trevi jams the micro-phone in her crotch and sprays Coca-Cola at her groin while talking and singing dirty words.[45] Even classical music seeks to wake up listen-ers. Deborah Warner distracted Glyndebourne audiences from their Fortnum & Mason picnic hampers and formal dress by having Don Giovanni treat a cemetery Madonna as one of his conquests. The direc-tor insisted: "The desecration of a religious place is fundamental to the opera." Peter Greenaway's opera *Rosa* lived up to his cinematic reputation. In an abattoir, whose workers wear only bloodstained white aprons, Esmeralda, nude through much of the opera, seeks to attract her fiancé's attention by painting herself black to impersonate the mare that obsesses him. After his murder she marries his corpse, enters the disemboweled body of his horse, and expires in flames. Greenaway claimed to be employing "the new vocabulary of the streets and cinema," and his composer called it all "very intellectual, very symbolic." *Der Spiegel* praised this "timely kick to the genre," and the entire Amsterdam run was sold out.[46]

Theater also must engage a public accustomed to being shocked. Ron Athey, an HIV-positive gay former heroin addict, stuck twenty hypodermic needles into his arm and knitting needles into his forehead to simulate the crown of thorns and then cut a design into the back of another man, hanging paper towels blotted with his blood over the audience. The American Conservatory Theater performance of Dario Fo's *The Pope and the Witch* outraged San Francisco's archbishop by portraying a crazed pontiff approving birth control and legalized her-oin. Audiences walked out when the theater's female director pre-sented the Duchess of Malfi naked from the waist down and bound in duct tape, while other women were tied to cell bars and had pincers on bare breasts. Peter Greenaway's film *The Baby of Macon* shows a theater audience watching church officials sentence a young woman to be raped 113 times. She steps out of character and jokes with fellow actors as she prepares to shriek behind a curtain, convincing the theater audience it is pretense. But the *cinema* audience sees her raped by lines of soldiers as bored church officials keep count. Greenaway did not "use violence as an instrument of pleasure. Here there is real retribution, and real hurt. Here there is cause and effect. Cinema is more powerful than the other so-called serious arts. We must insure that it contains challenging and provocative ideas."[47]

But art's claim of a license to shock does not elevate everything shocking to art. Pop star Marky Mark dedicated a recent book to his penis and put a photo of himself holding it on the frontispiece. Madonna's MTV teaser for her single "Erotica" and coffee-table book *Sex* showed her with eyes masked, dressed in leather, being ridden like a horse; pulling the reins of bondage boys; and in a lesbian love scene and ménage à trois—all shot in the grainy black-and-white of snuff films. Fay Weldon put Michelangelo's *David* on the cover of a novel, with a flap covering his genitals. Beavis and Butthead earned the highest ratings for MTV by picking their noses, urinating, and having erections. The Los Angeles store Necromance sells jewelry made from animal and human bones. Pretty Boy Floyd's bass player was a patron: "Wearing bones grosses people out, keeps them on edge. We like that." When the *Economist* illustrated an article about mergers with a cover photograph of camels copulating, half its readers were disgusted and half greatly amused.[48]

The fashion industry is unscrupulous in appropriating the avant-garde for commercial purposes. *Paper* magazine's entry in the "Inspiration '95" show was a woman "who dragged herself down the runway with blue-dyed skin, blackened teeth and bowling balls strapped to her feet." Joop Jeans pictured a baby with a leash around its neck and the caption "A child is the ultimate pet." Women appear naked from the waist up or lying on their backs in bathing suits with their legs spread in ads for Guess and Express Jeans. Calvin Klein photographs a woman on a couch naked from head to thigh to advertise Obsession for Men. Valentino shows two naked men embracing a woman in a short slip and another naked man clinched with a woman in a position that would suggest intercourse but for her checked suit. Gianni Versace poses men and women in transparent clothing or partly or completely nude, in sexually provocative poses, sometimes ménages à trois, holding each other or their own breasts or crotches. The designer said: "See-through has been modern for 20 years. People go naked. Are you shocked? Violence is shocking." Even Bloomingdale's full-page *New York Times* ad showed two couples in Jockey underwear embracing and a man with a bulging crotch.[49] Benetton has drawn attention to its clothes with a bombed-out car, a dying AIDS patient, oil-soaked seabirds, a military cemetery, Albanian refugees swarming aboard an overcrowded ship, a murdered Mafia victim, a Croatian soldier in a bloody uniform, and third-world child laborers. British protests forced it to remove billboards showing a bloody newborn attached to its umbilical cord. Europeans boycotted when an ad showed a male arm and chest tattooed "H.I.V. Positive." Ads showing fifty-six male and female genitalia, and a black woman suckling a white baby, were never seen in the United States. Luciano Benetton appeared naked except for glasses, urging readers to donate clothes to the poor (and perhaps replace them with his products). His director of communication was shameless:

> It takes a shocking image sometimes to jar people out of complacency. The purpose of these ads is not to sell clothing, but the caveat is that Benetton is in business to sell apparel. These ads are designed, at the same time as they raise awareness of a serious issue, to make awareness of our label.[50]

DIVINING MOTIVE

Whereas mens rea usually just modifies the seriousness of criminal acts, a speaker's motives can convert the contemptible into the praiseworthy. The cast of *Shimada*, forced to close after a few performances, protested against harsh reviews that "had missed what the play was about, that it was designed to stimulate questions . . . please do not impugn our honor by calling us prejudiced when we employ our God-given gifts to tell our deepest truths about the moral failure of prejudice." A Sunset Boulevard billboard of three sexy women looked like all the others on the strip until you read the caption "Hey Bud, Quit Using Our Cans to Sell Yours," and saw it had been erected by Consumers to Stop Sexist Alcohol Advertising. A full-page fashion ad flaunted a black woman in red-leather bustier and thigh-high boots lying on her back with her legs spread. But it was the transvestite model RuPaul, whose motto is "You're born naked and the rest is drag." His poses spelled out MAC's Viva Glam lipstick, which declared that "every cent of the retail selling price . . . is donated to the fight against AIDS."[51]

Because motive can be opaque, speakers sometimes seek to neutralize harm by claiming good intentions. In "a staff discussion of how not to perpetuate stereotypes" during American military intervention in

Somalia, the executive producer of NBC's *Nightly News* referred to Gen. Mohammed Farah Aidid as an "educated jungle bunny." The network's news president quickly announced that "the term does not reflect the producer's feeling, beliefs and personal history." Film directors Albert and Allen Hughes claimed they wanted *Menace II Society* "to show the realities of violence . . . to have the audience turn away." When they issued the video, however, they added a preface in which an actor steps out of character to declare his abhorrence of violence.[52]

If motives are essential to meaning, however, they also are mixed: blackface is a good example.[53] A fine line separates journalistic courage from sensationalism: Frederick Wiseman's documentary of mental patients; Eugene Richards's photographs of cocaine users; the graphic portrayal of sex, drugs, and crime among New York teenagers in *Kids* and the city's transvestites and transsexuals in *Paris Is Burning;* or Michael Ryan's sexual autobiography.[54] On his highly profitable television talk show Geraldo Rivera paired Roy Innis of the Congress on Racial Equality with a White Aryan Resistance member, goaded Innis into assaulting the racist, and made further shows about the fistfight. Taping a Klan rally a few months later, Rivera responded to slurs by fighting and was arrested—but got out of jail in time to film the cross burning. *Nightline* does stories on how the tabloids cover Joey Buttafuoco and Leona Helmsley. Why did the *New York Times* front page contain a pinup in a thong bikini, taken from the inspector general's report on the Tailhook scandal? Or South Africa's prize-winning progressive weekly reproduce four pictures of topless women for an article entitled "Too Many Tits, Not Enough Text," ostensibly criticizing hypocrisy in the government's pornography policy? What motivated Bill Buford to hang out with neo-Nazis and write "objectively" about their thuggery, or the Australian whose best-selling novel portrayed skinhead attacks on Vietnamese immigrants?[55] I cannot vouch for the purity of my own motives in presenting these anecdotes.

Artists manipulate motivational ambiguity to deflect criticism. John Updike insisted his retelling of Tristan and Isolde in *Brazil* criticized rather than expressed racism. When a school canceled *Peter Pan* for its stereotyped Indians, a defender maintained that James Barrie was actually satirizing "American caricatures of Indians."[56] Paramount's female president of production said *Fatal Attraction* was "a morality tale from the wife's point of view." Paramount head Sherry Lansing called *Indecent Proposal*—in which Robert Redford offers Demi Moore a million dollars to sleep with him—"the ultimate feminist statement" because Moore decides "what she wants to do with her body." In *Sliver*, Lansing said, Sharon Stone "goes through an arc of passivity that leads to strength. By the end, she is in total control." Director Joe Eszterhas justified the film's voyeurism by presenting it as a film *about* voyeurism—a pretext as old as Renaissance paintings of Susannah and the Elders or nudes admiring themselves in mirrors. Oliver Stone claimed *Natural Born Killers* was "meant to reflect on our depraved culture." In *Man Bites Dog* the Belgian "film crew" making a mock documentary about a serial killer eventually joins him in a rape. The director stressed the "similarity between the film crew, which is seduced by the killer character, and the viewer, who . . . may go along with the character until a certain point. And we knew we needed one point in the film when you can't watch it any more."[57]

Speaker protestations, therefore, are suspect. Audiences conflate author with character, accusing Philip Roth of anti-Semitism, John Updike and Saul Bellow of male chauvinism. It was not just Muslim masses who heard Rushdie's voice in each fantastic creature populating *The Satanic Verses*. An Indian drama critic refused to "accept that a writer could distance himself from the words his characters speak . . . how can he not be responsible for his entire representation?" Each author might have echoed Bret Easton Ellis's defense of *American Psycho*.

> I would think most Americans learn in junior high to differentiate between the writer and the character he is writing about. . . . Bateman is the monster. I am *not* on the side of that creep. . . . [T]he murder sequences are so over the top, so baroque in their violence, it seems hard to take them in a literal context. And there are dozens more hints that direct the reader toward the realization that for all the book's surface reality, it is still satirical, semi-comic and—dare I say it?— playful in a way.

This further infuriated women, who made thirteen death threats, some containing photographs of the author with his eyes poked out and an axe through his head. The Los Angeles NOW president reiterated her boycott call: "This is not art. Mr. Ellis is a confused, sick young man with a deep hatred of women who will do anything for a fast buck." His British publisher retorted: "It is a book about terrible things, but it is not a terrible book."[58]

Viewers are equally suspicious about the visual arts. Galería Otra Vez in Los Angeles removed Manuel Ocampo's *Vade Retro*—a cartoonish black with gigantic genitals urinating on the cross—from its Columbus quincentennial exhibit, rejecting the Filipino-American artist's contention that it criticized European colonialism. Critics of Richard Haas's bas relief on the history of immigration to New York saw a closed bodega as "Hispanic failure" where the artist had intended to express Sunday, a prostitute in a woman who had caught his eye skating in Central Park, and a homeless man as stereotyping rather than consciousness raising. Haas painted over the mural. James Ahearn lived in the South Bronx for years before making his realistic sculptures of a fourteen-year-old girl on roller skates, a twenty-four-year-old man with basketball and boom box, and an older neighborhood character and his pit bull. But a Latina whose apartment overlooked the outdoor installation denounced the "evil, ugly images," and her daughter saw "totems of racism." Minority civil servants whose department had regulatory authority called them "negative elements." "To the art world, my bronzes were serious, ironic," said Ahearn. "They had oomph, they were strong. They were an 'artist's' pieces . . . but I thought that day, They'll never look like this again." He removed them.[59]

Some speaker rationalizations are patently hypocritical. The *Mirror* tabloids published surreptitious photographs of the Princess of Wales working out on her back in lycra, calling them evidence that "she could have been a sitting target for an I.R.A. terrorist." The manufacturer of True Crime trading cards said they "document the roots and the history of crime" for "crime buffs and crime-science professors." The 99-cent pack included Jeffrey Dahmer amid spattered blood and the text "After getting them drunk or drugging them, Dahmer photographed, strangled, and dismembered his victims, mostly young Asian and African-American men." When police found doodles of bullet-riddled bodies and plans for a "terror box" detonated by remote control in the home of a suspect in a New York subway bombing, his lawyer called them notes for a "high-tech suspense thriller."[60] The mass media depend on such mutual deception. Producer Joel Silver defended box office successes like *Lethal Weapon,* the *Die Hard* series, *Demolition Man,* and *The Last Boy Scout* as "fun." "Is that violence? Yes. Is it a fantasy? Yes. It's not meant to be taken seriously." Joe Eszterhas called *Showgirls* "a morality tale . . . about a young woman who refused to be corrupted at the deepest part of her being. . . . Not to allow teen-agers under 17 to hear this very moral message because it is set against the world of nude Vegas dancing is pious nonsense." He should know: the studio produced 250,000 promotional copies of an eight-minute sneak preview featuring the nudity. Opposing bans by Canada, New Zealand, and Scandinavia, the producers of *Mighty Morphin Power Rangers* called it "essentially a life-action cartoon, with the battles between good and evil enacted in a fantasy world between superheroes and outrageous and obviously unreal monsters." It contained "strong positive messages" and encouraged "pro-social behavior." Gangsta rapper Ice Cube called women "bitches" and "hos" because "I have to speak the language of the street to get their ear." Ricardo "Kurupt" Brown of Tha Dogg Pound declared: "[W]hat we do is just a form of poetry."[61]

Motive is essential, transformative, subtle, ambiguous, obscure, and manipulable. Legal regulation is poorly suited to making the necessary discriminations.

CONTEXTUALIZING SPEECH

Regulation also is inattentive, even oblivious, to context. America Online, whose programs automatically eliminate "obscene or vulgar" language, censored "breast" in a network devoted to cancer information and "fuck" from a discussion of the famous "Fuck the Draft" case—rendering the controversy incomprehensible.[62]

But context shapes meaning as powerfully as motive. Creative identity valorizes expression. Doris Lessing's two regular publishers rejected her pseudonymous manuscript; when another published the book, no Lessing authority would read it and no serious journal would review it.[63] At the other extreme, Salvador Dali and Andy Warhol shamelessly exploited their fame (unfortunately, more than fifteen minutes long) to inflate the prices of their productions. Speaker identity equally affects the harmfulness of words. Images that would be pornographic if produced by or for men become feminist erotica when crafted by and for women, for instance Judy Chicago's *Dinner Party*, honoring thirty-nine great women by decorating dinner plates with vaginas. Imagine the outcry if the Connecticut casino that dressed cocktail waitresses as Pocahontas, with feathers in their hair and miniskirts slit to the thigh, had been operated by Anglos rather than Pequot Indians.[64] The difference between Aunt Jemima on the pancake box or Sambo in the restaurants and "Black Is Beautiful" dolls lies in who produces them for whom, as well as the images themselves. But identity does not immunize from criticism. When the Israeli rock group Duralex Sedlex played "Zyklon B" at Auschwitz to symbolize Jewish survival, many Israelis protested, and an Auschwitz survivor condemned the "desecration of the memory of the victims."[65]

Audiences can reach diametrically opposed interpretations of the same artifact, as shown by the feminist split over lesbian S/M pornography.[66] The *New York Times Magazine* cover picturing the actress Matuschka baring her mastectomy for a story on breast cancer produced four times the usual number of letters to the editor, a third of them angry at this "shock therapy" but the rest enthusiastic. Two Jewish Columbia College seniors found an anti-Semitic subtext in the hugely popular *Batman Returns*. Another successful American film, *Free Willy*, convulsed audiences in Britain, where the eponymous whale's name means penis. Although adults have criticized Maurice Sendak's picture books as negative and frightening, the author persuasively contends that children see these perennial favorites as celebrating their capacity to survive.[67]

As we saw in chapter 4, political statements also permit divergent readings. Anselm Kiefer, one of the first postwar German artists to deploy Nazi symbols, photographed himself giving the *Sieg Heil* salute in Roman amphitheaters, ambiguously titling the volume *Besetzungen* (Occupations). Germans suspected Nazi sympathies, but American Jews embraced him as an anti-Nazi. When the fall of the Berlin Wall exposed Hitler's bunker, the city's chief archeologist wanted to incorporate it into the new German Parliament to "remind [politicians] every day of how evil governments can become." At a public hearing one Berliner attacked this "continuity of history" as "a way of honoring the perpetrators." Another, however, wanted "the fact that there were specific people who ordered these crimes" not to be forgotten. General Hideki Tojo and other war criminals were tried in Tokyo's Imperial Army Headquarters; three decades later Yukio Mishima disemboweled himself after calling for a coup to restore Japan's military honor. The Japan Civil Protection Association wanted it preserved to inspire patriotism; the Left wanted schoolchildren to visit it as a symbol of national shame; but a history professor feared it would "become a holy place, with the war criminals reinstated as martyrs."[68]

A 1993 incident at Williams College illustrates the complex interaction of speaker identity, motive, and audience. Just before Black History Month racial slurs appeared on the door of the Black Student Union. Three days later an African American student told the college administration he had written them for a course on anarchism to promote discussion of racism. The administration disclosed a student had taken responsibility but did not identify his race for nine days. The BSU plastered the campus with posters condemning the act and urging students to interrogate their racism, which they did not remove when the student confessed to them. The student paper said this silence perpetuated "an implicit lie." The administration suspended the student for a semester, with BSU approval. The student denied malicious intent, however, insisting "[A] lot more people are talking now."[69]

CONFUSED CONSEQUENTIALISM

Because utilitarianism is the dominant contemporary justification for criminal justice—indeed for the entire technocratic state—government regulation of speech rests on consequentialist arguments.[70] Censors have always blamed speech for action. In 1774 German communities banned *The Sorrows of Young Werther*, Goethe's fictionalized account of his love triangle, accusing it of inspiring romantic suicides. A century later, two sensational murders were attributed to dime novels like *Desperate Dan* and *The Dastard* (although the fourteen-year-old perpetrator had never read any). A 1959 rapist-murderer claimed to have been inspired by the golden calf sequence in Cecil B. DeMille's *Ten Commandments*. Similar charges were made against the Russian roulette scene in *The Deer Hunter*, and Britain banned *A Clockwork Orange* for allegedly provoking rape and assault.[71] Robin Morgan gave feminists the catchy slogan "Pornography is the theory, and rape the practice."[72] (One of Times Square's leading pornographers retorted that his sex shops were "a deterrent to rape.")[73]

The empirical research, however, offers little support for this ideology. Exposure to violent images elicits aggressive feelings, not acts; and sexualization of violent representations has no independent effect. Violent behavior among children is related to the amount of television they watch but not program content.[74] The only verifiable consequence of tolerating pornography is more pornography. Porn stars are appearing in mainstream films (Traci Lords in *Cry-Baby*) and as fashion models (Jeff Stryker for Thierry Mugler). Top model Naomi Campbell posed with Madonna in *Sex*; comedian Sandra Bernhard stripped for *Playboy*. The commercial success of *Basic Instinct* produced a rash of imitative erotic thrillers: *Caged Fear, Sunset Heat, Fatal Instinct, Animal Instincts*, and *Red Shoe Diaries*.[75]

Moral crusaders appear impervious to data. After her Indianapolis ordinance was declared unconstitutional, Catharine MacKinnon pushed the bill in Massachusetts and in Congress: "It's for the woman whose husband comes home with a video, ties her to the bed, makes her watch, and then forces her to do what they did in the video." A Virginia Coalition against Porn sought to ban a strip show from the county fair because two women "were abused after their husbands attended the show."[76] Demonstrators at the opening of *Rising Sun* blamed media stereotypes for racial attacks on Asians. And Ross Perot—rarely associated with feminism or civil rights—followed the dubious lead of Dan Quayle (his 1992 rival's running mate) by attacking a *Doogie Howser* episode in which the eponym and his girlfriend, both eighteen, lost their virginity. "Some 15-year-old girl that's been thinking about it hadn't done it yet. 'Hell, Doogie's girl did it. It must be all right.'"[77] Sponsors of the Child Pornography Prevention Act of 1996 justified the prohibition of computer-generated images, which exploited no child model, on the ground that they whetted the appetites of pedophiles.[78]

PROBLEMATIZING PATERNALISM

Some prohibitionists, including MacKinnon, invoke solicitude for porn actors. But society tolerates, indeed glamorizes, many far more dangerous occupations: soldier, police or fire officer, astronaut, circus performer, car racer, stunt person, dancer, athlete.[79] Many fashion models use drugs, partly to stay thin.[80] After decades of popularity in Brazil, "The Ultimate Fighting Championship" premiered in the United States in 1993. The only protective gear it permits is a mouthpiece and cup; the only moves it prohibits are eye gouges, biting, and groin shots. Fights continue until the loser is unconscious, he or his corner concedes, or a doctor intervenes. A promoter said hopefully: "There's a potentially huge audience for this. . . . In every little bitty town in America there's a karate studio. Kids really get into martial arts in some way or another, even if it's only in video games." Commenting on fights in the audience throughout the evening, announcer Jim Brown (former pro football star turned community activist) called them "the most alive group of people I've ever seen." Pay-per-view subscribers grew to 300,000 by the fifth event.[81]

I do not mean to belittle the pervasiveness of sexual and other forms of exploitation. But paternalism always must answer the conventional arguments: *de gustibus non disputandum, chacun à son goût*. Was Josephine Baker exploiter or exploited when she danced nude before adoring Parisians and took hundreds of lovers?[82] Each month New York's Art Students League turns away twenty-five to thirty life modeling applicants. A woman who posed explained: "[T]he focus is completely on you, and some people really appreciate that attention." A painter who also modeled called it "a way . . . for artists to do things together in a noncompetitive atmosphere."[83] Asian male actors are posing as hunks on calendars and greeting cards. Ray Chang called it "a chance to say . . . we are sexual beings." Tamlyn Tomita agreed: "Sex is power."[84] Some porn actors enjoy performing sex in public. A South African male stripper liked "being in the limelight. I like the women going crazy." Others engaged in "courtship" routines, offering women admirers champagne and roses (a powerful scene in the film *Bhaji on the Beach*). A woman secretary who performed sex on stage with volunteers said: "[I]t stimulates our sex life."[85] The threat of discovery can also intensify amateur lovemaking, as D. H. Lawrence described in *Sons and Lovers* and Philip Roth in *Goodbye, Columbus*. Graham Greene claimed that he and Jocelyn Rickards had sex behind every high altar in Italy. Daring each other to defy English prudery, a young unmarried couple stripped and had intercourse in daylight on a traffic circle in the town where the man's father had been mayor.[86]

Even pain can be self-inflicted and enjoyed, as in the rites of passage in many cultures. The fascination with Christian martyrs—pierced with arrows, burned, stoned, flayed alive, torn by wild beasts, miraculously receiving the stigmata, and of course crucified—dramatically exposes human ambivalence. In the Philippines, many scourge themselves in public parades on Good Friday; a few have themselves crucified. The church does not actively discourage these practices, though it officially disapproves.[87] Many religions mandate or honor fasting. San Francisco's "modern primitives" engage in "body modification" and "body play." "Piercing is just like life," explained one woman. "It hurts. It heals. And then you live with it. Forever." Another added: "[W]hen the needle is going through, it's agonizing. You get an incredible rush of endorphins." Is this different in kind from the millions of physical fitness fanatics whose motto is "no pain, no gain"? After piercing comes branding, which is physically as well as psychically permanent. Some African American fraternities brand their initials on pledges. Pain, like porn, is going mainstream. Universal Studios in Florida considered showcasing the Jim Rose Circus at Halloween. Rose swallows razor blades, lies on a bed of nails, and hammers spikes into his nose. The Sword Swallower eats live slugs, while Matt "the Tube" Crowley drinks quarts of beer, chocolate sauce, and ketchup through his nose. Fans fight for front-row seats to see the tears in Mr. Lifto's eyes as he lifts weights with his pierced nipples.[88]

TAKING CAUSES SERIOUSLY

Real concern for consequences would require us to trace the effects—about whose harmfulness many agree—back to the most powerful causes, rather than targeting those that appear more vulnerable to regulation or conveniently coincide with other agendas.[89] The harshness of legal penalties, however, limits their application to the aberrant extremes of hard-core pornography and neo-Nazi hate speech. Indeed, the modern state's entire regulatory apparatus is predicated on the dubious strategy of increasing the severity of punishment to compensate for its infrequency.

If the evils of pornography are sexual objectification and violence, the fashion and beauty industries are far greater offenders. We can see this more easily in other societies. The Padaung of Myanmar use brass rings to stretch the necks of women—up to twenty pounds for each foot gained. In their village—now a tourist attraction—one said: "When the neck is longer, you are prettier. There is some pain, but the body gets used to it." Imitating the eighteen-inch shoes of Renaissance Venetian courtesans, a contemporary designer defended her platform shoes: "I pander to the common idea of what is attractive—the idea of height being slimming. . . . I wanted to put women on a pedestal. You feel so much more feminine and the center of attention."[90] Fashion often infantilizes women. Spring 1993 featured baby-doll dresses, pleated schoolgirl skirts, Mary Janes, and ankle socks. Although "little-girl dresses . . . looked so sexy," Anna Sui insisted it had "nothing to do with perverted sexuality—that's not what I was trying to titillate." Betsey Johnson used baby bonnets, rompers, diapers, and pacifiers. Gianni Versace put Kate Moss in a skirt exposing matching panties, knee-high stockings, and stiletto heels. Martine Sitbon dressed her models in transparent baby-dolls.[91] A woman who designed "steamy dresses" for *Playboy* called it "the only magazine of that type not demeaning. The women are empowered by their sexuality."[92] We heard similar rationalizations from filmmakers.

Fashion shapes bodies as well as clothes. On a randomly chosen day the *Los Angeles Times* news section contained nine advertisements for weight loss, totaling more than three full pages, displaying women in sexually provocative poses over captions like "Lose Up to 3 Dress Sizes in 10 Weeks," "Body of the '90's," "Now I can wear the clothes my skinny sister wears."[93] Only 22 percent of white high school girls are satisfied with their appearance—unsurprising since fashion models are 16–23 percent thinner than average. Half of women college students said magazines like *Cosmopolitan* made them less confident; more than two-thirds felt worse about their looks. Although all were normal weight, four-fifths had dieted, and 10 percent had eating disorders.

Boycott Anorexic Marketing attacked Diet Sprite for featuring Kristin McMenamy (nicknamed "Skeleton") and Calvin Klein for using Kate Moss. A feature story on aspiring "supermodels" described Meghan Douglas as "an exotic 117-pound sylph who 'loves candy' but tries to visit the gym every day." Nadja Auermann eats desert only once a week: "My job is to be skinny." On the facing page of this "Fashions of the Times" special, a Maidenform ad ridiculed wasp-waist corsets with the heading "Imagine for a moment what it must have been like to be a woman in the 1800s," followed by two pages of bras captioned "Okay, you can exhale now." It neglected to mention that you cannot eat. Half of American women have considered cosmetic surgery; there were 643,910 such operations in 1990. Even (perhaps especially) women whose bodies are envied or desired by millions—Cher, Mariel Hemingway, Jane Fonda—have had breast augmentations, which enhance attractiveness to men while reducing their own sexual pleasure. The Wonderbra and Hanes Hosiery's Smooth Illusions panty-hose, which promises the advantages of liposuction without surgery, have been best-sellers. A year after fashion models sported body rings, tattoos, and other piercings, Gauntlet on Fifth Avenue stayed open seven days a week, employing four piercers to operate on twenty customers a weekday and a hundred on weekends.[94]

Male bodies are being similarly fetishized. Male celebrities in *People* magazine have waists under thirty inches. The director of the men's division at LA Models explained: "Ultimately, we're selling sex, and women like to see men with nice bodies, broad shoulders, and the V-shape." The proportion of cosmetic surgeries performed on men increased from 5 percent in the 1980s to 20 percent in the early 1990s. They include hair, calf, and pectoral implants, chest-hair dying, and face patterning. For years Dr. Melvyn Rosenstein advertised penile enlargement in the *Los Angeles Times,* promising "Immediate results. Self-improvement. Self-confidence. Totally Natural! . . . Most patients will double in size. . . . Dreams DO come true." A Park Avenue doctor promoted male breast reduction in the *New York Times Magazine.* Men's cosmetics total $2.5 billion a year (compared to $20 billion for women). More male anorexics and bulimics are seeking treatment. Girdles and corsets are selling rapidly.[95]

Advertising also reproduces racial subordination. One in five Japanese commercials features Caucasian models, who earn 50 percent more than their local counterparts. Just as Jewish mothers encouraged their daughters to have nose jobs, so Asian mothers urge removal of the epicanthic fold—an operation that can take six months to heal.[96] In the 1950s Dr. Fred Palmer's Skin Whitener urged African American women to "Be lovely, be loved with lighter, brighter skin." After four decades of civil rights agitation and black pride, it still promises to make "your skin just one shade. Beautiful." Opposite an ad for Vantex Skin Bleaching Creme, *Ebony* magazine ran an article about darker adoptive parents' preference for lighter adopted children. In Africa these products use higher concentrations of hydroquinone, which reduces melanin and increases the risk of skin cancer.[97]

SHOOTING MESSENGERS

Contemporary attacks on speech echo attempts to blame postwar crime waves on the emergence of television.[98] Rep. Edward J. Markey (D-

Mass.), House Telecommunications and Finance Subcommittee chair, declared: "The sheer saturation of all the violent programming creates a culture of tolerance for it . . . we can't pretend there isn't some connection." The *New York Times* quoted Yale psychologist Leonard D. Eron asserting that the scientific debate on causation was "over." A *Journal of the American Medical Association* article "proved" that television causes violence by correlating white homicide rates with the introduction of that medium in the United States, Canada, and South Africa! The AMA asserted that "evidence is mounting of a correlation between aggression and listening to violent lyrics." After the Oklahoma City bombing, the *New York Times* blamed the violent exhortations of far-right radio talk shows, such as G. Gordon Liddy's advice to "shoot to the groin area" if you miss Alcohol, Tobacco, and Firearms agents' heads.

> [T]he cumulative force of their words can create a generalized atmosphere of violence in which unstable individuals feel they have a license for crime. . . . [just as the exhortations of George Wallace, Ross Barnett and Lester Madox] to defy federal law and their castigations of the national government and the civil rights movement created the climate that produced a flurry of murders by gun and bomb . . . [and] hysteria at the fringes of [the antiwar] movement contributed to the paranoid and delusional anarchism of the weather underground bombings.[99]

An American "expert" asserted that exposure to video games and violent television desensitized Americans to killing in the same way military training had done during the Vietnam War.[100] Trying to revive his flagging presidential campaign, Robert Dole said: "[T]here can be no question that the perceptions of a 15-year-old are shaped by music and movies and fashion. And there can be no question that the trendiest trend of our popular culture is the return of drug use."[101]

Playing on these fears, the American Family Association took full-page ads in major newspapers.

> We're DISMAYED that today 1.1 million girls between the ages of 15 and 19 get pregnant each year.
> We're SHOCKED when we learn that two thirds of all births to 15 and 19 year old girls are out of wedlock.
> We're FRIGHTENED at the way violence and crime are spreading everywhere and threatening our children, our families and our homes.
> We say it's time to put the blame where we think it belongs. . . .
> The REASON for all the sex, violence, filth and profanity is with the writers, directors, producers, singers, actors, etc.

Rev. Calvin O. Butts 3d of Harlem's Abyssinian Baptist Church proclaimed a "direct relationship" between rap and a "9-year-old bumping and grinding on the street after school and her becoming the next casualty, if you will, of an early and untimely pregnancy." National Political Congress of Black Women director DeLores Tucker said rap lyrics incited male abuse of black women. By boasting about their positive influence, the mass media concur. The owner of Bravo and American Movie Classics declared: "Television changes behavior . . . for the bad . . . and it can change it for the good." A Viacom senior vice president concurred: "[I]f television doesn't have the ability to influence behavior, then a lot of advertisers have been conned." The advertising industry exposed a billion people in thirty countries to a poster with the word "violence" being erased. A judge who selected the winning poster said they were looking for "something that incited action. . . . You almost want to take part in the erasing." Such propaganda seems to have affected beliefs, if not actions: nearly two-thirds of children under eighteen thought television encouraged peers to have sex, and four-fifths thought it made them disrespect parents.[102]

Heinous crimes often arouse simplistic explanations. When it emerged that the father of one of the ten-year-olds who abducted and brutally murdered two-year-old Jamie Bulgar had rented *Child's Play 3* several weeks earlier, the trial judge speculated that "exposure to violent video films may be part of an explanation." British politicians and church leaders agreed, urging tighter restrictions. But there was no evidence that the murderers had seen the video. After seventeen-year-olds Romain Laine and Cedric Noyrigat died from an explosion of crystallized sugar and weedkiller stuffed in a bicycle handlebar, Romain's mother blamed the American television program *MacGyver*. But though she was supported by politicians, teachers, and a child psychologist recently retired as research director of the Centre National de Recherche Scientifique, the station that had transmitted the popular program noted it had ended two months before the tragedy, showed no chemical manipulations, and had been seen in eighty-seven countries without incident. Norway banned *Mighty Morphin Power Rangers* after the program allegedly inspired viewers to kick a five-year-old girl to death; the ban survived exposure of the story as apocryphal. After Martin Bryant massacred thirty-five people in Tasmania, a commission of inquiry pronounced a link between media depictions and violence. Rumors quickly spread that some of the 2,000 videos in his house were violent and sexually explicit; but they were innocent, and most belonged to an elderly woman he had befriended. Attackers burned a subway booth attendant to death in an incident resembling *The Money Train*, shortly after its release—the first such crime in seven years. The New York City police commissioner called it "a strong coincidence."

The president of the Transit Authority (which had refused to allow violent scenes to be filmed in the subway) was even more confident: "We know from experience that when you get movie and television depictions of criminal activity, it is often copycatted." Mayor Giuliani called the crime "very similar to scenes in the movie." Presidential aspirant Robert Dole urged a boycott. But those charged with the crime had never even heard of the film.[103]

As these examples show, the facile inference of *propter* from *post* is tempting but dubious. After they saw *Interview with the Vampire*, a man threatened his girlfriend: "I'm going to kill you and drink your blood." He stabbed her later that night; but though claiming to have been "influenced by the movie," he conceded: "I cannot sit here and blame the movie." During a screening of *Schindler's List* a man shot a woman in the back just when Nazis were shooting Jews. The suspect claimed to be a Roman Catholic convert to Orthodox Judaism who wanted to test God and protect Jews from harm. "I feel for these people so much. . . . To see that happen, I just took out my gun from my back pocket and began squeezing the trigger." The prosecutor maintained "the movie definitely factored into it." But Spielberg's marketing director retorted: "If ever a movie speaks against things like that, it's this film." When a front-page *New York Times* article noted that Wayne Lo wore a Sick of It All T-shirt during a shooting rampage at Simon's Rock College, band members expressed sympathy for the murder victims but protested that their lyrics condemned violence and concluded: "Mr. Lo's problems, no doubt, go much deeper than his t-shirt."[104]

Other media suffer similar accusations. Bertrand de Jouvenal sued Zeev Sternhell for libel for calling him an example of fascist "impregnation" of French politics in the 1930s. When Raymond Aron testified for the plaintiff and then collapsed on the courthouse steps and died, some blamed Sternhell for writing the book.[105] When former prime minister Pierre Beregovoy committed suicide after the press exposed his interest-free loan from a businessman later indicted for insider trading, Defense Minister François Léotard accused "several news media" of "murder," and Prime Minister Laurent Fabius asserted: "[T]here are words, caricatures and images that have the force of bullets."[106] Richard Nixon blamed Pat's 1976 stroke on her reading of Woodward and Bernstein's Watergate expose. A white supremacist who murdered a San Francisco hairdresser in 1987 and a Chicago plastic surgeon he picked out of a telephone directory six years later declared at trial: "I condemn bleach-blond hair and tinted eyes. I condemn fake Aryan features brought about by plastic surgery." Some attributed responsibility to the neo-Nazi literature he devoured.[107] After a quadriplegic eight-year-old, his mother, and his nurse were murdered by a contract killer who followed detailed instructions in *Hit Man: A Technical Manual for Contractors*, the mother's relatives sued the book's publisher for wrongful death.[108] Some blamed Derek Humphrey for the increase in suicides by the method described in his *Final Exit* (although total suicides remained constant).[109] Others attributed the assassination of Yitzhak Rabin to caricatures of him in a Gestapo uniform and religious justifications for the act.[110] After Theodore John Kaczynski was charged with being the Unabomber, commentators noted that he had booked into hotels under the name Conrad, had read the author's complete works twelve times, and seemed to imitate *The Secret Agent*.[111]

Yet skepticism about unscientific correlations and anecdotal (sometimes apocryphal) atrocity stories does not relieve speech of all culpability. Each additional 10 percent of cigarette advertising produces a 9 percent increase in that brand's teenage market share.[112] Screenings of *New Jack City, Menace II Society, Poetic Justice,* and *Higher Learning* were followed by at least four deaths, dozens of woundings, and much property damage. Defenders justifiably complained that equally violent films by Bruce Willis, Arnold Schwarzenegger, and Clint Eastwood were not blamed for violence. Yet African American filmmakers clearly exploit youthful obsession with violence. The poster advertising *Juice* showed four young black men with the caption "Juice. Power. Respect. How far will you go to get it?" The writer-director of *Boyz N the Hood* insisted the trailer emphasize violence: "I wanted that action crowd."[113] Gangsta rap has been accused not only of misogyny, racism, and homophobia but also of provoking attacks on police. Tupac Amaru Shakur's *2Pacalypse Now* contained half a dozen songs describing killing police, including "Soulja's Story."

> Cops on my tail, so I bail till I dodge them,
> They finally pull me over and I laugh,
> Remember Rodney King
> And I blast this punk ass . . .
> What the fuck would you do?
> Drop them or let them drop you?

This was found in the tape deck of a car stolen by a black nineteen-year-old charged with murdering the white state trooper who had pulled him over after a high-speed chase. The officer's widow sued Shakur and his record company, declaring "There isn't a doubt in my mind that my husband would be alive if Tupac hadn't written those violent anti-police songs and the companies involved hadn't published and put them out on the street." Promising the help of his Freedom

Alliance, Oliver North said the "case provides us with a painfully vivid example of why this kind of music is so dangerous" (making you wonder what he was listening to when he ran Iran Contra). The defense lawyer also planned to use the record in the penalty phase to seek life imprisonment instead of death.[114] Should we hold *The Crying Game* liable because an eighteen-year-old American murdered his three roommates by shooting them in the head after listening to the phrase "2 da head" on the film track?[115]

Attacks on abortion clinics also offer disturbing examples. The lawyer defending Michael F. Griffin on charges of murdering Pensacola abortion-clinic doctor David Gunn claimed that minister John Burt drove Griffin to a "nervous breakdown" with antiabortion propaganda. Shortly after the shooting Burt said on television: "If I am a general with troops under me and I give them a game plan and send them out, I can't be responsible for every soldier in that army." *Life Advocate* reported the name and hometown of Gunn's successor, accusing him of "the deaths of thousands of babies," shortly before Paul. J. Hill murdered him and his security escort. After Hill's conviction the antiabortion group White Rose honored him: "The just sanction for the capital crime of abortion, as with any other murder, is death." When John Salvi was apprehended armed outside a Virginia clinic, after killing and wounding workers and patients at Boston clinics, the director of Pro-Life Virginia declared that if the suspect had been seeking "to defend the lives of unborn babies, it's justified, it's moral, it was a righteous act." Citizens for Justice agreed: "Deadly force is being used against the unborn, so people are now willing to use that same kind of force against the abortion industry." The Planned Parenthood League of Massachusetts warned that "when people call those of us who provide a constitutionally protected medical service 'murderers,' the outcome is increased violence." A few days later Planned Parenthood of New York City took a full-page ad asserting "WORDS KILL. . . . Words of hate helped pull the trigger last Friday in Massachusetts." After antiabortion posters of bloody fetuses were found in Salvi's apartment, the Planned Parenthood Federation of America insisted: "This is not a free speech issue. This is tantamount to shouting 'Fire' in a crowded theater."[116]

When tested against the stringent requirements of legal causation, however, most tort claims blaming speech for violence fail: a nine-year-old girl raped with a soda bottle a few days after television portrayed a rape with a plumber's helper;[117] adolescent boys who attempted or committed suicide after listening to heavy-metal recordings by Judas Priest and Ozzy Osbourne;[118] an adolescent who died of autoerotic asphyxiation after reading a *Hustler* article entitled "Orgasm of Death";[119] a suicide by a youth playing Dungeons and Dragons;[120] a murder by a boy who had just seen the gang film *The Warriors*;[121] a boy who hanged himself after seeing a professional perform a similar trick on *The Tonight Show*.[122] Yet some courts have imposed liability: a $7 million judgment against the United Klans of America for provoking a lynching; a $12.5 million award against Tom and John Metzger and the White Aryan Resistance for inspiring skinheads to murder an Ethiopian immigrant; $4.4 million against *Soldier of Fortune* magazine for an advertisement through which a contract killer was hired; and a judgment against a radio station for encouraging teenagers to race around the San Fernando Valley in pursuit of a prize, killing a motorist in the process.[123]

Nevertheless, the relationship between speech and act rarely displays this unidirectional influence. Rather, life imitates art imitating life like two flawed mirrors reflecting each other's image in infinite regress but with increasing distortion. This is not a postmodernist discovery. A producer publicized a 1930s movie by sending an extra dressed in black to Rudolph Valentino's grave and telling the press she mourned his death every year. Enjoying the attention, she returned unpaid on the next anniversary, only to encounter a rival claimant to public grief. Sixty years later, several women still appeared annually, accusing each other of seeking publicity and sometimes grabbing at veils and bouquets.[124] The cast of *L.A. Law* were often invited to advise lawyers on advocacy and legal secretaries on sexual harassment. Dana Carvey's impersonation of Bush on *Saturday Night Live* led speechwriters to seek hints about the president's mannerisms. Defending his relationship with Mia Farrow's adopted daughter Soon-Yi Previn, Woody Allen told *Time*: "The heart wants what it wants. There's no logic to those things." In *Husbands and Wives* Allen says about Rain—a college student Soon-Yi's age—"My heart does not know from logic." Rejecting his disclaimer that "movies are fiction. The plots of my movies don't have any relationship to my life," Los Angeles and New York audiences booed the film's trailer. Farrow's press agent felt compelled to insist she knew nothing of the relationship while the film was being shot and her apparent affectlessness was not attributable to drugs. "Her behavior on screen is all acting." When a film director was arrested while shooting *Tito for the Second Time among the Serbs* in Belgrade, the police apologetically released him after the actor playing the deceased leader walked into the station in character and said: "Come on, let my friend go. He's a harmless movie actor." The same month a man jumped up in New Haven's Long Wharf Theater and denounced the actress playing the distraught wife in Brian Friel's *Faith Healer*. "This is disgraceful. You're going to kill yourself the amount you smoke." Pointing to the No Smoking sign, he stalked out. Although the actress was using herbal cigarettes, Friel rewrote the script to have her drink more and smoke less, and the theater warned audiences that actors smoked on stage. Responding to critics of media violence, magicians Penn and Teller made a public service announcement for cable television. Dipping his hand into a bucket, Penn said: "This is a vat of viscous red fluid. Stage blood. When we play with this on stage, we celebrate life and give people a rage to live." After Teller pricked his finger, Penn added: "Now this . . . is real blood." "Only dangerous psychotics celebrate real blood."[125]

Gangster films create the greatest confusion. A scriptwriter for *Married to the Mob* based protagonist Tony "the Tiger" Russo partly on John Gotti's performance at his 1986 trial. The actor playing Russo stayed in character off the set: "I would get the most extraordinary reactions. Waiters, cabbies, they would do anything for me. I was like a king." The 1992 trial heard a taped telephone conversation of Gotti saying "He didn't rob nothin'. You know why he is dying? He's gonna die because he refused to come when I called." A prosecutor said Gotti was copying Al Capone in *The Untouchables*. Salvatore Locascio, son of a codefendant, vented his outrage when the judge disqualified one of his father's lawyers. "This is America; haven't they ever heard of the Bill of Rights? We have a Bill of Rights in this country. It's right over there, on the wall. Tell them to go over there and read it." A reporter was reminded of Rod Steiger playing Al Capone in the 1959 movie: "We have a constitution in this country. The Constitution—ever heard of it? I suggest that when you go to your office you read it." Joseph Colombo Sr., *capo di tutti capi*, agreed to help film *The Godfather* if his people were hired as extras and the words "Cosa Nostra" were never uttered. James Caan, who played Sonny Corleone, spent so much time hanging out with Carmine "the Snake" Persico that undercover agents once mistook him for the mobster. At Persico's 1985 trial Caan publicly kissed him on the cheek: "I would never deny that my friend is my friend." In 1992 Caan pledged his house as collateral for the release of Ronald A. Lorenzo, a gangster he had met fifteen years earlier during the filming of *Chapter Two*. After Lorenzo's conviction a juror commented it was "a little ironic, this guy in the 'Godfather' movie testifying here." Henry Hill, whose biography was the basis for Martin Scorsese's *Goodfellas*, said: "[T]he dress, the manner, the cockiness—a lot of it comes from the movies." He remembered the older neighborhood "wiseguys" walking "round like actors—it was like being a movie star." The first time he had seen Gotti, thirty years earlier, "John was at the card table" and suddenly started beating a man. "I mean there was blood splashing over the walls." Asked if he were not confusing memory with a scene from *Goodfellas*, Hill insisted it was much closer to *The Untouchables*. Since the fall of communism, Russian hoodlums also have begun imitating Hollywood, dressing in Italianate zoot suits, and calling themselves "killers." John Le Carré described a gangster in black Ray-Ban sunglasses: "Grigori has been studying old episodes of 'Kojak,' which would explain his shaven head and sneer."[126]

PERVERSE PENALTIES

Although all regulation contains loopholes and creates perverse incentives, these drawbacks are accentuated when the state controls speech.

ENCOURAGING EVASION

Entrepreneurs deploy all the conventional techniques to circumvent regulation. When American television banned tobacco ads in 1971, Philip Morris initiated the Virginia Slims women's tennis tournament and R. J. Reynolds launched the Winston Cup auto race—both seen by large television audiences. They soon had many imitators: the Vantage Golf Scoreboard, Salem Pro-Sail races, Lucky Strike bowling competitions, Winston rodeos, Benson & Hedges ice skating, and Marlboro horse racing. In 1988/89 twenty-two of the twenty-four major league baseball stadiums advertised cigarettes in locations likely to be televised during games; rates varied with the amount of coverage. At the 1986 World Cup in Mexico City R. J. Reynolds erected four twenty-foot signs next to the playing field, seen by 650 million viewers. The Marlboro logo has appeared on television more than 6,000 times during the Grand Prix.[127] Voluntarily banned from radio since 1936 and television since 1948, distillers have been infiltrating back through horse shows sponsored by Seagram and guides to night life by Finlandia; both deny these are "commercials."[128]

Speakers can employ the whole gamut of poetic techniques to disguise and multiply meaning: simile, metaphor, conceit, personification, hyperbole, litotes, synecdoche, metonymy, paradox, irony, ellipsis, and punning. Some attempts are crude: a Van Halen album entitled *For Unlawful Carnal Knowledge*, or Up sportswear's logo—a 45-degree large red arrow (suggesting an erect penis) over the caption "Keep It Up." Californians got around the Department of Motor Vehicles censor with vanity license plates like "IVNIC8," "UGETNNE," "S888N," and "JTAMGZL." Subscribers avoid Prodigy's keyword search for obscenities and slurs with imaginative spellings and euphemisms. Frank Lautenberg skirted rules of senatorial courtesy by saying that Alfonse M. D'Amato's performance smelled of the barnyard. Reviewing *NYPD Blue*, the *Los Angeles Times* critic evaded his paper's bowdlerizers by referring to "occasional coarse utterances that include the rhymes-with-zits synonym for female breasts and the rhymes-with-curd word for excrement."[129] Pornographers comply with the letter of the law by focusing on the pubic areas of girls in bathing suits or leotards.[130] When the Children's Television Act of 1990 required stations to increase educational programming some simply claimed that *Superboy* "presents GOOD as it triumphs over EVIL" and *Super Mario Brothers* taught self-confidence.[131] Indian films feature song lyrics like "my engine is hot / please give me a push," "Yesterday my lover bowled such a torrid spell, / I couldn't sleep a wink all night," "He climbed on me . . . / the pigeon on the terrace." American singer Tom Jones was no more subtle: "Pussycat, pussycat, I've got lots of hours to spend with you . . . / I'll soon be kissing your sweet little pussycat lips . . . "and "Maybe it's the way you wear your bluejeans so tight. / I can't put my finger on what you're doing right."[132]

Political dissidents use similar devices. When General Jaruzelski banned Solidarity, slogans covered Polish walls, pamphlets, and banners in the distinctive Solidarność script. ANC and IRA supporters gave forbidden songs new words or just hummed the tunes. Palestinian youths defiantly ate sliced watermelon to represent the red, black, and green of the banned PLO flag. After Tiananmen, Chinese youths wore T-shirts with slogans like "I'm bored" or "I'm the emperor." One displayed a black cat, evoking 1960s reformer Deng Xiaopeng's epigram "It doesn't matter if a cat is black or white. As long as it catches mice, it's a good cat." Posters ostensibly honoring Mao actually discredited communism by juxtaposing his photo with Western products. The *Beijing Daily* questioned whether the city's deputy mayor had actually committed suicide by discussing an analogous event two millennia earlier. Forbidden to use Nazi insignia, German fascists substitute the imperial war flag, whose large black cross Hitler reconfigured into the swastika; some give the *Sieg Heil* with three fingers instead of five. American family-planning clinics responded to the Bush administration's antiabortion gag rule by using federal money to evaluate pregnancy and referring women who tested positive to an advice session when the state was paying employee salaries. When Quebec mandated French on outdoor signs, an advertisement sought protection as political speech by appending "Before Bill 101, This Sign Was Legal. Vote to Make This Legal Again."[133]

Electoral politics insinuates what it cannot say. The Roman Catholic Archdiocese of New York protected its tax-exempt status by giving parishioners more than 100,000 voter guides in which school board candidates answered questions posed by Pat Robertson about classroom prayer and parental control over curriculum. During the 1992 campaign Bush publicist Mary Matalin called Clinton "evasive and slick. We've never said to the press that he's a philandering, pot-smoking draft dodger." "The way you just did?" asked the interviewer. "The way I just did," she gloated. Others called Clinton a "skirt chaser" and said marital fidelity "should be one of the yardsticks by which candidates are measured" and then apologized—further spreading the dirt. When the *New York Post* reported that a forthcoming book accused Bush of adultery, Clinton piously declared, "I don't think it has any place in this campaign"—thereby ensuring republication of the charge. The *Los Angeles Times* wrote a story on the insufficiency of the evidence to warrant covering the allegation![134]

LICENSING HARM

Even the most enthusiastic regulators tolerate a great deal of harmful speech. Fiction distresses living subjects: Jesse Chambers, the model for Miriam in *Sons and Lovers;* Gerald and Sara Murphy, the inspiration for the Divers in *Tender Is the Night;* a murdered University of Chicago graduate student in Saul Bellow's *The Dean's December;* the Rosenberg sons in E. L. Doctorow's *The Book of Daniel.* Claire Bloom had to threaten to sue Philip Roth to get him to make changes in a forthcoming novel in which "Philip" seduces a younger woman behind the back of his wife "Claire," a whiny English Jewish actress.[135] Humorists get away with murder. *Adbusters* magazine reproduced a photo of the notorious slow chase over the caption "O.J. never stood for 'Orange Jumpsuit'.... When it comes to backing a PR nightmare, it Herts."[136] Critics demolish creative artists. The *New York Times* review of the new novel by the *Bridges of Madison County* author (who had sold 10 million copies of his two previous books) was devastating. "Robert James Walker has fed his hackneyed romance recipe back into the computer and come up with his worst book yet, a truly atrocious ballad . . . that gives new meaning to the words sappy, sexist, mannered and cliched. . . . spectacularly awful—not to mention offensive—writing permeates "Border Music" . . . [which] must surely rank as one of the most dreadful novels to come along in a long time."[137]

Almost anything goes in politics. Antiwar demonstrators shouted, "Hey, Hey, LBJ / How many kids did you kill today?" Antiabortionists yell "Murderer" at clinic patients and staff. When ABA president George Bushnell called House Republicans "reptilian bastards" for cutting Legal Services Corporation funding, they denounced the "reprehensible and unforgivable insult" and demanded his resignation. A week later, furious at the prospect of losing federal money, California governor Pete Wilson called Congress "whores to the public employee unions."[138] IRA members otherwise banned from British television can speak as political candidates. Long before Bush featured Willie Horton's rape during a weekend prison furlough, British fascists used elections to propagate racism, picturing a seventy-five-year-old white woman "savagely beaten by two young black thugs" or (sounding like Patrick Buchanan) denouncing the Persian Gulf War as an attempt to "reinstall the oppressive and corrupt pro-Jew, the emir of Kuwait and in the process sacrifice the lives of our young men and women who have been sent there by the Jewish stooge John Major . . . [backed by] the Jewish owned press (Maxwell & Murdoch are Jews) whipping up war hysteria."[139] Jean-Marie Le Pen declared the "superiority of France's civilization." The "inequality of the races" show they "do not have the same evolutionary capacity." Desperately trying to rescue his doomed presidential campaign at the last hour, Robert Dole condemned aliens "for committing crimes, getting drivers' licenses, using public services." He asked voters: "[W]hy are thousands of Californians the victims of violent crimes committed by people who should have been stopped at the border before they so much as stepped foot in this country?"[140]

Entertainers assume the mantle of politics to deflect criticism. Wearing red panties, bra, and combat boots and literally wrapping herself in the flag, Madonna rapped: "Dr. King, Malcolm X / Freedom of speech is as good as sex." Paddled by two flag-waving male dancers in tight shorts and army boots, she warned: "If you don't vote, you're going to get a spankie." Although a VFW spokesman said this "bordered on desecration," her publicist pointed to the 10,000 college students the concert had registered. MTV's "Choose or Lose" campaign featured Aerosmith guitarist Joe Perry shouting "Freedom is the right . . . to wear whipped cream as clothing" while he licked it off a woman's breasts. Two other women in American-flag suits held the rim of a gigantic condom as a voice intoned, "Freedom to wear a rubber all day—if necessary."[141] Politically motivated literature claims similar license. German playwright Rolf Hochhuth accused the pope of complicity in the Holocaust, held Churchill responsible for firebombing Dresden, blamed Americans for proliferating chemical weapons, exposed the Nazi past of German leaders, and applauded the assassination of the head of Treuhand (charged with privatizing East German state property). George Cruikshank caricatured King George IV and Queen Caroline, Honoré Daumier lampooned Louis-Philippe, José Guadalupe Posada attacked Porfirio Díaz; Francis Bacon paints popes sitting on the toilet; the Guerrilla Girls and Robbie Conal continue the tradition.[142] Journalists feel obligated to publish the truth regardless of consequences. Responding to Hillary Clinton's criticism of television for screening violent events, the Fox News president insisted: "We can't create programs for a mass audience through the prism of 13-year-olds." The same *New York Times* that reported the conference "Children and the New Media" reproduced photographs from a "Farewell to Bosnia" exhibit, showing a victim with head wounds, a boy without hands, prosthetic feet, and a young girl's legs torn by shrapnel.[143]

All actual or proposed regulation of race hatred exempts science. Racists exploit this loophole by substituting regression analyses for vulgarities. In *The Secret Relationship between Blacks and Jews,* the Nation of Islam purported to document Jewish responsibility for slavery with 1,275 footnotes. Holocaust revisionists feign scholarship. Robert Faurisson claimed to expose "The Rumor of Auschwitz" and Dr. Arthur R. Butz "The Hoax of the Twentieth Century." Ditlieb Felderer called Anne Frank's diaries forgeries, and Fred Leuchter concocted engineering "evidence" showing the impossibility of gas chambers. The outrageously misnamed *Historical Review* extols such travesties as "a truly comprehensive compendium of primary research that challenges all major orthodox 'Holocaust' claims" and "hundreds of critical commentaries on the Nuremberg Trials by leading western military men." David Irving's 1977 BBC lecture calling Hitler "as evil as Churchill, as evil as Roosevelt, as evil as Truman" prefigured Reagan's speech commemorating the SS guards buried at Bitburg as "victims of nazism . . . just as surely as the victims of the concentration camps." Emulating David Duke's newly sanitized racism, Colorado's KKK leader ran for city council in a Denver suburb on the slogan "Equal rights for all; special privileges for nobody." The national head insisted the Klan does not hate blacks but just loves whites. In a British pamphlet misleadingly entitled "Jewish Tributes to Our Child Martyrs," Lady Jane Birdwood used such "conciliatory tones" to repeat the blood libel that "Christian children . . . were crucified, tortured and bled to death all over Europe in Mediaeval times to satisfy Jewish religious rituals" that the attorney general refused to prosecute. Condemning the Talmud for "incitements to hatred of gentiles in general and Christian people in particular," which "are *still* a part of the catechism of Jewish belief," she asked with false naiveté: "Could these awful texts have prompted

the child murders?" The events she characterized as "an unprecedented display of Jewish contrition and humility" for a "mass suicide
of Jews" actually were a *Christian* apology for a twelfth-century massacre of hundreds of Jews.[144]

VALORIZING DEVIANCE

Ineffective state regulation might be viewed as an acceptable price for
propitiating victims. But punishment can be positively perverse. Just
as women are raped twice—the second time by defense counsel—so
those who sue for defamation or invasion of privacy may suffer more
from the trial's repetition, elaboration, proof, and rebuttal, often before
a larger audience, than they did from the initial utterance.[145] Bill
Roache, who played Ken Barlow on the hugely popular British soap
Coronation Street for thirty-one years, sued the *Sun* for a center-page
spread entitled "Boring Ken was girl-crazy stud," which portrayed him
as smug, boastful, wooden, lucky not to have been fired, a joke to
scriptwriters, and universally hated by the cast. Roache "felt humiliated and so embarrassed that I didn't want to see people or talk about
it." But of course he did both in the courtroom. Although he had not
challenged certain accusations to spare his wife, newspapers spread
the trial's salacious accounts of his alleged one-night stand with one
actress and his seduction of another on the floor of his house after a
party. Awarded £50,000 and costs, Roache complained: "We've been
through hell and back." But the *Sun*'s legal officer was unrepentant:
"We offered Bill Roache £50,000 about a month ago. He could have
had an apology and could have had his costs paid."[146]

Even when legal regulation does not prompt evasion or aggravate
harm, it constructs and encourages deviance (as labeling theory argues). Victorian repression fostered prostitution and child pornography. Although Iran banned all videos except children's cartoons, and
the Force to Combat the Corruption of Society confiscated more than
20,000 tapes in seven months, Iranians can see anything, including
hard-core porn. Tobacco Institute campaigns ostensibly designed to
discourage children from smoking do just the opposite.[147] MPAA ratings tempt children to sneak into forbidden films by jumping theaters
in cineplexes or getting adults to buy them tickets.[148]

Regulation can confer moral stature on infantile rage. State repression provokes German skinheads to sport swastikas, sing "Deutsch-
land über Alles," and give *Sieg Heil* salutes and the KKK to wear white
hoods and burn crosses. The editor of the British National Front's *Bull-
dog* challenged the government to prosecute him or "we will print a

special victory issue . . . with even more racialist articles."[149] Prohibition even helps comedians. Bill Maher, host of Comedy Central's *Politically Incorrect,* said "a restrictive mood . . . gives us something to rebel against. . . . There's no way any censor can really win with a comic. We'll always have the last word, and, more importantly, the funnier word." In Jackie Mason's one-man stage show *Politically Incorrect,* that Howard Stern of the retirement set complained: "They called me a bigot because I called Dinkins a shvartzer. [Pause] The man is a shvartzer. What do you want from me?" When the California State Bar president pleaded for an end to lawyer jokes, after a disgruntled former client committed mass murder in a law firm, he promptly became the biggest joke of all.[150]

Entrepreneurs welcome repression as an opportunity to disguise promotional activities as civil libertarianism. A full-page ad in British newspapers in fall 1991 declared:

> This commercial has been banned from British television. As usual, it all comes down to a question of taste. Voice over: "For years we had a love affair. We thought it was over. But now passions are soaring once again since we discovered the taste of . . . 'I Can't Believe It's Not Butter!'. . . . " Looks innocent enough, doesn't it? Well, believe it or not, our commercial's got some people—including a certain food lobby—very hot under the collar.

The next day's variation partly obscured "butter," noted the product could be advertised in the United States, and commented: "Now America is the land of free speech. If you want to say 'I can't believe it's not butter!' you can come right out and say so. . . . But not in Britain."[151]

A contemporaneous tobacco industry campaign began with St. Augustine's admonition "Hear the Other Side" (*audi alteram partem*). "When fundamental freedoms are at stake, it's particularly vital to hear the other side. . . . [A] Court struck down Canada's tobacco advertising ban as 'a form of censorship and social engineering which is incompatible with the very essence of a free society.' " To raise the specter of Puritan intolerance, the next full-page ad quoted Oliver Cromwell, "Not what they want but what is good for them," adding "there's something inherently anti-democratic in imposing upon people your view of what's best for them." A third invoked Juvenal, "Let my will replace reasoned judgement," and sought to inflame British resentment of Eurocrats: "That's not fair or democratic. But that seems to be Brussels' view when it comes to tobacco advertising." To undercut a French requirement that packages warn that smoking "seriously harms health" and mention one of five specified risks, tobacco companies added "according to Law 91-32"—an implicit appeal to French anti-statism.[152]

Philip Morris regained a foothold on television after nearly two decades by subsidizing the National Archives bicentenary celebration of the Bill of Rights, mailing 4 million copies under its corporate logo. A few years earlier it persuaded the New York Public Library to host an awards ceremony for the best essay about the First Amendment. Seeking to identify the right to smoke and to advertise cigarettes with civil rights, feminism, and artistic expression, it also bought large newspaper advertisements featuring Judith Jamison, the black director of the Alvin Ailey American Dance Theatre, and her ambiguous quote: "If anyone loses even a single right, we risk losing them all. . . . We must keep a watchful eye, a sharp mind, and most of all, a willingness to ensure that everyone is afforded the same freedom."[153]

Racists do the same thing. Chapter 2 described how the NSPA shifted public debate from its hateful message to its constitutional right to march. Tom Metzger of the White Aryan Resistance declared: "I believe everything I publish is protected by the First Amendment." Black organizers who invited Holocaust revisionists to a civil liberties conference sounded like the British tobacco industry: "It's time we hear all sides of this thing of holocausts. And that is what the 1st Amendment is all about." The revisionist California Institute for Historical Review bought ads in student newspapers under the name Committee for Open Debate on the Holocaust. The Canadian revisionist Ernest Zundel disseminated fifty half-hour programs on American cable television entitled *Another Voice of Freedom.*[154] Inverting this strategy, Scientology took weekly full-page ads in the *New York Times,* cleverly exploiting German repression of their "Church" to insinuate parallels with the Holocaust.[155] Rap musicians have caught on: Tha Dogg Pound boasted that their new album *Dogg Food* "is about as raw and uncut as it gets. . . . We believe in free speech, man, and we ain't holding nothing back."[156]

Punishment confers visibility. Frank Collin and his pitiful band would have languished in obscurity had Skokie not forbidden the march. When the KKK demonstrated at the Colorado statehouse, vilifying Martin Luther King's birthday as a "Day of Infamy for America," 400 police had to protect the 100 Klansmen from 1,000 opponents, who fought the cops and trashed nearby stores, ensuring extensive media coverage. The state Klan leader welcomed the "million dollars worth of publicity." Whenever Klansmen distributed the *White Patriot* and other racist literature, "somebody usually gets mad and makes a few calls. And bingo! We're back on television." Jean-Marie Le Pen and the National Front gained publicity and even sympathy during regional French elections when demonstrators prevented their plane from landing, mayors banned their gatherings, and police disrupted marches.[157]

As we saw above, art's shock heightens aesthetic effect; its suppression also attracts audiences. When the Salon rejected Gustave Courbet's *Return from the Conference,* he boasted: "I painted the picture so it would be refused. I have succeeded. That way it will bring me some money."[158] Three years after the secretary of the navy seized Paul Cadmus's *The Fleet's In!* his first New York one-man show drew an unprecedented 7,000 visitors.[159] The Brooklyn Museum featured artists censored by the NEA in its "Too Shocking to Show" because "it's a matter of standing up and being counted."[160] When the Singapore film festival awarded top prizes to films banned there and in China, a jury member said the censorship constituted "all the more reason why [they] should be recognized."[161] The Senate hold on CPB funding and the subpoena threat against NPR reporter Nina Totenberg for allegedly leaking Anita Hill's accusations against Clarence Thomas substantially increased donations to public radio and television.[162] After Christian conservatives tried to block the Charlotte, North Carolina, premiere of Tony Kushner's *Angels in America,* the theater sold more tickets than on any other day in its eighteen-year history.[163] Efforts to suppress James Joyce, D. H. Lawrence, and Henry Miller greatly increased sales (if not always readers). Literature that thrived in samizdat under communism has languished in the newly free market. After Stephen Spender attacked David Leavitt for appropriating his life in the novel *While England Sleeps,* Spender was able to publish his first book of poetry in a decade and reissue his "plagiarized" autobiography *World within World,* which had been out of print for twelve years. Gore Vidal's publisher marketed *Live from Golgotha* by quoting reviewers calling it blasphemous and the bishop of Killaloe's assertion "I will not read the book." A. N. Wilson seemed to hope his biography of Jesus would provoke similar outrage in England. Having narrowly missed the Booker Prize three times, Timothy Mo boasted that his latest book, *Brownout of Breadfruit Boulevard,* had "the filthiest opening chapter of any book ever published."[164]

Popular culture is even more calculating—and effective. Dan Quayle's attack on *Murphy Brown*—already CBS's highest-rated entertainment series—allowed the network to charge an average of $310,000 for a thirty-second spot, the most for any regular network program, and sell out commercial time through December even before the season began. A sponsor's ad agency said: "I love being associated with 'Murphy Brown.' . . . the controversy has worked in a positive sense." The hour-long season premiere was seen by 44 million—4 million more than watched the Republican convention. Newspapers carried photos of Dan (accompanied by single mothers) watching Murphy watching Dan criticizing Murphy. ABC's debate over whether Roseanne would be allowed to kiss a woman sent its ratings to the highest in the nation. Ellen DeGeneres seems to be flirting with the same tactic as I write this. When Howard Stern debuted as a disk jockey, his scatological humor and attacks on gays, women, minorities, and the homeless repelled fifty advertisers. A year after the FCC cited him for indecency, however, he had become the most popular morning radio personality among men in New York, Philadelphia, Washington, and Baltimore. The next year he claimed a national audience of 16 million, generating advertising revenue of $360,000 a week.[165]

The print media have learned the same lesson. Attempts to boycott or outlaw True Crime trading cards increased sales to ten times those of any other series. The manufacturer gloated: "[T]he notoriety proved to be the best publicity we could have hoped for." A federal injunction against the true crime book *A Dark and Bloody Ground* produced a second printing. A player's attack on an author of *The Worst Team Money Could Buy: The Collapse of the New York Mets* helped sell nearly 50,000 copies. In a full-page ad touting David Brock's vicious attack on Anita Hill, the Free Press cited Freud, "Many enemies—much honor," and inverted the usual practice by quoting the *worst* bits of three hostile reviews, adding "Anita Hill's admirers *really* don't want you to read this book." It also denounced the *New Yorker* for refusing to print Brock's eight-page reply to Hill's defense by Jane Mayer and Jill Abramson and offered free copies.[166]

Film producers have begun releasing "director's cuts" on video, restoring sex and violence eliminated to secure an acceptable rating: the monster throwing a girl into the lake in the 1932 *Frankenstein,* a gay love scene between Tony Curtis and Laurence Olivier in the 1960 *Spartacus,* and sex scenes between Madonna and Willem Dafoe in *Body of Evidence,* Jeremy Irons and Juliette Binoche in *Damage,* Sharon Stone and Michael Douglas in *Basic Instinct,* and Kim Basinger and Mickey Rourke in *9½.* MPAA president Jack Valenti denounced as "fraudulent blathering" Doug McHenry's complaint about the NC-17 rating for *Jason's Lyric.* Producers "get millions of dollars of free publicity by accusing the rating system of everything but child molestation. It's a marketing gambit." Clearly hoping to repeat or exceed the success of the R-rated *Basic Instinct,* which earned $352 million, Paul Verhoeven issued

Showgirls with an NC-17 rating. All 250,000 copies of an eight-minute promotional tape with the hottest scenes rented immediately, and an estimated million people daily visited the Web site. When it appeared on video, consumers overwhelmingly preferred the NC-17 to the R version. Disney's *Program* was doing poorly until copycat deaths and injuries made it cut the scene in which a football hero lies down in the middle of a highway. Television promptly showed that clip to millions who would never have seen the film.[167]

Black rappers have capitalized on repression of their lyrics. 2 Live Crew used their Florida obscenity trial to promote a new video, about to be premiered on MTV, "about how 2 Live Crew gets punished and sent to Cuba and Castro is waiting for them." The album on which their banned nightclub act was based had peaked when born-again Miami lawyer Jack Thompson began a campaign against it, nearly doubling previous sales. After Broward County sheriff Nick Navarro—nicknamed "Prime Time" Nick for his frequent media appearances—put undercover deputies on the case, he appeared with group leader Luther Campbell on Geraldo Rivera's television talk show, while Phil Donahue paired Campbell with Thompson. The group responded with "Banned in the USA," described as "a rap ode to the First Amendment." Ice-T's "Cop Killer" appeared to prefigure the Los Angeles riots: "I got my 12-gauge sawed off / I got my headlights turned off / I'm 'bout to bust some shots off / I'm 'bout to dust some cops off." After twentieth-century America's worst civil disturbance, the Combined Law Enforcement Association of Texas, the Los Angeles Police Protective League, and the Fraternal Order of Police declared a boycott. A Latina Los Angeles city councilor running for Congress urged Time Warner to withdraw it and local radio stations to pull it. The Houston City Council denounced the lyrics. The California attorney general wrote to eighteen record chains, three of which pulled the song from more than 1,000 outlets. The effect was predictable: sales jumped 60 percent in Los Angeles, 100 percent in Austin, San Antonio, and Dallas, and 370 percent in Houston; the album climbed from 62 to 49 on the charts, selling 330,000 copies in seventeen weeks. Ice-T sold out a live performance in Los Angeles. Claiming to be uninterested in profit, he withdrew the album—provoking a run on the remaining 150,000. At a San Diego concert several months later he read an angry letter from the San Diego Police Officers Association, stuffed it in his crotch, and sang the song defiantly, while the audience yelled, "Die, pig, die." The cover of his next album, *Home Invasion*, had images of men in ski masks beating an older white man bloody and tearing the clothes off a voluptuous young woman. One track warned "From now on, any cops get in our way . . . " followed by the sound of gunfire; another threatened to decapitate Charlton Heston for denouncing "Cop Killer."[168]

RIGHTING WRONGS, WRONGING RIGHTS

Government bans on speech magnify all the usual problems of state regulation and create some new ones. Law dichotomizes experience, rupturing its inherent continuities. Boundaries are incurably arbitrary and therefore indeterminate—such as the Canadian distinction between playful spanking and reddening the buttocks. Gaping loopholes are built into proscriptions. It is impossible to distinguish unlawful speech from the routine opportunism of politicians pandering to popular prejudice: an Enoch Powell, Jean-Marie Le Pen, Patrick Buchanan, David Duke, Dan Quayle, Pete Wilson, or Newt Gingrich decrying the "costs" of immigration, calling for "law and order," depicting AIDS as divine retribution, attacking "racial quotas," or cutting welfare benefits. Legal distinctions elevate form over substance. Skeptics may attack religion but not mock believers. (Which did Rushdie do, or Andres Serrano?) Filmmakers may exploit sex if the actors strip off period costumes. Racists and anti-Semites can cloak their vileness as pseudoscience or history. We concede art's license to shock but cannot circumscribe art.

Legal efforts to regulate speech founder on the ineradicable ambiguity of meaning deployed by the ludic imagination. Context is all: violence may be comedic or newsworthy; both a Star of David and a crucifix may become gang symbols. How do action films, video games, or television cartoons differ from comic books, Punchinello shows, Shakespearean or Greek tragedies, or world mythology? Because the moral content of symbols depends on the identities of and relationship between speaker and audience it can reverse instantaneously, like the optical illusion in which figure and ground oscillate between a vase and profiled faces. Whereas circumstances just modify the severity of other wrongs, they can invert speech from abhorrent to laudable and back. Subordinated groups neutralize stigmata through playfulness: lesbians enjoy erotica that would be pornographic if produced or consumed by men; African Americans call each other "nigger," women use "bitch," gays toss around "queer" and "faggot." Legal formalism's aspiration to universalism blinds it to context, as shown by British prosecutions of black power advocates for racial hatred. The moral content and harmfulness of symbols depend on motives that are difficult or impossible to discern and often mixed. Even the best intentions may mitigate rather than excuse. Extreme examples may be defended as parody, as Bret Ellis protested about *American Psycho* and Henry Louis Gates Jr. said of 2 Live Crew. Audience response, though pivotal, is unpredictable, divided, and fickle—consider the contested interpretations of Sally Mann's photographs or Anselm Kiefer's art. The history of art, literature, politics, religion, morality, and even science should inspire healthy skepticism about the durability of contemporary judgments.

Law can justify the severity of its remedies only by misrepresenting the consequences of speech. Paternalistic concern for pornographic performers may be misplaced. The causes of violence are complex and the culpability of speech unproved. All audiences actively engage in interpretation and criticism—even children seemingly mesmerized by television. Images may inspire projection and fantasy rather than emulation. Preoccupation with extremes—which alone provoke the outrage necessary to mobilize political support for prohibition—diverts attention from the quotidian—which inflicts far greater harm. Posturing politicians propagate apocryphal atrocity stories. Hard-core porn and neo-Nazi rants contribute much less to reproducing attitudes about race, ethnicity, gender, sexual orientation, and physical difference than do the mass media, advertising, popular and high culture, religion, political rhetoric, child-rearing practices, and education. But law cannot mold modal behavior.

If the consequences of speech are too indeterminate to justify punishment, the effects of punishment vary between insignificance and perversity. Law's severity and uncertainties and disagreements about the moral quality of speech make prosecutors reluctant to charge, juries to convict, and judges to punish. Formal law diverts attention from the content of speech to the procedures used to suppress it. The ambiguity of symbols facilitates evasion, allowing speakers to don the raiment of art, science, or politics—forms that law's literalism cannot penetrate. Regulation may fail most profoundly when it appears most successful. Because speech is the offense, the repeat performance at trial aggravates the injury. The process is the punishment—but of victims rather than perpetrators. Far from silencing harmful speech, law encourages, valorizes, and publicizes it, transforming offender into victim and offense into romantic defiance or fundamental right.

CHAPTER SEVEN

. . . .

Taking Sides

Respect has become a central goal in the eternal resistance to subordination.[1] Just as bourgeois revolutions sought political equality and pro-
letarian movements aspired to transform relations of production, so
identity politics strives for dignity. It extends the socialist dream of a
democratized workplace and the social democratic project of material
equality to the realm of reproduction—families, schools, media, culture—which have become pivotal battlegrounds in postindustrial society. The object is control over the means of *re*production: symbols. True
to their postmodern location, protagonists in this contest are complexly
fragmented, without pretensions to be, or become, a universal class.

   Because these cultural wars are waged with words, liberalism is torn
between the extreme responses of libertarianism and authoritarianism,
uncritical tolerance and perfectionist control, idolatry of the market
and obeisance to the state. Both sides incite moral panics. Libertarians
warn that any restraint on speech steps on the slippery slope leading
inexorably to totalitarianism; prohibitionists justify regulation by invoking the specter of assaults on women and minorities. Having argued in chapters 5 and 6 that pure libertarianism is neither possible
nor desirable but state regulation invites excess and error, I now confront the daunting task of charting a path that reduces one harm *of*
speech—disrespect—while minimizing the harms *to* speech—suppressing or distorting expression, provoking and valorizing deviance.[2]
I begin by arguing the need to take sides, drawing lessons from earlier
experiments in particularism. After briefly considering efforts to amplify silenced voices, I focus on responses to disrespectful speech. I
agree that the best antidote to degrading speech is more speech, but
of a particular kind: only an apology can rectify the status inequality
constructed by harmful words. To achieve this, the social settings
within which respect is conferred should encourage victims to complain through an informal process that evaluates speech in context and

makes offenders render an apology acceptable to both victim and community.

THE EVASIONS OF NEUTRALITY

Liberalism is enthralled by the chimera of neutrality, hoping to escape politics and evade responsibility for choice by defining universal principles for the impartial exercise of state power. As rumors of the Holocaust reached Britain in 1943 and local fascists parroted Nazi anti-Semitism, the Socialist home secretary refused to outlaw incitement to hatred against Jews because "it would be contrary to public policy to single out one section of the community for preferential treatment and protection . . . we must maintain the principle that the law is no respecter of persons."[3] Yet critics have shown repeatedly that willful blindness to inequality inevitably perpetuates and magnifies it.[4] Half a century later, unwittingly paraphrasing Anatole France's famous aphorism that "the law, in its majestic equality, forbids the rich as well as the poor to sleep under bridges," the British home secretary defended his denial of political asylum against a charge of racism: "Our policy is colour blind. It applies to people wheresoever they come from, whether it is Africa, Asia, or Eastern Europe."[5] His omissions were eloquent: few North Americans or Western Europeans were clamoring at the gates of Britain's depressed economy.

Daily experience exposes the myriad ways formal equality reproduces substantive inequality. Gender-blind allocation of public toilets creates angry lines outside women's bathrooms. Signs on British pubs exclude "anyone wearing soiled clothing or work boots." Programs designed to reduce material barriers to medical care may amplify racial differences: elderly American whites receive four to seven times as many heart bypasses as blacks, and white kidney-disease victims are significantly more likely to obtain transplants.[6] Boys do better on eleven ETS achievement tests (fifty-seven points better on physics), girls on only three (two to four points). Consequently, more than twice as many boys qualify to compete for National Merit scholarships.[7]

Liberalism rationalizes the persistence of inequality under conditions of political freedom as the expression of private "choice." Sometimes this rhetoric degenerates into self-caricature. When California executed its first prisoner in twenty-five years, criticisms of the cruelty of the gas chamber led it to authorize the alternative of lethal injection. The *New York Times* headline read "California Inmates Get Choice in Executions." A Hong Kong refugee coordinator defended the repatriation of Vietnamese boat people: "If somebody is being carried as gently as you possibly can, I don't call that force."[8] The principal arena within which constrained "choice" amplifies inequality, of course, is the "free" market. Its penetration of the third world—and now the second, with the collapse of communism—offers new opportunities for women (and boys) to be sexually exploited and parents to sell their children for adoption. In 1991 the most popular career aspiration among Moscow teenage girls was "escorting" foreigners for hard currency. Fair-skinned adoptive babies fetched more than $40,000 in Berlin.[9]

The "choices" that reproduce hierarchy can be constrained as greatly by culture as by political power and market forces. Some women seeking sexual equality uncritically emulate patriarchal models. *American Gladiators*, appearing on 156 television stations, has attracted more than 15,000 to audition for the chance to scrap with men and women professionals. One mother regularly exposes her four-year-old daughter to its positive role models: "[F]ive women out there, kicking butt, just like the men." A decade after women were admitted to Princeton, they joined their male classmates in "streaking" through town on the first snowfall. "Here's a male tradition," said one. "I not only wanted to be part of it, I wanted to try to take it over." The Princeton women's rugby team chants "Beat 'em, bust 'em" and "Fight, score, win, eviscerate." The captain felt a sense of power "knocking someone else down and coming out on top." Many feminists applauded Dalma Heyn's call to eliminate the double standard by demanding the freedom from marital fidelity enjoyed by men. Camille Paglia has achieved celebrity status by declaring that a woman must "take personal responsibility for her sexuality," be "cautious about where she goes and with whom," and "accept the consequences" of rape caused by her "mistake." She was "delighted that [William Kennedy] Smith was acquitted."[10]

EXPERIMENTS IN PARTICULARISM

Acknowledging that "neutral" passivity is a decision to reproduce the status quo, liberal polities sometimes take responsibility for redressing social, economic, and cultural inequalities: nineteenth-century legislation for women and child workers, Reconstruction for former slaves, and reparations for victims of the Holocaust, the Japanese invasion of Asia, and communist expropriation.[11] More recently the British Labor Party allowed constituencies to exclude male candidates from short lists, and a former French Socialist prime minister agreed to head his party's ticket for European Parliament only if it nominated an equal number of men and women.[12] The College Board is adding a writing component to the PSAT to equalize the chances of girls and boys to become National Merit scholarship semifinalists.[13] Yet liberalism cannot resolve the tension between particularism and universalism. Thousands of Indian students demonstrated against affirmative action in 1990, leading to many deaths and injuries and at least 150 attempted suicides. After the London police altered height and weight requirements to increase minority representation (there were no Chinese, and the proportion who were black was a tenth that of the population), a majority of officers denounced this as prejudice. When the University of Cambridge announced an affirmative action plan affecting less than a dozen of its 10,000 undergraduates, Harrow's headmaster warned against this "dangerous road of social engineering," complaining that "it is not the fault of Harrow boys that they are well taught." Although the lord chancellor began monitoring the ethnicity of applicants for Queen's Counsel (who alone are eligible for the bench), noting that no High Court judge and only two circuit judges were black, the master of the rolls asked: "[W]hy is there a right number of . . . men or women judges?" He simply recommended the best person for the job.[14]

The United States exhibits an equally incoherent mix of rhetorical posturing and political struggle. Women have had some success in achieving "potty parity" in public accommodations and longer bathroom breaks in the workplace.[15] Shaker Heights subsidizes the mortgages of buyers who make neighborhoods more reflective of the racial composition of greater Cleveland. A Chicago suburb advertised for white home buyers after its black population increased from 12 to 48 percent in fifteen years.[16] Yet the Senate rejected what Alfonse M. D'Amato denounced as a "quota bill" that would allow challenges to the death penalty based on statistical evidence of racial disparities: blacks and Hispanics were 25 percent of those charged under federal death penalty statutes but 89 percent of those for whom prosecutors sought the death penalty.[17] And the Bush administration ended the ranking of federal civil service examinees within ethnic groups to equalize representation.[18]

Education is a central battleground. Elementary school boys complain when teachers call on girls just as often.[19] A black Richmond, Virginia, elementary school principal sought to retain the 12 percent of her pupils who were white by grouping them within a single classroom in each grade. Although many parents of both races supported her, some black parents complained, and a state judge barred any transfers before a hearing. The school superintendent ordered her to redistribute the pupils, but white parents submitted evidence that their children exhibited nervous tension or threatened suicide at the prospect. Pressed by black ministers, the NAACP, and the ACLU, the school board voted along racial lines to end clustering; and the federal government threatened to withhold its $14 million annual support if this were not done.[20] Politicians are mining the rich lode of votes to be gained by attacking affirmative action. Liberal Democratic Sen. Joseph I. Lieberman (D-Conn.) called "group preferences" "unAmerican." Running for the Republican presidential nomination, Robert Dole declared: "[A]fter nearly 30 years of government-sanctioned quotas, time-tables, set-asides and other racial preferences, the American people sense all too clearly that the race-counting game has gone too far." "Let's stop dividing Americans by race."[21]

Just as liberalism resists particularistic admission to or treatment within schools, so it is uncomfortable with separatism. The ACLU vigorously challenged a Milwaukee plan to create elementary and middle schools for black boys. The New York Civil Liberties Union condemned a proposed high school emphasizing the experience and culture of black and Hispanic men, located in a minority neighborhood (though nominally open to all). The noted black psychologist Kenneth B. Clark, who had testified for the plaintiffs in *Brown v Board of Education*, criticized the proposal as telling students "'You're different . . . black males have more social and crime problems than others.' . . . This is an approach that stigmatizes rather than educates." An ACLU and NOW Legal Defense Fund lawsuit stopped the Detroit school board from launching an all-male K–8 school, which would be black given the racial composition of the public schools.[22] Yet African American politicians and educators are increasingly divided over the use of busing to achieve desegregation.[23] Most "historically black" public universities want to retain their racial identity. Integrated institutions have reserved classes and especially residence halls for minorities, though the New York Civil Rights Coalition forced a state investigation of them at Cornell, and the university president refused to approve a gay and lesbian dorm because "we're increasingly fragmenting the campus." Some whites have responded by establishing white student unions to defend their privileges and assert cultural superiority.[24]

Other subordinated categories struggle with the contradictions of separatism. Feminists have defended girls' schools, pointing to the success of their graduates and the tendency of coeducational settings to favor boys. Yet a recent study suggests sex segregation may reinforce feminine stereotypes of obedience, conformity, passivity, and niceness. The U.S. Department of Education tolerates classes for the "mathematically challenged," which several states have construed to mean girls (as long as boys are not excluded). Students at Mills College and Texas Women's University resisted pressure to become coed, and enrollment at single-sex institutions increased 19 percent from 1981 to 1993. A renegade feminist supported Virginia Military Institute's proposal to remain all male by creating a parallel program at a women's college emphasizing "cooperative confidence building" and golf and tennis rather than the "rat line" initiation rite. "We really don't need to beat uppityness and aggression and all that out of young women."[25] Activists created the West Hollywood Institute for Gay and Lesbian Education because "we need to unite and come together, developing our culture. Once we've done that, we can integrate and become full participants in a transformed society." The Lesbian Herstory Archives in Brooklyn bars men from some materials. An organizer of the Australian Mardi Gras and Sleaze Ball sought to exclude straights who "have no understanding and no respect for our culture whatsoever." But the editor of a gay newspaper opposed those who "want to go back into segregating themselves again."[26] Disabled university students enthusiastically supported their own center to celebrate "the culture [that] is part of the disability that distinguishes us, the same as people of color organize around their culture." A blind organizer added: "For years we have been asked to live in this able-bodied world, trying to become able-bodied people. The idea here is, I'm proud of my disability and I don't need to be fixed."[27]

Partisanship and exclusivity are indispensable to any struggle against inequality but pose great difficulty for liberal ideals.

EQUALIZING VOICES

Adversaries in the cultural wars employ two particularistic strategies, which require equally particularistic responses. One disseminates symbols through texts, curricula, advertising, elite and popular culture, journalism, and public monuments and rituals, thereby influencing a mass audience, if often superficially. The other targets individuals or small groups, affecting fewer people but often more intensely. Although I am primarily concerned with the latter—institutionalized reactions to harmful speech—this section briefly addresses proactive strategies.

Expression is inescapably partisan, enhancing the visibility and esteem of some by upstaging others. Some liberals follow Holmes in defending the existing mix of messages as the inexorable result of the "marketplace of ideas." Media apologists call this giving consumers what they want. But such rationalizations ignore differences in buying power and the capacity of supply to shape demand while purporting to satisfy it. Both the state and private philanthropy, therefore, respond to market failure by subsidizing cultural production. Women, racial, ethnic, and religious minorities, gays and lesbians, and the physically challenged claim ownership of or space within museums, galleries, exhibitions, libraries, dance troupes, orchestras, films, recorded music, theater companies, choruses, parades, sports teams, and competitions. Affirmative action in the industries that produce and disseminate information and values is one means of equalizing cultural capital—access to and position within symbolic space.[28]

Even trivial changes in the symbolic hierarchy can be momentous. Seeking to erect a memorial to Eleanor Roosevelt in a Manhattan park, an advocate noted that not one statue in the city represented an American woman. (Only 5 percent of the 25,000 national historic landmarks are dedicated to women, and there are only forty public outdoor statues nationwide—five of Lewis and Clark's Indian guide.) Proposing to commemorate Marie Curie sixty years after her death, President Mitterrand said: "It is not normal that no woman has been admitted in the Panthéon on her own merit." Hurricanes, previously named after women (for their unpredictable fury?), now alternate between male and female. Writers and publishers use gender-neutral language and avoid slurs. The new American Methodist *Book of Worship* describes God as "our Mother and Father," "bakerwoman" leavening hopes, and giving "birth to our world." But when York cast a woman as God in the Mystery Plays, the archdeacon expostulated: "It's modern political correctness gone mad." After forty years of assigning men to the Jungle Cruise and women to Storybook Land, however, Disneyland declared all jobs unisex.[29]

Symbolic equality among races is more contested and less advanced. Seeking to respond to *Birth of a Nation*, Oscar Micheaux made "race movies" between the wars, glorifying black life. Two weeks after the Florida legislature required public schools to teach about the Holocaust, it also mandated instruction in black history, which Gov. Lawton Chiles declared "must not be minimized or trivialized." Minority actors have sought to transcend racial stereotypes—successfully in multiethnic performances of *Antigone* and *Uncle Vanya* at San Francisco's American Conservatory Theater. Although African Americans augmented their proportion of prime-time television roles from 0.5 to 17 percent between 1955 and 1992, Latinos declined from 3 to 1 percent. Encouraged by tax incentives, minority ownership of radio and television stations increased from 1 to 3 percent from 1974 until 1994, when Congress ended this program. Racial and ethnic minorities have sought to eliminate offensive images. After two decades of debate, the Virginia Senate voted to rewrite the lyrics of "Carry Me Back to Old Virginia."

When black legislators protested this was insufficient, the lower house voted 87-9 to replace it as the state song. The Arab-American Anti-Discrimination League persuaded a television station in Detroit, which contains the country's largest Arab American community, not to re-broadcast *The Little Drummer Boy*, a 1968 show stereotyping evil Arabs. The Council of Islamic Education objected to textbooks portraying all Muslims as Bedouins who rub sand over their faces and using a camel to symbolize Islam's "moment in time" while representing Spain by cartographers, Japan by Samurai warriors, Austria by the Crusaders, and England by printers. The U.S. House of Representatives asked Imam Siraj Wahaj to give the invocation in 1991; the Senate heard Imam Wallace D. Mohammed do so the following year. The American Muslim Council thanked Russell Baker for referring to "Judeo-Christian-Islamic culture." "Muslim America has been longing to hear and read this sweet expression."[30]

Gays and lesbians are just gaining public recognition. Oscar Wilde finally received a Westminster Abbey memorial nearly a century after his death. New York's "Children of the Rainbow" first-grade curriculum urges teachers to be "aware of varied family structures, including ... gay or lesbian parents." When Ikea pictured a gay couple in main-stream media ads, the editor of *Advertising Age* called it "one small step for Madison Avenue, but ... one giant leap for the gay community" and GLAAD-NY said, "[I]t humanizes us." *Poz* magazine applauded a Nike commercial featuring an HIV-positive legal secretary for "break[ing] down the wall of 'otherness.'"[31]

The "Black Is Beautiful" dolls of the 1970s have inspired other attempts to enhance self-image. When her black three-year-old son cried because he could not grow up to be master of the universe, Yla Eason made him a black Sun-Man, which toy companies then produced commercially. Girls did not notice that an anatomically correct doll had a shorter neck, higher waist, and larger feet than Barbie, but their mothers exclaimed: "Wow! a doll with hips and a waist!" Angered by a Barbie who simpers, "Math class is hard!" East Village performance artists calling themselves the Barbie Liberation Organization bought some 300 other dolls and infiltrated them into stores with new voice boxes. The transformed "Teen Talk" Barbie spit out: "Attack. Vengeance is mine. Eat lead, cobra." Duke cooed: "Will we ever have enough clothes? Let's plan our dream wedding." The parents of an autistic child created a Down-syndrome doll after hearing such a child ask her parents why she did not look like them. A mother described her fourteen-year-old Down-syndrome daughter's response: "She set up all her other dolls around Dolly and was explaining ... [that] Dolly's different than everybody else, even though she'd like to be the same, but it's O.K. to be different . . . everybody's different in their own way."[32] The messages of such media, events, and artifacts appear partisan only because they are counterhegemonic.

CALIBRATING SPEECH HARMS

The previous chapter's critique of state regulation noted the many ways in which the meaning and impact of speech vary with context. In order to think about how speech constructs—and thus might reconfigure—the hierarchy of respect, we must analyze this variation further. Texts, for instance, fall along a stylistic continuum from simplistic propaganda through the subliminal messages of advertising to the irreducible ambiguity of art. Content varies from demotic to esoteric: compare tabloids with scholarly journals, or soap opera with literary criticism. Writing is more permanent than speech but less immediate. Peoples of the book revere writing; oral traditions respect rhetorical and narrative skills. With declining literacy and attention spans, visual images become more powerful than words and appear more truthful. Moving images capture attention more fully than stills but are less omnipresent. Live interaction increases emotional power, but reproduction reaches larger audiences and allows repetition. Spontaneity may excuse and deliberation aggravate. A message expressing the hegemonic culture has greater influence than one challenging received wisdom (which evokes resistance). Audiences may be critical or credulous, attentive or distracted. We have developed a protective carapace against the media's unrelenting assault; all writers and teachers know how little their readers and students absorb or retain. How much do you remember of the last page? the last paragraph?

SPEAKER IDENTITY

Those who speak for collectivities, rather than as individuals, endow their messages with authority and moral consensus. Although James Watt, Reagan's first secretary of the interior, could wreak havoc on the environment with impunity, he was forced to resign after boasting of appointing a committee containing "a black, a woman, two Jews . . . and a cripple."[33] Jesse Jackson's reference to New York as "Hymietown" and Bill Clinton's comment that Mario Cuomo acted as though he had Mafia connections continued to haunt both politicians.[34] J. Peter Grace, chairman and CEO of the chemicals conglomerate W. R. Grace & Company and director of Reagan's Private Sector Survey on Cost Control, had to apologize for saying of Wisconsin's Republican governor

"He doesn't have much competition. Where I come from we have Cuomo the homo, and then in New York City, we have Dinkins the pinkins."[35] Recognizing that the disciplinary powers of police, prison warders, and teachers magnify their words, American courts have upheld limitations on their speech.[36] Reputation can dilute as well as aggravate harm. When Patrick Buchanan sought to revive his failing 1992 presidential campaign by maligning a public television program about gay black men, an ActUp spokesman explained the muted response: "Buchanan is just so vile it's almost redundant to say it." Another activist called Buchanan "an established homophobe."[37] A spoiled moral identity contaminates all future utterances: Paul de Man's and Martin Heidegger's support for Nazism, François Mitterrand's prewar fascism, Philip Larkin's racism, Woody Allen's relations with his stepchildren, T. S. Eliot's anti-Semitism and racism.[38]

SPEAKER MOTIVE

Good motives, if credited, can nullify harm. The *New York Times* reproduced a Nazi caricature of Jews captioned "Don't Trust a Fox in the Chicken Coop or a Jew at His Word" to illustrate a story about the city's proposed Holocaust museum. No one objected when Berlin and Los Angeles museums reconstructed the 1937 "Entartete Kunst" (Degenerate Art) exhibit a half century later. Yet a Berlin critic was upset when a record company issued an "Entartete Musik" series after a similar lapse of time: "To produce records, books and posters with this word across them is the final victory of the Nazis."[39] Blacks, especially women, were insulted when George Mason University fraternity members donned blackface and fright wigs and padded breasts and buttocks for an "ugly woman" skit. And blacks walked out of the Friars Club when Ted Danson appeared in blackface even though (especially because?) Whoopi Goldberg was complicit. But South African "Coloureds" celebrate the New Year's Coon Carnival by painting their faces and dressing in outlandish costumes. Some of the 5,000 Parisians protesting government policy toward immigrants wore blackface. And women expressed no anger when the gay West Hollywood Cheerleaders marched in drag in the eighth annual AIDS Walk Los Angeles or flaming queens annually celebrate Wigstock in the West Village.[40] Although freak shows are condemned as degrading, Jennifer Miller's Circus Amok features her in a (real) beard, wearing padded shorts to simulate male genitals. "Hair is a symbol of power," she declared. "It goes all the way back to Samson." She defended her work as "a strong feminist piece of theater." "I use the platform of the sideshow to de-

freakify." It was unclear, however, whether a modern book reproducing P. T. Barnum's nineteenth-century freaks—albinos, a giantess, Tom
Thumb, a living skeleton, Siamese twins, and of course a bearded
lady—was historical documentation or further exploitation.[41]

Motive is often opaque. What was the intent of the graffiti artist who
amended a "Jesus Saves" poster in a New York subway by adding
"Moses Invests"? Audiences may impute diametrically opposed motives. Alan Dershowitz complained that the *New York Times Book Review*
had "really gone over the edge" and abdicated "responsibility" by publishing a reader's letter denying *both* the Holocaust and the moon land-
ings. Others were "saddened" and called it "obscene." But the editor
of a Jewish newspaper said it helped explain "why some people deny
the Holocaust." Another reader added: "We must be reminded that
'educated' people like [the letter writer] were standing at the train track
watching while the Nazis packed their freight cars."[42]

Even explicit disclaimers may not dispel suspicion. Students at a
Los Angeles community college complained about an AIDS awareness
poster showing HIV-positive victims being bashed by bigots, losing
weight, contracting cancer, and dying—even though it declared: "[N]o
disrespect is intended by this depiction of human suffering."[43] When
Michael Jackson sang "Jew me, sue me, everybody do me / Kick me,
kike me, don't you black or white me," the Simon Wiesenthal Center
dean accepted his claim that the song was "about the pain of prejudice
and hate . . . I am the voice of the accused and the attacked." But the
ADL regional director objected that "hate is too serious a subject for
subtleties. Why single out Jews?" He was unmollified by Jackson's insistence "It's not anti-Semitic because I'm not a racist."[44] At the 1996
Olympics the French synchronized swimming team planned to enact
the German extermination of Jewish women. But though the trainer
insisted, "[T]he routine is in no way a parody. Our message is an appeal
to combat racism," the Council of French Jewish Organizations called
it "tactless and in poor taste," and the French minister of sports canceled it: "There are subjects where we cannot run the risk of communicating messages which could be misinterpreted."[45] Many African
Americans refused to accept Rutgers president Francis L. Lawrence's
repeated declaration that his "slip of the tongue" about racial differences in SAT scores was "precisely opposed to my beliefs."[46]

Some audiences stubbornly disregard motive. Orthodox Jews demanded that Yad Vashem remove photographs of naked concentration-camp inmates being led to their deaths, although an Auschwitz
survivor protested: "Are the pictures indecent, immodest, demeaning,
humiliating? The facts are, not the pictures. We couldn't cover our na-

kedness then. Don't cover it up now." The *New York Times* agreed, illustrating its article with one of the photographs.[47] Although dictionaries long have defined obscenities and racial slurs, an African American sued a CD-ROM encyclopedia for references to "nigger," including Joseph Conrad's *Nigger of the Narcissus*, Dick Gregory's autobiography *Up from Nigger*, and Martin Luther King's memory of being called nigger as a child. Did the plaintiff object the next day when newspapers reported O. J. Simpson's defense lawyers' impeaching Mark Fuhrman's testimony by showing that he lied in denying he had used "nigger" for years?[48]

TARGET

Abstract slurs to collectivities affect larger numbers less intensely; face-to-face affronts may indelibly imprint individuals. Compare pornography on newsstands or in movie theaters with sexual harassment, blasphemous books with desecration of religious sites or disruption of rites, racial hatred by soapbox orators with workplace taunts. The damage inflicted tends to vary inversely with the target's status. Unredressed speech harms fester, proclaiming the victim's vulnerability, transforming tendentious allegation into acceptable stereotype. Insults sting more if directed at ascribed rather than achieved characteristics, because the former implicate personhood more deeply. After a Marseilles street vendor called Albert Cohen "salle youpin" on his tenth birthday, the novelist spent the rest of his long life writing about the shock of being labeled an outsider.[49]

SPEAKER-TARGET RELATIONSHIP

Directionality is critical in asymmetrical relationships. Emma Bovary's desperate pursuit of Rudolphe differs vastly from Philip Carey's obsession with Mildred Rodgers in *Of Human Bondage*. A cartoon in Tina Brown's first *New Yorker* issue showed hard-hatted women making wolf whistles at a man walking by their construction site and yelling "Yo! Nice Butt!" "I think I'm in love!" and "Looking for me, Sweetie?"[50] Many feminists were angry that the first film about sexual harassment, based on Michael Crichton's *Disclosure*, trivialized the harm by making a man the victim.[51] A comment that can be ignored from a cheeky inferior rankles from a superior. Both races enjoyed the film *White Men Can't Jump*, but they split over the struggle between a white adoptive mother and a black birth mother in *Losing Isaiah*. Under the title *White Men Can't Drum*, an American Indian lampooned those who appropriated his culture in wilderness bonding ceremonies. It is no longer acceptable to make a film entitled "Women Can't Add" or even to laud black athletic prowess. During a Michigan State University presidential search it was disclosed that the Florida State president, a leading candidate, once praised the "natural athletic abilities" of blacks, citing data that "a black athlete can actually outjump a white athlete on average." Although he instantly apologized—"The last thing I wanted to do was offend people"—a former president of the undergraduate black association objected: "To try to justify racist views as science is preposterous. When other people in sports and entertainment have come up with these statements, they were axed immediately." So was this candidate.[52]

Groups encourage language among insiders that would be intolerable from outsiders. Blacks play the dozens. Lenny Bruce made a career of telling anti-Semitic jokes to Jewish audiences; the Jewish Museum produced a "Too Jewish" exhibit. Eddie Murphy satirized Jesse Jackson on *Saturday Night Live*. Jeff Foxworthy earned millions ridiculing fellow rednecks on television and records and in books. Cairo critics and sold-out audiences cheered a merciless four-hour satire of Arab sins and character failings. Women writers and artists neutralize misogynist stereotypes by appropriating them. Philip Kan Gotanda's plays caricature Japanese Americans. African American literature professor Henry Louis Gates Jr. waxed nostalgic about the "colored" world depicted in *Amos 'n' Andy*. Although many African Americans have condemned the portrayal of "Nigger Jim" in *Huckleberry Finn*, Gates welcomed evidence that Mark Twain had modeled Huck's speech on a black boy: "[I]t is the black American linguistic voice which forms the structuring principle of the great American novel, and that ain't bad." *The Piano Lesson*, August Wilson's second Pulitzer Prize–winning play, broadly stereotyped blacks dancing, grinning, drinking, gambling, whoring, believing in ghosts, and speaking black English. But blacks condemned *Show Boat* (by Jerome Kern and Oscar Hammerstein, both Jewish) for portraying them as "shuffling, mumbling, dancing, singing caricatures." Hanif Kureishi makes highly critical films about Pakistani immigrants to Britain, Spike Lee about African Americans, and Woody Allen about Jews (although it was unclear whether Diane Keaton's long association with him gave her similar license in *Unstrung Heros*). Maxine Hong Kingston can write about Chinese Americans, Ishmael Reed about African Americans, and James Welsh about American Indians in ways outsiders cannot. *Once Were Warriors*, written, directed, and acted by Maoris, graphically portrayed their family violence, sexual abuse, alcoholism, and poverty. In response to Maori criticism the female lead asked: "How do you expect to grow as a race if you're not prepared to look at the ugliness within it?"[53] Yet common identity can intensify betrayal when community members address outsiders, as shown by the response of Muslims to Salman Rushdie, Jews to Philip Roth, and African American men to Alice Walker.[54]

One subordinated group may allow another liberties that would be deeply offensive if taken by the dominant. Since the late nineteenth century, African Americans have dressed as Indians and adopted tribal names for the Mardi Gras—behavior some Indians accept as expressing gratitude for sanctuary their ancestors offered runaway slaves. Quebec separatists called themselves "white niggers" in the 1970s. "Rock 'n' Roll Nigger" made Patti Smith famous. But after Richard Riordan had to apologize for relating a Richard Pryor joke about the size of a black man's penis, a Latino comedian reminded the Los Angeles mayor of the "unwritten rule in comedy that if you're white you cannot tell ethnic jokes." I doubt many Asian Americans were amused by African American novelist Ishmael Reed's *Japanese by Spring*.[55]

Subordinated groups draw the sting of the worst epithets by domesticating them. Women call each other bitches, and the differently abled call themselves crips.[56] *NYQ*'s publisher explained that "the word queer started up as a way to say it's not derogatory to be a homosexual." Larry Kramer named his play *Faggots*. The opera *Harvey Milk* is full of gay stereotypes. Explaining why he wrote about "opera queens," Yale literature professor Wayne Koestenbaum declared: "I embrace and impersonate the degrading image because there is no way out of stereotype except to absorb it, to critique it by ironically assuming its vestments. . . . I say: Degenerate, c'est moi."[57] The black author of *Negrophobia* portrayed a white teenager transported to a world of bigoted stereotypes: "black people should start taking back these images from our iconography that have been stolen and corrupted through the years by racists. . . . it's a statement of our power instead of self-loathing. . . . It is subverting the perversion."[58] Rap flaunts the "n-word"—Niggaz with Attitude, Ice-T's "Straight Up Nigga," 2-Pac's "Strictly 4 My N.I.G.G.A.Z.," Eazy-E's "Zaggin4evil"; so do the film *Trespass*, Russell Simmons's *Def Comedy Jam*, and Paul Mooney's comedy tape *Race*. The rap magazine *The Source* titled a story about Spike Lee and Charles Barkley "Nineties Niggers." An African American editorial page writer for the *New York Times* denounced *The Bell Curve* as "just a genteel way of calling somebody a nigger." The publicity director for Death Row Records maintained that "in the African American world, we address people with it with much love." But former NAACP head Benjamin F.

Chavis insisted "that term makes us less than human. . . . We cannot let that term be trivialized."[59]

Chapter 6 showed the volatility of the line between pornography and eroticism. Feminist erotica may become pornography in the eyes of men.[60] The meaning of female nudes changes with the artist's gender—consider Kim Dingle's wildly fighting little girls, some in frilly dresses, others naked.[61] What would feminist critics of pornography make of the 1995 convention of romance book publishers, at which Cover Model contestants scantily dressed as pirates, Indians, and firefighters strutted before 4,000 women yelling and barking like dogs? (Romance books account for nearly half of all paperback fiction sales.) Or the photograph of a nude, muscular, hairless man, which launched the eau de toilette Nightflight, targeted at gays?[62] Denounced by feminists for pornography, Dorothy Allison defended the book that won an award for best lesbian fiction: "The huge issue for any incest survivor is learning to enjoy sex. It is why I do the sexually explicit writing that I do." A West Hollywood club suits (or unsuits) its acts to different audiences: "Sin-a-matic" whipping for the S/M crowd on Saturday, audience striptease for the black lesbian community on Tuesday, and topless for straight men on Thursday. Ellen Stohl, a paraplegic, has posed nude in *New Mobility* and *Playboy;* the *Los Angeles Times* photographed her straddling a wheelchair dressed only in high heels and net stockings. When model Linda Sobek was murdered, a memorial magazine pictured her in a string bikini on the front cover and little more on the next forty-six pages. Her photographer said such recognition was "something she was striving for," and her mother agreed there was no better way to honor her daughter.[63]

The interaction between speaker, target, and audience can greatly complicate meaning. When a black artist painted an enormous portrait of a white, blond, blue-eyed Jesse Jackson, captioned "How Ya Like Me Now?" two black men attacked it with hammers while white workers were installing it. The black curator defended it as "an important image that had to be seen, concentrated upon, talked about." Jackson had the last word: "I encourage artistic expression and full artistic freedom. Sometimes art provokes. Sometimes it angers, which is a measure of its success. Sometimes it inspires creativity. Maybe the sledgehammers should have been on display too."[64] Shortly after African American Mayor Harold Washington died of a heart attack, the Art Institute of Chicago displayed a white student's portrait of him in frilly white bra, panties, garter, and stockings, entitled "Mirth and Girth." Three black aldermen stormed into the private show and ordered the police to confiscate the painting, warning it "increased tensions in the African-American community to the point where violence on the scale of the 1960's West Side riots was imminent."[65]

The contestability and mutability of interpretation are illustrated by reactions to Colonial Williamsburg's enactment of a slave auction. Although it had reconstructed slave quarters and developed programs on runaway slaves, the Virginia NAACP declared that "people are outraged" about the auction. The African American department director acknowledged that "this is a very, very sensitive and emotional issue. But it is also very real history." Yet a black minister called it "despicable and disgusting. This is the kind of anguish we need not display." NAACP demonstrators pushed through the audience singing "We Shall Overcome," and the protest organizer objected: "You cannot portray our history in 21 minutes and make it some sideshow." The director stepped out of her character as a house servant, broke down crying, and grabbed the microphone. "You all are going to watch! I want you to judge with honest hearts and minds." Two black ministers sat down on the stage and challenged her to call the police. But the audience of 2,000, three-fourths white, watched silently, and some wept. Afterward the protest organizer lauded the performance: "Pain had a face. Indignity had a body. Suffering had tears."[66]

History also shapes the interpretation of messages. The Crusades informed Muslim response to *The Satanic Verses*, slavery colors American race relations, the Holocaust makes Jews perpetually suspicious of German motives. Absent history and context, offensive speech may remain enigmatic. Den Fujita, an enormously successful Osaka businessman who has sold millions of copies of *The Jewish Way of Doing Business* and *How to Blow the Rich Man's Bugle Like the Jews Do,* claims to be a philo-Semite. "I'm trying to do something good for the Jewish people. Most Jewish people speak two or three languages. They're good at mathematics. The Japanese should learn from that. . . . Business people in and out of Japan call me a 'Ginza Jew.' I am satisfied with that." The Japanese-Israel Friendship Association commented cryptically: "In Japan, there is no anti-Semitism. But many Japanese accept this Nazi-style stereotype that Jews control the world."[67] Karl May, the most popular novelist in German history, fueled his compatriots' fascination with American Indians. Dresden, his hometown, contains a museum, an open-air theater where Winnetou's adventures are enacted each summer, and an annual fair with two miles of exhibits of Indian life, staffed by 700 costumed Germans joined by some real Indians. One German visited reservations biannually to buy artifacts: "Indians

. . . say 'You're European. Go be Vikings.' They think we're crazy. . . .
Hey, I can't help it. I just don't dream about being a Bavarian."[68]

REDRESSING SPEECH HARMS

Although civil libertarians object to any interference with "freedom
of expression," speakers always negotiate style and content with their
auditors. Speech could be "liberated" from such constraints only by
dispensing with an audience—which would render it solipsistic and
pointless. Even (perhaps especially) in the most intimate relationships,
people choose their words with care, thinking and feeling much they
never verbalize; marriage counseling often focuses on problems of
communication.[69] Parents and teachers socialize children to address
siblings and friends properly.[70] All successful performers seek to
please. A century before filmmakers slavishly courted preview audiences, Anthony Trollope, writing *The Last Chronicle of Barset* in the
drawing room of the Athenaeum, heard two clergymen disparaging
his characters, with particular animus toward Mrs. Proudie. Declaring
"I will go home and kill her before the week is over," Britain's best-
selling author promptly did so.[71] When 500 million people in twenty-
seven countries saw the premiere of Michael Jackson's video "Black or
White," some protested a scene of him rubbing his pelvis and un-
zipping his fly and another in which he smashed up cars. Jackson immediately cut both, claiming (bizarrely) "I've always tried to be a good
role model."[72] A month after being acquitted of beating Rodney King,
Stacey Koon "wrote" a book about the LAPD, referring to the victim
as "Madingo" and the amateur video taker as "George of the Jungle."
Koon boasted of viciously kicking a Latino drug suspect in the testicles
and described fellow officers joking that a black man he had repeatedly
shot would survive because blacks "are too dumb to go into shock."
When the book appeared five months later (and Koon was facing federal prosecution), all this was gone. The author said: "[T]hat was part
of the editing process. Those were just raw notes." Daryl F. Gates, just
forced to retire as LAPD chief, debuted on a local radio talk show the
day of the second indictment, exulting "I don't have the restraints that
I had before. . . . Now I can say almost anything I want to say."[73]

Chapter 5 detailed the numerous ways social environments constrain speech. These influences can do much to equalize respect. If
mechanisms for screening and modifying disrespectful messages fail,
however, we need to react to the harm retrospectively. This section
proposes a response.

Victims have the greatest incentive to challenge symbolic subordination. Yet the weakest link in any remedial process is victim passivity (not detection, conviction, and sentencing, as law-and-order demagogues tirelessly repeat). In all regulatory procedures dependent on complaint, most attrition occurs at the earliest stages: naming an experience as harmful, blaming another, and claiming redress.[74] As Gramsci's concept of hegemony emphasized, consciousness is the greatest obstacle because it is invisible, taken for granted. Sexual offenses clearly illustrate this. When France strengthened its law against sexual harassment, a survey revealed that 20 percent of women would not consider themselves wronged if asked to undress during a job interview and 45 percent would not if a male superior asked them to spend a weekend discussing a requested promotion. Only a fourth of British women sexually harassed at work complained to a third party, and just 2 percent took legal action. Despite Americans' reputation for litigiousness, the proportions in Los Angeles were almost identical. Among American rape victims, 70 percent did not want their families to learn, two-thirds feared being blamed themselves, and only a fifth complained to police. An estimated three-fourths of spousal-abuse victims and five-sixths of homophobic assault victims never report.[75]

If such extraordinarily high proportions of physical injuries go unredressed, I would expect even fewer victims of purely dignitary harms to complain. Many will confront social superiors (whereas crime victims generally accuse social inferiors). Publicity aggravates dignitary wrongs. Victims are blamed or have their motives impugned by those they accuse, for example, William Kennedy Smith, Mike Tyson, and Clarence Thomas. Many suffer institutional retaliation: 16 percent of Los Angeles municipal women employees who complained of sexual harassment encountered increased hostility from coworkers and superiors.[76]

Given the overwhelming social disincentives to complain, subordinated peoples must be helped to challenge disrespectful speech. Just as liberal theory limits partisanship when the state speaks, so it constrains partisanship on behalf of speech victims. Yet the state constantly intervenes to remedy the failures of markets (antitrust, consumer protection, labor law, regulated industries), politics (campaign finance, lobbying), and law (legal aid). Victim assistance can dramatically influence how many complain and who they are. The British Law Society's offer of free initial consultations to tort victims increased the proportions of women and unwaged clients. The provision of free cellular phones to racial and sexual harassment victims encouraged them to seek police assistance. A free help line for boarding school pupils received 12,000 calls in its first year (10 percent of the student population), three-fourths from girls.[77] Like any behavior, complaining is learned; official support and tangible rewards encourage repetition and imitation.[78] The Tulsa Sexual Assault Nurse Examination program greatly increased complainant cooperation and prosecutorial success. Racial harassment complaints in Leeds, England, grew tenfold when the Housing Department started responding. Complaints to the Equal Employment Opportunity Commission rose more than 50 percent in the wake of Anita Hill's accusations. In Hollywood many women who had accepted harassment as the occupational hazard of an industry dedicated to selling sex challenged it for the first time. Telephone calls to Los Angeles spousal-abuse hot lines rose dramatically after Nicole Brown Simpson's murder.[79] Because liberal theory and limited resources constrain state assistance, support from private collectivities is essential. Just as trade unions and aggregations of tort victims press their members' claims, so subordinated categories—all of whom lose status when any one suffers disrespect—must support complaints of harmful speech (another reason to allow such groups to strengthen unity through separatism).[80] Since most victimized groups are minorities, they must form coalitions with each other and with principled opponents of subordination.

PROCESSING GRIEVANCES INFORMALLY

The very act of challenging hurtful speech begins to redress the status inequalities speech constructs (just as passivity affirms and encourages them). Yet chapter 6 adduced powerful reasons for minimizing state regulation: procedural fetishism, excessive severity, formalism, inaccessibility, delay, and the danger that perverse incentives will provoke defiance and invite martyrdom. Although I share women's outrage at catcalls and wolf whistles, criminalization seems an inappropriate response.[81] Instead, the communities of civil society should redress harmful speech.[82] Because face-to-face interaction in these settings constructs social status, such confrontations also can alter it. Communities can encourage complaints and offer victims support. Members linked by significant social bonds can exert influence through gossip, cooperation and obstruction, deference and contempt, inclusion and ostracism. Because behavior within communities is more visible and motive more transparent, evasion is more difficult. The redress of speech harms can strengthen community by enhancing civility. Individual communities are not limited to the lowest common denominator of societal consensus about respect but can prefigure a more inclusive equality.

The identity of such communities varies with time and place, but they include schools and universities, workplaces, trade unions, neighborhoods, libraries, stores and shopping malls, the media, public transportation, voluntary associations, sports stadiums, political parties and movements, and religious congregations.[83] Perhaps emulating the Danes who donned yellow stars to defy Nazi demands to identify Jews, the citizens of Billings, Montana, responded to attacks on an interracial couple and Jewish households by filling their windows with menorahs donated by churches and local businesses. The attacks ceased, according to the police chief, because "it became physically impossible for the hate groups to harass and intimidate thousands and thousands of Billings citizens."[84]

Communities should regulate speech informally. Although I elsewhere criticized informalism for extending state power while offering false hope to the powerless, informal community responses to speech harms do just the opposite, exerting influence in situations where state power is inappropriate but indifference unacceptable.[85] Informalism maximizes access and speed, inverting the limitations of legal deterrence by compensating through extensiveness (application to as many speech harms as possible) what it lacks in intensity (the power to deprive offenders of wealth or freedom). The ambiguity of symbol, nuance of meaning, opacity of motive, and richness of history and context—all of which make formal law's dichotomies intolerably crude instruments for regulating speech—create the space and flexibility that allow parties to renegotiate respect. Since a principal goal of the remedial process is to empower victims, it must be controlled by them (not by the professionals who dominate formal procedures). Victims need support from other members of their subordinated category and allies. Both substantive norms and intermediaries must be openly partisan: the object is to equalize status, not resolve conflicts or settle disputes. Because the norms governing status relations are inchoate and evolving, informalism legislates while adjudicating—a confusion of roles that liberal legalists seek to conceal. The norms that emerge from the experience empower future victims.

THE GRAMMAR OF APOLOGY

What do victims want? They want offenders to acknowledge the injury and apologize. Speech can heal as well as harm; the process is the punishment.[86] Just as insults are performative utterances, elevating the speaker's status at the victim's expense, so the only corrective is more speech. The Supreme Court once denied First Amendment protection to "fighting words"; what civil libertarians refuse to acknowledge is that words do not just provoke fights, they *are* fights. Status degradation can be just as harmful as contusions; recognizing its importance avoids the fatal flaw in consequentialist justifications for regulation—the unanswered (and perhaps unanswerable) empirical questions about the behavioral effects of speech.

The response to harmful speech, therefore, should be a structured conversation between victims (with their supporters) and offenders.[87] Once the victim has voiced the grievance, the accused must be allowed to offer an account—an alternative interpretation of ambiguous words and obscure motives.[88] The victim's acceptance may expunge the injury. But because few accounts are entirely credible, an apology may also be necessary. An apology is a ceremonial exchange of respect. Just as harmful speech impairs the status of victims, so apologies are degradation rituals for offenders, who must affirm the norm of status equality, admit violating it, and accept responsibility. Offenders owe, offer, or give apologies, thereby acknowledging moral inferiority. Victims readmit offenders to the moral community by accepting apologies or preserve the moral imbalance by rejecting them. Thus, victims not only initiate the remedial process but also control its outcome by deciding when offenders have been rehabilitated. An audience (equivalent to the one who heard the original insult) often witnesses the apology and evaluates its adequacy.[89]

That apologies are performative is shown by the necessity for following a precise formula—as in prayers, or legally operative language. In Japan, where apology plays a vital social role, the government calibrates its phraseology with scrupulous care. The Liberal Democrats were prepared to express "hansei" (regret) for military cruelties but initially balked at admitting that "our country's invasions and colonization caused unbearable suffering and misery to huge numbers of people." Soon thereafter Socialist prime minister Murayama used those words in China and wrote a scroll saying "I face up to history." When the Diet debated an apology, however, it changed "aggressive acts" to "aggressive-like acts." Yet in accepting responsibility for the comfort woman, Murayama "deeply apologize[d] to all those who . . . suffered emotional and physical wounds that can never be healed." The Chinese Foreign Ministry applauded the substitution of "owabi" for the blander and more ambiguous "hansei."[90]

Successful American apologies display similar elements. When Rep. Patricia Schroeder, an outspoken critic of sexual harassment in the military, was caricatured engaging in oral sex by sailors at Miramar Naval Air Station, the chief of naval operations was in her office apologizing even before she heard of the incident. The commander of Naval Air Force for the Pacific (responsible for Miramar) said he was "humiliated, disgusted, frustrated." "We are going to change . . . a decaying culture that has proven more and more unproductive and unworthy." The Tailhook Association chairman wrote the acting navy secretary: "We apologize to the women involved, the Navy and the nation for our part in what has become a source of embarrassment."[91] George Wallace confessed his sins and sought black forgiveness before the 1976 Alabama gubernatorial race. After winning it with nearly unanimous black support he went unannounced to Montgomery's Dexter Street Baptist Church, where Martin Luther King had launched his civil rights movement, and apologized to the congregation. He crowned the black homecoming queen at the University of Alabama, whose integration he had violently opposed. He apologized to Vivian Malone Jones, whose enrollment he had blocked by "standing in the schoolhouse door." King's widow, Medgar Evers's brother, and Jesse Jackson all forgave Wallace. When he joined in "We Shall Overcome" at the thirtieth anniversary of the Selma march, the Southern Christian Leadership Conference president thanked him "for his act of courtesy. . . . We could not, would not, deny him an act of repentance."[92] In response to Denver Nuggets basketball star Mahmoud Abdul-Rauf's refusal to stand for "The Star Spangled Banner," KBPI shock jocks invaded the suburban Denver mosque where he prays, wearing their shoes, and blasted the anthem on trumpet and bugle, broadcasting this on the radio. The station suspended the offenders, aired an apology daily for a week, and bought newspaper and television ads doing so.[93]

The importance of reciting the offensive acts is shown by singer and model Marky Mark's apology for racism: "In 1986 I harassed a group of school kids on a field trip, many of them African-American. And in 1988, I assaulted two Vietnamese men over a case of beer. I know there are kids out there doing the same stuff now and I just want to tell them, don't do it."[94] By contrast, when Sen. Robert Packwood (R-Ore.) finally took "full responsibility" for sexual harassment that was "just plain wrong," he still would not acknowledge what he had done.[95] The Japanese historian who exposed World War II comfort women said a "sincere apology" sufficient "to restore the dignity of the victims" would require the government to unveil "the entire scope of the military's sexual slavery and admit historical facts."[96] The danger of giving detail, however, is that victims may contest it. Acknowledging that "hundreds of Lithuanians took direct part" in the Holocaust, the new prime minister "assume[d] responsibility for prosecuting those who participated in murder." But the Simon Wiesenthal Center in Jerusalem retorted: "Thousands of Lithuanians were involved in the murder of Jews, not hundreds. And second, their pledge to go forward with prosecutions is a lot of baloney."[97]

Offenders often balk at the self-abasement essential to effective apologies. By offering exculpatory accounts, they resist full responsibility. Although the New York Yankees issued an unequivocal apology for racist remarks by their vice president for community relations, he continued to deny having compared African Americans to monkeys. Eden Jacobowitz was "willing to apologize for calling [black women students at the University of Pennsylvania] water buffalo, but not for racial harassment" because at his Jewish day school "nobody [took] offense" at being called "behameh."[98] When it was disclosed in 1992 that the noted German political scientist Elisabeth Noëlle-Neumann, then visiting at the University of Chicago, had displayed anti-Semitism in her dissertation and articles written in the 1930s, she mixed rationalization with apology.

> Anyone who has dealt with texts written under a dictatorship knows that certain phrases serve an alibi function and are a necessity if one is to be able to write what is in fact prohibited. I am terribly sorry if any hurt was caused by what I wrote 50 years ago. I certainly can say that when I wrote that passage at the time, I had no intention of doing any harm to the Jews.

The Chicago department chair was not satisfied: "Knowing what we know about the Holocaust, there is no reason for her not to apologize. To ask somebody who played a contributing role in the greatest crime of the twentieth century to say 'I'm sorry' is not unreasonable."[99]

Like her, many admit the words but deny evil motives. Nixon is a perfect example. His resignation speech "regret[ted] deeply any injuries that may have been done in the course of events that led to this decision. I would say only that if some of my judgments were wrong, and some were wrong, they were made in what I believed at the time to be the best interest of the Nation." He then flashed his trademark double victory sign and frozen smile from the helicopter steps on the White House lawn. Some listeners may have been reminded of his earlier disclaimer "I am not a crook."[100] Criticized for a derogatory reference to "Japs," Bush's treasury secretary replied: "At no time did I intend to offend anyone. If I did, I apologize." Rebuked for distributing a racist poem at the Republican caucus, a California assemblyman declared: "I am not a racist by any stretch of the imagination. I didn't mean to offend anyone." Soon thereafter an assemblywoman talked about "Jewing down" building subcontractors. Explaining she "had used the term in the past and never thought of the offense," she admitted, "I needed correcting." The *Los Angeles Times* editorialized about both incidents: "'sorry' somehow doesn't quite take back the insidious effects of uttering racist poems and ethnic slurs."[101] After Marlon Brando said on Larry King that "Hollywood is run by Jews. It's owned by Jews and they should have greater sensitivity about the issue of people who are suffering," he expressed "remorse" but denied that the comments were meant to be anti-Semitic.[102]

Some offenders seek to shift responsibility for the harm to oversensitive or miscomprehending victims. When John Cardinal O'Connor celebrated Black History Month in St. Patrick's Cathedral by expressing "shame" at racism in the church, he qualified this nostra culpa by speaking of "bilateral racism" and making blacks partly responsible for integrating Catholicism.[103] Assailed for calling a black woman's bid to market New York City bonds a "watermelon," Deputy Mayor John S. Dyson replied: "If someone takes this as a racial comment, I'm sorry for that. I apologize for anybody who felt that. I think my record of 20 years in public life shows that I'm not racially motivated one way or the other." Mayor Giuliani backed his deputy: "[A] watermelon . . . in and of itself doesn't suggest [a racial slur]. You can interpret it either way you want. . . . if someone says that's not what I intended . . . I believe a person who says that." The *New York Times* criticized Dyson's "apology" for "put[ting] the burden of misunderstanding on the hearer rather than on the speaker, where it belongs." Dyson should "admit, publicly and without qualification, that he used language that most blacks and many whites would recognize instantly as racist. That should be followed by a promise to avoid both language and behavior that cast doubt on the administration's racial fairness."[104] When white suburban St. Louis police held at gunpoint a Washington University professor and his wife (vice president of the St. Louis Junior League), both black, the mayor regretted "that Prof. and Mrs. Gerald Early felt uncomfortable and unwelcome." The Urban League objected: "That's no apology. [The mayor] could have simply said, 'We apologize to Professor Early and his family, not for their uneasiness but for their treatment.'"[105]

By throwing doubt on the offender's repentance, such reservations may require more abject expressions of contrition. After mocking Judge Lance Ito in a crude Japanese accent, Sen. Alphonse D'Amato (R-N.Y.) said: "If I offended anyone, I'm sorry. I was making fun of the pomposity of the judge and the manner in which he's dragging the trial out."

When the Asian-American Legal Defense and Education Fund said, "[T]he apology doesn't cover the manner in which he made these statements, which was very offensive," D'Amato declared: "I am deeply sorry for the pain that I have caused Judge Ito and others." The fund called this "a good-faith effort to take back what he said" but reiterated its "gut feeling" that "the statements made and the first apology still ring true."[106] After Edward J. Rollins's anti-Semitic remarks managed to insult Willy Brown as well as Harold Berman and Henry Waxman, the political consultant said the "joke" "was not intended to be offensive and was intended to be a humorous comment. If anyone was offended I absolutely apologize." When this proved insufficient, he apologized "profusely" for his "totally inappropriate remark." "My lack of sensitivity is totally inexcusable." He expressed "full repentance" while acknowledging that his new apology "may be unacceptable and inadequate." He was right—several Jewish New York representatives convinced Dole to fire him.[107] Mayor Omar Bradley, condemning Eazy-E for the derogatory portrayal of their town in Niggaz with Attitude's "Straight Outta Compton," simultaneously affirmed his own black identity by criticizing "the specific racial group that's using you, brother . . . and destroying us and having a lunch and a bar mitzvah at the same time." Although he "apologize[d] for the word bar mitzvah," he maintained "that the majority of these black exploitation films and music videos are . . . controlled by people of the Jewish faith." Nevertheless, Los Angeles Jewish leaders accepted his second apology "for any comments made that were anti-Semitic or hurt the Jewish faith or Jewish people in any way."[108]

The status implications of apology become even clearer, and more momentous, when they involve collectivities. The Southern Baptist Convention—founded to defend slavery—declared in 1995: "We lament and repudiate historical acts of evil such as slavery from which we continue to reap a bitter harvest, and we recognize that the racism which yet plagues our culture today is inextricably linked to the past." American Methodists adopted "The Sand Creek Apology," in which they "extend[ed] to all Cheyennes and Arapahos a hand of reconciliation and ask[ed] forgiveness for the death of over 200 mostly women and children" in the 1864 massacre. The Catholic Church apologized for its assimilation policy, which included removing Indian children from their parents. In one of his first actions, French president Jacques Chirac apologized to Jews for Nazi collaboration, whose "dark hours forever sully our history and are an insult to our past and our traditions . . . the criminal folly of the occupiers was seconded by the French, by the French state." The chief rabbi of Paris was "fully satisfied," the president of the European Jewish Congress was "delighted," and Nazi-hunter Serge Klarsfeld said the "speech contained everything we hoped to hear one day."[109]

When the original offense involves acts as well as words—as in many of the above examples—apology may be coupled with material redress. Signing the bill authorizing reparations for wartime internment of Japanese Americans, President Reagan declared it "has less to do with property than with honor. For here we admit we were wrong." The Japanese American Citizens League, which had campaigned for the legislation for decades, emphasized that money showed the apology was "sincere" but "could not begin to compensate a person for his or her lost freedom, property, livelihood or the stigma of disloyalty." By contrast, Philippine "comfort women" denounced Japan's belated apology as "not enough. They should give us the compensation we are seeking."[110] Offenders can strengthen words in other ways. One of Japan's most prestigious publishers apologized for a Holocaust revisionist article that appeared on the fiftieth anniversary of the liberation of Auschwitz and also closed the 200,000-circulation magazine in which it appeared.[111] But just as the Japanese American example reveals that accepting money may taint the victim as greedy, so punishment of offenders can transform outcasts into martyrs. A New York Mets player found committing adultery and using drugs "apologize[d] publicly to my wife and children, the Mets' ownership and management, my teammates, to all Met fans and to baseball in general for my behavior in St. Petersburg." But when the Mets chairman fined him $2,000, the fans' outrage turned to sympathy.[112]

Some offenses are too heinous to admit of apology. Japan refused to allow the American pilot whose plane dropped the atomic bomb to visit the country to apologize. When Israel resumed diplomatic relations with the Vatican, *Haaretz* said the church "should not be forgiven" its long history of persecution.[113] Czech Protestants were equally unmoved by John Paul II's apology for the Counter Reformation: "Today I, the Pope of the church of Rome, in the name of all Catholics, ask forgiveness for the wrongs inflicted on all non-Catholics during the turbulent history of these peoples."[114] Although the newly independent Lithuania draped public buildings in black crepe on the thirty-first anniversary of the destruction of the Vilnius ghetto, "repent[ing] and ask-[ing] the Jewish people for forgiveness," the Simon Wiesenthal Center in Jerusalem said the admissions did not "go far enough." The Knesset president expected demonstrations when the Lithuanian prime minister visited Israel. "There are some people in Israel, especially those with Baltic heritage, who think of Lithuania as one big tragic terrible and surrealistic cemetery of our nation. This is not an easy stereotype to change."[115] Yet an apology's unexpectedness may offset its inadequacy. Although the Soviet Union denied that Jews were the dominant victims of the Babi Yar massacre, the Jewish director of the Babi Yar Center was surprised and gratified when Leonid Kravchuk, president of the newly independent Ukraine, apologized to Ukrainian Jews on the fiftieth anniversary and said Ukrainians must accept "part of the blame." "He came to me personally and apologized. I was at a loss, frankly speaking. We aren't used to apologies." The center made Kravchuk an honorary member.[116]

Even words may be unforgivable. André Bettencourt wrote more than sixty articles in the German-financed *La Terre Française* during the Occupation. On Easter 1941 he called Jews "hypocritical Pharisees" whose "race has been forever sullied by the blood of the righteous. They will be cursed." The following Christmas he wrote:

> Jews thought they had won the game. They succeeded in laying hands on Jesus and crucifying him. Rubbing their hands, they cried out, 'Let his blood fall upon us and upon our children.' You know how it fell and still is falling. Prescriptions in the eternal book must be fulfilled.

Bettencourt subsequently joined the Resistance (earning the croix de guerre), served in the senate and the cabinets of Mendès-France, de Gaulle, and Pompidou, was deputy chairman of l'Oréal, and became a chevalier of the Légion d'Honneur. When two Jewish researchers uncovered the articles in 1995, Bettencourt declared: "I have repeatedly expressed my regrets concerning them in public and will always beg the Jewish community to forgive me for them." But Serge Klarsfeld would not and asked the United States to ban Bettencourt.[117]

Just as inadequate apologies impugn the authenticity of repentance, making victims suspicious of subsequent attempts, so apologies incommensurate with the wrong can trivialize the entire remedy. A former Argentine solider, describing the "dirty war" on a radio talk show, responded to caller Sara Steimberg, whose twenty-two-year-old son had been killed: "I ask your forgiveness again. I threw your son alive into the sea." Chechen rebels sought pardon from their hostages (some of whom were killed in the seizure).[118] Routinization can render collective apologies superficial: Christians to Muslims for the Crusades, Lutherans to Jews for their founder's anti-Semitism, New Zealanders to Maoris, Pope John Paul to Africa for the slave trade and Native Americans for missionary exploitation, whites for slavery, Germans to Dutch for the invasion, Americans to Indians. Moral entrepreneurs make a living organizing such events.[119] A cartoon headlined "Japan to World:

'Sorry about W.W. II!'" nicely captured such vacuity. "For a limited time only, the WORLD'S BEST APOLOGIZER is now available to deliver your expression of regret." Hugh Grant would tell the Bosnian Serbs: "Terribly, terribly sorry about that. Simply no excuse for it." Iraq was a "perfectly ghastly affair, really. Feel just awful about it. Sleepless nights and all that."[120]

Some victims deliberately rebuff apologies to preserve their moral superiority (although an unwarranted rejection may appear prideful or oversensitive). African Americans and other minorities refused the Rutgers University president's apology for racist statements he called a slip of the tongue. Dr. Joycelyn Elders made amends for criticizing the Catholic Church's silence on slavery and opposition to abortion by offering sincere apologies to Archbishop William H. Keller. But the church still forced the surgeon general's resignation within eighteen months.[121] When Shusuke Nomura, a former associate of Yukio Mishima, launched his rightist Society of the Wind movement in 1992, the liberal *Asahi Weekly* modified the party's ideogram to "Society of the Lice." After he protested for a year, the paper declared: "We apologized because this cartoon was published in the midst of a political campaign." After they promised a fuller apology, in response to his continued complaints, he arrived to receive it dressed in a kimono and criticized the paper for nearly an hour. When its president called for end to the tirade, Nomura asked which side faced the Imperial Palace, bowed in that direction, declared he would kill Asahi and himself, and committed suicide (like his mentor).[122] In 1986 the moderator of the United Church of Canada told a gathering of native Canadian elders: "We ask you to forgive us. In our zeal to tell you about Jesus Christ, we were blinded to your spirituality. We imposed our civilization on you as a condition for accepting our gospel. As a result, we are both poorer." The church's National Native Council said: "[T]he happiness felt in the council teepee was almost unbelievable." When the church's general council reconvened two years later, however, the All-Native Circle Conference refused to accept the apology.[123]

Instead of rejecting apologies, victims can further elevate their moral stature by offering forgiveness *without* them. Pope John Paul II visited his attempted assassin in jail and publicly forgave him. Steven Cook accused Chicago archbishop Joseph Cardinal Bernardin of having sexually abused him as a teenager two decades earlier. When Cook's $10 million lawsuit was dismissed after he admitted his recollections under hypnosis were unreliable, Cardinal Bernardin sought him out and offered forgiveness. Although neither Newt Gingrich nor his mother apologized for her statement that Newt had called Hillary Clinton a bitch, the First Lady sent a handwritten note inviting them to a private White House tour. A Gingrich aide conceded that this "gracious" response "showed a lot of class" and said mother and son were looking forward to the visit.[124]

Some offenders, of course, refuse to acknowledge their own misbehavior or the moral superiority of their victims. Insisting that the atomic bombing of Japan was justified, President Bush declared: "No apology is required and it will not be asked of this President, I can guarantee you that."[125] Although New Jersey governor Christine Todd Whitman apologized "to anyone who is offended" by her charge that young black men competed in fathering illegitimate children, she "really [couldn't] pretend that it doesn't happen." Rep. Randy "Duke" Cunningham (R-Calif.) attributed his reference to "homos" to time pressure and promised not to use the slur again but insisted that gays "degrade" military readiness.[126]

HARD QUESTIONS

My proposal that communities secure apologies from those whose words reproduce status inequality raises difficult questions. First, some harmful speech occupies the core of any conception of free expression: self-realization, sociability, religious controversy, political debate, journalistic investigation, artistic creativity, scientific research. Fighting for the souls of Russian Jewish immigrants in Far Rockaway, the Lion of the Tribe of Judah Bible Church screamed at the Jewish Action Group, "You're blind," provoking the retort, "You're a dead carcass swinging on a string."[127] A Taxpayer Party candidate for senator from Illinois ran prime-time television ads showing children singing "How long must the killing go on? How long must the blood be on our hands?" as an adult palm opens to disclose an aborted fetus. His campaign manager said the purpose was to attract children who would make their parents explain abortion.[128] Such harms are the price of freedom; the balance between them must depend on content and context.

Second, my proposal is consciously partisan. It represents a decision not only to value status equality but also to favor some categories over others. In the zero-sum competition for status it is impossible to respect *both* Jews and anti-Semites, gays and homophobes, minorities and racists, women and misogynists. Communities charged with redressing harmful speech will make different choices. Fundamentalist Christian colleges will continue to view homosexuality as sin; some all-male workplaces will flaunt pornography; white militias will assert their racial superiority. No response to this dilemma is entirely satisfactory. A "neutral" principle like "champion the lower of two contending status groups" might favor anti-Semites over Jews in some environments and homophobes over gays and lesbians in others. As I argued at the beginning of this chapter, neutrality is a chimera, choice unavoidable. Once again, this must be informed by history and context. For instance, I would seek respect for nonbelievers in situations where religious belief is hegemonic, but I also sympathize with British Muslims who felt that Rushdie's ridicule reinforced stereotypes of Islamic fundamentalism.

Even if these choices are entrusted to communities, however, there are ways to shape their exercise. One is by example: egalitarian environments may inspire emulation. Spurred by competition from other high tech companies, IBM has joined more than 300 other employers (including Time Warner, Disney, and Xerox) in conferring benefits on the unmarried partners (homosexual and heterosexual) of its 110,000 employees.[129] Without wanting to seem unduly Whiggish, I see post-Enlightenment history extrapolating equality from religious, ethnic, and racial minorities to women, gays and lesbians, and the physically and mentally different. A second influence is integration: prejudice is partly a function of ignorance bred by distance. Dominant groups should not be able to exclude subordinate, therefore, and subordinate groups must reckon the perpetuation of prejudice among the costs of self-segregation. A third set of pressures are informal—exhortation, demonstration, and boycott—the decades-long quarantine of South Africa, for instance, or the successful campaign against Arizona's refusal to commemorate Martin Luther King's birthday. The last recourse is state regulation. Although many other liberal democracies have forbidden egregiously offensive speech, the U.S. Supreme Court has excluded that option.[130] Nevertheless, polities can encourage respect through precept and purse strings, if not prohibition.

The third problem is the intransigent. The degree of constraint should vary inversely with community size (as it does empirically). Although liberal theory imbues the private with an aura of liberty, such environments actually impose greater constraint: people often speak more freely to strangers than to intimates. As the regulatory jurisdiction expands, the increasingly momentous consequences of silencing dissent should prompt greater caution. (This is *not* the conventional public-private distinction; my criterion is the scope of constraint rather than state involvement.) The vice of pluralistic regulation is tolerance of prejudice; its virtue is fostering the greatest variety of messages. Because communities will make different choices about what to allow, members dissatisfied with what they can say or hear in one setting and unable to persuade it to change can move to another. The cost of doing so increases with community inclusiveness. That may explain the safety value of a Hyde Park speaker's corner (where everything is permitted and nothing matters). But a community must be able to back its choices about respect by compelling participation in structured conversations about disrespectful speech while rejecting flimsy excuses and hypocritical regrets. Although informal sanctions may be generally sufficient, a community must be able to expel incorrigibles who continue to violate its norms of respect.[131]

Let me instantiate these prudential judgments by returning to the three narratives with which I began. (This exercise is necessarily provisional; if my multitudinous examples serve no other purpose, they surely demonstrate that the meanings of words depend profoundly on context and require the thickest description for any adequate understanding.) I am unconvinced by consequentialist arguments for state regulation of pornography, especially given the difficulty of distinguishing it from erotica. Yet I am fully persuaded that most pornography objectifies women, denying them respect. This might justify a ban on the display of pornography in workplaces, university dormitories, and public accommodations, its sale in a student bookstore or army PX, even consumption by men in settings where women must observe. The harm, however, is not limited to pornography. All those using sexualized images to sell entertainment or commodities share responsibility for reproducing sexual hierarchy. Yet the meaning of such images varies with context: sexual representation can play an essential role in art, for instance, or in heightening erotic pleasure between equals (both heterosexual and homosexual couples).

Racial hatred does not present the same ambiguities as sex. Our tortured history has led us to enshrine the repudiation of racism in constitutions, statutes, and judicial decisions. My skepticism about state regulation here is strategic, not principled. Both criminal and civil penalties may publicize, valorize, and confer martyrdom on offenders. Had Skokie emulated the silence of other Chicago suburbs, the NSPA would not have persisted. Once the handful of Nazis decided to march, the 6,000 counterdemonstrators easily drowned them out. But this leaves unanswered the hardest question. What if racism, which has been the national ideology in the past and remains hegemonic in many regions, threatened to become dominant once again, as may be happening in the thinly veiled campaigns against affirmative action, immigration, welfare, crime, drugs, and foreign languages? Must a liberal democracy allow its freedoms to be abused by those who would eradicate them if they seized power? The Supreme Court has made it difficult to resist such threats. But its constitutional interpretations do not limit private institutional efforts to ban hate speech and secure apologies from offenders. The commitment of universities to education and truth, for instance, is inconsistent with racist and sexist language by faculty and students. They have properly acted against a man who called a woman a "cunt" and a "fucking bitch," whites who donned blackface to mock Clarence Thomas and Anita Hill, a white man who told an Asian American "it's people like you—that's the reason this country is screwed up . . . you don't belong here . . . whites are always getting screwed by minorities," a white man who called a black woman a "fat-ass nigger," and a fraternity that held a racist "South of the Border" party.[132]

The Satanic Verses poses both moral and strategic issues. Rushdie may be a blasphemer, but so were Moses, Socrates, and Jesus. His novel has great literary merit, but many Muslims felt its stereotypes justified their outcaste status in Europe and especially Britain. Rushdie claimed to have intended just the opposite, invoking his antiracist activities, but many Muslims saw him pursuing fame and fortune at their expense. As I argued earlier, motive is unknowable. Rushdie might have written the novel with greater sensitivity to Muslim feelings; but such self-censorship inhibits creativity, and shock can heighten aesthetic experience.

The Muslim response to publication ranged from misguided to grossly reprehensible. Most demonstrators had not read the book; many of their complaints were unfounded or exaggerated. The threats were intolerable, especially Khomeini's fatwa. By apologizing and embracing Islam, Rushdie did everything he could to restore the honor and respect of his people and religion (short of withdrawing the book—which could not be unwritten). The refusal to forgive him greatly enhanced his moral standing and diminished Iran's (if possible).

If Rushdie was entitled to write and Muslims were morally obligated to accept his apology, other issues are less clear. Face-to-face slurs have a unique power to hurt. Although Rushdie flatly insisted that "free speech is the whole thing, the whole ball game," his own experience belied such absolutism. When a Rugby classmate scrawled "Wogs Go Home," he recalled, "I went insane. I grasped that boy by the collar with my left hand and by the belt with my right hand, and I banged him as hard as I could against the wall he was writing on." This experience indelibly defined his relationship to England. Other school memories rankled more than a quarter century later: a debate about immigration in which his adversary ridiculed his "peculiar brownish color" and urged his exclusion from Britain, and the line about him in the graduation satire: "What is this shape 'midst the nebulous fog? / Merely the resident Bradley House wog."[133] Rushdie's own reaction to such insults, therefore, might justify Muslim bookstores, libraries, and schools in excluding his book. (My emphasis on context urges attention to the medium, means of dissemination, and relationships between speaker and audience—race, religion, education, and class.) The ban by Muslim nations is more troubling. I argued above that the broader the prohibition, the harder it is to justify. Yet if Weimar Germany would have been right to outlaw the National Socialist party before 1933, why should Islamic nations not repel attacks on their religious core? Is it possible to answer that question without passing judgment on the relative merits of democracy and fascism, theocracy and secularism?

THE PRICE OF PERFECTIONISM

If subordinated peoples struggling for respect despair at the resilience of status hierarchies based on religion, ethnicity, race, gender, sexual orientation, and physical difference, even partial victories incur costs: backlash and trivialization, the conceits of identity politics, and revolutionary excess. Adversaries denigrate claims for respect as "political correctness"—a redundant tautology, since politics is inescapable and we all believe ours are correct.[134] What is denigrated as politically correct today may be taken for granted tomorrow. At the instance of two Chippewa high school girls, Minnesota Indians are campaigning to eliminate "squaw" from state place-names because that corruption of an Algonquin word for woman had become the equivalent of "cunt." Although the state department of natural resources viewed it as "a matter of civility," Lake County refused to cooperate, proposing to rename Squaw Creek "Politically Correct Creek." Yet three decades earlier California changed 143 place-names from Nigger to Negro and 26 from Jap to Japanese; the originals would be unthinkable today.[135]

Politicians fuel popular resentment against those seeking respect. Speaking at the 1991 University of Michigan commencement, President Bush warned:

> [W]e find free speech under assault throughout the United States, including some college campuses. The notion of political correctness has ignited controversy across the land . . . replac[ing] old prejudice with new ones. . . . [it] has soured into a cause of conflict and even censorship. Disputants treat sheer force . . . as a substitute for the power of ideas. Throughout history, attempts to micromanage casual

conversation have only incited distrust. They've invited people to look for an insult in every word, gesture, action.[136]

Parodists have a field day: an anguished family at Thanksgiving dinner asking "Are we willing to condone state-sanctioned prayer . . . blatant exploitation of the Native-American . . . and the rampant slaughter of wildlife?" or a Smithsonian exhibit on Hiroshima, with the bomber captioned "Built by oppressed female workers and piloted by the white male establishment, the Enola Gay's mission was the destruction of Japanese culture."[137] The film *PCU* mocked a Politically Correct University. James Garner's politically correct retellings of fairy tales sold more than three million copies in eighteen languages. *Duckman*, which lampoons political correctness, was ranked one of the ten best television shows by the *Wall Street Journal*, attracted a million households, and became the focus of college parties.[138]

Dominant groups seek to delegitimate challenges by retailing reverse atrocity stories that ridicule victims or transmute them into oppressors. The National Scrabble Club of Britain criticized the game's official American dictionary for "carrying political correctness a little too far" by purging racial slurs and derogatory ethnic and religious terms. California kooks are a favorite target. Although respectable jurisdictions like Michigan and the District of Columbia outlaw discrimination based on height, weight, and appearance, a proposed Santa Cruz ordinance led to feature stories about a recently fired psychiatric aide with a tongue plug, purple hair, five earrings, and nose ring, a short Mexican American lesbian who complained about being "vertically challenged," and Sara "Hell," who tattooed her shaved head to highlight a single lock of fuchsia hair. When San Francisco's Ritz-Carlton Hotel rewrote its personnel standards "to specifically deem as unacceptable the matter of facial hair on female employees," a fired employee declared: "I am proud of my mustache. It has been painful and embarrassing to me that someone took away my job based on looks rather than merit." When the city added "gender identity" to categories protected against discrimination, another hotel asked: "If someone comes in with a beard and a miniskirt, do I have to hire them?" A companion ordinance allowed transvestites to choose which public restroom to use, as long as it offered privacy. A Berkeley waitress who refused to serve a man reading *Playboy* generated irate phone calls from male and female soft-porn fans, a boycott, and a "read-in" at the diner, offering free copies from the publisher, delighted by the publicity.[139]

The subordinate, in turn, abuse their moral leverage by playing identity politics, claiming exclusive rights to speak for or about their groups.[140] Three decades ago blacks condemned William Styron for daring to write *The Confessions of Nat Turner* and Laurence Olivier for his portrayal of Othello. By the 1990s only an Asian could be the lead in *Miss Saigon*, and only Latinos could appear in American productions of Ariel Dorfman's *Death and the Maiden*. Latinos objected to Anglos starring in the film of *The House of Spirits* and formed Latinos for Positive Images to protest the same in *The Perez Family*. Canadian blacks attacked the portrayal of American blacks in *Show Boat*, partly because both author and composer were Jewish. Castigating the film of *The Color Purple*, Ishmael Reed declared: "The way that was treated by Spielberg is the best argument I know for African-Americans' control of their projects." Warner Brothers initially hired Norman Jewison, the Jewish director of the highly acclaimed *A Soldier's Story* (about a Southern black regiment during World War II), to direct its film about Malcolm X. After receiving hundreds of protest letters, the studio substituted Spike Lee. While denying he had orchestrated the campaign, Lee acknowledged: "I had problems with a white director directing this film. Unless you are black, you do not know what it means to be a black person in this country." "Most black people are suspicious of white people and their motives. That's just reality." Finally getting it, Disney hired Native Americans to consult and record all the Indian voices in *Pocahontas*. American Indian Movement founder and Wounded Knee protest organizer Russell Means, who played the heroine's father, said the film "presents a host of lousy settlers . . . and there's not a bad Indian in sight. But there's nothing wrong with telling the truth." The American Indian Dance Theater's artistic director, who helped choreograph the animation, insisted "the thrust is authentic . . . and since Russell Means is a tough cookie, they ain't going to be profaning or defaming too much."[141] The Irish American community demanded a greater say in the exhibit "Gaelic Gotham: A History of the Irish in New York" and forced the Museum of the City of New York to replace the guest curator with an Irish American.[142] A Gentile expert in Yiddish and advocate for Soviet Jews, who had taught Jewish studies at Queens College for twenty-five years, was forced to quit as head of the department two weeks after being named. A Jewish colleague said the appointment was "like making me head of the black studies program. . . . Jewish studies exists to give Jewish students a role model."[143]

We know, of course, that identity is neither necessary nor sufficient to ensure a spokesperson's integrity. The list of those who attained community leadership by virtue of identity but engaged in treachery, corruption, or autocracy is depressingly long. And numerous artists have been applauded as authentic exponents of traditions they did not inherit. Two-thirds of Los Angeles ethnic restaurants have Latino chefs—including Cafe Athens, Anna Maria Ristorante Italiano, Four Rivers Chinese Cuisine, Chutney's Indian Fast Food, and Shemiran (Iranian). But Raphael Lopez, who cooked at Izzy's Deli for eighteen years, insisted that Mexican food was "like a tradition. [Anglos] might put in the same thing, but it doesn't taste the same."[144] After Danny Santiago won an Academy of Arts and Letters award for his moving portrayal of East Los Angeles Chicano life in *Famous All over Town*, he embarrassed many admirers by revealing he was a seventy-year-old Jewish graduate of Andover and Yale.[145] *The Education of Little Tree*, which purported to be the true story of a ten-year-old orphan who learned Indian ways from his Cherokee grandparents, sold 600,000 copies, won the American Booksellers Award for the title they most enjoyed selling, and was purveyed on Indian reservations and assigned in Native American literature courses. *Booklist* praised its "natural approach to life." In Tennessee, where the story was situated, the *Chattanooga Times* called it "deeply felt." Lauding it as "one of the finest American autobiographies ever written," an Abnaki poet compared it to a "Cherokee basket, woven out of the materials given by nature, simple and strong in its design, capable of carrying a great deal." The distinguished American Indian law professor Rennard Strickland wrote the foreword to the 1990 reissue. The *New Mexican* raved: "I have come on something that is so good, so good, I want to shout 'Read this! It's beautiful. It's real.'" But it wasn't. The pseudonymous Forrest Carter was actually the late Asa Earl Carter, "a Ku Klux Klan terrorist, right-wing radio announcer, home-grown American fascist and anti-Semite, rabble-rousing demagogue" and author of George Wallace's notorious 1963 speech pledging "Segregation now . . . Segregation tomorrow . . . Segregation forever."[146]

Like all political conflicts, struggles for respect breed excess. Two decades after the University of Massachusetts replaced its Indian mascot with a Minuteman, students criticized the latter as insufficiently "inclusive." Schools have banned *The Autobiography of Miss Jane Pittman* for quoting racial slurs, a student production of *Peter Pan* for stereotyping Indians, and the ballet *Romeo and Juliet* for privileging heterosexuality.[147] Japanese newspapers and television prohibit such words as "burakumin" (outcaste), "blind," "crazy," "ugly," "bald," and "short."[148] The portrayal of the adolescent seductress in *Poison Ivy* infuriated most of the audience at the Seattle International Festival of Women Directors. At the New York Museum of Modern Art two months later "half the audience thought it should be seen and talked about . . . the rest found it beneath consideration." When a woman asked, "How could you, as a woman, write a character like Ivy?" the director retorted: "You can't censor art to be the way you want it depicted. Because pretty soon no one can be bad. There can't be bad men. There can't be bad black people."[149]

Status harms and resentments inhibit scientific discourse as well as arts and media. Oscar Lewis was criticized for writing about the culture of poverty, Daniel Patrick Moynihan for speaking of dysfunctional African American families, Hannah Arendt for decrying Jewish passivity in the Holocaust, Fogel and Engermann for suggesting that not all slaves suffered terrible living conditions, Lawrence Harrison for reasserting the link between culture and material inequality.[150] The NIH withdrew support for a conference called "Genetic Factors in Crime" after attacks by black scholars and the Congressional Black Caucus. The African American deputy director of extramural funding at NIH objected to research "offering the prospect of identifying individuals who may be predisposed to certain kinds of conduct." The president of the Association of Black Psychologists denounced the meeting as "a blatant form of stereotyping and racism."[151]

CONCLUSION

In pursuit of the chimera of neutrality, liberalism embraces a passivity that reproduces inequality. By doing so it engages in the very choice it purports to abhor—and makes the wrong one. Affirmative action in education and employment candidly acknowledge the need to correct past injustice and pursue substantive, not merely procedural, equality. This book charts the extension of that struggle from the arena of production to the realm of reproduction, the material to the cultural, wealth and power to respect. All representations elevate the status of some at the expense of others. The contemporary cultural wars express resistance to such symbolic subordination through demands for visibility, attacks on stereotypes, and challenges to insults. Because the last response is psychically (and sometimes materially) costly, victims should be assisted to voice grievances. Just as expression can reproduce and intensify status degradation, so it can restore and confer respect through an apology acceptable to victims. Communities should be encouraged to enact and administer standards of mutual respect, requiring offenders to apologize and expelling incorrigibles.

Commentators who ridicule such efforts as "politically correct" apparently believe that the existing distribution of respect is appropriate and that relations between dominant and subordinate would recover a mythic peace and harmony if only a few troublemakers would just shut up. That, of course, is the delusion of every oppressor: workers would be content absent union organizers, southern blacks without "outside agitators," women without bra-burning feminists, South African blacks without communists, Palestinians without the PLO. Once awakened, however, the aspiration to equality cannot easily be stifled. If progress is fitful and costly, it is important to recall how many forms of status degradation long taken for granted have been delegitimated. Racist, anti-Semitic, and sexist slurs that routinely infected daily discourse have been banished to the margins of deviance. The rants of shock jocks titillate precisely because audiences know that such language is harmful and have largely abandoned it themselves. Indulgence in crude stereotypes by politicians or the mass media has become sufficiently rare to provoke public outcry, which usually compels retraction and apology. In most Western nations hegemonic religion has yielded to pluralistic tolerance. Public disapproval is curtailing sexual harassment. The differently abled, long forced to hide, beg, or display themselves as "freaks," have gained greater access to public life. Even homophobia is in retreat. Communal support for respectful speech builds on these small victories in the eternal struggle for a more humane society.

NOTES

●●

Abbreviations

CHE	*Chronicle of Higher Education*
G	*Guardian*
I	*Independent*
IOS	*Independent on Sunday*
LAT	*Los Angeles Times*
NY	*New Yorker*
NYRB	*New York Review of Books*
NYT	*New York Times*
NYTB	*New York Times Book Review*
NYTM	*New York Times Magazine*
O	*Observer*
T	*The Times*
WMG	*Weekly Mail and Guardian* (Johannesburg)

Chapter 1

1. NYT A3 (9.20.95), A3 (10.5.95), A4 (10.16.95), A6 (11.2.95), §1 p. 6 (12.3.95), §1 p. 11 (1.21.96); LAT A6 (9.22.95), A7 (9.27.95), A11 (10.6.95), A2 (1.13.96), A11 (1.26.96), A4 (1.30.96).
2. NYT 9 (9.23.95), §1 p. 16 (9.24.95).
3. LAT B1 (9.29.95), B3 (9.30.95).
4. NYT A5 (9.29.95), §1 p. 12 (10.8.95), A7 (10.12.95), §1 p. 24 (10.15.95); LAT A4 (10.7.95), A12 (10.18.95).
5. LAT A1 (10.30.95), A3 (11.13.95); NYT A12 (11.9.95).

Chapter 2

1. Downs (1989: 1, 10–23).
2. Quoted in Lederer (1980b); see also Lederer (1980a: 15).
3. Russell & Lederer (1980: 28).
4. Quoted in Lederer (1980b: 127–28).
5. Rubin (1984: 298).
6. Quoted in Echols (1984: 54–56).
7. Alderfer et al. (1982); Perry (1992).

8. Ferguson et al. (1984); 9 (1) *Feminist Studies* 180–82 (1983); see also Linden et al. (1982); Gubar & Hoff (1989); for comparable British debates, see Barrett (1982); Bower (1986); Chester & Dickey (1988); Assiter (1989); *Marxism Today* 22 (July 1990).

9. Vance (1984).

10. Downs (1989: 27–28).

11. This account is taken from Downs (1989: 61–89) and Brest & Vandenberg (1987).

12. Dworkin (1989).

13. MacKinnon (1987: 15).

14. David Rubinstein, "The Porn Law," *City Pages* (1.4.84).

15. Theresa Stanton, "Fighting for Our Existence," *New York Native* (2.25.85).

16. This account is taken from Downs (1989: 95–139) and Brest & Vandenberg (1987: 656–57).

17. Hunter & Law (1987–88).

18. *American Booksellers Association, Inc. v Hudnut*, 598 F. Supp. 1316 (S.D. Ind. 1984).

19. Ibid., 1327.

20. Ibid., 1335–36.

21. 771 F. 2d 323 (7th Cir. 1985).

22. Ibid., 328.

23. *American Booksellers v Hudnut*, 475 U.S. 1001 (1986).

24. Duggan, Hunter, & Vance (1985: 130); NYT A15 (1.17.92); NYTBR 1 (3.29.92); *Time* 52 (3.30.92).

25. NYT A5 (11.24.92).

26. NYT B16 (3.12.93). The 1992 Barnard controversy was echoed a decade later when a feminist law journal at the University of Michigan, where MacKinnon taught, censored videos about prostitution, NYT

B12 (11.13.92). MacKinnon continued to clash with anticensorship feminists, NYT B12 (11.5.93); Strossen (1995); Pally (1994); Kaminer (1992); Heins (1993). She reacted to Ronald Dworkin's serious but critical review by lumping him with "kept writers in pornography magazines," NYRB 36 (10.21.93), reviewing MacKinnon (1993); NYRB 47–49 (3.3.94). For other exchanges, see NYTM 40 (3.13.94); NYTBR 4 (10.1.95).

27. On the history of racial hatred in Chicago and throughout the country, see Walker (1994).

28. *Beauharnais v Illinois*, 353 U.S. 250 (1952).

29. *Chicago v Lambert*, 47 Ill. App. 2d 151 (1964). For a history of the pre-Skokie cases, see Arkes (1975).

30. This account is taken from Neier (1979); Hamlin (1980); Downs (1985); Barnum (1982) (survey research); Gibson & Bingham (1985) (effect on ACLU and support for civil liberties).

31. *Skokie v NSPA*, 366 N.E. 2d 347, 352–53 (1977).

32. *Collin v Smith*, 578 F. 2d 1197 (7th Cir.), cert. denied, 439 U.S. 916 (1978).

33. For a survey of laws, see Anti-Defamation League (1994).

34. *RAV v City of St. Paul, Minnesota*, 112 S.Ct. 2538, at 2541–50 (Scalia, with Rehnquist, Kennedy, Souter, and Thomas, 1992), reversing *In re the Welfare of RAV*, 464 N.W. 2d 507 (Minn. 1991).

35. *RAV v City of St. Paul*, at 2550–

60 (White, with Blackmun and O'Connor, and Stevens in part), 2560–61 (Blackmun), 2561–71 (Stevens, with White and Blackmun in part).

36. NYT §1 p. 1 (12.1.91), B19 (12.5.91), A1, A10 (6.23.92); Cleary (1994).

37. 169 Wis. 2d 153, 485 N.W. 2d 807 (1992).

38. *Wisconsin v Mitchell*, 113 S.Ct. 2194 (1993); NYT A20 (4.20.93), A16 (4.22.93), 1 (6.12.93). See generally Anti-Defamation League (1994). The New Jersey Supreme Court followed the U.S. Supreme Court's distinction in reversing convictions of two men who painted a swastika and "Hitler Rules" on a synagogue and a satanic pentagram on the driveway of a Roman Catholic Church but upholding the conviction of a man for harassment for painting "Dots U Smell" on the garage of a Pakistani family, NYT 9 (10.2.93), A11 (10.13.93), B1 (5.27.94).

39. See Levy (1993); Lawton (1993).

40. *Taylor's Case* (1676) 1 Vent. 293, 86 E.R. 189; Webster (1990: 22).

41. *R v Moxon* (1841) St. Tr. N.S. 693; *R v Hetherington*, 4 St. Tr. N.S. 693 (1841).

42. *Whitehouse v Lemon, Whitehouse v Gay News Ltd.*, QB 10 [1979], AC 617 [1979]; Jones (1980); *New Statesman and Society* 74 (7.15.77).

43. 389 *Hansard* cols. 302, 316, 321, 335 (5th series).

44. Levy (1993: 566–67).

45. The principal source for this account is Appignanesi & Maitland (1989). In one of the nu-

merous ironies of this ongoing tragedy, their original publisher, Collins, withdrew after signing a contract; and when Fourth Estate took over publication, the printer withdrew from its contract, pp. vii–viii.

46. I (3.8.89), cited in Qureshi & Khan (1989: 30).

47. Ruthven (1990: 85).

48. Akhtar (1989a: 12); Ruthven (1990: 87–89); Law Commission (1981: 48).

49. Ruthven (1990: 85). I discuss the Ayodhya conflict in chapter 4. For a study of the "cultural politics" of responses to the book, focusing on India and Islam, see Spivak (1989, 1990).

50. Appignanesi & Maitland (1989: 45–59); Bedford (1993: 127).

51. *Sunday* (9.18–24.88), quoted in Appignanesi & Maitland (1989: 40–41).

52. Appignanesi & Maitland (1989: 42–44).

53. Ruthven (1990: 90).

54. Hamilton (1995–96: 104).

55. Louw (1989); see Coetzee (1996).

56. Appignanesi & Maitland (1989: 24–27, 31–33, 56–57); Ruthven (1990: 84, 86, 91–94, 96).

57. Akhtar (1989b: 238–41); Akhtar (1989a: 1, 6, 11–12, 25, 35, 102); Qureshi & Khan (1989: 1).

58. Qureshi & Khan (1989: i).

59. Qureshi & Khan (1989: 14–15).

60. Modood (1990: 154).

61. Ruthven (1990: 29); Qureshi & Khan (1989: 10).

62. Lecture at Cornell (3.1.89), in Appignanesi & Maitland (1989: 220–28); Ruthven (1990: 29); see also Mazrui (1990).

63. Ruthven (1990: 36). A decade

earlier a British court punished two men under the Public Order Act of 1936 for throwing a pig's head into a mosque while Muslims were present, Law Commission (1981: 156).

64. Ruthven (1990: 62).
65. Jussawalla (1989: 107–8).
66. Akhtar (1989a: 61); Qureshi & Khan (1989: 25); Appignanesi & Maitland (1989: 215–16).
67. *Jewish Chronicle* (2.24.89), in Appignanesi & Maitland (1989: 135).
68. Qureshi & Khan (1989: 25); Appignanesi & Maitland (1989: 181–82).
69. Appignanesi & Maitland (1989: 143); Qureshi & Khan (1989: 26).
70. Ruthven (1990: 102–3); Appignanesi & Maitland (1989: 56–57).
71. Ruthven (1990: 103).
72. Akhtar (1989a: 42).
73. Ruthven (1990: 103).
74. I (1.16.89).
75. Appignanesi & Maitland (1989: 27–29, 67–69, 74–77).
76. No one at the time mentioned Rushdie's devastating portrait of Khomeini as the imam determined to end history, who sacrifices millions of his followers in the pursuit of power, Rushdie (1988: 205–16, 234). Four years later Rushdie denied the influence of those passages: "[T]he book did not exist in a Farsi edition, and there were no copies of the book available in Iran at that time anyway. It's since been admitted by quite high-ranking Iranian offi-

cials that Khomeini never saw a copy of the book; whatever he did he did on the basis of hearsay," Banville (1993). That hardly disproves the connection.

77. Appignanesi & Maitland (1989: 25, 64–65, 92–95, 103); Akhtar (1989a: 80, 93).
78. Saadi (1994).
79. *Times of India* (1.27.89), quoted in Nair & Battacharya (1990: 21).
80. Bedford (1993: 134–36).
81. Webster (1990: 19).
82. Appignanesi & Maitland (1989: 123–24, 126–27); Ruthven (1990: 119–21); Bedford (1993: 132).
83. Appignanesi & Maitland (1989: 102, 127, 171, 174); Qureshi & Khan (1989: 39); Jenkins (1989); Webster (1990: 43).
84. Marnham (1990). Rushdie had received an $850,000 advance, Hamilton (1995–96: 112).
85. Appignanesi & Maitland (1989: 217); Barnes (1994: 102).
86. Appignanesi & Maitland (1989: 69, 101, 134, 140–41); Akhtar (1989a: 26); Qureshi & Khan (1989: 5, 19); Ruthven (1990: 118).
87. Appignanesi & Maitland (1989: 128–29); Qureshi & Khan (1989: 12–13); Bedford (1993: 146); *R v Chief Metropolitan Stipendiary Magistrate, ex parte Choudury* [1991] 1 All E.R. 306.
88. Ruthven (1990: 81); Webster (1990: 107–9, 132); Modood (1990: 143).
89. Appignanesi & Maitland (1989: 132, 142, 145, 154, 191–93);

Ruthven (1990: 114–17);
Coetzee (1994); Bedford (1993:
136–39).

90. Appignanesi & Maitland (1989:
106, 118, 122, 127, 130, 137–38,
185).

91. D'Souza (1993).

92. On relations between Islamic
immigrants and western Europeans, see Gerholm & Lithman
(1988).

93. Appignanesi & Maitland (1989:
183–84, 186).

94. Ibid., 143, 154–56, 159, 164–65).

95. Ibid., 180–81, 185–87; *Mother
Jones* (April 1990) in LAT A16
(3.14.90).

96. Ruthven (1990: 1, 4–5); Rutherford (1990: 25).

97. Akhtar (1989a: 112); Ruthven
(1990: 151–52); Bedford (1993:
154–55).

98. IOS (2.4.90), reprinted in Rushdie (1992: 393–414).

99. Reprinted in Rushdie (1992:
315–29).

100. Webster (1990: 86, 112); Lee
(1990: 98, 103); *Daily Telegraph*
(5.8.90), cited in Bedford (1993:
153).

101. T (12.28.90); Bedford (1993:
158).

102. 20 (2) *Index on Censorship* 34
(February 1991); Rushdie
(1991), reprinted in Rushdie
(1992: 430); Bedford (1993: 161–
62, 169).

103. *Article 19 Bulletin* 12 (July
1991); IOS 1 (11.3.91); G 9
(11.7.91); Bedford (1993: 165).

104. G 20 (11.14.91).

105. NYT §1 p. 2 (12.8.91).

106. NYT A1, B8 (12.12.91), reprinted in Rushdie (1992: 430–
39).

107. NYT 8 (12.28.91) (letter dated
12.16).

108. NYT A19 (2.12.92).

109. MacDonogh & Article 19
(1993); Rushdie (1993).

110. LAT A1 (3.25.92).

111. NYT B2 (1.29.92), B1 (2.14.92),
B2 (2.20.92), B2 (2.29.92), 12
(3.14.92), A18 (3.26.92), A6
(5.1.92), A4 (6.18.92), 1
(7.25.92); LAT A16 (3.26.92);
NYRB 31 (5.14.92); Banville
(1993); Bedford (1993: 175–76).

112. NYT B3 (8.5.92), 8 (10.15.94), §1
p. 15 (10.16.94), A4 (11.15.94),
A6 (3.30.95); Coetzee (1994).

113. NYT A24 (11.4.92), 4 (2.6.93),
§4 p. 21 (2.6.93), A3 (2.15.93),
B2 (2.17.93), A4 (3.9.93); LAT
A5 (2.12.93), B6 (2.17.93); Banville (1993); Barnes (1994: 103–
4).

114. NYT §4 p. 19 (7.11.93) (op ed).

115. Nesin (1994); NYT 4 (7.3.93),
A12 (7.7.95); LAT A5 (7.3.93);
WMG 39 (9.17.93). The last arti-
cle was accompanied by a very
unflattering caricature of
Rushdie.

116. NYT B1 (9.21.93).

117. NYT A3 (10.12.93).

118. *Pour Rushdie* (1993); NYT B1
(11.4.93). Naguib Mahfouz and
eight others were conspicu-
ously absent from the American edition the following year,
For Rushdie (1994).

119. NYT A13 (7.1.93), A1 (11.25.93),
1 (11.27.93), B2 (2.9.94), B6
(2.14.94); LAT A1 (11.29.93), B7
(11.30.93), A1 (12.1.93), B7
(2.14.94); NYTM 9 (1.2.94);
WMG 29 (2.18.94).

120. LAT A4 (3.21.95).

121. NYT B1 (9.8.95); Rushdie

(1996). The ban was struck down in court on the sixth anniversary of the fatwa, NYT B4 (2.14.96).

122. Lee (1990: 103); NYTBR 7 (1.14.96).

123. LAT E1 (9.14.95).

124. NYT §1 p. 9 (10.3.93), A17 (11.30.93), A6 (6.8.94), §4 p. 7 (7.3.94), A3 (7.13.94), A17 (7.14.94), 1 (7.16.94), §4 p. 3 (7.31.94), A7 (8.19.94), §4 p. 4 (8.28.94); WMG 26 (12.30.93); LAT A6 (6.27.94), A23 (7.1.94), A7 (8.11.94), B4 (6.19.95); Weaver (1994).

Chapter 3

1. Hamilton (1995–96: 104).
2. See Jones (1990).
3. Morgan (1977: 169).
4. NYRB 48–49 (3.3.94).
5. Weber (1978: 306).
6. Weber (1978: 391, 932, 937).
7. Gusfield (1963: 14). See also Stone & Form (1953). Page & Clelland (1978: 266) criticize later theorists for replacing Weber's emphasis on lifestyle with the concept of social prestige defined as "approval, respect, admiration or deference."
8. Veblen (1979).
9. Weber (1978: 391).
10. Bourdieu (1984); see Joppke (1986).
11. Hofstadter (1955: 43–44); see also Trow (1958); cf. Elliott & McCrone (1987).
12. Hofstadter (1963: 81–86); cf. Bell (1962).
13. Lipset (1963a: 167–68; 1963b); cf. Rush (1967).
14. Scheler (1961).
15. Ranulf (1964).
16. Gusfield (1963: 3); see also Gusfield (1967, 1968). Gusfield (1962; 1963: 23) explicitly distinguished this from Hofstadter's "expressive politics."
17. Gusfield (1963: 27).
18. Ibid., 4.
19. Adam (1978: 42); Schur (1980).
20. Gusfield (1963: 21, emphasis added).
21. For an attempt to generalize about social movements as a function of status inconsistency, see Wilson & Zurcher (1976).
22. E.g., Peristiany (1965); Fürer-Haimendorf (1967); Bailey (1971); Miller (1993).
23. E.g., Goffman (1951, 1955, 1956, 1959, 1961).
24. Goode (1978).
25. E.g., the work of Alfred Adler; see Jones (1955: 131).
26. Granberg (1978).
27. See Clarke (1987a, 1987b); Wallis (1977); Wood & Hughes (1984).
28. Brandmeyer & Denisoff (1969: 5–6); Billings & Goldman (1979).
29. Edelman (1971: 17); Beisel (1990: 46).
30. Doyle (1937); Myrdal (1944).
31. E.g., Ehrenreich (1981); English (1981); Luker (1984); Petchesky (1984); Joffe (1985); Granberg (1978).
32. Edelman (1960, 1964, 1971, 1976).
33. E.g., Clarke (1987a, 1987b); Wood & Hughes (1984); Wallis (1977, 1979); Bland & Wallis (1977); Wallis & Bland (1979).
34. Williams (1987); see also Cose (1993).

35. Fanon (1965, 1967); Memmi (1965).
36. Gusfield (1963: 178); cf. Hirsch (1976) (positional scarcity).
37. Gusfield (1963: 1).
38. Ibid., 11, 23.
39. Ibid., 6–7; Clarke (1987b: 144).
40. NYT §2 p. 5 (1.12.92).
41. Harding (1991: 380–86).
42. Gusfield (1963); see also Timberlake (1966); Mennell (1969).
43. Hofstadter (1925: 140).
44. Gusfield (1963: 10–11); National Education Association (1951). The "school wars" have been a recurrent theme of American history, Wade (1972); Ravitch (1974).
45. Viereck (1955: 103).
46. NYT (12.5.92); Gusfield (1963: 172); Mankin (1980).
47. Riesman & Denney (1951); Gusfield (1963: 22–23).
48. Nelson (1968); Mennell (1969); Gunnlaugsson & Galliher (1986) (beer in Iceland); Reinarman (1990) (drunk driving).
49. Galliher, McCartney, & Baum (1974); Galliher & Basilick (1979); Galliher & Cross (1982, 1983); Scheerer (1978) (Germany and the Netherlands); Himmelstein (1983).
50. Reinarman (1979); Reinarman, Waldorf, & Murphy (1988); Reinarman & Levine (1989); Duster (1970).
51. Spector & Kitsuse (1977: 13–16, 211, 221).
52. Dienes (1972).
53. Kirkpatrick, Cushing, and Bowman (1973); Wallis (1976); Morrison & Tracey (1978); Tracey & Morrison (1979); Zurcher et al. (1971, 1973); Curtis & Zurcher (1973); Commission on Obscenity and Pornography (1971); Zurcher & Kirkpatrick (1976); Rodgers (1975); Beisel (1990); but see Wood & Hughes (1984).
54. Platt (1977).
55. Cohen (1972).
56. Tierney (1982); Nelson (1984); Johnson (1989); Loeske (1989).
57. Koch & Galliher (1993).
58. Edelman (1971: 27, 49); National Advisory Commission (1968).
59. Westby & Braungart (1970); Braungart (1971); Miller & Sjoberg (1973).
60. Whitehouse (1993).
61. Parkin (1968).
62. Ehrenreich (1989).
63. Beaney & Beiser (1964); Birkby (1966); Page & Clelland (1978); Wade (1972); Hunter (1991, 1994).
64. Gamson (1978) (fluoridation); Douglas & Wildavsky (1982) (environmentalism). In 1995 Californians were still resisting legislation intended to increase the proportion of those drinking fluoridated water from 17 percent to the national level of 62 percent, LAT A3 (4.18.95).
65. Troyer (1989); Rabin & Sugarman (1993).
66. NYT A9 (3.18.94), §1 p. 15 (5.8.94); LAT A1 (4.15.94), A5 (5.3.94).
67. LAT E1 (4.27.94); NYT §1 p. 27 (9.18.94), A16 (9.26.94).
68. Sixth letter concerning the English nation, quoted in Holmes (1995: 51).
69. Weber (1978: 936).
70. See, e.g., Packard (1961); Riesman (1950).
71. On the symbolic dimensions of

class struggle, see Sennett &
Cobb (1972).

72. Hunter (1991).

73. Edelman (1971: 26–27).

74. Gusfield (1963: 18).

75. Weber (1978: 938). Gusfield
(1963: 26–27) drew the opposite conclusion—that economic
recession accentuates class politics, whereas prosperity highlights status.

76. There is significant overlap, if
also divergence, between status
politics and "revitalization
movements." See Wallace
(1956).

77. See Wattenberg (1995); Aronowitz (1992, 1993).

78. De Tocqueville (1958, 1:3).

Chapter 4

1. E.g., Elon (1994); Silberman
(1993).

2. See Bodnar (1991); Rodriguez-
Salgado (1992); cf. Schmidt
(1995).

3. See Bach (1992).

4. Goldstein (1995, 1996).

5. NYT 4 (12.6.91), A4 (1.6.92), §1
p. 4 (2.23.92), A8 (4.17.92), A13
(11.16.93), §4 p. 4 (1.15.95), A4
(1.25.95); LAT A4 (2.13.95), A8
(2.14.95).

6. LAT A4 (3.18.94), A4 (6.1.94);
NYT A19 (6.7.94), §1 p. 8
(4.2.95).

7. NYT A12 (12.2.91), A28
(12.5.92), D20 (12.6.91), 9
(12.7.91), §1 pp. 1, 24, 26
(12.8.91).

8. NYT A7 (5.18.94); LAT A4
(6.4.94).

9. Nobile (1995).

10. LAT A5 (1.3.94), A25 (1.27.95),
A1 (1.31.95), A1 (3.16.95), A5
(7.3.95); NYT §1 p. 12 (8.28.94),
A9 (8.30.94), 14 (9.10.94) (letters
to the editor), B4 (9.26.94), 10
(10.1.94), §4 p. 15 (10.9.94) (op
ed), A20 (10.10.94) (letters to
the editor), A12 (11.28.94), A12
(1.20.95), A6 (1.26.95), 8
(1.28.95), A14 (1.30.95) (editorial), A1, A15 (1.31.95), §4 p. 5
(2.5.95), 14 (2.26.95), A9
(5.3.95), A6 (5.19.95), §1 p. 4
(5.21.95), §4 p. 15 (6.25.95), A9
(7.10.95), §5 p. 3 (8.6.95); Nobile
(1995); Linenthal & Engelhardt
(1996); Harwitt (1996).

11. NYT §1 p. 25 (12.4.94), A5
(12.8.94), A19 (12.9.94).

12. LAT B1 (7.9.93), E1 (7.14.93).

13. LAT B1 (9.29.93), A3 (5.13.94),
A1 (6.23.94), A3 (1.10.96), A3
(1.18.96).

14. LAT B1 (2.1.95), B1 (2.3.95), B1
(2.4.95), B3 (2.7.95), A12
(2.8.95), B1 (2.9.95), B7 (2.10.95),
B1 (2.11.95), B3 (7.6.95), B3
(10.3.95), B5 (11.27.95); NYT §1
p. 10 (2.12.95).

15. Carter (1995); see also O'Reilly
(1995).

16. NYT §4 p. 7 (11.27.94). David
Duke carries on the same tradition; see Rose (1992).

17. NYT B12 (12.11.91), A1
(1.15.92), A12 (1.29.92), A14
(2.21.92), 8 (2.29.92), §1 p. 15
(3.1.92), B1 (3.24.92); LAT A1,
A18 (2.22.92), A22 (2, 27.92), A1
(2.28.92), A20 (2.29.92), A1
(3.9.92), A12 (3.10.92), A12
(3.16.92), A14 (3.19.92), A18
(4.15.92).

18. NYT C23 (1.30.96).

19. NYT A12 (1.29.92), A12
(1.30.92), A19 (3.26.92), A14

(4.1.92), A17 (4.2.92), §1 p. 14 (4.5.92); LAT A17 (2.22.92), A24 (3.20.92).

20. NYT A1 (11.10.94), A1, B8 (12.6.94), B11 (12.7.94); LAT A13 (1.9.95).

21. LAT A10 (11.22.95); NYT B18 (11.23.95).

22. Cf. Webb (1995); Goldberg (1994).

23. Cf. Waltman (1991).

24. See Juergensmeyer (1993).

25. NYT A12 (3.22.96), §1 p. 18 (3.24.96).

26. G 29 (11.5.91); IOS 8 (11.10.91).

27. NYT §1 p. 5 (11.12.89), A6 (1.21.92), 7 (8.14.93), A6 (1.21.94), §1 p. 5 (9.11.94), 4 (10.29.94); G 29 (11.5.91); IOS 8 (11.10.91); LAT A13 (11.10.95); WMG 19 (5.27.94), 15 (9.23.94).

28. NYT A3 (6.22.95).

29. NYT 5 (1.25.92).

30. LAT B4 (10.2.93), A1 (6.19.95), E1 (6.27.95); NYT §1 p. 3 (4.3.94), 10 (4.23.94), 10 (2.26.95).

31. NYT A8 (2.22.93), A5 (2.25.93); G 22 (12.14.93); WMG 23 (9.30.94); Trillin (1994).

32. See Menendez (1993).

33. Quoted in NYRB 21 (2.2.95) from Midge Decter, "The ADL vs. the Religious Right," Commentary (September 1994).

34. NYT 15 (11.12.92).

35. LAT B7 (9.8.94).

36. NYT (8.29.94), A8 (9.2.94).

37. NYT 7 (7.10.93), C18 (9.1.93), 1, 22 (12.10.94), §1 p. 13 (1.8.95); LAT A2 (7.31.93), A20 (6.24.94), A33 (6.25.94); Elders & Chanoff (1996).

38. NYT B4 (3.24.95), A15 (4.10.95), A19, B3 (4.20.95); LAT A25 (3.25.95).

39. NYT 4 (12.6.91), A4 (1.6.92), §1 p. 4 (2.23.92), A8 (4.17.92), A7 (1.26.93), A4 (2.4.93), A5 (2.15.93), A6 (4.8.93), A5 (5.28.93), A4 (9.10.93), A6 (10.26.93), 4 (1.8.94), A2 (1.21.94), A7 (4.14.94), A13 (4.26.94), §4 p. 6 (5.14.95), 1 (8.5.95), A4 (9.5.95), A7 (9.6.95), A6 (9.14.95); LAT B8 (11.5.92), A1 (1.27.94), A9 (2.15.94), A4 (3.4.94), A1 (6.3.94), A6 (10.6.95); G 5, 7, 12 (12.11.92), 4 (12.12.92), 6 (12.18.92); Laqueur (1993); Poulton (1995); Glenny (1995).

40. NYT A1 (12.6.91), §1 p. 9 (2.23.92), A2 (8.5.93), 2 (8.21.93); LAT A9 (1.15.92), A6 (1.17.92), A9 (8.6.93); Hicks (1995).

41. LAT A10 (8.11.93), A9 (8.14.93), A12 (5.5.94), A5 (5.7.94), A7 (5.11.94), A4 (6.23.94), A8 (8.13.94), A4 (8.24.94), A1 (8.30.94), A1 (4.8.95), A10 (4.18.95), A1 (7.19.95), A4 (8.11.95), A30 (11.14.95); NYT §1 p. 7 (4.25.93), A1 (7.16.93), A7 (5.5.94), 5 (5.7.94), §1 p. 8 (5.8.94), A6 (5.31.94), A7 (8.15.94), A5 (8.16.94), A4 (3.6.95), A6 (5.4.95), §4 p. 3 (5.7.95), A1 (6.7.95), A25 (6.15.95), A1 (8.16.95), A5 (11.14.95), A7 (11.15.95). For a comparison of responses to war guilt in Germany and Japan, see Buruma (1994).

42. NYT C1 (4.9.92), A1 (4.13.92), A6 (8.15.95).

43. NYT B1 (1.18.93), B1 (9.9.93), 12 (9.18.93), B1 (12.22.93), §2 p. 1

(1.2.94), A10 (1.3.94), C2
(1.6.94), §2 p. 1 (1.30.94), C7
(3.23.95), C1 (8.7.95); LAT D1
(9.25.93), A2 (1.28.95).

44. NYT §1 p. 1 (10.1.95).

45. NYT B1 (5.25.93), A4 (11.23.93),
§1 p. 2 (12.26.93), A6 (3.10.94),
A4 (5.15.96).

46. NYT B1 (5.25.93); LAT H2
(3.21.95), A2 (8.24.96).

47. NYT A8 (5.25.94); *Star* (Johannesburg) 1 (7.24.94); *Weekend
Star* 2 (7.30–31.94); LAT H4
(5.9.95), A5 (7.26.96); see generally Matsuda (1991).

48. G 10 (10.17.91); NYT A4
(11.29.91), C1 (2.18.91), §1 p. 4
(2.23.92), A1 (3.15.94), §1 p4
(7.3.94), §1 p6 (8.7.94), A4
(3.20.95); WMG 16 (8.5.94);
Seattle Post-Intelligencer A2
(7.6.94).

49. LAT A1 (1.21.92), A1 (2.3.92),
H4 (4.21.92), A13 (4.9.93); NYT
A6 (5.14.93), A15 (11.2.95);
Globe and Mail A3 (6.5.95);
Richler (1992, 1993).

50. See Baron (1990, 1991); Arington (1991); Shell (1993); Tatalovich (1995). The Supreme
Court is reviewing the Arizona
statute during the 1996 term,
*Arizonans for Official English v
Arizona*, 116 S.Ct. 1316 (1996)
(granting cert.).

51. NYT B13 (3.19.93), A7 (5.14.93),
A8 (5.19.93), §1 p. 1 (6.20.93);
LAT A10 (5.19.93).

52. NYT B7 (12.9.91), §1 p. 4
(1.18.92), A2 (4.17.92), 5
(4.18.92), A18 (12.9.94), A22
(6.8.95), A8 (9.5.95), A11
(7.25.96), §4 p. 7 (7.28.96); LAT
A27 (3.28.92), B1 (4.2.92), B1
(4.17.92), A3, A5 (4.23.92), A13
(10.31.95), A1 (8.2.96).

53. NYT A8 (1.8.93), A1 (1.27.93),
A11 (4.30.93), A8 (1.27.94), A10
(2.24.94), A12 (8.11.94), 7
(9.5.94), §4 p. 5 (1.21.96); LAT
A5 (1.13.93), A5 (2.11.93), A14
(3.10.93), A23 (1.28.94), A6
(7.2.94), 8 (9.24.94), A16
(10.10.94), A1 (3.1.96); see
Forman (1991).

54. NYT C2 (5.10.93), A10 (7.23.93).

55. CHE A39 (1.8.92); NYT §1 p. 20
(12.3.95).

56. NYT 10, 14 (4.21.90); NYTM 21
(5.23.93). On the symbolic sa-
lience of blood donations, see
Titmuss (1972).

57. NYT A1 (1.29.96), A5 (7.29.96);
LAT A1 (1.29.96).

58. IOS 16 (12.6.92); NYT A1
(5.1.93), A16 (7.20.94).

59. NYT §4 p. 5 (6.12.94), D21
(3.27.96) (Muskie obituary).

60. NYT A8 (4.3.92), 8 (4.4.92);
LAT A1 (4.3.92).

61. I 11 (12.9.92); NYT 9 (6.9.90),
B3 (12.17.91), A18 (10.6.93), A14
(10.12.93); LAT A20 (3.13.92).

62. NYT A14 (7.1.94), 14, 16
(7.2.94); cf. Davies (1982).

63. E.g., Fletcher (1988).

64. NYT A7 (12.24.91); LAT A19
(1.13.92), B1 (1.23.92), A22
(1.30.92), A1 (4.22.92), B1
(9.5.96).

65. See Dubin (1987); Perkins
(1995).

66. LAT B1 (2.12.93), B1 (1.23.95),
A5 (3.2.95).

67. NYT A22 (10.19.94); LAT A27
(9.17.93); NYTM 6–7 (7.3.94);
Turner (1994).

68. NYT A1 (12.16.91), §2 p. 4
(2.2.92), §2 p. 25 (8.14.94), §2
p. 1 (9.4.94), C20 (6.15.95), D20
(6.16.95), 14 (6.17.95); LAT F2
(12.21.91).

69. NYT A7 (3.29.93), §2 p9 (7.25.93), B1 (4.27.94), A18 (5.12.94); LAT F1 (7.28.93), B3 (7.31.93); Griffith (1967); Fleener-Marzec (1980); Cutlip (1994).

70. LAT F1 (7.10.93); NYT §2 pp. 1, 22 (6.11.95), A16 (7.12.95).

71. NYT 8 (2.22.92), A7 (2.28.92), 1 (9.5.92), B5 (9.15.92), A18 (10.2.92), §1 p. 8 (2.19.95), B5 (9.19.95); LAT B1 (10.14.93), A1 (12.30.93); 12 (4) *Consortium of Social Science Associations Washington Update* 6–7 (2.22.93); NY 68 (3.13.95).

72. LAT B1 (4.14.93), A1 (5.10.93), A2 (5.15.93), A9 (5.25.93), A1 (11.11.93), A11 (11.17.93); NYT B7 (5.12.93), 6 (5.15.93), B9 (11.3.93); Bernstein (1994); NYRB 16 (10.6.94).

73. *Levin v Harleston et al.*, S.D. N.Y. 90 Civ. 6123 (KC) (9.4.91); Rohde (1991).

74. CHE A4–5 (9.25.91), A19 (11.6.91), A19 (2.5.92); NYT A13 (4.20.90), A18 (3.27.92), A17 (4.23.93), 16 (4.24.93), A1 (5.12.93), A14 (5.19.93), §4 p. 7 (5.23.93), A9 (8.5.93), §1 p. 22 (9.12.93), §1 p. 17 (2.13.94), A16 (4.19.94), A1 (11.15.94), B5 (11.28.94), B3 (12.9.94), A14 (12.29.94), A1 (4.5.95), B12 (6.28.95), A10 (10.3.95).

75. NYT B8 (12.29.93), 15 (1.8.94), §1 p. 11 (1.16.94), §1 p. 14 (1.23.94), A12 (1.25.94), A11 (1.28.94), A8 (2.1.94), A1 (2.4.94), A11 (2.23.94), A9 (2.28.94), A12 (3.1.94), A11 (3.2.94), A1 (3.3.94), A1 (4.21.94), §1 p. 8 (4.24.94), §1 p. 13 (5.1.94), A15 (5.13.94), §1 p. 14 (5.15.94), A1 (12.14.94);

LAT B7 (1.28.94), A12 (2.3.94), A15 (3.1.94), A7 (3.8.94), A5 (4.30.94), A4 (5.2.94). On Black-Jewish relations, see Lerner & West (1995); Friedman & Binzen (1995).

76. Young (1993). On revisionists, see Lipstadt (1993); Vidal-Naquet (1993).

77. NYT A1 (1.20.92), B1 (1.28.92), A5 (2.19.92), A4 (3.23.92), 1 (3.28.92), A6 (3.30.92), §1 p. 4 (1.24.93), §1 p. 10 (1.31.93); LAT A1 (4.1.92).

78. NYT A1 (12.31.93); A10 (9.23.94), A8 (11.16.94), A1 (7.17.95).

79. LAT A1 (7.30.93); NYT A4 (7.30.93).

80. NYT A1 (4.22.93), A1 (4.23.93), A4 (2.15.94), 6 (9.24.94).

81. NYT A3 (5.31.94), 6 (1.14.95).

82. NYT A2 (1.16.95), A4 (1.20.95), A4 (1.26.95), 4 (1.28.95); LAT A6 (1.27.95), A1 (1.28.95), A4 (1.30.95).

83. LAT F1 (1.22.94), F1 (3.1.94), F1 (3.12.94), F1 (3.24.94), A2 (4.12.94); NYT §4 p. 17 (2.6.94), 9 (2.19.94), A9 (2.21.94), B1 (4.7.94).

84. NYT A14 (8.13.93), 5 (3.26.94), §1 p. 8 (9.4.94).

85. LAT A1 (5.25.93), A22 (5.21.94), A18 (8.13.94), A19 (6.29.94); NYT §1 p. 12 (2.13.94), 9 (2.19.94), A10 (5.2.94), A8 (5.18.94), A10 (5.23.94), A8 (8.11.94), A26 (10.7.94), A6 (1.27.95), A12 (1.31.95), 8 (6.3.5), 1 (8.19.95).

86. NYT A1, B10 (3.27.92), §1 p. 1 (4.5.92), B3 (6.15.95), 19 (6.17.95).

87. G 13 (10.10.91), 1 (10.12.91); NYT A1 (4.19.93). For opposing

views on this episode, see
Brock (1993); Danforth (1994);
Mayer & Abramson (1994).
88. G 6 (10.22.91).
89. NYT 7 (5.14.94), A9 (6.17.94).
90. NYT 10 (2.24.90), A14 (3.27.90),
A1 (11.1.90); LAT A17 (11.1.90).
91. I 13 (11.8.91); NYT §2 p. 13
(1.19.92), §2 p. 17 (3.15.92);
WMG 37 (3.25.94); Stoller
(1991); Lederer (1980c: 65).
92. NYT §1 p. 1 (8.15.93).
93. Crenshaw (1991).
94. See, e.g., Chauncey (1994);
Woog (1995); for England, see
Kaufmann & Lincoln (1991).
95. LAT B7 (1.28.93); NYTBR
(12.12.93), 35 (1.16.94); NYT
A10 (3.6.95), A11 (3.8.95);
Bawer (1993).
96. NYT A1 (3.3.94); Farrakhan
(1993).
97. NYT A13 (3.10.92), A15 (3.2.93),
A10 (8.19.93); §1 p. 17
(10.31.93), A1 (12.2.93), A18
(2.1.95), A11 (2.7.95), A10
(12.11.95); LAT A5 (4.26.94);
Baehr v Lewin, 852 P. 2d 44 (Ha.
1993).
98. LAT A3 (1.25.96); NYT A11
(5.31.96), 6 (8.24.96).
99. NYT A6 (7.1.93), A8 (7.30.93),
A11 (11.4.93), A9 (1.12.94), A8
(8.11.94), A1 (10.12.94), §4 p. 6
(10.16.94), §1 p. 10 (5.14.95), 7
(5.20.95), A1, C19 (5.21.96);
LAT A5 (6.9.94), A12 (7.12.94),
A1 (2.22.95), A1 (10.9.95), A12
(11.8.95); *Seattle Post-
Intelligencer* A1 (7.9.94).
100. NYT A11 (3.13.91), 7 (3.14.91),
B17 (12.10.91), A20 (11.23.94);
Wolinsky & Sherrill (1993).
101. LAT F1 (1.9.93), A20 (1.29.93),
A1 (1.30.93), A1 (5.11.93), A1
(5.12.93); NYT A1 (1.13.93), 1

(1.23.93), A1 (2.1.93), A8
(3.25.93), 8 (5.8.93), A1
(5.11.93).
102. NYT A1 (5.28.93), A1 (7.2.93),
A1 (7.14.93), A7 (7.16.93), 1
(7.17.93), A14 (7.20.93), A9
(9.29.93); LAT A19 (7.28.93),
A11 (11.17.93), A12 (4.5.94).
103. NYT A22 (6.9.95), B10 (6.10.95),
A22, 26 (6.16.95).
104. NYT 10 (4.17.93), A11 (2.3.95),
A14 (7.5.95); LAT A3 (5.20.93).
105. NYT A8 (3.19.93).
106. NYT 1 (1.28.95), §4 p. 14
(1.29.95), A14 (1.30.95); LAT A4
(1.28.95).
107. NYT A15 (5.12.95); LAT A27
(5.13.95).
108. NYT A15 (8.25.95), 1 (9.2.95);
LAT A20 (10.18.95).
109. NYT A18 (3.13.91), A15
(3.14.91), §1 p. 1 (3.17.91), A16
(1.22.92), 10 (1.25.92), B16
(1.31.92), B12 (2.26.92), B15
(2.29.92), B12 (3.3.92), §1 p. 21
(3.15.92), B12 (3.16.92), A14
(3.17.92), A16 (3.18.92), §4 p. 16
(3.22.92); LAT A18 (1.25.92).
110. NYT 16 (1.9.93), 16 (1.16.93), 12
(2.13.93), A12 (2.23.93), 9
(2.27.93), A15 (3.11.93), A1
(3.18.93), A13 (8.24.93), A14
(3.4.94), B3 (12.15.94), B8
(3.16.95), 16 (3.18.95), A8
(3.20.95), A14 (6.20.95), A12
(6.29.95).
111. LAT A21 (4.21.94); NYT §1
p. 18 (5.1.94), A11 (6.23.94).
112. NYT B1 (1.30.92), §2 p. 17
(3.29.92), B8 (4.13.92); LAT F2
(12.21.91), F1 (3.16.92).
113. NYT §2 p. 25 (4.22.90), 6
(1.11.92).
114. See Signorile (1993).
115. NYT §4 p. 3 (10.1.95).
116. LAT A4 (2.11.93).

117. LAT A1 (10.12.93); NYT 11 (12.24.94).

118. LAT B1 (8.1.92), B1 (8.12.92), B7 (6.15.93), A18 (10.31.95); NYT A8 (3.22.93), A1 (7.16.93), A12 (11.2.95); Gorski & Allen (1992); Bailey et al. (1993); Dawidoff & Nava (1994); Zhou et al. (1995); Hamer & Copeland (1995); LeVay (1995, 1996); Burr (1996). Even book reviews provoked furious letters, NYRB (7.13.95), 66 (11.2.95).

119. NYT A10 (4.16.93), B8 (2.1.94), A12 (9.6.94), B8 (10.18.94); LAT A18 (10.12.93); McConaghy, Buhrich, & Silove (1994); Laumann et al. (1994).

120. LAT A3 (4.27.94).

121. NYTBR 35 (7.11.93); NYT §1 p. 21 (6.6.93), B1 (6.16.95), 14 (1.27.96).

122. NYT §1 p. 1 (5.16.93), A7 (6.22.94), C1 (10.27.94), §1 p. 33 (11.6.94), A14 (5.2.96); Sacks (1989; 1995: 295); Gallagher (1985).

123. NYT §1 pp. 1, 18 (11.22.92), 16 (1.13.93).

124. LAT A1 (5.23.93).

125. NYT A13 (9.7.93); LAT B3 (9.7.93).

126. NYT §1 p. 10 (9.8.96).

127. NYT 4 (7.8.95).

128. NYT 1 (2.10.96), 1 (7.13.96).

Chapter 5

1. See also Dooling (1996).

2. NYT A4 (11.22.93), §4 p. 1 (5.29.94), A1 (1.17.96); G 1 (12.18.93).

3. NYT A6 (8.5.93), A9 (11.7.94), A5 (1.10.95), A5 (1.18.95), A7 (7.27.95), A10 (11.29.95); LAT A7 (2.25.94).

4. See Hirano (1993) (American postwar occupation of Japan).

5. Miller (1996); NYTBR 11 (1.14.96).

6. LAT H2 (4.7.92); Lee (1990: 109).

7. NYT §1 p. 12 (4.14.91); LAT A15 (4.17.91).

8. LAT A11 (1.31.91), A9 (2.15.91), A3 (2.20.91).

9. LAT A11 (1.31.91), A9 (2.15.91), A3 (2.20.91).

10. NYT 7 (8.14.93), §1 p. 15 (8.29.93), 1 (1.2.95), §1 p. 9 (1.15.95), A10 (1.17.95).

11. NYT A12 (5.4.94), A8 (10.4.94), B11 (11.15.95); LAT A18 (2.19.94); Matthiessen (1983, 1991); Moldea (1989); Logan (1995); *Moldea v New York Times*, 15 F. 3d 1137, modified, 22 F. 3d 310 (D.C. Cir. 1994); see Gillmor (1992).

12. NYT §1 p. 26 (10.16.94), D6 (11.14.94), A1 (8.22.95); LAT A20 (8.24.95).

13. NYT A32 (12.13.91), A16 (1.17.92), §4 p. 4 (1.19.92), A4 (2.14.92), C1 (2.18.92), A11 (4.6.92).

14. NYT A12 (11.4.94), A4 (1.17.96); LAT A8 (1.19.96).

15. LAT A12 (7.31.93); NYT A3 (11.9.93); WMG 23 (11.19.93).

16. NYT A21 (11.30.94), B4 (12.1.94), A24 (12.3.94).

17. NYT B4 (7.19.93).

18. LAT F1 (8.4.93); NYT B1 (8.4.93).

19. NYT B4 (6.30.03), B2 (8.9.93), B4 (10.27.93), B3 (1.28.94), B2 (2.2.94), B3 (2.17.94), B11 (7.18.95) (Spender's obituary); NYTBR 10 (9.4.94), 43 (10.2.94); Leavitt (1993, 1994).

20. NYTBR 35 (7.11.93); NYT §1

p. 24 (10.6.96) (Woody Allen, Eudora Welty, Susan Sontag).

21. Hamilton (1992).

22. NYTBR 34 (1.17.93); NYT A15 (1.22.93); Hamilton (1993).

23. NYT B2 (2.23.94); NYRB 49 (10.20.94); Lesher (1994).

24. NYT C16 (9.21.94).

25. Harris (1980); Malcolm (1993, 1994).

26. NYT B1 (4.6.93).

27. NYTM (1.15.95) (cover story); LAT A4 (1.21.95), A17 (1.28.95).

28. NYT C4 (7.24.95).

29. NYT A4 (12.29.94).

30. NYT §4 p. 2 (12.20.92), A1 (12.31.93), B2 (1.5.94), C1 (2.1.94); LAT F1 (3.12.93), A24, F1 (8.13.93).

31. G 2 (12.15.93); WMG 37 (4.22.94); LAT F1 (5.17.94), F10 (6.3.94).

32. NYT B1 (1.11.94), A9 (11.4.94), §4 p. 6 (12.18.94).

33. LAT F12 (5.24.93), A1 (6.30.93), F1 (8.4.93), F1 (10.14.93), F1 (10.20.93), A1 (10.21.93), A1 (2.1.94), A21 (3.5.94), F1 (6.8.94); NYT A1 (6.30.93), §3 p. 14 (7.18.93), B1 (8.3.93), 1 (1.22.94), 9 (3.5.94), §4 p. 17 (5.1.94), C7 (5.9.94).

34. NYT A1 (6.1.95), D8 (6.5.95), A25 (6.15.95), A1 (7.11.95), A6 (7.30.96); LAT A1 (7.30.95), F1 (5.1.96).

35. LAT A1 (7.2.93), A25 (11.17.93), B1 (11.22.93), G11 (12.18.93), A4 (3.5.94), A18 (4.12.94); NYT C3 (1.11.94).

36. NYT B16 (6.16.92).

37. WMG 23 (11.19.93) (United Kingdom); Abel (1995: chap. 8) (South Africa); O'Malley (1987a, 1987b) (Australia).

38. NYT §4 p. 6 (12.18.94); Wertham (1954).

39. LAT B1 (1.29.92), B1 (1.30.92), F1 (2.5.92), F2 (3.24.92); NYT §2 p. 20 (5.30.93), B3 (9.16.93), B1 (2.4.94); Randall (1968); Walsh (1996).

40. NYT B1 (1.30.92), §2 p. 17 (3.15.92), B1 (12.22.92), §2 p. 11 (2.20.94), B2 (3.30.94), B1 (9.6.94), §2 p. 1 (2.12.95), B3 (6.30.95); LAT F1 (1.18.93), F1 (5.6.93), F1 (9.22.93), F8, F20 (9.24.93), F1 (4.23.94).

41. LAT F1 (1.29.93), A1 (9.28.95); NYT C2 (5.19.95), A1 (6.22.95), C1 (8.10.95), D1 (1.19.96).

42. O 15 (11.17.91); G 8 (11.18.91); NYT B2 (12.16.91), A3 (12.19.91); *Searchlight* 178:15 (April 1990), 179:12 (May 1990), 183:14 (September 1990), 187: 10, 17 (January 1991), 188:7, 17 (February 1991), 190:17 (April 1991), 191:16 (May 1991), 192:5 (June 1991); European Parliament (1985: 81–82); Gordon (1982: 28–36); Coliver (1992); du Plessis & Corder (1994: 122–23, 158–59).

43. NYT A1 (1.19.90), A1 (1.20.90), §1 p. 4 (2.18.90); LAT B3 (3.17.95).

44. NYT A12 (2.21.90), D22 (12.11.91), D1 (12.12.91), A1 (3.10.92), A5 (3.13.92), C20 (9.22.93), A7 (7.14.93), 23 (4.2.94), A15 (12.23.94), A10 (8.15.96); O 6 (11.17.91).

45. NYT 16 (6.27.92), §1 p. 7 (9.6.92), B12 (5.17.93), C1 (7.14.93), 23 (4.2.94), 8 (6.4.94), A15 (12.23.94), C19 (5.3.96).

46. NYT C1 (5.12.92), C16 (4.14.93), A1 (4.16.93), B5 (4.28.93), A1 (11.8.96); LAT A16 (5.20.92), A22 (4.20.95), F2 (1.21.95); *Rubin v Coors Brewing Co.*, 115 S.Ct. 1585 (1995); *44 Liquormart,*

Inc. v Rhode Island, 116 S.Ct. 1495 (1996).

47. NYT B? (6.23.93), A16 (5.5.95), A14 (6.22.95); LAT A5 (8.4.93); *Florida Bar v Went for It, Inc.,* 115 S.Ct. 2371 (1995).

48. LAT A3 (7.6.93), A12 (7.31.93), A5 (2.15.94); NYT A14 (1.11.94).

49. *Discovery Network Inc. and Harmon Publishing Co. v Cincinnati,* 113 S.Ct. 1505 (1993); NYT A11 (3.25.93).

50. NYT 19 (3.19.94).

51. NYT C3 (1.19.94); NYTM 19 (2.13.94).

52. NYT A8 (11.1.94), A8 (11.16.94).

53. NYT C1 (3.5.92), C? (3.16.92), C5 (3.27.92).

54. LAT A21 (3.30.93); NYT C16 (4.8.94), §3 p. 9 (1.29.95); Jacobson (1994); Jacobson & Mazur (1995).

55. LAT A14 (3.9.95).

56. O 6 (11.17.91); LAT A1 (5.19.94); NYT A8 (5.20.94).

57. LAT D1 (6.22.95).

58. NYT C18 (10.6.93).

59. NYT C17 (12.2.93), C18 (4.6.94); LAT F1 (1.10.94).

60. NYT A11 (6.16.93), A1 (5.13.94), A1 (11.23.94); LAT B1 (10.7.93).

61. NYT A7 (11.27.90), §1 p. 34 (12.8.91), §1 p. 9 (3.22.92), A7 (3.31.93), A19 (8.19.94), A6 (10.17.95), A8 (11.9.95), A1 (1.30.96); G 14 (10.11.91); *Mail on Sunday* 3 (11.17.91); NYTBR 1 (3.29.92); Webster (1990: 26–27).

62. NYT §1 p. 1 (12.27.92), B1 (1.18.93), B6 (3.5.93), 12 (9.18.93), B1 (12.22.93), A10 (1.3.94), C2 (1.6.94), B1 (1.11.94), C3 (2.22.94), A1 (6.3.94), §3 p. 7 (10.23.94), A1 (11.30.94), C5 (2.20.95), C2 (2.12.96), C9 (10.7.96); LAT D1

(9.25.93), A2 (1.28.95), A1 (2.8.95), D1 (2.10.96); *Business Day* (South Africa) 2 (8.5.94); WMG 3 (1.27.95).

63. LAT A9 (2.15.94), A10 (2.17.94); NYT §1 p. 8 (9.3.95).

64. LAT A11 (1.21.91), A9 (2.15.91), A3 (2.20.91), A9 (11.4.93), 7 (1.29.94), A35 (11.6.96); NYT §4 p. 2 (12.25.94).

65. LAT A1 (10.7.93), A20 (10.28.93), B1 (12.1.93), B6 (12.2.93), E1 (1.10.94), A3 (1.12.94), B1 (4.9.94), A3 (9.6.94), A15 (4.15.95); NYT A1 (12.11.91), C1 (6.15.92), A16 (8.7.92), A13 (10.7.92), §1 p. 10 (12.26.93), §1 p. 11 (1.8.95), §4 p. 14 (6.4.95); California Senate Bill 1330, Assembly Bill 501.

66. Bezanson (1994).

67. NYT C7 (11.13.95), C4 (1.12.96) (tax abandoned).

68. NYT B4 (2.18.93).

69. NYT A1 (8.27.93).

70. LAT A1 (10.13.93); NYT A12 (11.7.94).

71. NYT §1 p. 14 (1.14.96).

72. NYT A11 (3.8.95), §1 p. 15 (6.25.95).

73. LAT B3 (2.18.93), A5 (11.17.93); NYT A1 (4.2.93), 17 (4.1.95), C11 (4.24.95), A1 (7.7.95), C6 (7.17.95), 17 (7.29.95), C5 (12.14.95); *Turner Broadcasting System, Inc. v Federal Communications Commission,* 114 S.Ct. 2445 (1994).

74. NYT C3 (11.2.93), §4 p. 6 (1.23.94).

75. NYT §2 p. 18 (7.11.93).

76. NYT C4 (9.13.93), A15 (10.26.93), C1 (4.6.94), 17 (7.4.94), C4 (9.27.95), C5 (10.9.95).

77. LAT A20 (11.24.93), A14 (5.12.94), A1 (2.22.95); NYT B5

(4.28.93), A10 (6.15.93), A8, B4 (8.12.93), §1 p. 11 (10.31.93), A1 (2.8.94), §1 p. 40 (12.4.94), 10 (10.8.94), §1 p. 6 (1.15.95).

78. NYT A9 (4.22.94), C6 (8.8.94), D1 (10.25.94), B20 (11.11.94), A18 (12.23.94), A1 (1.30.95), A1 (2.10.95), §4 p. 4 (2.19.95), A1 (2.27.95), A7 (7.27.95); LAT F1 (2.7.95), A17 (7.11.95).

79. LAT A3 (7.5.93).

80. NYT A9 (9.29.93).

81. LAT A3 (9.16.93), A32 (5.10.95).

82. NYT A12 (1.20.95).

83. NYT A1 (10.21.94), 8 (10.22.94), B14 (10.27.94), A20 (11.9.94).

84. *Gentile v Nevada,* 111 S.Ct. 2720 (1991).

85. NYT B1 (4.2.93), A14 (4.27.93).

86. LAT A1 (8.30.94); NYT 7 (9.24.94), A19 (10.4.94), 10 (10.8.94), B15 (10.20.94), A1 (10.21.94), 8 (10.22.94), A16 (11.8.94), B17 (12.1.94), A6 (8.26.96) (civil trial); California Assembly Bill 501, Senate Bill 254; Resnick (1994).

87. LAT B3 (2.18.94) (his suit was dismissed).

88. LAT F1 (4.19.93); NYT §4 p. 4 (9.25.94), A10 (9.28.94), A1 (3.13.96).

89. NYT A15 (8.19.93), B1 (9.8.93), §1 p. 13 (9.26.93), A11 (11.2.93); Irons & Guitton (1993).

90. NYT C5 (2.26.96); Ritchie (1991).

91. WMG 24 (8.27.93) (citing *The Table*).

92. South African *Hansard* cols. 53–325 (1.31.93).

93. NYT §4 p. 4 (2.26.95).

94. LAT B3 (7.9.93); NYT §1 p. 14 (6.5.94), B3 (12.13.94).

95. NYT A1 (12.6.94), A20 (12.9.94).

96. LAT A12 (1.26.95); NYT A8 (1.26.95).

97. NYT A11 (2.23.95).

98. NYT A1 (6.2.93), A12 (6.3.93), A1 (6.4.93), 14 (6.5.93); LAT A14 (6.5.93).

99. NYT A9 (3.31.93), A6 (7.21.93), A7 (4.19.94), B11 (5.13.94), A20 (11.9.94), A12 (2.23.95); LAT A11 (9.22.93); *U.S. v National Treasury Employees Union,* 115 S.Ct. 1003 (1995).

100. NYT §1 p. 16 (6.12.94).

101. LAT A16 (8.11.92), A3 (2.15.94), A3 (4.8.94); NYT §1 p. 18 (9.27.92), A19 (11.7.94), C18 (11.8.94), D25 (11.9.94), A15 (12.27.94); WMG 12 (8.13.93).

102. *Reporting World War II* (1995); Stenbuck (1995).

103. LAT A7 (6.9.93), A10 (6.16.93), 9 (6.19.93); NYT A8 (7.2.93).

104. NYT §1 p. 15 (5.3.92), A23 (6.25.92), 1 (10.3.92), §1 p. 20 (9.12.93), §1 p. 13 (10.10.93), 15 (10.20.93), §1 p. 14 (2.13.94), §1 p. 11 (4.24.94); LAT A17 (10.3.92), A3 (4.8.94), A3 (9.6.94), A24 (1.21.95); Singer (1992); California Senate Bill 1260, Assembly Bill 1685.

105. NYT A13 (1.22.92), B7 (3.30.94); LAT B1 (3.19.94), B1 (5.17.94), B1 (12.7.95); California Senate Bill 1269 (1995).

106. LAT B1 (1.24.92), B1 (4.26.93), A3 (10.1.93); NYT §1 p. 19 (5.1.94), B11 (6.7.95); California Assembly Bill 2543, 2752 (1995); compare *Bright v Los Angeles Unified School District,* 18 Cal. 3d 450 (1977) (protecting student speech under state constitution) with *Hazelwood School District v Kuhlmeier,* 484 U.S. 260 (1988) (rejecting protection under federal constitution).

107. NYT A18 (9.22.93), 10 (10.9.93),

Notes to Pages 148–154 299

A13 (3.14.94), A14 (6.8.94), B8 (10.11.95); LAT A3 (5.4.94), A3 (6.29.94).

108. NYT B8 (10.13.93), A12 (9.1.94), 23 (10.1.94), §1 p. 14 (1.22.95); LAT A3 (4.4.94); Ravitch (1974); Arons (1983); Kirp (1991); Del-Fattore (1992); People for the American Way (1993, 1994); Foerstel (1994); Johnson (1994).

109. NYT A9 (2.21.93); LAT A3 (3.10.94), A23 (3.11.94).

110. LAT A3 (7.28.92).

111. NYT A1 (11.10.89), §1 p. 11 (10.14.94), §1 p. 10 (3.22.92).

112. NYT §1 p. 1 (3.10.96), B7 (9.4.96).

113. *Sunday Times* §10 p. 4 (7.14.96).

114. NYT 18 (4.8.95).

115. LAT F17 (3.13.92).

116. LAT B9 (11.21.95).

117. NYT A16 (8.25.94).

118. NYT 34 (1.1.92), B1 (2.24.94), A16 (3.4.94), AB6 (10.27.94), §2 p. 20 (11.19.95); LAT B1 (2.14.92), F1 (4.23.92). A federal court later found the New Jersey action unconstitutional.

119. The literature on intellectual property is huge; see, e.g., Stewart (1991); Gaines (1991); Boyle (1992); Saunders (1992); Rose (1993); Lury (1993); Goldstein (1994); Branscomb (1994).

120. LAT A12 (3.30.93); NYT A8 (3.30.93), 11 (11.13.93), A1 (3.8.94); *Campbell v Acuff-Rose Music, Inc.*, 114 S.Ct. 1164 (1994).

121. NYT B10 (4.3.92), A9 (10.14.92).

122. NYT B4 (6.23.93), A1 (7.2.93); Hal (1993).

123. NYT 19 (9.17.94); LAT D1 (2.22.95); Sheff (1993).

124. NYT B1 (4.28.92).

125. LAT F1 (3.24.92); NYT §2 p. 23 (7.5.92).

126. NYT A14 (3.29.93), B5 (6.1.93), A9 (6.9.93); Thomas (1952); Oates (1978); see Mallon (1991).

127. LAT D1 (1.25.95), B3 (2.14.95); NYT A7 (8.14.95), A11 (9.14.95), 19 (1.20.96).

128. NYT §2 p. 27 (8.1.93).

129. NYT B4 (6.17.93).

130. NYT A10 (3.18.94), B1 (5.11.94), B1 (9.1.94), 12 (12.2.95).

131. LAT F1 (2.18.95).

132. CHE A35 (4.8.92).

133. NYT C1 (10.21.96).

134. NYT A4 (7.2.93), C2 (7.1.94), B1 (8.29.94), §1 p. 6 (1.1.95), A1 (2.27.95), A1 (4.11.95); LAT A9 (1.5.95).

135. *Outlook Mail* (Santa Monica) A2 (4.27.94).

136. NYT §4 p. 14 (3.26.95); *Daily Bruin* (UCLA) 13 (10.11.95).

137. NYT C1 (2.18.92); LAT D1 (3.15.92).

138. NYT C2 (5.10.93), A10 (7.23.93).

139. NYT C2 (3.15.93).

140. NYT B1 (3.7.94).

141. NYT §1 p. 12 (12.26.93).

142. LAT A19 (8.13.93).

143. NYT A1 (1.16.95).

144. NYT C4 (7.15.93).

145. Observed December 1994.

146. Adbusters Media Foundation (1995).

147. NYT C1 (1.4.95).

148. NYT C4 (4.8.94), 1 (6.11.94), C2 (8.8.94), C2 (5.8.95).

149. NYT A16 (10.8.92), A11 (2.11.94).

150. NYT C2 (1.30.95), D1 (6.8.95), A14 (4.3.96) (U.S. D.C. rejected patent).

151. See Fischer (1992) (telephone); Rheingold (1993) (computer networks); Garry (1994); Boyle (1996).

152. NYT §1 p. 1 (10.24.93); LAT B7 (2.2.95).

153. NYT §4 p. 6 (3.21.93), C10 (8.9.93), C1 (3.2.94), A17 (3.4.94), §4 p. 6 (3.27.94), C20 (3.30.94), C1 (5.31.94), §3 p. 1 (1.22.95), C1 (3.14.95), A17 (3.16.95), C1 (9.14.95), 8 (10.28.95); LAT A1 (9.5.94); NYRB 37 (2.16.95).

154. LAT A1 (6.29.94); NYT A1 (2.23.94), C1 (6.23.94), C1 (2.2.95), C7 (3.24.95), A1 (5.26.95).

155. NYT §3 p. 11 (10.23.94), A6 (2.7.95), A13 (3.24.95); *Moser v Federal Communications Commission*, 46 F. 3d 970 (9th Cir.), cert. denied, 115 S.Ct. 2615 (1995).

156. NYT A9 (3.15.93), A1 (4.16.93), C1 (7.13.93), C1 (9.21.93), 1 (2.12.94), §4 p. 3 (2.13.94), A1 (2.28.94), 17 (3.26.94), §3 p. 5 (4.24.94), D1 (6.8.94), C1 (7.21.94), C2 (8.12.94), 37 (9.17.94), C2 (10.13.94), 1 (12.31.94), C6 (2.2.95), C1, C10 (4.10.95), C5 (5.5.95), C5 (9.11.95), C1 (1.12.96), C2 (9.6.96); LAT D1 (2.2.95), A1 (8.31.96).

157. NYT §2 p. 26 (4.12.94), A1 (7.27.92), A1 (4.11.94), A25 (10.18.94), §1 p. 43 (10.39.94).

158. NYTBR 32 (10.30.94).

159. NYT B1 (3.11.94); WMG 31 (7.1.94); Beard (1994).

160. NYT C8 (3.20.95), A1 (6.15.95), A1 (6.22.95).

161. NYT A1 (6.13.95).

162. LAT A14 (2.11.95); NYT 7 (2.11.95), A9 (2.17.95).

163. LAT A1 (3.19.93); NYT 25 (7.16.94), D1 (11.16.94), C4 (5.26.95), C2 (7.25.95), C1 (10.25.95), C2 (12.14.95); *Cubby v CompuServe*, 776 F. Supp. 135 (S.D. N.Y. 1991).

164. NYT A1 (12.29.95); LAT A1 (12.29.95).

165. NYT A1 (9.22.94), §4 p. 3 (9.25.94).

166. NYT 1 (4.9.94), 10 (12.31.94).

167. NYT C1 (5.11.94); LAT J3 (5.19.94).

168. NYT A1 (6.29.94), B7 (6.30.04), §4 p. 3 (9.25.94), §4 p. 2 (2.26.95), C2 (9.5.96); LAT E1 (9.9.96).

169. Shea (1994); Seabrook (1994); Turkle (1995); Stone (1995).

170. NYT C1 (11.1.93), 1 (7.4.94), A1 (7.21.94), 12 (1.14.95), A1 (1.23.95), B? (1.26.95), 17 (1.28.95), C1 (2.20.95), §1 p. 15 (9.3.95), C5 (11.27.95); LAT A1 (8.12.94); Slatalla & Quittner (1994); Sterling (1992); Hafner & Markoff (1991).

171. *UCLA Today* 8 (11.4.94); NYT B1 (1.11.95).

172. NYT A1 (6.6.94), C1 (10.6.94); Godin (1994).

173. NYT C1 (4.19.94), C1, C5 (5.11.94), A1 (6.29.94), C4 (8.31.94), C4 (9.8.94), C16 (9.21.94); LAT D1 (12.28.94); Canter & Siegel (1994).

174. LAT A5 (7.28.93); NYT B12 (9.24.93), B9 (11.3.93), B16 (4.8.94).

175. I 16 (12.9.92); NYT A9 (9.15.92), A1 (4.26.94), A14 (3.1.95), A1 (4.28.95).

176. NYT A14 (2.18.92), 10 (3.21.92), 13 (4.18.92), A12 (9.10.92), A14 (9.23.92), A19 (10.2.92), B5 (8.2.95), A1 (11.9.95), 20 (12.30.95); LAT F1 (11.16.90), F1 (1.2.91); Trump (1994).

177. LAT D1 (7.2.94) (false advertising), A1 (9.6.94) (misrepresentation of academic rating); NYT C2 (7.21.94) (false advertising), §2 p. 1 (9.4.94) (rigged quiz shows); Leff (1976).

178. NYT A1 (5.10.94).
179. *Soldier of Fortune Magazine v Braun*, 757 F. Supp. 1325 (M.D. Ala. 1991), aff'd, 968 F. 2d 1110 (11th Cir. 1992), cert. denied, 113 S.Ct. 1028 (1993).
180. NYT 1 (5.14.94).
181. *Weirum v RKO General, Inc.*, 15 Cal. 3d 40 (1975).
182. Fisher (1991); cf. NYT B1 (11.30.94).
183. LAT B6 (8.20.93); Simon (1994).
184. See Gardbaum (1991); Maltese (1992); Doss (1995).
185. NYT A? (12.21.95), 21 (12.25.95); "Fissures at an Exhibition," 7 *Lingua Franca* (July–August 1996). The curator of "Back of the Big House," a professor of African American studies and anthropology at George Washington University, based the exhibit on his book, Vlad (1993).
186. NYT §1 p. 27 (9.18.94); LAT A5 (10.31.95).
187. NYT §1 p. 26 (5.31.92), §1 p. 8 (6.27.93), 7 (7.10.93), §1 p. 7 (10.31.93), §1 p. 4 (3.20.94); LAT A4 (11.24.93).
188. LAT A1 (2.11.93).
189. NYT A6 (1.9.95), A1 (1.10.95), A11 (1.11.95); LAT A1 (1.10.95), A10 (1.11.95).
190. LAT A1 (2.22.92), A3 (6.23.92); NYT A12 (3.11.93), A1 (5.5.93), 19 (5.31.93), 1 (8.14.93), §1 p. 11 (8.29.93), §1 p. 1 (1.1.94), A11 (3.3.94), A1 (3.18.94), A9 (3.24.94), A24 (11.11.94), 8 (2.26.95); Roeder (1993).
191. NYT A20 (12.14.94), A10 (1.10.95).
192. NYT 31 (11.4.95).
193. NYT 5 (3.7.92), 1 (3.28.92), A14 (4.13.92), A7 (5.12.92), 6 (5.23.92). DaPonte gained rein-

statement by threatening litigation.
194. NYT A20 (12.20.91), A1 (4.14.92), A1 (4.15.92); Robbins (1992).
195. NYT A8 (1.9.92), A10 (3.19.92), A9 (4.8.92); Smolla (1992: 266–67). On government manipulation of wartime news, see MacArthur (1992); Miller (1992).
196. NYT §2 p. 35 (3.8.92).
197. NYT 14 (2.29.92), §2 p. 36 (4.29.95); Mankin (1980).
198. NYT A27 (6.7.95).
199. Hawthorne (1992); Marquis (1995).
200. CHE A12 (3.11.92); Mulcahy & Swaim (1982); Pindell (1990).
201. NYT B13 (11.10.89).
202. NYT B3 (11.10.89), 14 (2.29.92), B1 (3.24.92), B1 (4.22.93); LAT F1 (2.5.92), A1 (2.22.92), F1 (3.19.92), A3, F1 (4.8.92), A10 (6.5.93); *Finley v NEA*, 795 F. Supp. 1457 (C.D. Calif. 1992); Bolton (1992); Frohnmayer (1993).
203. LAT F1 (5.4.92); NYT B1 (5.13.92), 12 (5.16.92), A1 (6.10.92), 13 (8.1.92).
204. LAT F2 (7.16.93), A3 (8.5.93); NYT §1 p. 1 (9.5.93).
205. LAT A7 (6.21.94), F1 (10.23.95); NYT B2 (6.29.94), B1 (11.3.94), A8 (8.10.95).
206. NYT 9 (12.17.94), A1 (1.9.95), A1 (1.25.95).
207. CHE A21 (2.19.92), A25 (4.8.92); NYT B1 (2.24.92), B1 (4.9.93), A10 (6.22.93), B1 (9.6.94).
208. LAT F1 (2.21.92), F1 (2.28.92); NYT A8 (3.4.92), A8 (3.5.92).
209. NYT A7 (5.17.94).
210. LAT F1 (3.31.93), F12 (8.10.93).
211. LAT F1 (8.24.92); NYT §4 p. 17 (4.17.94), A18 (4.28.94).

212. CHE A1 (10.2.91); *Consortium of Social Science Associations Washington Update* 1 (8.5.91), 1 (4.6.92), 1–2 (6.1.92), 3 (2.22.93); NYT B5 (9.5.92), B5 (9.15.92), A11 (10.16.95); NYTBR 3 (10.30.94); Laumann et al. (1994); Maynard-Moody (1995).

213. *International Guardian* 3, 9 (9.14.91); NYT C1 (9.7.93), B6 (11.24.93).

214. *International Guardian* 3, 9 (9.14.91); NYT 12 (9.4.93), C1 (9.7.93), B6 (11.24.93). For a critique of commodification, see Collins & Skover (1996).

215. See, e.g., *Blount v SEC,* 116 S.Ct. 1351 (1996) (refusing to review a court of appeals decision upholding a rule prohibiting municipal bond dealers from contributing to state and local campaigns of officials who can send them business).

216. LAT A21 (11.10.93); NYT 1 (11.13.93), A11 (11.16.93), 15 (11.20.93); Rollins & DeFrank (1996).

217. LAT A1 (11.3.90), A32 (5.1.94), A3 (6.2.94).

218. NYT A1 (7.7.93), §1 p. 32 (11.20.94), 15 (10.21.95).

219. LAT B1 (8.14.93); NYT A11 (7.30.93), A16 (9.26.94), §1 p. 1 (3.26.95), C5 (8.28.95); Kluger (1996).

220. NYT §3 p. 9 (3.5.95), A9 (3.9.95); LAT A3 (3.9.95), A1 (7.7.95), A26 (7.14.95).

221. NYT A1, A7 (4.15.02), C1 (12.6.93), A1 (2.14.94), A8 (3.11.94), A14 (3.15.94), B1 (11.15.95).

222. NYT A15 (5.26.94), A16 (5.27.94).

223. NYT A11 (12.12.90), A12 (6.24.92), A1 (9.28.92), A14 (6.16.93), A1 (8.15.94), 7 (9.24.94), §1 p. 30 (9.25.94), C3 (10.4.94), A23 (10.7.94), §1 p. 12 (3.12.95), C? (9.11.95), C2 (8.20.96). On the role of pharmaceutical advertisements in shaping the content of medical journals, see Wilkes, Doblin, & Shapiro (1992).

224. NYT A1 (9.8.95), A10 (9.18.95).

225. NYT A10 (4.18.91), B1 (12.12.94), A1 (3.15.95), §4 p. 5 (3.20.95), B8 (9.13.95).

226. NYT 7 (2.24.96).

227. LAT B1 (2.18.94).

228. NYT 6 (9.4.93), A10 (2.20.95); Sabato & Simpson (1996).

229. Abel (1995: 303).

230. NYT §1 p. 3 (1.8.95); Koch (1993).

231. NYT 13 (12.2.89).

232. NYT C6 (1.31.93), A9 (7.21.95), A8 (8.11.95); *TV Guide* (12.93); Knowlton (1994); Auletta (1994).

233. NYT C2 (2.20.95), §3 p. 1 (7.23.95), 21 (10.28.95), C1 (1.4.96), 21 (10.5.96).

234. LAT D1 (1.17.95), A1 (1.3.96); NYT B1 (1.25.96); Haring (1995).

235. NYT A15 (3.15.94).

236. Robinson (1994).

237. NYT B3 (9.22.93).

238. NYT C5 (12.11.95).

239. NYT B4 (3.9.92), B1 (3.11.92).

240. NYT 4 (5.12.90), §1 p. 6 (9.9.90), A20 (12.11.91), A3 (12.28.92), B1 (2.22.94), A1 (7.31.96); LAT A3 (6.9.90), H4 (11.9.93), A1 (10.19.96); NYTBR 14 (7.12.92); NYRB 64 (10.20.94).

241. Fish (1994).

242. LAT A26 (11.3.90), A25 (11.8.90); NYT A15 (11.5.90), A1 (3.20.92).

243. NYT §1 p. 1 (3.26.95), A12

(4.12.95), D6 (6.15.95), §1 p. 1
(7.2.95), 24 (7.3.95), A1
(2.14.96), C2 (2.29.96), §4 p. 5
(8.11.96); LAT D1 (2.16.96), A1
(5.10.96); *Nation* 10 (7.3.95).

244. NYRB 13 (6.27.93), 53 (1.12.95);
Sweetman (1993); Parini
(1995).

245. NYT B? (6.6.94); Gaines &
Churcher (1994).

246. Wiener (1996); Glantz et al.
(1996).

247. NYT A3 (6.28.95); Power
(1995).

248. NYT B2 (12.6.90); NYTM 13
(6.19.94); Graham (1994).

249. NYT C4 (4.5.96).

250. Abel (1994a, 1994b).

251. WMG 23 (6.3.94); Edwards
(1991); Webster (1990: 26–27,
130); GLC Gay Working Party
(1985: 13–14, 23); Lewis (1994).

252. NYT A15 (8.3.92).

253. LAT A1 (9.10.96).

254. NYT B1 (7.19.93), C16
(11.12.93).

255. NYT B4 (11.3.93).

256. NYT 13 (12.2.89), C8 (3.16.92),
B4 (7.27.95), B2 (7.28.95);
Treacy & Wiersema (1995). *Billboard*'s chart of pop music also
may be manipulable, Haring
(1995); NYT B1 (1.25.96).

257. NYT A14 (10.24.90).

258. NYT B12 (9.11.92).

259. NYT C10 (8.9.93).

260. LAT B1 (1.10.95), B1 (1.13.95).

261. NYT A1 (12.12.90).

262. NYT A9 (5.4.95), A12 (8.4.95);
Mack (1994).

263. NYT A10 (4.18.91), B1
(12.12.94), A1 (3.15.95), §4 p. 5
(3.20.95), B8 (9.13.95); CHE A31
(1.22.92); Alliance for Justice
(1993).

264. See Squires (1993); Underwood
(1995).

265. LAT H2 (4.7.92); Griffith (1995);
see also Shepard (1996).

266. NYT C1 (6.27.94).

267. LAT A1 (3.16.93).

268. NYT C4 (7.26.96).

269. NYT §1 p. 3 (11.20.94).

270. NYT A4 (7.12.94), 14 (2.4.95).

271. NYT A6 (3.2.93).

272. NYT §1 p. 14 (5.30.93).

273. NYT A1 (5.4.93), A12 (11.4.94);
LAT A4 (5.17.93).

274. LAT E1 (4.13.95).

275. NYT A11 (12.23.94).

276. NYT C8 (4.19.93), 25 (7.5.93).

277. NYT C6 (4.18.94), B16 (1.13.95),
A12 (1.14.95).

278. NYT 10 (4.24.93), 6 (8.10.96).

279. NYT §1 p. 13 (3.28.93).

280. LAT E3 (11.9.93); NYT 6
(6.11.94), B11 (11.7.94); Boswell
(1994).

281. NYT C17 (12.20.94); NYTBR 11
(2.12.95).

282. NYT C5 (6.20.94).

283. LAT A3 (3.16.92), A14 (4.21.92),
A12 (6.11.92).

284. NYT A15 (11.5.90), A8 (7.3.92),
A10 (6.18.93), C8 (5.9.94), A1
(6.20.94); LAT F1 (10.23.93).

285. LAT A11 (2.26.91).

286. NYT A11 (1.5.95); LAT F1
(1.6.95), F2 (1.9.95).

287. NYT 13 (6.29.93), 6 (11.13.93),
§2 p. 29 (1.2.94); LAT F1
(10.30.93).

288. LAT F2 (4.28.95).

289. LAT A16 (4.27.95), A6 (5.2.95);
NYT §1 p. 18 (4.30.95), A8
(5.18.95), A10 (6.26.95).

290. NYT §1 p. 11 (1.1.95).

291. LAT A18 (10.6.95); NYT A1
(10.11.95), A1 (10.12.95).

292. NYT §2 p. 27 (2.20.94).

293. NYT §1 p. 16 (3.1.92).

294. LAT A3 (4.28.95).

295. NYT A6 (3.2.93).

296. NYT A7 (6.3.94).

297. NYT §2 p. 1 (12.8.91), §2 p. 1 (5.23.93), §4 p. 5 (12.18.94); LAT F1 (6.11.93), F1 (7.10.93), F1 (9.21.93), F4 (10.26.93).

298. NYT §2 p. 1 (12.8.91), B3 (2.2.93), §2 p. 1 (9.5.93), §2 p. 29 (1.9.94), B2 (2.9.94); LAT F1 (4.28.93), F1 (3.1.94), F1 (3.3.94), F14 (3.19.94).

299. See, e.g., King (1994).

300. NYTBR 3 (11.14.93); Butler (1993).

301. NYT §2 p. 27 (1.9.94).

302. NYTBR 24 (2.5.95).

303. LAT F2 (4.27.94), F4 (3.3.95); NYT B13 (3.10.95); NYRB 40 (5.13.93); McBride (1996).

304. NYT B1 (2.5.92), B1 (3.9.92), §2 p. 11 (4.19.92), B6 (10.2.92), B1 (7.29.93), B1 (9.9.93), B1 (9.28.93), §2 p. 26 (5.15.94), §3 p. 10 (2.12.95); LAT F12 (10.2.92), A1 (12.23.92), F1 (5.6.93), A1 (3.21.94), F1 (7.11.94), F1 (5.22.96).

305. LAT F1 (7.26.93), B1 (7.27.93), F1 (8.5.93); NYT B1 (3.9.93), C18 (11.2.94); NYTM 13 (6.24.94).

306. See Collins (1992); C. E. Baker (1994).

307. LAT F1 (1.17.92), F1 (2.29.92), F1 (9.1.92); NYT C15 (11.14.89), §2 p. 1 (12.8.91), §2 p. 1 (5.31.92), C17 (9.23.93), C16 (11.2.93), C7 (4.4.94), C6 (6.6.94), B2 (3.3.95).

308. NYT §2 p. 1 (12.8.91), §2 p. 1 (7.10.94).

309. LAT F1 (4.2.92).

310. NYT C2 (6.7.96).

311. NYTBR 20 (1.17.93); Stempel (1993); Kisseloff (1995).

312. LAT A27 (1.30.92); Warner, Goldenhar, & McLaughlin (1992).

313. NYT A1 (9.26.94), A1 (10.5.94), B8 (10.13.94).

314. NYT B1 (6.15.93).

315. NYT C1 (2.25.92).

316. NYT D1 (6.1.92), B3 (6.10.92).

317. NYT C9 (6.26.92), A1 (2.11.93), A8 (2.12.93), C15 (9.17.93), C3 (8.2.95); LAT A1 (2.9.93), A1 (2.10.93).

318. NYT §1 p. 10 (10.24.93).

319. NYT C8 (11.15.95).

320. LAT B3 (8.13.93), F1 (5.24.95); NYT B1 (7.13.95).

321. NYT 8 (5.8.93), §1 p. 23 (10.17.93), §4 p. 3 (5.22.94); LAT A1 (5.1.93).

322. NYT A11 (3.10.93), B1 (9.7.93), 7 (6.11.94); LAT A3 (3.23.93), B3 (1.28.94), B1 (2.11.94), A11 (1.14.95).

323. NYT A11 (3.10.93), A16 (4.21.93), A11 (6.11.93), 10 (5.7.94), B20 (2.9.96).

324. NYT §1 p. 1 (5.30.93), C1 (7.13.93).

325. NYT §1 p. 16 (2.23.92), C3 (1.11.94).

326. NYT A6 (6.29.93), A5 (7.2.93).

327. LAT A1 (9.13.93), B1 (11.1.93), B3 (11.3.93); NYT A12 (6.17.93), A21 (4.1.94), A1 (4.15.94), A1 (4.29.94), §1 p. 50 (11.13.94), B11 (12.7.94).

328. LAT A1 (5.31.96).

329. NYT A14 (2.24.95), 15 (2.26.95).

330. NYT B1 (2.25.92).

331. NYT B2 (6.17.93), B2 (6.24.93).

332. NYT C1 (2.22.93), A17 (7.7.93), §4 p. 16 (8.22.93), §4 p. 18 (3.23.94), §4 p. 16 (1.21.96), A17 (12.8.95), B1 (12.20.95); LAT H8 (6.1.93); G 12 (12.17.93); Montgomery (1989).

333. NYT A8 (2.18.94); LAT A12 (6.24.94).

334. LAT F1 (8.18.92), F1 (8.20.92).

335. NYT 1 (12.21.90).

336. LAT F2 (4.13.95), F1, F2 (4.27.95).

337. LAT F1 (10.6.92); NYT B4
(11.23.93), A13 (5.31.94), C1
(2.3.95); Redgrave (1994).
338. LAT A33 (3.12.92); NYT A1
(3.12.92), A1 (5.11.93), A4
(9.1.93), A13 (10.26.93), C5
(4.11.94), A8 (10.21.94), A19
(12.1.94); Nerone (1994).
339. NYT A1 (9.19.95).
340. NYT §1 p. 5 (4.3.94), A10
(10.31.95).
341. LAT A4 (2.17.95).

Chapter 6

1. For critiques of censorship, see
Randall (1989); Rodgerson &
Wilson (1991); Hentoff (1992);
Heins (1993); Gates (1993); Easton (1994); Strossen (1995);
Dooling (1996).
2. Except where otherwise noted,
my source is Gordon (1982: 1–
22); for the American experience, see Walker (1994).
3. House of Commons Debates,
vol. 711, col. 940 (5.3.65),
quoted in Dickey (1968: 490).
4. T (12.22.66), rev'd, QB 51
(1967); T (1.26.67).
5. Home Office (1975).
6. *Daily Telegraph* (7.25.78).
7. *Daily Telegraph* (10.31.78).
8. Home Affairs Committee
(1980).
9. *Green Paper* (1980).
10. See Burt (1993) (seventeenth-
century England); Beisel (1990)
(nineteenth-century America);
Arnold (1992) (Joyce's *Ulysses*).
11. Friedrich (1992); Wilson-
Bareau, House, & Johnson
(1993); NYRB 27 (4.22.93).
12. NYT B3 (3.5.92), §2 p. 68
(9.8.96); NY 32 (10.5.92); see
also Peter Cohen, *The Architec-

ture of Doom (documentary);
Cone (1992) (Vichy France);
Ades et al. (1995).
13. NYT §2 p. 6 (10.18.92), B1
(7.29.93), B3 (1.4.95); NYTBR 14
(6.26.94); Hemingway (1986);
Chauncey (1994); March
(1995).
14. LAT F1 (5.19.93), B1 (1.19.96),
B1 (1.20.96).
15. LAT D1 (2.16.96); see also
Walsh (1996).
16. NYT B3 (8.30.94), A1 (12.14.94).
17. NYT A9 (11.4.93), 12 (4.9.94),
B1 (9.6.94), A10 (3.22.95), §2
p. 1 (2.18.96), B10 (4.3.96); LAT
F14 (11.19.93); on the MPAA
see Vizzard (1970).
18. NYT A7 (11.5.93), §1 p. 11
(1.9.94), B10 (6.3.94), A6
(2.7.95); LAT B1 (4.27.94).
19. On the sorry history of blasphemy, see Jones (1980); Webster (1990); Levy (1993).
20. Steinem (1980: 37); see also Longino (1980).
21. See Kaite (1995). On the difficulty of bounding pornography, see Barthes (1976); Sontag
(1982); Lindgren (1993); Cole
(1994); Arcand (1993); Baird
& Rosenbaum (1991); Keller
(1993); Stan (1995). For the dismal history of the American attempt, see de Grazia (1992); on
Britain, see Barker (1984).
22. Rubin, Seckel, & Cousins
(1995).
23. Bettelheim (1976); Tatar (1992).
24. *American Booksellers Association,
Inc. v Hudnut*, 598 F. Supp.
1316, at 1339 n. 6 (S.D. Ind.
1984).
25. *R. v Butler*, 89 D.L.R. (4th) 449
(1992); Toobin (1994). Robin
Morgan denies that *Butler* was
used against lesbians, NYTBR

29 (2.19.95), but the prosecution of *Bad Attitude* postdated that decision.

26. NYT B1 (3.21.95), §4 p. 6 (6.18.95), B1 (11.7.95); Lutz & Collins (1993); Gingrich & Fortschen (1995); see also Clayson (1991) (Impressionist paintings of prostitutes).

27. Matsuda (1989: 2357, 2367); cf. Delgado (1982, 1991); Lawrence (1990); Matsuda et al. (1992); Lederer & Delgado (1995); Freedman & Freedman (1995).

28. NYT A13 (7.20.92), 14 (8.29.92); Coon (1962); Eysenck (1971); Jensen (1969); Herrnstein (1971); 59 *U.S. News and World Report* 68 (11.22.65); Bradley (1992); Herrnstein & Murray (1994); Itzkoff (1994); Rushton (1994).

29. Colford (1993); Arkush (1993); Laufer (1995); Limbaugh (1992, 1993).

30. NYT B2 (8.5.92), A13 (8.11.92).

31. NYT A14 (8.27.93); LAT F1 (2.15.94); NYTBR 13 (11.27.94); Binder (1993); H. A. Baker (1994); Dyson (1994, 1996).

32. Quoted in Edwards (1991). The language resembles Rushdie's open letter to Rajiv Gandhi, quoted in chapter 2.

33. NYT §2 p. 31 (1.10.93); Kappeler (1986); Berger et al. (1972: chaps. 2–3).

34. NYT B1 (8.10.95); LAT D1 (9.2.95); Mulcahy & Swaim (1982: 7 n. 14).

35. G 25 (11.21.91); NYT C29 (11.25.94); NYTBR (1.28.96); Gardner (1978: 135); Freed (1991); Arbus (1972, 1995); Danly & Leibold (1994).

36. NYT 8 (9.2.95); Kinzer (1992: 50).

37. NYTM 29 (9.27.92); NYRB 7 (2.3.94); Mann (1988, 1992); cf. NYT §2 p. 28 (1.28.96) (Mapplethorpe photos of nude children).

38. NYT A1 (1.30.95), §4 p. 4 (2.19.95), §1 p. 15 (1.4.96).

39. NYT §1 p. 17 (12.6.92), B1 (8.3.93), B12 (1.10.95); LAT F1 (8.3.93); NYTM 17 (5.22.94); Philip Haas's documentary "Money Man" in the PBS *P.O.V.* series.

40. LAT F1 (5.6.93), A2 (12.31.94).

41. See Hughes (1980).

42. NYT 15 (12.4.93); Hunt (1992, 1993); Darnton (1995a, 1995b); Gardner (1978: 170); Kendrick (1987); Dubin (1992); Steiner (1995); Kipnis (1996).

43. G 33 (10.10.91), 27 (11.9.91); NYT B1 (3.24.92), C28 (10.14.94), §4 p. 35 (1.22.95), B1 (3.3.95), §2 p. 45 (10.22.95), §2 p. 68 (9.8.96) ("Making Mischief: Dada Invades New York," at the Whitney Museum); Lippard (1990); Carr (1993); Mapplethorpe (1993, 1995); Danto (1995); Morrisroe (1995); Fritscher (1994); Gonzalez-Crussi (1995).

44. LAT E1 (4.8.93); NYT §3 p. 7 (10.24.93), §1 p. 1 (4.3.94); NYTBR 14 (9.18.94); Ellis (1991, 1994); N. Baker (1992, 1994); R. Baker (1993); Stern (1993).

45. NYT §2 p. 32 (11.21.93), B6 (11.24.93); LAT F1 (6.8.93).

46. NYT §2 p. 18 (2.6.94), B1 (8.11.94), 13 (11.26.94).

47. NYT §2 p. 5 (6.13.93), §2 p. 18 (2.6.94), §2 p. 31 (10.23.94); LAT A7 (6.21.94).

48. NYT B2 (9.28.92), §2 p. 28 (10.18.92), §2 p. 33 (10.17.93), §4 p. 5 (9.18.94); LAT F4

(10.5.92), E1 (3.12.93); Weldon (1992).

49. NYT C8 (10.4.93); C16 (3.25.94), B9 (5.16.95), A4 (8.2.95); LAT J2 (4.21.94); NYTM 2–5 (3.13.94), 2–3 (12.18.94), 2 ff. (2.3.95); NY 59 (10.1.93), 32–35 (8.21.95); Steele (1995).

50. NYT §2 p. 33 (5.3.92), C18 (7.29.93), B4 (11.23.93), C18 (2.3.95); WMG 12 (1.14.94).

51. NYT A18 (5.8.92), §2 p. 23 (7.11.93); NYTM pt. 2 (8.27.95); cf. Garber (1992).

52. LAT F1 (5.26.93); NYT B3 (6.10.93), C10 (10.18.93), B6 (1.28.94).

53. NYT B2 (10.27.93); Lott (1993).

54. NYT B1 (4.6.93), B11 (3.11.94); Richards (1994); M. Ryan (1995).

55. LAT F1 (2.5.92), A12 (8.17.92); NYT 1 (4.24.93); WMG 6 (9.4.92); Nachman (1994: 29); Buford (1992a, 1992b); Harewood (1993).

56. NYT A10 (3.18.94); Updike (1994).

57. NYT B1 (6.2.93); LAT F1 (4.6.93), A1 (7.30.95); Berger et al. (1972: chap. 3); cf. Hubner (1993) (pornographers claiming to champion counterculture).

58. NYT B1 (3.6.91); Edwards (1991); Bharucha (1990: 64); cf. Tanner (1994).

59. LAT F1 (10.10.92); Kramer (1992).

60. NYT §1 p. 20 (12.6.92), A3 (11.9.93); LAT A17 (1.3.95).

61. NYT A1 (12.28.93), A9 (11.4.94), B1 (9.14.95); LAT F1 (7.11.95), F1 (9.16.95); NYTM 40–45 (4.3.94).

62. LAT D1 (12.2.95), A1 (12.11.95); Rosen (1995: 78–79); see Turkle (1995).

63. Lessing (1984: vii–xii); Kappeler (1986: 125–26).

64. NYT A8 (1.29.92), §1 p. 15 (2.16.92); LAT E1 (2.21.92).

65. NYT B2 (8.5.92).

66. Assiter & Avedon (1993); Herman (1994); hooks (1992).

67. NYT A17 (7.2.92), B1 (9.20.93); LAT F1 (11.23.93); NYTM (8.15.93), 6 (9.5.93).

68. NYT A5 (2.29.92), A1 (2.17.93); LAT A3 (7.25.92); Flam (1992).

69. NYT B6 (2.17.93).

70. E.g., Riesman (1942); Delgado (1982); Matsuda (1989: 2327).

71. NYT B1 (8.7.92), 9 (2.6.93), §4 p. 15 (12.3.95); LAT F1 (10.23.93); Schechter (1994).

72. Morgan (1977: 169); see Itzin (1992).

73. NYT §1 p. 17 (10.29.95).

74. NYT §4 916 (8.9.92); LAT F1 (2.7.96); Yaffe & Nelson (1982); Winn (1985); Donnerstein, Linz, & Penrod (1987); Schauer (1987); Zillmann & Jennings (1989); Childress (1991).

75. NYT B4 (5.11.92), B5 (10.8.92).

76. NYT §1 p. 10 (3.15.92), §1 p. 8 (9.4.94).

77. LAT B3 (7.3.93), B7 (8.13.93) (Mexico-bashing leads to hate crimes); NYT A9 (6.22.92).

78. NYT A11 (10.3.96).

79. NYT A18 (8.12.92), §4 p. 4 (7.28.96), B3 (9.23.96); LAT F1 (2.19.96); Burstyn (1985); Gordon (1983); J. Ryan (1995). Furthermore, computer simulation now allows the production of pornography without actors, LAT B9 (6.6.96).

80. NYT B5 (6.21.94); NYTM 26 (2.4.96); Fried (1993).

81. LAT F1 (11.10.93), F1 (11.15.93), F18 (4.7.95); NYT 18 (11.18.95),

§4 p. 5 (11.26.95), §1 p. 12 (12.10.95).

82. Baker & Chase (1994); cf. Daniell (1984) (woman's account of enjoying rough sex).

83. NYT 9 (9.6.93).

84. LAT D1 (2.23.95).

85. LAT A3 (1.10.94); WMG 11 (9.9.94); Stoller (1991); Williams (1989); Delacoste & Alexander (1987).

86. G 2 (11.22.91); NYRB 25 (6.22.95); Lawrence (1955: 358); Roth (1959); Sheldon (1994); Sherry (1989).

87. LAT A8 (4.10.93), A12 (4.2.94); NYT 5 (4.15.95) (Poland).

88. LAT E1 (9.1.92), B7 (9.9.95); NYT B4 (6.15.92); Marchand (1992); cf. Deleuze (1971); Bogdan (1988).

89. See Marchand (1985); Buchwald, Fletcher, & Roth (1993); Ruskkoff (1994). On "everyday racism," see Essed (1991); van Dijk (1987).

90. LAT H6 (3.9.93); NYT B1 (8.16.93), C13 (11.3.95); Marchand (1985).

91. NYT B4 (3.29.94).

92. Ibid.

93. LAT A6, A8, A12, A14, A17, A18, A19, A22 (3.25.91); see Bordo (1993).

94. NYT A1 (2.6.92), B4 (11.23.93), C16 (4.26.94), 15 (9.10.94), 25 (11.12.94), B14 (12.13.94), §3 p. 5 (3.12.95), 4 (10.19.96); LAT E1 (11.14.89), E1 (8.18.92); NYTM pt. 2, pp. 42–45 (2.23.92); 254 (5) *Nation* 155 (2.10.92); Goffman (1976); Steele (1985: 65–67); Wolf (1991); Faludi (1991); Goldman (1992); Davis (1994); Steele (1995); Lord (1995).

95. LAT E1 (8.7.92), A20 (12.27.93); NYT A13 (1.4.96); NYTM 85 (9.8.96); Glassner (1993).

96. NYT A3 (11.17.95); LAT E1 (1.23.96).

97. NYT B7 (2.26.92); LAT E1 (4.17.92).

98. See Mander (1978); Medved (1992); Barry (1993); Cowan (1979); Minow & LaMay (1995); for more nuanced or skeptical views, see NYT 11 (8.14.93); Lichter et al. (1991); Davis (1993); Kruger (1993); Stockdale (1995).

99. NYT A12 (7.27.92), A1 (12.14.94), A18 (4.27.95), A10 (6.23.95); LAT B7 (4.8.93), F5 (5.12.93), A1 (4.25.95), A1 (4.26.95), B7 (4.27.95), F1 (2.7.96); Centerall (1992).

100. Grossman (1995); cf. Provenzo (1991); Sheff (1993).

101. LAT A1 (9.19.96).

102. NYT §4 p. 24 (1.10.93), 16 (5.8.93), 1 (1.8.94), C7 (1.30.95), B1 (2.27.95), C6 (3.13.95), 1 (8.20.95); LAT A1 (2.27.95).

103. LAT F1 (3.19.93), A1 (11.28.95), A23 (12.16.95), A40 (12.19.95); NYT A5 (7.23.93), A5 (8.13.93), A3 (11.25.93), A13 (11.26.93), §2 p. 9 (7.10.94), A9 (11.4.94), §4 p. 6 (12.18.94), B12 (11.27.95), A12 (12.11.95), A21 (12.12.95); WMG 37, 39 (4.22.94); G 8 (12.15.93); T 13 (7.10.96).

104. LAT B1 (1.7.94), A3 (2.8.94); NYT A1 (12.28.92), A16 (1.15.93), A18 (11.30.94).

105. NYTBR 51 (6.23.94); Assouline (1984); Sternhell (1986).

106. NYT A1 (5.4.93), A7 (5.4.95); LAT A4 (5.17.93).

107. LAT A1 (6.23.93), A3 (8.11.93).

108. NYT A8 (2.14.96); NYTM 12–13 (8.19.96).

109. NYT 9 (11.6.93), A10 (12.11.95); Marzuk et al. (1993); Humphrey (1991).

110. LAT A14 (10.16.95), A1 (11.7.95), A6 (11.8.95), A1, A18 (11.10.95); NYT A19 (11.7.95), A1 (11.9.95), 1 (11.11.95), §1 p. 1 (11.12.95), A21 (11.17.95); NYRB (12.21.95).

111. T 11 (7.10.96).

112. NYT A15 (4.4.96); Pollay et al. (1996); see also Evans et al. (1995); Pierce et al. (1992, 1994).

113. LAT F1 (2.22.91), B6 (3.9.91), F1 (2.22.92), F1 (9.1.92), B1 (7.27.93), F1 (8.5.93), F2 (1.20.95); NYT A10 (3.13.91); 7 (4.13.91), B1 (1.22.92), A14 (2.4.92), A14 (2.21.92), B1 (4.21.93).

114. LAT A1 (9.17.92), A12 (9.23.92), F1 (10.13.92).

115. LAT A3 (9.27.96).

116. NYT 6 (3.5.94), A12 (8.26.94), §1 p. 8 (1.1.95), 1 (1.2.95), A9 (1.5.95), §1 p. 9 (1.15.95); LAT A7 (1.24.96).

117. *Olivia N v National Broadcasting Co.*, 126 Cal. App. 3d 488, 178 Cal. Rptr. 888 (1981), cert. denied, 458 U.S. 1108 (1982).

118. *Waller v Osbourne*, 763 F. Supp. 1144 (M.D. Ga. 1991); *McCollum v CBS, Inc.*, 202 Cal. App. 3d 989, 249 Cal. Rptr. 187 (1988); NYT B4 (8.3.92), B1 (9.23.92).

119. *Herceg v Hustler Magazine, Inc.*, 814 F. 2d 1017 (5th Cir. 1987), cert. denied, 485 U.S. 959 (1988).

120. *Watters v TSR, Inc.*, 715 F. Supp. 819 (W.D. Ky. 1989), aff'd, 904 F. 2d 378 (6th Cir. 1990).

121. *Yakubowicz v Paramount Pictures Corp.*, 404 Mass. 624, 536 N.E. 2d 1067 (1989).

122. *DeFilippo v NBC*, 446 A. 2d 1036 (R.I. 1982).

123. NYT §1 p. 10 (2.23.92), A12 (8.19.92), A7 (3.10.95), C5 (12.11.95); LAT A1 (1.12.93); *Ellmann v Soldier of Fortune Magazine, Inc.*, 680 F. Supp. 863 (S.D. Tex. 1988); *Soldier of Fortune v Braun*, 757 F. Supp. 1325 (M.D. Ala. 1991), aff'd, 968 F. 2d 110 (11th Cir. 1992), cert. denied, 113 S.Ct. 1028 (1993); 190 *Searchlight* 18 (April 1991); *Weirum v RKO Gen. Inc.*, 15 Cal. 3d 40, 123 Cal. Rptr. 468 (1975); Dees & Fiffer (1993).

124. LAT B1 (8.17.92).

125. LAT F2 (9.22.92), B1 (9.23.92); NYT §2 p. 20 (8.16.92), B1 (8.31.92), §2 p. 6 (9.6.92), B1 (9.14.92), B1 (9.25.92), C18 (11.10.93), B2 (4.29.94), 4 (4.30.94); cf. Gitlin (1986).

126. NYT B1 (2.21.92); LAT F1 (9.30.92), B1 (10.16.92), A1 (8.13.93); NYTBR 3 (2.19.95); Pileggi (1986); le Carré (1995).

127. NYT §4 p. 5 (3.4.90), A16 (8.25.92), C1 (3.3.94), 23 (4.2.94), D3 (6.7.95).

128. NYT C1 (5.3.96).

129. LAT F1 (9.21.93); NYT A14 (9.2.94), §1 p. 1 (3.26.95).

130. NYT A14 (9.28.93), A11 (11.2.93), 9 (11.13.93), A13 (11.29.93), §1 p. 16 (6.12.94), A12 (1.18.95); *Knox v U.S.*, 115 S.Ct. 1106 (1995).

131. NYT A1 (9.30.92), A1 (3.4.93), C6 (6.27.94).

132. LAT F6 (1.28.94); NYT C3 (8.14.95).

133. *New Statesman and Society* 17

(10.4.91); NYT A4 (2.4.93), 2 (10.16.93), A3 (4.24.95); LAT A1 (1.21.92), A1 (10.2.92), A5 (10.1.93); Schell (1994).

134. NYT A14 (8.5.92), A7 (8.20.92), A16 (4.16.93); LAT A20 (8.13.92).

135. NYTBR 7 (10.13.96); Bloom (1996).

136. 3 (3) *Adbusters* 24–25, 34, 97 (winter 1995).

137. NYT B13 (1.27.95); see also NYTBR 13 (6.12.94).

138. LAT A18 (2.18.95), A1 (2.23.95).

139. 179 *Searchlight* 7 (May 1990), 189:5 (March 1991); Lee (1990: 120).

140. NYT A7 (10.2.96); LAT A3 (10.18.96).

141. NYT 7 (10.20.92); NYTM 30 (10.11.92).

142. NYT B3 (2.11.93); "The Art of Attack: Social Commentary and Its Effect," Armand Hammer Museum of Art (10.12.93– 1.2.94); Guerrilla Girls (1995).

143. NYT 9, 17 (3.5.94); LAT A21 (3.5.94).

144. NYT §1 p. 10 (2.23.92), A13 (7.20.92); 182 *Searchlight* 3 (August 1990), 183:5 (September 1990), 185:17–19 (November 1990); Nation of Islam (1991).

145. See Ernst & Lindey (1936); Dean (1953); Lewis (1992); cf. Matoesian (1993); Pally (1994).

146. G 1–2 (10.30.91), 2 (11.1.91), 1 (11.5.91).

147. NYT 12 (3.28.92), A13 (9.2.92); Kincaid (1992).

148. NYT §2 p. 1 (2.18.96).

149. Greater London Council (1984d: 21).

150. LAT A1 (7.6.93), A1 (7.8.93), F1 (11.22.93), F1 (1.11.94); NYT B10 (7.9.93).

151. G 5 (10.2.91), 7 (10.30.91).

152. G 9 (10.14.91), 5 (10.23.91), 9 (10.28.91); NYT A4 (6.23.95), A6 (9.22.95) (Canada's highest court voided the total ban while indicating that a more limited one would be acceptable).

153. LAT A17 (5.8.90); NYRB 32 (7.11.96).

154. NYT A27 (12.11.91), A14 (12.30.91), §4 p. 6 (1.9.94); LAT B1 (1.31.92); Bill Moyers, *Hate on Trial*, PBS documentary (2.5.92).

155. NYT A21 (10.13.94), A? (10.20.94), A13 (11.28.94), A9 (10.17.96).

156. LAT F1 (7.11.95).

157. LAT A14 (1.21.92); NYT §1 p. 10 (2.23.92), A8 (3.10.92).

158. Quoted in Barnes (1992: 3).

159. NYT §2 p. 35 (3.8.92).

160. NYT B8 (6.19.92); Friedberg (1992).

161. LAT F3 (5.3.94).

162. LAT F1 (2.21.92).

163. NYT A8 (3.22.96).

164. NYT B3 (9.23.92), B2 (9.24.92), B2 (10.2.92), B2 (2.2.94), B2 (3.1.95); Vidal (1992); Wilson (1992); Leavitt (1993, 1994); Spender (1994, 1997).

165. NYT C8 (9.17.92), A17 (9.23.92), §3 p. 7 (10.24.93); LAT F1 (7.30.92), F14 (3.9.94).

166. NYT §1 p. 20 (12.6.92), C6 (5.17.93); NYTBR 6 (8.1.93); Coburn (1992); Klapisch & Harper (1993); Brock (1993); Mayer & Abramson (1994).

167. NYT §2 p. 23 (5.16.93), B1 (10.22.93), B1 (9.6.94), §2 p. 1 (2.12.95), B8 (1.19.96); LAT F1 (9.20.95).

168. NYT A1 (10.17.90), B1 (7.8.92),

§2 p. 27 (12.13.92); LAT A20 (10.20.90), F1 (6.13.92), F1 (6.16.92), F1 (6.18.92), F1 (6.19.92), A33 (7.3.92), D1 (7.4.92), B3 (7.25.92), A1 (7.29.92), D1 (7.30.92), A3 (10.1.92).

Chapter 7

1. For sensitive discussions of the centrality of public recognition, see Minow (1990); Guttmann (1992a, 1992b); Karst (1993). On the role of representation, see Brown (1995); Cornell (1995).
2. Cf. LaMarche (1995). On the effect of disrespectful representations on audience perception of target, see Greenberg & Pyszcynski (1985); on stereotyping, see Helmreich (1982).
3. Lester (1987: 21) (quoting permanent secretary).
4. See, e.g., Galanter (1974); Young (1990).
5. France (1927: chap. 7); G 8 (11.14.91).
6. LAT A3 (1.31.92), A1 (8.26.93), B1 (3.18.94), B1 (4.20.94); NYT A14 (3.18.92), A7 (2.15.95); Whittle et al. (1993); Kahn et al. (1994); Lamas et al. (1995). All the studies held medical condition constant.
7. NYT §1 p. 14 (2.13.94).
8. NYT A7 (8.31.92); IOS 11 (11.10.91).
9. I 10 (10.15.91); G 28 (11.1.91); NYT A19 (1.25.91), B12 (12.11.91), B1 (4.15.92).
10. NYT B1 (1.23.91), §1 p. 69 (12.15.91), B2 (6.17.92), A1 (5.8.95); Heyn (1992); Roiphe (1994); Paglia (1990, 1992, 1994); Denfeld (1995).

11. NYT A4 (5.14.92), A2 (8.10.92); Bentley (1955); McFeely (1968); Crouch (1992).
12. *New Statesman and Society* 20 (10.4.91); NYT A5 (12.31.93).
13. NYT A14 (10.14.96).
14. NYT A9 (9.26.90), A3 (9.27.90), A2 (9.28.90), A4 (10.9.90), A4 (3.4.91); LAT A1 (10.20.90); G 6 (9.19.91), 5 (10.12.91), 2 (10.14.91); 187 *Searchlight* 8 (January 1991), 190:7 (April 1991); Galanter (1984).
15. NYT §4 p. 3 (3.20.94); LAT A3 (1.9.95).
16. NYT A1 (12.30.91), §1 p. 20 (4.30.95).
17. NYT A10 (5.12.94).
18. NYT 1 (12.14.91).
19. Orenstein & AAUW (1994).
20. NYT A9 (2.2.93), A7 (7.9.93); LAT A1 (2.25.93).
21. NYT A8 (3.10.95), A1 (3.16.95), A8 (9.5.95); see also Roberts & Stratton (1995).
22. NYT §1 p. 1 (9.30.90), A17 (1.10.91), §1 p. 15 (1.13.91), A12 (3.1.91), §4 p. 20 (7.11.93), 16 (3.18.95), A1 (7.16.96) (East Harlem Young Women's Leadership School), A16 (8.14.96) (idem); LAT A1 (1.15.94).
23. NYT A10 (3.1.93); LAT A1 (11.16.93).
24. NYT A20 (1.29.92), A7 (12.24.92), A14 (5.28.93), B8 (4.20.94), A10 (5.2.94), B8 (3.16.95), 15 (4.1.95), A17 (9.24.96) (Cornell dorms upheld); Hacker (1992: 154–58).
25. LAT A1 (2.12.92), A3 (11.8.93), A3 (2.6.95), A3 (3.8.95); NYT A1 (2.12.92) A1 (11.24.93), 1 (1.15.94), §1 p. 12 (2.13.94), A1 (9.22.94), §1 p. 48 (11.6.94), A34 (12.16.94); IOS 8 (11.3.91);

WMG 28 (5.6.94); Wellesley College (1992); Brown & Gilligan (1992).
26. LAT B1 (2.28.92); 3 (1) *Ms* 59 (July–August 1992); WMG 17 (11.18.94).
27. NYT §1 p. 45 (4.26.92).
28. Bourdieu (1991); Curran et al. (1986); Karst (1990); Bérubé (1994); Bleifer (1996).
29. NYT §1 p. 14 (5.17.92), 14 (8.29.92), 10 (7.31.93), B5 (3.9.94), 6 (4.20.96), A12 (9.27.96), 20 (10.5.96); LAT D1 (5.12.95); Schwartz & Task Force (1995); cf. Gold et al. (1995); United Church of Christ (1995).
30. NYT 47 (12.14.91), 9 (2.22.92), §2 p. 5 (6.13.93), A8 (5.16.94), C1 (5.31.94), C1 (6.23.94), 19 (3.25.95), A14 (9.27.96); LAT B4 (10.3.92), A18 (3.4.94), F1 (9.8.94); *The American Experience*, "Midnight Ramble," PBS (10.26.94); Jhally & Lewis (1992).
31. NYT A1, C9 (3.2.92), §4 p. 16 (9.27.92), C6 (3.7.94), §4 p. 11 (4.3.94), C17 (6.24.94), C7 (3.2.95).
32. NYT 11 (12.12.92), B1 (12.31.93); WMG 12 (8.16.91).
33. LAT A6 (1.3.96).
34. NYT A12 (1.29.92), A12 (1.30.92), A19 (3.26.92), A14 (4.1.92), A17 (4.2.92), §1 p. 14 (4.5.92), A1 (7.8.92); LAT A1 (7.8.92).
35. LAT A20 (10.8.92).
36. Delgado (1982); Volokh (1992).
37. NYT §1 p. 17 (3.8.92).
38. NYT B2 (3.10.93) (Larkin), §2 p. 1 (8.15.93) (Allen), A3 (9.13.94) (Mitterrand); Pels (1991); Lehman (1991); Sheehan (1993); Wolin (1991); Nolte (1987a, 1987b); Péan (1994); Motion (1993); Thwaite (1993); Julius (1996); Eliot (1997).
39. NYT B3 (3.5.92), §2 p. 29 (4.25.93), B3 (10.22.93), A17 (8.19.94); NYRB 16 (4.21.94); Adam (1992); Barron (1991).
40. NYT A12 (8.29.91), A4 (1.3.94), A12 (10.13.93), 4 (10.16.93); CHE A1 (10.23.91); LAT B1 (9.21.92), B4 (10.12.93), B7 (10.13.93), F1 (10.21.93), A3 (8.24.96).
41. NYT C1 (6.9.95), B12 (7.24.95); Kumhardt, Kumhardt, and Kumhardt (1995); cf. Bradford & Blume (1992) (display of African pygmy); Postman (1985).
42. NYTBR 23 (8.29.93).
43. LAT B1 (3.6.92).
44. NYT C20 (6.15.95), D20 (6.16.95).
45. NYT A6 (6.6.96).
46. NYT A14 (2.1.95), A12 (2.2.95), A8 (2.6.95), A1 (2.9.95), 15 (2.11.95); LAT A13 (2.11.95).
47. NYT A6 (3.7.95).
48. NYT A8 (3.9.95), A10 (3.10.95).
49. NYRB 29 (7.11.96); Cohen (1996).
50. NY 114 (10.26.95).
51. Crichton (1994).
52. NYT A12 (7.22.93), A9 (7.29.93); NYTM 30 (10.4.92).
53. NYT B1 (1.31.92), A1 (7.7.92), 13 (5.1.93), §2 p. 13 (2.19.95), B1 (2.7.96), B1 (3.8.96); NYTM 28 (5.15.94); Gotanda (1991); Fishkin (1993); Delany, Delany, & Hearth (1993); Watkins (1994); Percelay (1994, 1995, 1996); Gates (1994); Warner (1995); Kleeblatt (1996).
54. See Walker (1996).

55. NYT §1 p. 1 (2.19.95); LAT B1 (1.11.94); Vallicrev (1971); Reed (1993).
56. Hockenberry (1995).
57. NYT A1 (3.2.93); Koestenbaum (1993).
58. NYT B3 (6.17.92); James (1992).
59. NYT §1 p. 1 (1.24.93), A27 (10.26.94); LAT A1 (8.31.95).
60. E.g., Gould (1976); Friday (1973, 1975, 1991); Barbach (1984); Kensington Ladies' Erotica Society (1984); Chester (1988); Lacombe (1988, 1994); Kiss & Tell (1991); Tisdale (1994); Bright (1995); McElroy (1995); cf. Kimmel (1991).
61. NYT §2 p. 37 (10.10.93); LAT F1 (2.7.95).
62. NYT A6 (4.3.95), C7 (5.2.95), B12 (10.26.95).
63. LAT F24 (3.24.95), E1 (3.29.95), B1 (1.27.96); NYTM 54 (12.17.95).
64. NYT B9 (12.1.89), B2 (12.4.89).
65. NYT A9 (8.12.92).
66. NYT 7 (10.8.94), A16 (10.11.94).
67. NYT A7 (2.19.91), §3 p. 1 (3.22.92); Goodman & Miyazawa (1993).
68. LAT E1 (1.28.92); NYT A4 (4.2.96).
69. Witness the extraordinary success of Deborah Tannen's books (1986, 1990, 1994).
70. E.g., Paley (1992).
71. G 25 (11.21.91); Hall (1991).
72. O 3 (11.17.91).
73. LAT B1 (5.16.92), B3 (5.21.92), B3 (10.15.92); NYT A8 (8.7.92).
74. Moriarty (1965); Nader (1980); Felstiner, Abel, & Sarat (1980–81); Mather & Yngvesson (1980–81); Harris et al. (1984); Abel (1985); Hensler et al. (1991); Merry (1990); Yngvesson (1988; 1993); Baumgartner (1986); Engel (1987); Greenhouse (1986); Greenhouse, Yngvesson, & Engel (1994).
75. NYT §4 p. 6 (11.24.91), A14 (4.24.92), §1 p. 10 (5.3.92); IOS 2 (10.20.91); LAT A1 (9.23.92), A2 (10.3.92).
76. NYT C1 (3.17.92). On retaliation against whistle-blowers, see G 7 (11.12.91); NYT A17 (4.24.90), C1 (3.17.92), A1 (3.22.91); Canan & Pring (1988); Canan et al. (1990); Pring & Canan (1996).
77. G 2 (10.31.91), 5 (11.20.91); O 7 (9.19.91); Genn (1982).
78. Curran (1977); Marks, Hallauer, & Clifton (1974).
79. NYT §1 p. 31 (4.26.92), A1 (7.13.92), A13 (12.30.94); G 29 (11.14.91); LAT F4 (2.15.92), A1 (6.24.94); Independent Commission (1986: 33–36); Phelps & Winternitz (1992); Morrison (1992).
80. On collective action by tort victims, see Ball (1986) (nuclear tests); Brodeur (1985) (asbestos); Erikson (1976) (Buffalo Creek); Stern (1977) (Buffalo Creek); Whiteside (1979) (dioxin); Levine (1982) (Love Canal); Gibbs (1982) (Love Canal); Schuck (1987) (Agent Orange); Insight Team (1979) (thalidomide); Teff & Munro (1976) (thalidomide).
81. NYT (7.2.93); Bowman (1993); Gardener (1994).
82. Cf. Michelman (1992); Greenawalt (1995).
83. O 9 (9.22.91); G 2 (11.14.91), LAT B1 (5.16.91), B1 (5.17.91), A3 (9.24.91), B3 (3.19.92), B1 (12.23.92), A3 (1.1.93), A3

(1.18.93), A1 (2.4.93), A1
(11.11.93); CHE A35 (2.12.92);
NYT A11 (1.23.91), A10 (6.2.93),
B4 (2.24.94); 191 *Searchlight* 13
(May 1991), 192:6 (June 1991),
193:6 (July 1991), 194:6 (August
1991); Commission for Racial
Equality (1988: 24). On the relationship between community
and democracy, see Sunstein
(1993); Post (1995: chap. 5).

84. NYT §1 p. 11 (2.20.94); Rosenblatt (1994).

85. Abel (1982); cf. Fitzpatrick
(1992); Merry & Milner (1993).

86. Feeley (1979) (paraphrasing
Marshall McLuhan); cf. Matsuda (1987).

87. Cf. Habermas (1984); de Haan
(1990: chap. 8).

88. Scott & Lyman (1968);
Blumstein et al. (1974).

89. Garfinkel (1956); Blum-Kulka,
House, & Kasper (1989); Schlenker & Darby (1981); Darby &
Schlenker (1982); Coulmas
(1981); 14 (1) *Patterns of Prejudice* (January 1980), 15 (4)
(October 1981) (publication of
apologies for racial hatred in
France); Gordon (1982: 34–36).

90. NYT A4 (3.6.95), §4 p. 3
(5.7.95), A1 (6.12.95); LAT A1
(7.19.95), A1 (8.16.95); Wagatsuma & Rosett (1986); Upham
(1987).

91. LAT A32 (7.3.92), A26 (8.8.92);
NYT A7 (7.3.92).

92. NYT 1 (3.11.95), A15 (3.24. 95);
LAT A16 (10.11.96); NYRB 49
(10.20.94); Lesher (1994).

93. NYT A12 (3.22.96), §1 p. 18
(3.24.96), §1 p. 21 (3.31.96).

94. NYT A13 (2.19.93).

95. NYT A12 (12.11.92).

96. LAT A2 (12.30.95).

97. NYT A10 (9.23.94).

98. NYT A16 (7.20.94); LAT A1
(5.10.93).

99. NYT B16 (11.28.91), 12
(12.29.91).

100. Tavuchis (1991).

101. NYT §1 p. 16 (8.2.92); LAT A3
(5.19.93), A3 (5.20.93), B3
(7.9.93), B7 (7.10.93).

102. LAT B8 (4.10.96); NYT B2
(4.10.96).

103. NYT §1 p. 24 (11.24.91).

104. NYT A14 (7.1.94), 14, 16
(7.2.94).

105. NYT §1 p. 24 (11.24.91); Early
(1994).

106. NYT B12 (4.6.95), A1 (4.7.95).

107. LAT A3 (5.19.95); NYT 7
(5.20.95).

108. LAT B1 (10.13.93), B1
(10.14.93).

109. NYT A1 (6.21.95), A1 (7.17.95),
10 (4.27.96), §1 p. 5 (7.20.96).

110. LAT A9 (8.6.93); Tavuchis
(1991); Hatamiya (1993).

111. NYT A5 (1.31.95); LAT A6
(1.31.95), A8 (2.3.95).

112. Tavuchis (1991).

113. NYT A1 (12.3.93).

114. NYT §1 p. 8 (5.21.95); LAT A4
(5.22.95).

115. NYT A10 (9.23.94).

116. NYT A3 (8.27.92).

117. NYT A11 (2.22.95).

118. LAT A1 (5.25.95), A1 (6.21.95).

119. LAT A1 (6.19.95), E1 (6.27.95);
Dawson (1994).

120. Ruben Bolling in NYT §4 p. 6
(9.3.95).

121. NYT C18 (3.1.93), §1 p. 42
(6.11.95).

122. NYT A7 (10.21.93).

123. Tavuchis (1991).

124. NYT 7 (1.7.95); LAT F1 (1.6.95),
A17 (1.7.95).

125. NYT A12 (12.2.91), A28

(12.5.91), D20 (12.6.91), 9 (12.7.91), §1 pp. 1, 24, 26 (12.8.91).
126. NYT A12 (4.15.95); LAT A27 (5.13.95).
127. NYT A7 (8.29.95); cf. Fox (1992) (rebuttal of Bible); Krassner (1993).
128. NYT A10 (10.23.96).
129. NYT A10 (9.20.96).
130. But see Fiss (1996a, 1996b).
131. On the experience of intentional communities, see Shapiro (1976); Hine (1973); Houriet (1971); Carden (1971); Zablocki (1971).
132. LAT B3 (3.19.92), A1 (11.11.93); CHE A35 (2.12.92); Fineman (1992).
133. Hamilton (1995–96: 94–95).
134. Attacks on political correctness include Bloom (1987); Sykes (1988, 1990, 1992); Bennett (1984, 1988); Cheney (1988, 1995); D'Souza (1991a, 1991b, 1991c); Kimball (1990); Presser (1991); Woodward (1991); Anderson (1992); Tyrell (1992); Schlesinger (1992); Getman (1992); Rauch (1993); Sowell (1993); Bernstein (1994); Smith (1994); Jacoby (1994); Henry (1994); Patai & Koertge (1994); Maher & Tetrault (1994); Horowitz (1994); Sacks & Thiel (1995); *Heterodoxy* (1992–). Defenses include Aufderheide (1992); Beckwith & Bauman (1993); Beers (1991); Berman (1992); Edmundson (1993); Friedman & Narveson (1995); Gates (1993); Gless & Smith (1992); Lauter (1993); Partisan Review (1991, 1993); Scott (1992); Williams (1994); Wilson (1995).
135. NYT A9 (9.4.96).
136. NYT §1 pp. 1, 16 (5.5.91). See also *New York Times* columnists Anthony Lewis and George Will, NYT B6 (5.13.91), 17 (5.27.91), A35 (10.14.94), A13 (11.27.95).
137. NYT §4 p. 4 (11.24.91), §4 p. 6 (9.11.94); see also Beard & Cerf (1992).
138. LAT F1 (6.25.94); NYT B1 (9.28.95); Garner (1994, 1995a, 1995b).
139. LAT A3 (1.24.92), A3 (5.25.92), A3 (12.26.94); NYT A8 (2.13.92), 5 (3.26.94); WMG 24 (5.13.94); Safire (1991).
140. See Gitlin (1995).
141. LAT F6 (4.23.92), F1 (1.25.94), F1 (4.4.94), F1 (2.9.95), F1 (5.18.95); NYT 12 (5.1.93), B1 (3.28.94); Styron (1967); Clarke (1968); Gates (1991).
142. NYT B1 (2.1.96), B1 (3.15.96).
143. NYT B1 (7.16.96).
144. NYT §1 p. 8 (1.8.95).
145. Santiago (1983).
146. Carter (1990); Gates (1991).
147. NYT B8 (12.29.93), §4 p. 17 (3.13.94), §1 p. 14 (1.22.95).
148. NYT §4 1 (12.18.94).
149. NYT §2 p. 13 (5.3.92).
150. Lewis (1961); Arendt (1963); Rainwater & Yancey (1967); Moynihan (1969); Fogel & Engermann (1974); Harrison (1992).
151. NYT 1 (9.5.92), B5 (9.15.92), A18 (10.2.92), B5 (9.19.95).

REFERENCES

Abel, Richard L. 1982. "The Contradictions of Informal Justice." In Richard L. Abel, ed., *The Politics of Informal Justice*. Vol. 1, *The American Experience*. New York: Academic Press.

———. 1985. "£'s of Cure, Ounces of Prevention." 73 *California Law Review* 1003.

———. 1994a. "Public Freedom, Private Constraint." 21 *Journal of Law and Society* 374.

———. 1994b. *Speech and Respect*. The 44th Hamlyn Lectures. London: Stevens & Sons.

———. 1995. *Politics by Other Means: Law in the Struggle against Apartheid, 1980–1994*. New York: Routledge.

Adam, Barry D. 1978. *The Survival of Domination*. New York: Elsevier North-Holland.

Adam, Peter. 1992. *The Art of the Third Reich*. New York: H. N. Abrams.

Adbusters Media Foundation. 1995. *Adbusters Culture Jammer's Calendar 1995*. Vancouver: Adbusters Media Foundation; Gabriola Island, British Columbia: New Society Publications.

Ades, Dawn, Tim Benton, David Elliott, and Iain Boyd Whyte. 1995. *Art and Power: Europe under the Dictators, 1930–1945*. London: Hayward Gallery/South Bank Centre.

Akhtar, Shabbir. 1989a. *Be Careful with Muhammad! The Salman Rushdie Affair*. London: Bellew Publishing.

———. 1989b. "The Case for Religious Fundamentalism." In Lisa Appignanesi and Sara Maitland, eds., *The Rushdie File*. London: Fourth Estate.

Alderfer, Hannah, et al., eds. 1982. *Diary of a Conference on Sexuality*. New York: Faculty Press.

Alliance for Justice. 1993. *Justice for Sale: Shortchanging the Public Interest for Private Gain*. Washington, D.C.: Alliance for Justice.

Anderson, Martin. 1992. *Impostors in the Temple*. New York: Simon & Schuster.

Anti-Defamation League. 1994. *Hate Crimes Laws: A Comprehensive Guide*. New York: Anti-Defamation League.

Appignanesi, Lisa, and Sara Maitland, eds. 1989. *The Rushdie File*. London: Fourth Estate.

Arbus, Diane. 1972. *Diane Arbus.* New York: Aperture.

———. 1995. *Untitled.* Ed. Doon Arbus and Yolanda Cuomo. New York: Aperture.

Arcand, Bernard. 1993. *The Jaguar and the Anteater: Pornography Degree Zero.* New York: Verso.

Arendt, Hannah. 1963. *Eichmann in Jerusalem: A Report on the Banality of Evil.* New York: Viking.

Arington, Michele. 1991. "English-Only Laws and Direct Legislation: The Battle in the States over Language Minority Rights." 7 *Journal of Law and Politics* 325.

Arkes, Hadley. 1975. "Civility and the Restriction of Speech: Rediscovering the Defamation of Groups." In Philip Kurland, ed., *Free Speech and Association.* Chicago: University of Chicago Press.

Arkush, Michael. 1993. *Rush!* New York: Avon Books.

Arnold, Bruce. 1992. *The Scandal of Ulysses: The Sensational Life of a Twentieth-Century Masterpiece.* New York: St. Martin's Press.

Aronowitz, Stanley. 1992. *The Politics of Identity: Class, Culture, Social Movements.* New York: Routledge.

———. 1993. *Roll over Beethoven: The Return of Cultural Strife.* Hanover, N.H.: University of New England Press.

Arons, Stephen. 1983. *Compelling Belief: The Culture of American Schooling.* New York: McGraw-Hill.

Assiter, Alison. 1989. *Pornography, Feminism, and the Individual.* London: Pluto Press.

Assiter, Alison, and Carol Avedon, eds. 1993. *Bad Girls and Dirty Pictures: The Challenge to Reclaim Feminism.* Boulder: Pluto Press.

Assouline, Pierre. 1984. "Enquête sur un historien condamné pour diffamation." 68 *L'histoire* 98.

Aufderheide, Patricia, ed. 1992. *Beyond P.C.: Toward a Politics of Understanding.* St. Paul: Graywolf Press.

Auletta, Ken. 1994. "Fee Speech." *New Yorker* 40 (September 12).

Bach, Penny Balkin. 1992. *Public Art in Philadelphia.* Philadelphia: Temple University Press.

Bailey, F. G., ed. 1971. *Gifts and Poison: The Politics of Reputation.* Oxford: Basil Blackwell.

Bailey, J. Michael, Richard C. Pillard, Michael C. Neale, and Yvonne Agyei. 1993. "Heritable Factors Influence Sexual Orientation in Women." 50 *Archives of General Psychiatry* 217.

Baird, Robert M., and Stuart E. Rosenbaum, eds. 1991. *Pornography.* Buffalo: Prometheus.

Baker, C. Edwin. 1994. *Advertising and a Democratic Press.* Princeton: Princeton University Press.

Baker, Houston A. Jr. 1994. *Black Studies, Rap, and the Academy.* Chicago: University of Chicago Press.

Baker, Jean-Claude, and Chris Chase. 1994. *Josephine: The Hungry Heart.* New York: Random House.

Baker, Nicholson. 1992. *Vox*. New York: Random House.

———. 1994. *The Fermata*. New York: Random House.

Baker, Robert. 1993. *Time and Pete*. New York: Simon & Schuster.

Ball, Howard. 1986. *Justice Downwind: America's Atomic Testing Program in the 1950s*. New York: Oxford University Press.

Banville, John. 1993. "An Interview with Salman Rushdie." *New York Review of Books* 34 (March 4).

Barbach, Lonnie, ed. 1984. *Pleasures: Women Write Erotica*. New York: Doubleday.

Barker, Martin, ed. 1984. *The Video Nasties*. London: Pluto Press.

Barnes, Julian. 1992. "'The Proudest and Most Arrogant Man in France.'" Review of Petra ten-Doesschate Chu, ed., *Letters of Gustave Courbet*. 39 (17) *New York Review of Books* 3 (October 22).

———. 1994. "Staying Alive." *New Yorker* 99 (February 21).

Barnum, David G. 1982. "Decision Making in a Constitutional Democracy: Policy Formation in the Skokie Free Speech Controversy." 44 *Journal of Politics* 480.

Baron, Dennis. 1990. *The English-Only Question: An Official Language for Americans?* New Haven: Yale University Press.

———. 1991. "English in a Multicultural America." 21 *Social Policy* 5.

Barrett, Michele. 1982. "Feminism and the Definition of Cultural Politics." In Rosalind Brunt and Caroline Rowan, eds., *Feminism, Culture, and Politics*. London: Lawrence & Wishart.

Barron, Stephanie, ed. 1991. *Degenerate Art: The Fate of the Avant-Garde in Nazi Germany*. Los Angeles: Los Angeles County Museum of Art; New York: H. N. Abrams.

Barry, David. 1993. "Screen Violence: It's Killing Us." *Harvard Magazine* 38 (November–December).

Barthes, Roland. 1976. *Sade Fourier Loyola*. New York: Hill & Wang.

Baumgartner, M. P. 1986. *The Moral Order of a Suburb*. New York: Oxford University Press.

Bawer, Bruce. 1993. *A Place at the Table: The Gay Individual in American Society*. New York: Poseidon.

Beaney, William H., and Edward N. Beiser. 1964. "Prayer and Politics: The Impact of *Engel* and *Schempp* on the Political Process." 13 *Journal of Public Law* 475.

Beard, Henry, and Christopher Cerf. 1992. *The Official Politically Correct Dictionary and Handbook*. New York: Villard.

Beard, Joseph L. 1994. "Casting Call at Forest Lawn: The Digital Resurrection of Deceased Entertainers: A 21st Century Challenge for Intellectual Property." 8 *High Technology Law Journal* 101.

Beckwith, Francis J., and Michael E. Bauman, eds. 1993. *Are You Politically Correct? Debating America's Cultural Standards*. Buffalo: Prometheus Books.

Bedford, Carmel. 1993. "Fiction, Fact, and the *Fatwa*." In Steve MacDonogh in association with Article 19, eds., *The Rushdie Letters: Freedom to Speak, Freedom to Write.* Lincoln: University of Nebraska Press; Dingle, County Kerry, Ireland: Brandon Book Publishers.

Beers, David. 1991. "Behind the Hysteria: How the Right Invented Victims of PC Police." *Mother Jones* 34 (September–October).

Beisel, Nicola. 1990. "Class, Culture, and Campaigns against Vice in Three American Cities, 1872–1892." 55 *American Sociological Review* 44.

Bell, Daniel. 1962. "Status Politics and New Anxieties: On the 'Radical Right' and Ideologies of the Fifties." In *The End of Ideology: On the Exhaustion of Political Ideas in the Fifties*, rev. ed. New York: Free Press.

Bennett, William J. 1984. *To Reclaim a Legacy: Report on the Humanities in Higher Education.* Washington, D.C.: National Endowment for the Humanities.

———. 1988. "Why the West?" *National Review* 37 (May 27).

Bentley, George R. 1955. *History of the Freedmen's Bureau.* Philadelphia: University of Pennsylvania Press.

Berger, John, Sven Blomberg, Chris Fox, Michael Dibb, and Richard Hollis. 1972. *Ways of Seeing.* London: BBC; Harmondsworth: Penguin.

Berman, Paul, ed. 1992. *Debating P.C.: The Controversy over Political Correctness on College Campuses.* New York: Dell.

Bernstein, Richard. 1994. *Dictatorship of Virtue: Multiculturalism and the Battle for America's Future.* New York: Knopf.

Bérubé, Michael. 1994. *Public Access: Literary Theory and American Cultural Politics.* London: Verso.

Bettelheim, Bruno. 1976. *The Uses of Enchantment: The Meaning and Importance of Fairy Tales.* New York: Vintage.

Bezanson, Randall P. 1994. *Taxes on Knowledge in America: Exactions on the Press from Colonial Times to the Present.* Philadelphia: University of Pennsylvania Press.

Bharucha, Rustom. 1990. "The Rushdie Affair: Secular Bigotry and the Ambivalence of Faith." 11 *Third Text* 61.

Billings, Dwight, and Robert Goldman. 1979. "Comment on the 'Kanawha County Textbook Controversy.'" 57 *Social Forces* 1393.

Binder, Amy. 1993. "Constructing Racial Rhetoric: Media Depictions of Harm in Heavy Metal and Rap Music." 58 *American Sociological Review* 753.

Birkby, Robert H. 1966. "The Supreme Court and the Bible Belt: Tennessee Reaction to the 'Schempp' Decision." 10 *Midwest Journal of Political Science* 304.

Bland, Richard, and Roy Wallis. 1977. "Comment on Wilson and Zurcher's 'Status Inconsistency and Participation in Social Movements.'" 18 *Sociological Quarterly* 426.

Bleifer, Craig B. 1996. "Looking at Pornography through Habermasian Lenses: Affirmative Action for Speech." 22 *New York University Review of Law and Social Change* 153.

Bloom, Allan. 1987. *The Closing of the American Mind.* New York: Simon & Schuster.

Bloom, Claire. 1996. *Leaving a Doll's House.* Boston: Little, Brown.

Blum-Kulka, Shoshana, Juliane House, and Gabriele Kasper, eds. 1989. *Cross-Cultural Pragmatics: Requests and Apologies.* Norwood, N.J.: Ablex Publishing.

Blumstein, Philip W., et al. 1974. "The Honoring of Accounts." 39 *American Sociological Review* 551.

Bodnar, John. 1991. *Remaking America: Public Memory, Commemoration, and Patriotism in the Twentieth Century.* Princeton: Princeton University Press.

Bogdan, Robert. 1988. *Freak Show: Presenting Human Oddities for Amusement and Profit.* Chicago: University of Chicago Press.

Bolton, Richard, ed. 1992. *Culture Wars: Documents from the Recent Controversies in the Arts.* New York: New Press.

Bordo, Susan. 1993. *Unbearable Weight: Feminism, Western Culture, and the Body.* Berkeley: University of California Press.

Boswell, John. 1994. *Same-Sex Unions in Premodern Europe.* New York: Villard.

Bourdieu, Pierre. 1984. *Distinction: A Social Critique of the Judgement of Taste.* Trans. Richard Nice. Cambridge: Harvard University Press.

———. 1991. *Language and Symbolic Power.* Cambridge: Polity.

Bower, Marion. 1986. "Daring to Speak Its Name: The Relationship of Women to Pornography." 24 *Feminist Review* 40.

Bowman, Cynthia Grant. 1993. "Street Harassment and the Informal Ghettoization of Women." 106 *Harvard Law Review* 517.

Boyle, James. 1992. "A Theory of Law and Information: Copyright, Spleens, Blackmail, and Insider Trading." 80 *California Law Review* 1413.

———. 1996. *Shamans, Software, and Spleens: Law and the Construction of the Information Society.* Cambridge: Harvard University Press.

Bradford, Phillips Verner, and Harvey Blume. 1992. *Ota: The Pygmy in the Zoo.* New York: St. Martin's Press.

Bradley, Michael. 1992. *The Iceman Inheritance: Prehistoric Sources of Western Man's Racism, Sexism, and Aggression.* New York: Kayode Publications.

Brandmeyer, G. A., and R. S. Denisoff. 1969. "Status Politics: An Appraisal of the Application of a Concept." 12 *Pacific Sociological Review* 5.

Branscomb, Anne Wells. 1994. *Who Owns Information? From Privacy to Public Access.* New York: Basic Books.

Braungart, Richard G. 1971. "Status Politics and Student Politics: An Analysis of Left- and Right-Wing Student Activists." 3 *Youth and Society* 195.

Brest, Paul, and Ann Vandenberg. 1987. "Politics, Feminism, and the Constitution: The Anti-pornography Movement in Minneapolis." 39 *Stanford Law Review* 607.

Bright, Susie. 1995. *Susie Bright's Sexwise.* Pittsburgh: Cleis.

Brock, David. 1993. *The Real Anita Hill: The Untold Story.* New York: Free Press.

Brodeur, Paul. 1985. *Outrageous Misconduct: The Asbestos Industry on Trial.* New York: Pantheon.

Brown, Lyn Mikel, and Carol Gilligan. 1992. *Meeting at the Crossroads: Women's Psychology and Girl's Development.* Cambridge: Harvard University Press.

Brown, Wendy. 1995. *States of Injury: Power and Freedom in Late Modernity.* Princeton: Princeton University Press.

Buchwald, Emilie, Pamela R. Fletcher, and Martha Roth, eds. 1993. *Transforming a Rape Culture*. Minneapolis: Milkweed Editions.

Buford, Bill. 1992a. *Among the Thugs*. New York: W. W. Norton.

―――. 1992b. "The Lads of the National Front." *New York Times Magazine* 32 (April 26).

Burr, Chandler. 1996. *A Separate Creation: The Search for the Biological Origins of Homosexuality*. New York: Hyperion.

Burstyn, Varda. 1985. "Beyond Despair: Positive Strategies." In Varda Burstyn, ed., *Women against Censorship*. Vancouver: Douglas & McIntyre.

Burt, Richard. 1993. *Licensed by Authority: Ben Jonson and the Discourse of Censorship*. Ithaca: Cornell University Press.

Buruma, Ian. 1994. *The Wages of Guilt: Memories of War in Germany and Japan*. New York: Farrar, Straus & Giroux.

Butler, Ruth. 1993. *Rodin: The Shape of Genius*. New Haven: Yale University Press.

Canan, Penelope, and George W. Pring. 1988. "Studying Strategic Lawsuits against Public Participation: Mixing Quantitative and Qualitative Approaches." 22 *Law & Society Review* 385.

Canan, Penelope, Gloria Satterfield, Laurie Larson, and Martin Kretzmann. 1990. "Political Claims, Legal Derailment, and the Context of Disputes." 24 *Law & Society Review* 923.

Canter, Laurence A., and Martha S. Siegel. 1994. *How to Make a Fortune on the Information Superhighway*. New York: HarperCollins.

Carden, Maren Lockwood. 1971. *Oneida: Utopian Community to Modern Corporation*. New York: Harper & Row.

Carr, C. 1993. *On Edge: Performance at the End of the Twentieth Century*. Hanover, N.H.: Wesleyan University Press.

Carter, Dan T. 1995. *The Politics of Rage: George Wallace, the Origins of the New Conservatism, and the Transformation of American Politics*. New York: Simon & Schuster.

Carter, Forrest. 1990. *The Education of Little Tree*. Albuquerque: University of New Mexico Press.

Centerall, Brandon S. 1992. "Television and Violence: The Scale of the Problem and Where to Go from Here." 267 *JAMA* 3059.

Chauncey, George. 1994. *Gay New York: Gender, Urban Culture, and the Making of the Gay Male World, 1890–1940*. New York: Basic Books.

Cheney, Lynne V. 1988. *Humanities in America: A Report to the President, the Congress, and the American People*. Washington, D.C.: National Endowment for the Humanities.

―――. 1995. *Telling the Truth: Why Our Culture and Our Country Have Stopped Making Sense—and What We Can Do about It*. New York: Simon & Schuster.

Chester, Gail, and Julienne Dickey, eds. 1988. *Feminism and Censorship: The Current Debate*. London: Prism Press.

Chester, Laura, ed. 1988. *Deep Down: The New Sensual Writing by Women*. Boston: Faber & Faber.

Childress, Steven Alan. 1991. "Reel 'Rape Speech': Violent Pornography and the Politics of Harm." 25 *Law & Society Review* 177.

Clarke, Alan. 1987a. "Moral Protest, Status Defence, and the Anti-abortion Campaign." 38 *British Journal of Sociology* 235.

———. 1987b. "Moral Reform and the Anti-abortion Movement." 35 *Sociological Review* 123.

Clarke, John Hendrik, ed. 1968. *William Styron's Nat Turner: Ten Black Writers Respond.* Boston: Beacon.

Clayson, Hollis. 1991. *Painted Love: Prostitution in French Art of the Impressionist Era.* New Haven: Yale University Press.

Cleary, Edward J. 1994. *Beyond the Burning Cross: The First Amendment and the Landmark R.A.V. Case.* New York: Random House.

Coburn, Walt A. 1992. *A Dark and Bloody Ground.* Ulverscroft.

Coetzee, J. M. 1994. "Fabulous Fabulist." *New York Review of Books* 30 (September 22).

———. 1996. *Giving Offense: Essays on Censorship.* Chicago: University of Chicago Press.

Cohen, Albert. 1996. *Belle du Seigneur: A Novel.* New York: Viking.

Cohen, Stanley. 1972. *Folk Devils and Moral Panics: The Creation of the Mods and Rockers.* London: MacGibbon & Kee.

Cole, David. 1994. "Playing by Pornography's Rules: The Regulation of Sexual Expression." 143 *University of Pennsylvania Law Review* 1.

Colford, Paul D. 1993. *The Rush Limbaugh Story: Talent on Loan from God: An Unauthorized Biography.* New York: St. Martin's Press.

Coliver, Sandra, ed. 1992. *Striking a Balance: Hate Speech, Freedom of Expression, and Non-discrimination.* London: Article 19; Colchester: Human Rights Centre, University of Essex.

Collins, Ronald K. L. 1992. *Dictating Content: How Advertising Pressure Can Corrupt a Free Press.* Washington, D.C.: Center for the Study of Commercialism.

Collins, Ronald K. L., and David M. Skover. 1996. *The Death of Discourse.* Boulder, Colo.: Westview Press.

Commission for Racial Equality. 1988. *Racism and Freedom of Speech on the Campus.* London: Commission for Racial Equality.

Commission on Obscenity and Pornography. 1971. *Technical Reports.* Vol. 5. Washington, D.C.: Government Printing Office.

Cone, Michele S. 1992. *Artists under Vichy: A Case of Prejudice and Persecution.* Princeton: Princeton University Press.

Coon, Carleton S. 1962. *The Origin of Races.* New York: Knopf.

Cornell, Drucilla. 1995. *The Imaginary Domain: Abortion, Pornography, and Sexual Harassment.* New York: Routledge.

Cose, Ellis. 1993. *The Rage of the Privileged Class.* New York: HarperCollins.

Coulmas, Florian. 1981. "'Poison to Your Soul': Thanks and Apologies Contrastively Viewed." In Florian Coulmas, ed., *Conversational Routine: Explorations in Standardized Communications Situations and Prepatterned Speech.* The Hague: Mouton.

Cowan, Geoffrey. 1979. *See No Evil: The Backstage Battle over Sex and Violence on Television.* New York: Simon & Schuster.

Crenshaw, Kimberlé. 1991. "Beyond Racism and Misogyny: Black Feminism and 2 Live Crew." 16 (6) *Boston Review* 6 (December).

Crichton, Michael. 1994. *Disclosure.* New York: Knopf.

Crouch, Barry C. 1992. *The Freedmen's Bureau and Black Texans.* Austin: University of Texas Press.

Curran, Barbara. 1977. *The Legal Needs of the Public.* Chicago: American Bar Foundation.

Curran, James, Jake Ecclestone, Giles Oakley, and Alan Richardson, eds. 1986. *Bending Reality: The State of the Media.* London: Pluto Press and Campaign for Press and Broadcasting Freedom.

Curtis, Russell L. Jr., and Louis A. Zurcher Jr. 1973. "Stable Resources of Protest Movements: The Multi-organizational Field." 52 *Social Forces* 53.

Cutlip, Scott M. 1994. *The Unseen Power: Public Relations: A History.* Hillsdale, N.J.: Erlbaum Associates.

Danforth, John C. 1994. *Resurrection: The Confirmation of Clarence Thomas.* New York: Viking.

Daniell, Rosemary. 1984. *Sleeping with Soldiers: In Search of the Macho Man.* New York: Holt Rinehart & Winston.

Danly, Susan, and Cheryl Leibold, eds. 1994. *Eakins and the Photograph.* Philadelphia: Pennsylvania Academy of the Fine Arts; Washington, D.C.: Smithsonian Institution.

Danto, Arthur C. 1995. *Playing with the Edge: The Photographic Achievement of Robert Mapplethorpe.* Berkeley: University of California Press.

Darby, Bruce W., and Barry R. Schlenker. 1982. "Children's Reactions to Apologies." 43 *Journal of Personality and Social Psychology* 742.

Darnton, Robert N. 1995a. *The Corpus of Clandestine Literature in France, 1769–1789.* Chapel Hill: University of North Carolina Press.

———. 1995b. *The Forbidden Best Sellers of Prerevolutionary France.* New York: W. W. Norton.

Davies, Christie. 1982. "Ethnic Jokes, Moral Values, and Social Boundaries." 33 *British Journal of Sociology* 383.

Davis, Douglas. 1993. *The Five Myths of Television Power; or, Why the Medium Is Not the Message.* New York: Simon & Schuster.

Davis, Kathy. 1994. *Reshaping the Female Body: The Dilemma of Cosmetic Surgery.* New York: Routledge.

Dawidoff, Robert, and Michael Nava. 1994. *Created Equal: Why Gay Rights Matter to America.* New York: St. Martin's Press.

Dawson, John. 1994. *Healing America's Wounds.* 2d ed. Ventura, Calif.: Regal.

Dean, Joseph. 1953. *Hatred, Ridicule, or Contempt: A Book of Libel Cases.* London: Constable.

Dees, Morris, and Steve Fiffer. 1993. *Hate on Trial: The Case against America's Most Dangerous Neo-Nazi.* New York: Villard.

de Grazia, Edward. 1992. *Girls Lean Back Everywhere: The Law of Obscenity and the Assault on Genius.* New York: Random House.

de Haan, Willem. 1990. *The Politics of Redress: Crime, Punishment, and Penal Abolition*. London: Unwin Hyman.

Delacoste, Frederique, and Priscilla Alexander, eds. 1987. *Sex Work: Writings by Women in the Sex Industry*. Pittsburgh: Cleis.

Delany, Sarah, and A. Elizabeth Delany with Amy Hill Hearth. 1993. *Having Our Say: The Delany Sisters' First 100 Years*. New York: Kodansha.

Deleuze, Gilles. 1971. *Masochism: An Interpretation of Coldness and Cruelty*. Leopold von Sacher-Masoch. *Venus in Furs*. Trans. Jean McNeil. New York: George Braziller.

DelFattore, Joan. 1992. *What Johnny Shouldn't Read: Textbook Censorship in America*. New Haven: Yale University Press.

Delgado, Richard. 1982. "Words That Wound: A Tort Action for Racial Insults, Epithets, and Name Calling." 17 *Harvard Civil Rights–Civil Liberties Law Review* 133.

———. 1991. "Campus Antiracism Rules: Constitutional Narratives in Collision." 85 *Northwestern University Law Review* 343.

Denfeld, Rene. 1995. *The New Victorians: A Young Woman's Challenge to the Old Feminist Order*. New York: Warner Books.

de Tocqueville, Alexis. 1958. *Democracy in America*. 2 vols. Ed. Phillips Bradley. New York: Vintage Books.

Dickey, Anthony. 1968. "Prosecutions under the Race Relations Act 1965, s.6 (Incitement to Racial Hatred)." 1968 *Criminal Law Review* 489.

Dienes, C. Thomas. 1972. *Law, Politics, and Birth Control*. Urbana: University of Illinois Press.

Donnerstein, Edward, Daniel Linz, and Stephen Penrod. 1987. *The Question of Pornography: Research Findings and Policy Implications*. New York: Free Press.

Dooling, Richard. 1996. *Blue Streak: Swearing, Free Speech, and Sexual Harassment*. New York: Random House.

Doss, Erika. 1995. *Spirit Poles and Flying Pigs: Public Art and Cultural Democracy in American Communities*. Herndon, Va.: Smithsonian Institution Press.

Douglas, Mary, and Aaron Wildavsky. 1982. *Risk and Culture: An Essay on the Selection of Technical and Environmental Dangers*. Berkeley: University of California Press.

Downs, Donald Alexander. 1985. *Nazis in Skokie: Freedom, Community, and the First Amendment*. Notre Dame: University of Notre Dame Press.

———. 1989. *The New Politics of Pornography*. Chicago: University of Chicago Press.

Doyle, Bertram. 1937. *The Etiquette of Race Relations in the South*. Chicago: University of Chicago Press.

D'Souza, Dinesh. 1991a. "Illiberal Education." *Atlantic Monthly* 51 (March).

———. 1991b. *Illiberal Education: The Politics of Race and Sex on Campus*. New York: Maxwell Macmillan International.

———. 1991c. "In the Name of Academic Freedom, Colleges Should Back Professors against Students' Demands for 'Correct Views.'" 37(32) *Chronicle of Higher Education* B1 (April 24).

D'Souza, Frances. 1993. Introduction to Steve MacDonogh in association with

Article 19, eds., *The Rushdie Letters: Freedom to Speak, Freedom to Write*. Lincoln: University of Nebraska Press; Dingle, County Kerry, Ireland: Brandon Book Publishers.

Dubin, Steven C. 1987. "Symbolic Slavery: Black Representations in Popular Culture." 34 *Social Problems* 122.

———. 1992. *Arresting Images: Impolitic Art and Uncivil Actions*. New York: Routledge.

Duggan, Lisa, Nan D. Hunter, and Carole S. Vance. 1985. "False Promises: Feminist Antipornography Legislation in the United States." In Varda Burstyn, ed., *Women against Censorship*. Vancouver: Douglas & McIntyre.

du Plessis, Lourens, and Hugh Corder. 1994. *Understanding South Africa's Transitional Bill of Rights*. Kenwyn, South Africa: Juta.

Duster, Troy. 1970. *The Legislation of Morality: Law, Drugs, and Moral Judgment*. New York: Free Press.

Dworkin, Andrea. 1989. *Pornography: Men Possessing Women*. New York: Dutton.

Dyson, Michael Eric. 1994. *Making Malcolm: The Myth and Meaning of Malcolm X*. New York: Oxford University Press.

———. 1996. *Between God and Gangsta Rap: Bearing Witness to Black Culture*. New York: Oxford University Press.

Early, Gerald. 1994. *Daughters: On Family and Fatherhood*. New York: Addison-Wesley.

Easton, Susan. 1994. *The Problem of Pornography: Regulation and the Right to Free Speech*. New York: Routledge.

Echols, Alice. 1984. "The Taming of the Id: Feminist Sexual Politics, 1968–1983." In Carole S. Vance, ed., *Pleasure and Danger: Exploring Female Sexuality*. Boston: Routledge & Kegan Paul.

Edelman, Murray. 1960. "Symbols and Political Quiescence." 54 *American Political Science Review* 695.

———. 1964. *The Symbolic Uses of Politics*. Urbana: University of Illinois Press.

———. 1971. *Politics as Symbolic Action*. New York: Academic Press.

———. 1976. *Political Language: Words That Succeed and Policies That Fail*. New York: Academic Press.

Edmundson, Mark, ed. 1993. *Wild Orchids and Trotsky: Messages from American Universities*. New York: Penguin.

Edwards, Susan. 1991. "A Plea for Censorship." 141 *New Law Journal* 1478 (November 1).

Ehrenreich, Barbara. 1981. "The Women's Movements: Feminist and Antifeminist." *Radical America* 98 (spring).

———. 1989. *Fear of Falling: The Inner Life of the Middle Class*. New York: Pantheon.

Elders, Joycelyn, with David Chanoff. 1996. *Joycelyn Elders, M.D.: From Sharecropper's Daughter to Surgeon General of the United States*. New York: William Morrow.

Eliot, T. S. 1997. *Inventions of the March Hare*. Ed. Christopher Ricks. New York: Harcourt Brace.

Elliott, Brian, and David McCrone. 1987. "Class, Culture, and Morality: A Sociological Analysis of Neo-Conservatism." 35 *Sociological Quarterly* 485.

Ellis, Bret Easton. 1991. *American Psycho.* New York: Vintage.

———. 1994. *The Informers.* New York: Knopf.

Elon, Amos. 1994. "Politics and Archaeology." *New York Review of Books* 14 (September 22).

Engel, David M. 1987. "The Ovenbird's Song: Insiders, Outsiders, and Personal Injuries in an American Community." 18 *Law & Society Review* 551.

English, Deirdre. 1981. "The War against Choice." *Mother Jones* (February–March).

Erikson, Kai T. 1976. *Everything in Its Path: Destruction of Community in the Buffalo Creek Flood.* New York: Simon & Schuster.

Ernst, Morris L., and Alexander Lindey. 1936. *Hold Your Tongue! Adventures in Libel and Slander.* London: Methuen.

Essed, Philomena. 1991. *Understanding Everyday Racism: An Interdisciplinary Theory.* Newbury Park, Calif.: Sage.

European Parliament. Committee of Inquiry into the Rise of Fascism and Racism in Europe. 1985. *Report of the Findings of the Inquiry.* Drafted by Dimitrios Evrigenis. Brussels: European Parliament.

Evans, N., A. Farkas, E. A. Gilpin, C. Berry, and J. P. Pierce. 1995. "Influence of Tobacco Marketing and Exposure to Smokers on Adolescent Susceptibility to Smoking." 87 *Journal of the National Cancer Institute* 1538.

Eysenck, H. J. 1971. *The I.Q. Argument: Race, Intelligence, and Education.* New York: Library Press.

Faludi, Susan. 1991. *Backlash.* New York: Crown.

Fanon, Frantz. 1965. *The Wretched of the Earth.* Trans. Constance Farrington. New York: Grove.

———. 1967. *Black Skin, White Masks.* Trans. Charles Lam Markham. New York: Grove.

Farrakhan, Louis. 1993. *A Torchlight for America.* Chicago: FCN Publ.

Feeley, Malcolm. 1979. *The Process Is the Punishment: Processing Cases in a Lower Criminal Court.* New York: Russell Sage.

Felstiner, William L. F., Richard L. Abel, and Austin Sarat. 1980–81. "The Emergence and Transformation of Disputes: Naming, Blaming, Claiming . . ." 15 *Law & Society Review* 631.

Ferguson, Ann, Ilene Philipson, Irene Diamond, Lee Quinby, Carole S. Vance, and Ann Barr Snitow. 1984. "Forum: The Feminist Sexuality Debates." 10 *Signs* 106.

Fineman, Martha Albertson. 1992. "Who Pays for Free Speech?" 9 (5) *Women's Review of Books* 17 (February).

Fischer, Claude S. 1992. *America Calling: A Social History of the Telephone to 1940.* Berkeley: University of California Press.

Fish, Stanley. 1994. *There's No Such Thing as Free Speech and It's a Good Thing, Too.* New York: Oxford University Press.

Fisher, Barry A. 1991. "Devotion, Damages, and Deprogrammers: Strategies and Counterstrategies in the Cult Wars." 9 *Journal of Law and Religion* 151.

Fishkin, Shelley Fisher. 1993. *Was Huck Black? Mark Twain and African-American Voices*. New York: Oxford University Press.

Fiss, Owen M. 1996a. *The Irony of Free Speech*. Cambridge: Harvard University Press.

———. 1996b. *Liberalism Divided: Freedom of Speech and the Many Uses of State Power*. Boulder, Colo.: Westview Press.

Fitzpatrick, Peter. 1992. "The Impossibility of Popular Justice." 1 *Social and Legal Studies* 199.

Flam, Jack. 1992. "The Alchemist." 39 (4) *New York Review of Books* 31 (February 13).

Fleener-Marzec, Nickieann. 1980. *D. W. Griffith's "The Birth of a Nation": Controversy, Suppression, and the First Amendment as It Applies to Filmic Expression*. New York: Arno Press.

Fletcher, George P. 1988. *A Crime of Self Defense: Bernhard Goetz and the Law*. New York: Free Press.

Foerstel, Herbert N. 1994. *Banned in the U.S.A.: A Reference Guide to Book Censorship in Schools and Public Libraries*. Westport, Conn.: Greenwood Press.

Fogel, Robert W., and Stanley L. Engermann, eds. 1974. *Time on the Cross: The Economics of American Negro Slavery*. New York: W. W. Norton.

Forman, James Jr. 1991. "Driving Dixie Down: Removing the Confederate Flag from Southern State Capitols." 101 *Yale Law Journal* 505.

For Rushdie: Essays by Arab and Muslim Writers in Defense of Free Speech. 1994. New York: George Braziller.

Fox, Robin Lane. 1992. *The Unauthorized Version: Truth and Fiction in the Bible*. New York: Knopf.

France, Anatole. 1927. *The Red Lily*. New York: Wm. H. Wise. First published 1894.

Freed, Leonard. 1991. *Photographs, 1954–1990*. Manchester: Cornerhouse Press.

Freedman, Monroe H., and Eric M. Freedman, eds. 1995. *Group Defamation and Freedom of Speech: The Relationship between Language and Violence*. Westport, Conn.: Greenwood Press.

Friday, Nancy. 1973. *My Secret Garden: Women's Sexual Fantasies*. New York: Trident Press.

———. 1975. *Forbidden Flowers: More Women's Sexual Fantasies*. New York: Pocket Books.

———. 1991. *Women on Top: How Real Life Has Changed Women's Sexual Fantasies*. New York: Simon & Schuster.

Fried, Stephen. 1993. *Thing of Beauty: The Tragedy of Supermodel Gia*. New York: Pocket Books.

Friedberg, David. 1992. *"The Play of the Unmentionable": An Installation by Joseph Kosuth at the Brooklyn Museum*. New York: New Press.

Friedman, Marilyn, and Jan Narveson, eds. 1995. *Political Correctness: For and Against*. Lanham, Md.: Rowman & Littlefield.

Friedman, Murray, with Peter Binzen. 1995. *What Went Wrong? The Creation and Collapse of the Black-Jewish Alliance*. New York: Free Press.

Friedrich, Otto. 1992. *"Olympia": Paris in the Age of Manet.* New York: Harper-Collins.

Fritscher, Jack. 1994. *Mapplethorpe: Assault with a Deadly Camera.* Mamaroneck, N.Y.: Hastings House.

Frohnmayer, John. 1993. *Leaving Town Alive: Confessions of an Arts Warrior.* New York: Houghton Mifflin.

Fürer-Haimendorf, Christoph von. 1967. *Morals and Merit.* Chicago: University of Chicago Press.

Gaines, Jane. 1991. *Contested Culture: The Image, the Voice, and the Law.* Durham: University of North Carolina Press.

Gaines, Steven, and Sharon Churcher. 1994. *Obsession: The Lives and Times of Calvin Klein.* New York: Birch Lane Press / Carol Publishing Group.

Galanter, Marc. 1974. "Why the 'Haves' Come Out Ahead: Speculations on the Limits of Legal Change." 9 *Law & Society Review* 95.

———. 1984. *Competing Equalities: Law and the Backward Classes in India.* Berkeley: University of California Press.

Gallagher, Hugh G. 1985. *F.D.R.'s Splendid Deception.* New York: Dodd, Mead.

Galliher, John F., and Linda Basilick. 1979. "Utah's Liberal Drug Laws: Structural Foundations and Triggering Events." 26 *Social Problems* 284.

Galliher, John F., and John R. Cross. 1982. "Symbolic Severity in the Land of Easy Virtue: Nevada's High Marijuana Penalty." 29 *Social Problems* 380.

———. 1983. *Morals Legislation without Morality: The Case of Nevada.* New Brunswick, N.J.: Rutgers University Press.

Galliher, John F., James L. McCartney, and Barbara E. Baum. 1974. "Nebraska's Marijuana Law: A Case of Unexpected Legislative Innovation." 8 *Law & Society Review* 441.

Gamson, William A. 1978. *The Strategy of Social Protest.* Homewood, Ill.: Dorsey Press.

Garber, Marjorie B. 1992. *Vested Interests: Cross-dressing and Cultural Anxiety.* New York: Routledge.

Gardbaum, Stephen A. 1991. "Why the Liberal State Can Promote Moral Ideals after All." 104 *Harvard Law Review* 1350.

Gardener, Carol Brooks. 1994. *Passing By: Gender and Public Harassment.* Berkeley: University of California Press.

Gardner, John. 1978. *On Moral Fiction.* New York: Basic Books.

Garfinkel, Harold. 1956. "Conditions of Successful Degradation Ceremonies." 61 *American Journal of Sociology* 420.

Garner, James Finn. 1994. *Politically Correct Bedtime Stories.* New York: Macmillan.

———. 1995a. *Once upon a More Enlightened Time.* New York: Macmillan.

———. 1995b. *Politically Correct Holiday Stories.* New York: Macmillan.

Garry, Patrick M. 1994. *Scrambling for Protection: The New Electronic Media and the First Amendment.* Pittsburgh: University of Pittsburgh Press.

Gates, Henry Louis Jr. 1991. "'Authenticity,' or the Lesson of Little Tree." *New York Times Book Review* 1 (November 24).

———. 1992. *Loose Canons: Notes on the Culture Wars.* New York: Oxford University Press.

———. 1993. "Let Them Talk." *New Republic* 37 (September 20, 27).

———. 1994. *Colored People: A Memoir.* New York: Knopf.

Genn, Hazel. 1982. *Meeting Legal Needs? An Evaluation of a Scheme for Personal Injury Victims.* Oxford: Centre for Socio-Legal Studies; Manchester: Greater Manchester Legal Services Committee.

Gerholm, Tomas, and Yngve Georg Lithman, eds. 1988. *The New Islamic Presence in Western Europe.* London: Mansell.

Getman, Julius. 1992. *In the Company of Scholars: The Struggle for the Soul of Higher Education.* Austin: University of Texas Press.

Gibbs, Lois. 1982. *Love Canal: My Story.* Albany: SUNY Press.

Gibson, James L., and Richard D. Bingham. 1985. *Civil Liberties and the Nazis: The Skokie Free-Speech Controversy.* New York: Praeger.

Gillmor, Donald M. 1992. *Power, Publicity, and the Abuse of Libel Laws.* New York: Oxford University Press.

Gingrich, Newt, and William R. Fortschen. 1995. *1945.* New York: Simon & Schuster.

Gitlin, Todd. 1986. *Watching Television: A Pantheon Guide to Popular Culture.* New York: Pantheon.

———. 1995. *The Twilight of Common Dreams: Why America Is Wracked by Culture Wars.* New York: Henry Holt.

Glantz, Stanton, Deborah Barnes, Lisa Bero, Peter Hanauer, and John Slade. 1996. *The Cigarette Papers.* Berkeley: University of California Press.

Glassner, Barry. 1993. *Bodies: Overcoming the Tyranny of Perfection.* New York: Simon & Schuster.

GLC Gay Working Party. 1985. *Changing the World: A London Charter for Gay and Lesbian Rights.* London: Greater London Council.

Glenny, Misha. 1995. "The Birth of a Nation." *New York Review of Books* 24 (November 16).

Gless, Darryl J., and Barbara Herrnstein Smith, eds. 1992. *The Politics of Liberal Education.* Durham, N.C.: Duke University Press.

Godin, Seth. 1994. *E-mail Addresses of the Rich and Famous.* Reading, Mass.: Addison-Wesley.

Goffman, Erving. 1951. "Symbols of Class Status." 2 *British Journal of Sociology* 294.

———. 1955. "On Face-Work." 18 *Psychiatry* 213.

———. 1956. "The Nature of Deference and Demeanor." 58 *American Anthropologist* 473.

———. 1959. *The Presentation of Self in Everyday Life.* New York: Doubleday.

———. 1961. *Encounters.* Indianapolis: Bobbs-Merrill.

———. 1976. "Gender Advertisements." 3 (2) *Studies in the Anthropology of Visual Communication* (fall). Reprint, New York: Harper & Row, 1979.

Gold, Victor Roland, et al. 1995. *The New Testament and Psalms: An Inclusive Version.* New York: Oxford University Press.

Goldberg, Steven. 1994. *Culture Clash: Law and Science in America.* New York: New York University Press.

Goldman, Robert. 1992. *Reading Ads Socially.* New York: Routledge.

Goldstein, Paul. 1994. *Copyright's Highway: From Gutenberg to the Celestial Jukebox.* New York: Hill & Wang.

Goldstein, Robert Justin. 1995. *Saving "Old Glory": The History of the American Flag Desecration Controversy.* Boulder, Colo.: Westview Press.

———. 1996. *Burning the Flag.* Kent, Ohio: Kent State University Press.

Gonzalez-Crussi, F. 1995. *Suspended Animation: Six Essays on the Preservation of Bodily Parts.* Photographs by Rosamond Purcell. New York: Harcourt Brace.

Goode, J. William. 1978. *The Celebration of Heroes: Prestige as a Control System.* Berkeley: University of California Press.

Goodman, David G., and Masanori Miyazawa. 1993. *Jews in the Japanese Mind: The History and Uses of a Cultural Stereotype.* New York: Free Press.

Gordon, Paul. 1982. *Incitement to Racial Hatred: A Brief Paper.* London: Runnymede Trust.

Gordon, Suzanne. 1983. *Off Balance: The Real World of Ballet.* New York: McGraw-Hill.

Gorski, Roger A., and Laura S. Allen. 1992. "Sexual Orientation and the Size of the Anterior Commissaure in the Human Brain." 15 *Proceedings of the National Academy of Sciences* 7199.

Gotanda, Philip Kan. 1991. *Yankee Dawg You Die.* New York: Dramatists Play Services.

Gould, Lois. 1976. *A Sea Change.* New York: Simon & Schuster.

Graham, Barbara. 1994. *Women Who Run with the Poodles.* New York: Avon.

Granberg, D. 1978. "Pro-Life or Reflection of Conservative Ideology? An Analysis of Opposition to Legalized Abortion." 62 *Sociology and Social Research* 414.

Greenawalt, Kent. 1995. *Fighting Words: Individuals, Communities, and Liberties of Speech.* Princeton: Princeton University Press.

Greenberg, Jeff, and Tom Pyszcynski. 1985. "Effect of an Overheard Ethnic Slur on Evaluation of the Target." 21 *Journal of Experimental Social Psychology* 61.

Greenhouse, Carol J. 1986. *Praying for Justice: Faith, Order, and Community in an American Town.* Ithaca: Cornell University Press.

Greenhouse, Carol J., Barbara Yngvesson, and David M. Engel. 1994. *Law and Community in Three American Towns.* Ithaca: Cornell University Press.

Green Paper on Public Order. 1980. Cmnd. 7891. London: HMSO.

Griffith, David Wark. 1967. *The Rise and Fall of Free Speech in America.* Hollywood: Larry Edmunds Book Shop. First published 1916.

Griffith, Thomas. 1995. *Harry and Teddy: The Turbulent Friendship of Press Lord Henry R. Luce and His Favorite Reporter, Theodore H. White.* New York: Random House.

Grossman, Dave. 1995. *On Killing: The Psychological Cost of Learning to Kill in War and Society.* Boston: Little, Brown.

Gubar, Susan, and Joan Hoff, eds. 1989. *For Adult Users Only: The Dilemma of Violent Pornography*. Bloomington: Indiana University Press.

Guerrilla Girls. 1995. *Confessions of the Guerrilla Girls*. New York: Harper Perennial.

Gunnlaugsson, Helgi, and John F. Galliher. 1986. "Prohibition of Beer in Iceland: An International Test of Symbolic Politics." 20 *Law & Society Review* 335.

Gusfield, Joseph R. 1963. *Symbolic Crusade: Status Politics and the American Temperance Movement*. Urbana: University of Illinois Press.

———. 1967. "Moral Passage: The Symbolic Process in Public Designations of Deviance." 14 *Social Problems* 175.

———. 1968. "On Legislating Morals: The Symbolic Process of Designating Deviance." 56 *California Law Review* 54.

Guttmann, Amy. 1992a. Introduction to A. Guttmann, ed., *Multiculturalism and "The Politics of Recognition."* Princeton: Princeton University Press.

———, ed. 1992b. *Multiculturalism and "The Politics of Recognition."* Princeton: Princeton University Press.

Habermas, Jürgen. 1984. *The Theory of Communicative Action*. Vol. 1, *Reason and the Rationalization of Society*. Boston: Beacon Press.

Hacker, Andrew. 1992. *Two Nations: Black and White, Separate, Hostile, Unequal*. New York: Charles Scribner's Sons.

Hafner, Katie, and John Markoff. 1991. *Cyberpunk: Outlaws and Hackers on the Computer Frontier*. New York: Simon & Schuster.

Hal, as told to Scott French. 1993. *Just This Once*. New York: Birch Lane Press.

Hall, N. John. 1991. *Trollope: A Biography*. New York: Oxford University Press.

Hamer, Dean, and Peter Copeland. 1995. *The Science of Desire: The Search for the Gay Gene and the Biology of Behavior*. New York: Simon & Schuster.

Hamilton, Ian. 1992. *Keepers of the Flame: Literary Estates and the Rise of Biography*. Winchester, Mass.: Faber & Faber.

———. 1995–96. "The First Life of Salman Rushdie." *New Yorker* 90 (December 25–January 1).

Hamilton, Nigel. 1993. *JFK: Reckless Youth*. New York: Random House.

Hamlin, David. 1980. *The Nazi/Skokie Conflict: A Civil Liberties Battle*. Boston: Beacon Press.

Harding, Susan. 1991. "Representing Fundamentalism: The Problem of the Repugnant Cultural Other." 58 *Social Research* 373.

Harewood, Jocelyn. 1993. *Romper Stomper*. Melbourne, Australia: Text.

Haring, Bruce. 1995. *Off the Charts: Ruthless Days and Reckless Nights inside the Music Industry*. New York: Carol Publishing Group.

Harris, Donald, Mavis Maclean, Hazel Genn, Sally Lloyd-Bostock, Paul Fenn, Peter Corfield, and Yvonne Brittan. 1984. *Compensation for Illness and Injury*. Oxford: Clarendon Press.

Harris, Mark. 1980. *Saul Bellow, Drumlin Woodchuck*. Athens: University of Georgia Press.

Harrison, Lawrence F. 1992. *Who Prospers? How Cultural Values Shape Economic and Political Success*. New York: Basic Books.

Harwitt, Martin. 1996. *An Exhibit Denied: Lobbying the History of Enola Gay.* New York: Copernicus.

Hatamiya, Leslie T. 1993. *Righting a Wrong: Japanese Americans and the Passage of the Civil Liberties Act of 1988.* Stanford, Calif.: Stanford University Press.

Hawthorne, Donald W. 1992. "Subversive Subsidization: How NEA Art Funding Abridges Private Speech." 40 *Kansas Law Review* 437.

Heins, Marjorie. 1993. *Sex, Sin, and Blasphemy: A Guide to America's Censorship Wars.* New York: New Press.

Helmreich, William B. 1982. *The Things They Say behind Your Back: Stereotypes and the Myths behind Them.* New York: Doubleday.

Hemingway, Ernest. 1986. *The Garden of Eden.* New York: Charles Scribner's.

Henry, William A., ed. 1994. *In Defense of Elitism.* New York: Doubleday.

Hensler, Deborah R., M. Susan Marquis, Allan F. Abrahamse, Sandra H. Berry, Patricia A. Ebener, Elizabeth G. Lewis, E. Allan Lind, Robert J. MacCoun, Willard G. Manning, Jeannette A. Rogowski, and Mary E. Vaiana. 1991. *Compensation for Accidental Injuries in the United States.* Santa Monica, Calif.: Rand Institute for Civil Justice.

Hentoff, Nat. 1992. *Free Speech for Me—but Not for Thee: How the American Left and Right Relentlessly Censor Each Other.* New York: HarperCollins.

Herman, Didi. 1994. "Law and Morality Re-visited: The Politics of Regulating Sado-Masochistic Porn and Practice." Presented to the annual meeting of the Law and Society Association, Phoenix, June.

Herrnstein, Richard J. 1971. "IQ." *Atlantic Monthly* 43.

Herrnstein, Richard J., and Charles Murray. 1994. *The Bell Curve: Intelligence and Class Structure in American Life.* New York: Free Press.

Heyn, Dalma. 1992. *The Erotic Silence of the American Wife.* New York: Turtle Bay Books.

Hicks, George. 1995. *The Comfort Women.* New York: W. W. Norton.

Himmelstein, Jerome L. 1983. *The Strange Career of Marijuana: Politics and Ideology of Drug Control in America.* Westport, Conn.: Greenwood Press.

Hine, Robert V. 1973. *California's Utopian Colonies.* New York: W. W. Norton.

Hirano, Kyoko. 1993. *Mr. Smith Goes to Tokyo: Japanese Cinema under the American Occupation, 1945–1952.* Washington, D.C.: Smithsonian Institute.

Hirsch, Fred. 1976. *Social Limits to Growth.* Cambridge: Harvard University Press.

Hockenberry, John. 1995. *Moving Violations: War Zones, Wheelchairs, and Declarations of Independence.* New York: Hyperion.

Hofstadter, Richard. 1925. *The Age of Reform.* New York: Knopf.

———. 1955. "The Pseudo-conservative Revolt." In Daniel Bell, ed., *The New American Right.* New York: Criterion.

———. 1963. "Pseudo-conservativism Revisited: A Postscript (1962)." In Daniel Bell, ed., *The Radical Right: The New American Right.* Garden City, N.Y.: Doubleday.

Holmes, Richard. 1995. "Voltaire's Grin." *New York Review of Books* 49 (November 30).

Home Affairs Committee. 1980. HC 756. London: HMSO.

Home Office. 1975. *Racial Discrimination*. Cmnd. 6234. London: HMSO.

hooks, bell [Gloria Watkins]. 1992. *Black Looks: Race and Representation*. Boston: South End Press.

Horowitz, David. 1994. *Liberal Racism: The College Student's Common-Sense Guide to Radical Ideology and How to Fight It*. Los Angeles: Center for the Study of Popular Culture.

Houriet, Robert. 1971. *Getting Back Together*. New York: Avon.

Hubner, John. 1993. *Bottom Feeders: From Free Love to Hard Core: The Rise and Fall of Counterculture Heroes Jim and Artie Mitchell*. New York: Doubleday.

Hughes, Robert. 1980. *The Shock of the New*. New York: Random House.

Humphrey, Derek. 1991. *Final Exit: The Practicalities of Self-Deliverance and Assisted Suicide for the Dying*. Eugene, Ore.: Hemlock Society.

Hunt, Lynn. 1992. *The Family Romance of the French Revolution*. Berkeley: University of California Press.

———, ed. 1993. *The Invention of Pornography: Obscenity and the Origins of Modernity, 1500–1800*. Cambridge: MIT Press.

Hunter, James Davison. 1991. *Culture Wars: The Struggle to Define America*. New York: Basic Books.

———. 1994. *Before the Shooting Begins: Searching for Democracy in America's Cultural Wars*. New York: Free Press.

Hunter, Nan D., and Sylvia A. Law. 1987–88. "Brief Amici Curiae of Feminist Anti-censorship Taskforce, et al., in *American Booksellers Association v. Hudnut*." 21 *Journal of Law Reform* 69.

Independent Commission of Enquiry into Racial Harassment. 1986. *Racial Harassment in Leeds, 1985–1986*. Leeds: Leeds Community Relations Council.

Insight Team of the Sunday Times. 1979. *Suffer the Children: The Story of Thalidomide*. New York: Viking.

Irons, Peter, and Stephanie Guitton. 1993. *May It Please the Court: The Most Significant Oral Arguments Made before the Supreme Court since 1955*. New York: Free Press.

Itzin, Catherine, ed. 1992. *The Case against Pornography: Sex Discrimination, Sexual Violence, and Civil Liberties*. Oxford: Clarendon Press.

Itzkoff, Seymour W. 1994. *The Decline of Intelligence in America: A Strategy for National Renewal*. Westport, Conn.: Praeger.

Jacobson, Michael F. 1994. *What Are We Feeding Our Kids?* New York: Workman Press.

Jacobson, Michael F., and Laurie Ann Mazur. 1995. *Marketing Madness: A Survival Guide for a Consumer Society*. Boulder, Colo.: Westview Press.

Jacoby, Russell. 1994. *Dogmatic Wisdom: How the Culture Wars Divert Education and Distract America*. New York: Doubleday.

James, Darius. 1992. *Negrophobia*. New York: Citadel Press.

Jenkins, Peter. 1989. "Is Rushdie Just the Tool of Allah's Will?" *Independent* 21 (March 1).

Jensen, A. R. 1969. "How Much Can We Boost IQ and Scholastic Achievement?" 33 *Harvard Education Review* 1.

Jhally, Sut, and Justin Lewis. 1992. *Enlightened Racism:* The Cosby Show, *Audiences, and the Myth of the American Dream.* Boulder, Colo.: Westview Press.

Joffe, Carole. 1985. "The Meaning of the Abortion Conflict." 14 *Contemporary Sociology* 26.

Johnson, Claudia. 1994. *Stifled Laughter: One Woman's Story about Fighting Censorship.* Golden, Colo.: Fulcrum.

Johnson, John M. 1989. "Horror Stories and the Construction of Child Abuse." In Joel Best, ed., *Images of Issues: Typifying Contemporary Social Problems.* New York: Aldine de Gruyter.

Jones, Ernest. 1955. *The Life and Work of Sigmund Freud.* Vol. 2, *Years of Maturity.* New York: Basic Books.

Jones, Peter. 1980. "Blasphemy, Offensiveness, and Law." 10 *British Journal of Political Science* 129.

———. 1990. "Rushdie, Race, and Religion." 38 *Political Studies* 687.

Joppke, Christian. 1986. "The Cultural Dimensions of Class Formation and Class Struggle: On the Social Theory of Pierre Bourdieu." 41 *Berkeley Journal of Sociology* 53.

Juergensmeyer, Mark. 1993. *The New Cold War? Religious Nationalism Confronts the Secular State.* Berkeley: University of California Press.

Julius, Anthony. 1996. *T. S. Eliot, Anti-Semitism, and Literary Form.* Cambridge: Cambridge University Press.

Jussawalla, Feroza. 1989. "Resurrecting the Prophet: The Case of Salman, the Otherwise." 2 *Public Culture* 106.

Kahn, K. L., M. L. Pearson, E. R. Harrison, K. A. Desmond, W. H. Rogers, L. V. Rubenstein, R. H. Brook, and E. B. Keeler. 1994. "Hospital Care for Black and Poor Hospitalized Medicare Patients," 271 *JAMA* 1169.

Kaite, Berkeley. 1995. *Pornography and Difference.* Bloomington: Indiana University Press.

Kaminer, Wendy. 1992. "Feminists against the First Amendment." *Atlantic Monthly* 110 (November).

Kappeler, Susanne. 1986. *The Pornography of Representation.* Cambridge: Polity.

Karst, Kenneth L. 1990. "Boundaries and Reasons: Freedom of Expression and the Subordination of Groups." 1990 *University of Illinois Law Review* 95.

———. 1993. *Law's Promise, Law's Expression: Visions of Power in the Politics of Race, Gender, and Religion.* New Haven: Yale University Press.

Kaufmann, Tara, and Paul Lincoln, eds. 1991. *High Risk Lives: Lesbian and Gay Politics after the Clause.* London: Prism Press.

Keller, Susan Etta. 1993. "Viewing and Doing: Complicating Pornography's Meaning." 81 *Georgetown Law Journal* 2195.

Kendrick, Walter. 1987. *The Secret Museum: Pornography in Modern Culture.* New York: Viking.

Kensington Ladies' Erotica Society. 1984. *Ladies' Own Erotica.* New York: Pocket Books.

Kimball, Roger. 1990. *Tenured Radicals: How Politics Has Corrupted Higher Education.* New York: Harper & Row.

Kimmel, Michael S., ed. 1991. *Men Confront Pornography.* New York: Crown.

Kincaid, James R. 1992. *Child-Loving: The Erotic Child and Victorian Culture.* New York: Routledge.

King, Margaret L. 1994. *The Death of the Child Valerio Marcello.* Chicago: University of Chicago Press.

Kinzer, Stephen. 1992. "East Germans Face Their Accusers." *New York Times Magazine* 24 (April 12).

Kipnis, Laura. 1996. *Bound and Gagged: Pornography and the Politics of Fantasy in America.* New York: Grove.

Kirkpatrick, R. George, Robert G. Cushing, and Charles K. Bowman. 1973. "Ad Hoc Anti-pornography Organizations and Their Active Members." 29 (3) *Social Issues* 69.

Kirp, David L. 1991. "Textbooks and Tribalism in California." 104 *Public Interest* 20.

Kiss and Tell. 1991. *Drawing the Line: Lesbian Sexual Politics on the Wall.* Vancouver: Press Gang.

Kisseloff, Joel. 1995. *The Box: An Oral History of Television, 1920–1961.* New York: Viking.

Klapisch, Bob, and John Harper. 1993. *The Worst Team Money Could Buy: The Collapse of the New York Mets.* New York: Random House.

Kleeblatt, Norman L., ed. 1996. *Too Jewish? Challenging Traditional Identities.* New Brunswick, N.J.: Rutgers University Press.

Kluger, Richard. 1996. *Ashes to Ashes.* New York: Knopf.

Knowlton, Steven R. 1994. *The Journalist's Moral Compass.* New York: Praeger.

Koch, Larry W., and John F. Galliher. 1993. "Michigan's Continuing Abolition of the Death Penalty and the Conceptual Components of Symbolic Legislation." 2 *Social and Legal Studies* 323.

Koch, Stephen. 1993. *Double Lives: Spies and Writers in the Secret Soviet War of Ideas against the West.* New York: Free Press.

Koestenbaum, Wayne. 1993. *The Queen's Throat: Opera, Homosexuality, and the Mystery of Desire.* New York: Poseidon.

Kramer, Jane. 1992. "Whose Art Is It?" *New Yorker* 80 (December 21).

Krassner, Paul. 1993. *Confessions of a Raving, Unconfined Nut: Misadventures in the Counterculture.* New York: Simon & Schuster.

Kruger, Barbara. 1993. *Remote Control: Power, Cultures, and the World of Appearances.* Cambridge: MIT Press.

Kumhardt, Philip B. Jr., Philip P. Kumhardt 3d, and Peter W. Kumhardt. 1995. *P. T. Barnum: America's Greatest Showman.* New York: Knopf.

Lacombe, Dany. 1988. *Ideology and Public Policy: The Case against Pornography.* Toronto: Garamond Press.

———. 1994. *Blue Politics: Pornography and the Law in the Age of Feminism.* Toronto: University of Toronto Press.

LaMarche, Gara, ed. 1995. *Speech and Equality: Do We Really Have to Choose?* New York: New York University Press.

Lamas, Gervasio A., Chris L. Pashos, Sharon-Lise T. Normand, and Barbara

McNeil. 1995. "Permanent Pacemaker Selection and Subsequent Survival in Elderly Medicare Pacemaker Recipients." 91 *Circulation* 1063.

Laqueur, Walter. 1993. *Black Hundred: The Rise of the Extreme Right in Russia.* New York: HarperCollins.

Laufer, Peter 1995. *Inside Talk Radio: America's Voice or Just Hot Air?* Secaucus, N.J.: Carol Publishing Group.

Laumann, Edward O., John H. Gagnon, Robert T. Michael, and Stuart Michaels. 1994. *The Social Organization of Sexuality.* Chicago: University of Chicago Press.

Lauter, Paul. 1993. "'Political Correctness' and the Attack on American Colleges." 44 *Radical Teacher* 34.

Law Commission. 1981. *Offences against Religion and Public Worship.* Working Paper no. 79. London: HMSO.

Lawrence, Charles. 1990. "If He Hollers Let Him Go: Regulating Racist Speech on Campus." 1990 *Duke Law Journal* 431.

Lawrence, D. H. 1955. *Sons and Lovers.* London: Collins.

Lawton, David. 1993. *Blasphemy.* Philadelphia: University of Pennsylvania Press.

Leavitt, David. 1993. *While England Sleeps.* New York: Viking.

———. 1994. "Did I Plagiarize His Life?" *New York Times Magazine* 36 (April 3).

le Carré, John. 1995. *Our Game.* New York: Knopf.

Lederer, Laura J. 1980a. Introduction to *Take Back the Night: Women on Pornography.* New York: William Morrow.

———. 1980b. "'*Playboy* Isn't Playing': An Interview with Judith Bat-Ada." In Laura J. Lederer, ed., *Take Back the Night: Women on Pornography.* New York: William Morrow.

———. 1980c. "Then and Now: An Interview with a Former Pornography Model." In Laura J. Lederer, ed., *Take Back the Night: Women on Pornography.* New York: William Morrow.

Lederer, Laura J., and Richard Delgado, eds. 1995. *The Price We Pay: The Case against Racist Speech, Hate Propaganda, and Pornography.* New York: Hill & Wang.

Lee, Simon, 1990. *The Cost of Free Speech.* London: Faber & Faber.

Leff, Arthur Allen. 1976. *Swindling and Selling.* New York: Free Press.

Lehman, David. 1991. *Signs of the Times: Deconstruction and the Fall of Paul de Man.* New York: Poseidon.

Lerner, Michael, and Cornel West. 1995. *Jews and Blacks: Let the Healing Begin.* New York: G. P. Putnam's Sons.

Lesher, Stephen. 1994. *George Wallace: American Populist.* New York: Addison-Wesley.

Lessing, Doris. 1984. *The Diaries of Jane Somers.* New York: Random House.

Lester, Anthony. 1987. "Antidiscrimination Legislation in Great Britain." 14 *New Community* 21.

LeVay, Simon. 1995. *The Sexual Brain.* Cambridge: MIT Press.

———. 1996. *Queer Science: The Use and Abuse of Research into Homosexuality.* Cambridge: MIT Press.

Levine, Adeline Gordon. 1982. *Love Canal: Science, Politics, and People.* Lexington, Mass.: Lexington Books.

Levy, Leonard W. 1993. *Blasphemy: Verbal Offense against the Sacred, from Moses to Salman Rushdie.* New York: Knopf.

Lewis, Anthony. 1992. *Make No Law: The Sullivan Case and the First Amendment.* New York: Random House.

Lewis, Heather. 1994. *House Rules.* London: Secker & Warburg.

Lewis, Oscar. 1961. *The Children of Sanchez.* New York: Random House.

Lichter, S. Robert, Linda S. Lichter, and Stanley Rothman, with the assistance of Daniel Amundson. 1991. *Watching America: What Television Tells Us about Our Lives.* New York: Prentice Hall.

Limbaugh, Rush. 1992. *The Way Things Ought to Be.* New York: Pocket Books.

———. 1993. *See, I Told You So.* New York: Pocket Books.

Linden, Robin Ruth, Darlene Pagano, Diana Russell, and Susan Star, eds. 1982. *Against Sado-Masochism.* San Francisco: Frog in the Wall Press.

Lindgren, James. 1993. "Defining Pornography." 141 *University of Pennsylvania Law Review* 1153.

Linenthal, Edward T., and Tom Engelhardt. 1996. *History Wars: The Enola Gay and Other Battles for the American Past.* New York: Henry Holt.

Lippard, Lucy R. 1990. "Andres Serrano: The Spirit and the Letter." *Art in America* 238 (April).

Lipset, Seymour Martin. 1963a. "The Sources of the 'Radical Right.'" In Daniel Bell, ed., *The Radical Right: The New Amercian Right.* Garden City, N.Y.: Doubleday.

———. 1963b. "Three Decades of the Radical Right: Coughlinites, McCarthyites, and Birchers." In Daniel Bell, ed., *The Radical Right: The New American Right.* Garden City, N.Y.: Doubleday.

Lipstadt, Deborah E. 1993. *Denying the Holocaust: The Growing Assault on Truth and Memory.* New York: Free Press.

Loeske, Donileen R. 1989. "'Violence' Is 'Violence' . . . or Is It? The Social Construction of 'Wife Abuse' and Public Policy." In Joel Best, ed., *Images of Issues: Typifying Contemporary Social Problems.* New York: Aldine de Gruyter.

Logan, David A. 1995. "Of 'Sloppy Journalism,' 'Corporate Tyranny,' and Mea Culpas: The Curious Case of *Moldea v. New York Times.*" 37 *William and Mary Law Review* 161.

Longino, Helen E. 1980. "Pornography, Oppression, and Freedom: A Closer Look." In Laura J. Lederer, ed., *Take Back the Night: Women on Pornography.* New York: William Morrow.

Lord, M. G. 1995. *Forever Barbie: The Unauthorized Biography of a Real Doll.* New York: William Morrow.

Lott, Eric. 1993. *Love and Theft: Blackface Minstrelsy and the American Working Class.* New York: Oxford University Press.

Louw, Chris. 1989. "Satan and Censorship." *Southern African Review of Books*

13 (February–March), translated and extracted from *Die Suid-Afrikaan* (December 1988–January 1989).

Luker, Kristin. 1984. *Abortion and the Politics of Motherhood.* Berkeley: University of California Press.

Lury, Celia. 1993. *Cultural Rights: Technology, Legality, and Personality.* New York: Routledge.

Lutz, Catherine A., and Jane L. Collins. 1993. *Reading National Geographic.* Chicago: University of Chicago Press.

MacArthur, John R. 1992. *Second Front: Censorship and Propaganda in the Gulf War.* New York: Hill & Wang.

McBride, Joseph. 1996. *Orson Welles.* Revised and expanded. New York: Da Capo.

McConaghy, Nathaniel, Neil Buhrich, and Derrick Silove. 1994. "Opposite Sex-Linked Behaviors and Homosexual Feelings in the Predominantly Heterosexual Male Majority." 23 *Archives of Sexual Behavior* 565.

MacDonogh, Steve, in association with Article 19, eds. 1993. *The Rushdie Letters: Freedom to Speak, Freedom to Write.* Lincoln: University of Nebraska Press; Dingle, County Kerry, Ireland: Brandon Book Publishers.

McElroy, Wendy. 1995. *XXX: Woman's Right to Pornography.* New York: St. Martin's Press.

McFeely, William S. 1968. *Yankee Stepfather: O. O. Howard and the Freedmen.* New Haven: Yale University Press.

Mack, John. 1994. *Abduction: Human Encounters with Aliens.* New York: Charles Scribner's Sons.

MacKinnon, Catharine A. 1987. *Feminism Unmodified: Discourses on Life and Law.* Cambridge: Harvard University Press.

———. 1993. *Only Words.* Cambridge: Harvard University Press.

Maher, Frances A., and Mary Kay Thompson Tetrault. 1994. *The Feminist Classroom.* New York: Basic Books.

Malcolm, Janet. 1993. "The Silent Woman." *New Yorker* 84 (August 23–30).

———. 1994. *The Silent Woman: Sylvia Plath and Ted Hughes.* New York: Knopf.

Mallon, Thomas. 1991. *Stolen Words: Forays into the Origins and Ravages of Plagiarism.* New York: Penguin.

Maltese, John Anthony. 1992. *Spin Control: The White House Office of Communications and the Management of Presidential News.* Chapel Hill: University of North Carolina Press.

Mander, Jerry. 1978. *Four Arguments for the Elimination of Television.* New York: Morrow.

Mankin, Lawrence David. 1980. *The National Government and the Arts from the Great Depression to 1973.* Ann Arbor: University Microfilms.

Mann, Sally. 1988. *At Twelve: Portraits of Young Women.* New York: Aperture.

———. 1992. *Immediate Family.* New York: Aperture.

Mapplethorpe, Robert. 1993. *Mapplethorpe.* New York: Random House.

———. 1995. *Altars.* With an essay by Edmund White. New York: Random House.

March, Joseph Moncure. 1995. *The Wild Party.* Illustrations by Art Spiegelman. New York: Pantheon.

Marchand, Roland. 1985. *Advertising the American Dream: Making Way for Modernity.* Berkeley: University of California Press.

Marchand, Shoshana. 1992. "Hooked: Mind and Body Games among the Modern Primitives." *Bay Guardian* 23 (May 27).

Marks, F. Raymond, Robert Paul Hallauer, and R. R. Clifton. 1974. *The Shreveport Plan: An Experiment in the Delivery of Legal Services.* Chicago: American Bar Foundation.

Marnham, Patrick. 1990. "Rushdie: A Classically French Affair." *Independent* (February 10).

Marquis, Alice Goldfarb. 1995. *Art Lessons: Learning from the Rise and Fall of Public Arts Funding.* New York: Basic Books.

Marzuk, Peter M., et al. 1993. "Increase in Suicide by Asphyxiation in New York City after the Publication of *Final Exit.*" 329 *New England Journal of Medicine* 1508.

Mather, Lynn, and Barbara Yngvesson. 1980–81. "Language, Audience, and the Transformation of Disputes." 15 *Law & Society Review* 775.

Matoesian, Gregory M. 1993. *Reproducing Rape: Domination through Talk in the Courtroom.* Chicago: University of Chicago Press.

Matsuda, Mari J. 1987. "Looking to the Bottom: Critical Legal Studies and Reparations." 22 *Harvard Civil Rights–Civil Liberties Law Review* 323.

———. 1989. "Public Response to Racist Speech: Considering the Victim's Story." 87 *Michigan Law Review* 2320.

———. 1991. "Voices of America: Accent, Accent Discrimination Law, and a Jurisprudence for the Last Reconstruction." 100 *Yale Law Journal* 1329.

Matsuda, Mari J., Charles R. Lawrence III, Richard Delgado, and Kimberlé Crenshaw. 1992. *Words That Wound: Critical Race Theory, Assaultive Speech, and the First Amendment.* Boulder, Colo.: Westview Press.

Matthiessen, Peter. 1983. *In the Spirit of Crazy Horse.* New York: Viking.

———. 1991. *In the Spirit of Crazy Horse.* New York: Viking.

Mayer, Jane, and Jill Abramson. 1994. *Strange Justice: The Selling of Clarence Thomas.* Boston: Houghton Mifflin.

Maynard-Moody, Steven. 1995. *The Dilemma of the Fetus: Fetal Research, Medical Progress, and Moral Politics.* New York: St. Martin's Press.

Mazrui, Ali. 1990. "Witness for the Prosecution: A Cross-Examination on *The Satanic Verses.*" 11 *Third Text* 31.

Medved, Michael. 1992. *Hollywood vs. America: Popular Culture and the War on Traditional Values.* New York: HarperCollins.

Memmi, Albert. 1965. *The Colonizer and the Colonized.* Trans. Howard Greenfield. New York: Orion Press.

Menendez, Albert J. 1993. *The December Wars: Religious Symbols and Ceremonies in the Public Square.* Buffalo: Prometheus Books.

Mennell, S. J. 1969. "Prohibition: A Sociological View." 3 *American Studies* 159.

Merry, Sally Engle. 1990. *Getting Justice and Getting Even: Legal Consciousness among Working Class Americans.* Chicago: University of Chicago Press.

Merry, Sally Engle, and Neal Milner, eds. 1993. *The Possibility of Popular Justice: A Case Study of Community Mediation in the United States.* Ann Arbor: University of Michigan Press.

Michelman, Frank. 1992. "Universities, Racist Speech, and Democracy in America: An Essay for the ACLU." 27 *Harvard Civil Rights–Civil Liberties Law Review* 339.

Miller, Mark Crispin. 1992. *Spectacle: Operation Desert Storm and the Triumph of Illusion.* New York: Simon & Schuster.

Miller, Paula Jean, and Gideon Sjoberg. 1973. "Urban Middle-Class Life Styles in Transition." 9 *Journal of Applied Behavioral Science* 144.

Miller, William Ian. 1993. *Humiliation, and Other Essays on Honor, Social Discomfort, and Violence.* Ithaca: Cornell University Press.

Miller, William Lee. 1996. *Arguing about Slavery: The Great Battle in the United States Congress.* New York: Knopf.

Minow, Martha. 1990. *Making All the Difference: Inclusion, Exclusion, and American Law.* Ithaca: Cornell University Press.

Minow, Newton N., and Craig L. LaMay. 1995. *Abandoned in the Wasteland: Children, Television, and the First Amendment.* New York: Hill & Wang.

Modood, Tariq. 1990. "British Asian Muslims and the Rushdie Affair." 61 *Political Quarterly* 143.

Moldea, Dan E. 1989. *Interference: How Organized Crime Influences Professional Football.* New York: Morrow.

Montgomery, Kathryn C. 1989. *Target, Prime Time: Advocacy Groups and the Struggle over Entertainment Television.* New York: Oxford University Press.

Morgan, Robin. 1977. "Theory and Practice: Pornography and Rape." In *Going Too Far.* New York: Random House.

Moriarty, Thomas. 1965. "A Nation of Willing Victims." *Psychology Today* 44 (April).

Morrison, David E., and Michael Tracey. 1978. "American Theory and British Practice: The Case of Mrs. Mary Whitehouse and the National Viewers and Listeners Association." In Rajeev Dhavan and Christie Davies, eds., *Censorship and Obscenity.* Totowa, N.J.: Rowman & Littlefield.

Morrison, Toni, ed. 1992. *Race-ing Justice, En-gendering Power.* New York: Pantheon.

Morrisroe, Patricia. 1995. *Mapplethorpe: A Biography.* New York: Random House.

Motion, Andrew. 1993. *Philip Larkin: A Writer's Life.* London: Faber & Faber.

Moynihan, Daniel Patrick, ed. 1969. *On Understanding Poverty.* New York: Basic Books.

Mulcahy, Kevin V., and C. Richard Swaim, eds. 1982. *Public Policy and the Arts.* Boulder, Colo.: Westview Press.

Myrdal, Gunnar. 1944. *An American Dilemma.* New York: Harper & Row.

Nachman, Jerry. 1994. "Are the Media out of Control?" *New York Times Magazine* 28 (June 24).

Nader, Laura, ed. 1980. *No Access to Law: Alternatives to the American Judicial System.* New York: Academic Press.

Nair, Rukmini B., and Rimli Battacharya. 1990. "Salman Rushdie: Migrant in the Metropolis." 11 *Third Text* 17.

National Advisory Commission on Civil Disorders. 1968. *Report.* New York: Philip Randolph Institute.

National Education Association. 1951. *The Pasadena Story.* Washington, D.C.: National Education Association.

Nation of Islam Historical Research Department. 1991. *The Secret Relationship between Blacks and Jews.* Chicago: Latimer Associates.

Neier, Aryeh. 1979. *Defending My Enemy: American Nazis, the Skokie Case, and the Risks of Freedom.* New York: E. P. Dutton.

Nelson, Barbara. 1984. *Making an Issue of Child Abuse: Political Agenda Setting for Social Problems.* Chicago: University of Chicago Press.

Nelson, Margaret. 1968. "Prohibition: A Case Study of Societal Misguidance." 12 *American Behavioral Scientist* 37.

Nerone, John. 1994. *Violence against the Press: Policing the Public Sphere in U.S. History.* New York: Oxford University Press.

Nesin, Aziz. 1994. "The Salman Rushdie Case in Turkey." In *For Rushdie: Essays by Arab and Muslim Writers in Defense of Free Speech.* New York: George Braziller.

Nobile, Philip, ed. 1995. *Judgment at the Smithsonian: The Uncensored Script of the Smithsonian's 50th Anniversary Exhibit of the Enola Gay.* New York: Marlowe.

Nolte, Ernst. 1987a. *Der europäische Burgerkrieg, 1917–1945: Nationalsozialismus und Bolschewismus.* Berlin: Propylaen Verlag.

———. 1987b. *Das Vergehen des Vergangenheid: Antwort an meine Kritiker im sogenannten Historikerstreit.* Berlin: Ullstein.

Oates, Stephen B. 1978. *With Malice toward None: The Life of Abraham Lincoln.* New York: New American Library.

O'Malley, Pat. 1987a. "Regulating Contradictions: The Australian Press Council and the 'Dispersal of Social Control.'" 21 *Law & Society Review* 83.

———. 1987b. "Regulation, Pseudo-regulation, and Counter-regulation: The Operation of the Australian Press Council." 9 *Media, Culture, and Society* 77.

O'Reilly, Kenneth. 1995. *Nixon's Piano: Presidents and Racial Politics.* New York: Free Press.

Orenstein, Peggy, and the American Association of University Women. 1994. *Schoolgirls: Young Women, Self-Esteem, and the Confidence Gap.* New York: Doubleday.

Packard, Vance. 1961. *The Status Seekers.* New York: Pocket Books.

Page, Ann L., and Donald A. Clelland. 1978. "The Kanawha County Textbook Controversy: A Study of Life Style Concern." 57 *Social Forces* 265.

Paglia, Camille. 1990. *Sexual Personae: Art and Decadence from Nefertiti to Emily Dickinson.* New York: Oxford University Press.

———. 1992. *Sex, Art, and American Culture: Essays.* New York: Vintage.

———. 1994. *Vamps and Tramps: New Essays.* New York: Vintage.

Paley, Vivian Gussin. 1992. *You Can't Say You Can't Play.* Cambridge: Harvard University Press.

Pally, Marcia. 1994. *Sex and Sensibility: Reflections on Forbidden Mirrors and the Will to Censor.* New York: W. W. Norton.

Parini, Jay. 1995. *John Steinbeck: A Biography.* New York: Henry Holt.

Parkin, Frank. 1968. *Middle Class Radicalism.* Manchester: Manchester University Press.

Partisan Review. 1991. "The Changing Culture of the University." 58 (2) *Partisan Review* (special issue).

———. 1993. "The Politics of Political Correctness: A Symposium." 60 (4) *Partisan Review* (special issue).

Patai, Daphne S., and Norette Koertge. 1994. *Professing Feminism: Cautionary Tales from Inside the Strange World of Women's Studies.* New York: Basic Books.

Péan, Pierre. 1994. *Une jeunesse française: François Mitterrand, 1934–1937.* Paris: Fayard.

Pels, Dick. 1991. "Treason of the Intellectuals: Paul de Man and Hendrik de Man." 8 *Theory, Culture, and Society* 21.

People for the American Way. 1993. *Attacks on the Freedom to Learn, 1992–1993.* Washington, D.C.: People for the American Way.

———. 1994. *Attacks on the Freedom to Learn, 1993–1994.* Washington, D.C.: People for the American Way.

Percelay, James. 1994. *Snaps.* New York: Morrow.

———. 1995. *Double Snaps.* New York: Quill.

———. 1996. *Triple Snaps.* New York: Quill.

Peristiany, J. G., ed. 1965. *Honour and Shame: The Values of Mediterranean Society.* London: Weidenfeld & Nicholson.

Perkins, William Eric. 1995. *Prisoners of the Image: Race and Ethnicity in American Popular Culture, 1840–1960.* New York: Harry Abrams.

Perry, Ruth. 1992. "Historically Correct." 9 (5) *Women's Review of Books* 15 (February).

Petchesky, Rosalind Pollack. 1984. *Abortion and Woman's Choice: The State, Sexuality, and Reproductive Freedom.* New York: Longman.

Phelps, Timothy M., and Helen Winternitz. 1992. *Capitol Games: Clarence Thomas, Anita Hill, and the Story of a Supreme Court.* New York: Hyperion.

Pierce, J. P., et al. 1992. "Does Tobacco Advertising Target Young People to Start Smoking: Evidence from California." 266 *JAMA* 3154.

Pierce, J. P., L. Lee, and E. A. Gilpin. 1994. "Smoking Initiation by Adolescent Girls, 1944 through 1988: An Association with Targeted Advertising." 271 *JAMA* 608.

Pileggi, Nicholas. 1986. *Wiseguy.* New York: Simon & Schuster.

Pindell, Howardena. 1990. "Covenant of Silence: De Facto Censorship in the Visual Arts." 11 *Third Text* 71.

Platt, Anthony M. 1977. *The Child Savers: The Invention of Delinquency.* 2d ed. Chicago: University of Chicago Press.

Pollay, Richard W., S. Siddarth, Michael Siegel, Anne Haddix, Robert K. Merritt, Gary A. Giovino, and Michael P. Eriksen. 1996. "The Last Straw? Cigarette Advertising and Realized Market Shares among Youths and Adults, 1979–1993." 60 *Journal of Marketing* 1.

Post, Robert. 1995. *Constitutional Domains: Democracy, Community, Management.* Cambridge: Harvard University Press.

Postman, Neal. 1985. *Amusing Ourselves to Death: Public Discourse in the Age of Show Business.* New York: Viking.

Poulton, Hugh. 1995. *Who Are the Macedonians?* Bloomington: Indiana University Press.

Pour Rushdie: Cent intellectuels arabes et musulmans pour la liberté d'expression. 1993. Paris: Editions la Découverte.

Power, Jonathan, ed. 1995. *A Vision of Hope: The Fiftieth Anniversary of the United Nations.* London: Regency.

Presser, ArLynn Leiber. 1991. "The Politically Correct Law School." 71 *American Bar Association Journal* 52 (September).

Pring, George W., and Penelope Canan. 1996. *SLAPPs: Getting Sued for Speaking Out.* Philadelphia: Temple University Press.

Provenzo, Eugene F. 1991. *Video Kids.* Cambridge: Harvard University Press.

Qureshi, Shoaib, and Javed Khan. 1989. *The Politics of the Satanic Verses: Unmasking Western Attitudes.* 2d ed. Leicester: Muslim Community Studies Institute.

Rabin, Robert L., and Stephen D. Sugarman, eds. 1993. *Smoking Policy: Law, Politics, and Culture.* Berkeley: University of California Press.

Rainwater, Lee, and William Yancey, eds. 1967. *The Moynihan Report and the Politics of Controversy.* Cambridge: MIT Press.

Randall, Richard S. 1968. *Censorship of the Movies: Social and Political Control of a Mass Medium.* Madison: University of Wisconsin Press.

———. 1989. *Freedom and Taboo: Pornography and the Politics of a Self Divided.* Berkeley: University of California Press.

Ranulf, Svend. 1964. *Moral Indignation and Middle Class Psychology.* New York: Schocken Books.

Rauch, Jonathan. 1993. *Kindly Inquisitors: The New Attacks on Free Thought.* Chicago: University of Chicago Press.

Ravitch, Diane. 1974. *The Great School Wars: New York City, 1805–1973.* New York: Basic Books.

Redgrave, Vanessa. 1994. *Vanessa Redgrave: An Autobiography.* New York: Random House.

Reed, Ishmael. 1993. *Japanese by Spring.* New York: Atheneum.

Reinarman, Craig. 1979. "Moral Entrepreneurs and Political Economy: Historical and Ethnographic Notes on the Construction of the Cocaine Menace." 3 *Contemporary Crises* 225.

———. 1990. "The Origins of Mothers against Drunk Driving and the Social Construction of the Teenage Drinking Problem." 17 *Theory and Society* 91.

Reinarman, Craig, and Harry Levine. 1989. "The Crack Attack: Politics and Media in America's Latest Drug Scare." In Joel Best, ed., *Images of Issues: Typifying Contemporary Social Problems.* New York: Aldine de Gruyter.

Reinarman, Craig, Dan Waldorf, and Sheigla B. Murphy. 1988. "Scapegoating and Social Control in the Construction of a Public Problem: Empirical and Critical Findings on Cocaine and Work." 9 *Research in Law, Deviance, and Social Control* 37.

Reporting World War II. 1995. 2 vols. New York: Library of America.

Resnick, Faye D. 1994. *Nicole Brown Simpson: The Private Diary of a Life Interrupted.* Beverly Hills: Dove Books.

Rheingold, Howard. 1993. *The Virtual Community: Homesteading on the Electronic Frontier.* Reading, Mass.: Addison-Wesley.

Richards, Eugene. 1994. *Cocaine True, Cocaine Blue.* New York: Aperture.

Richler, Mordechai. 1992. *Oh Canada! Oh Quebec! A Requiem for a Divided Country.* New York: Knopf.

———. 1993. "On Language: Gros Mac Attack." *New York Times Magazine* 10 (July 18).

Riesman, David. 1942. "Democracy and Defamation: Control of Group Libel." 42 *Columbia Law Review* 727.

———. 1950. *The Lonely Crowd.* New Haven: Yale University Press.

Riesman, David, and Reuel Denney. 1951. "Football in America." 3 *American Quarterly* 309.

Ritchie, Donald. 1991. *Press Gallery: A History of Washington Correspondents.* Cambridge: Harvard University Press.

Robbins, Natalie. 1992. *Alien Ink: The F.B.I.'s War on Freedom of Expression.* New York: William Morrow.

Roberts, Paul Craig, and Lawrence M. Stratton. 1995. *The New Color Line: How Quotas and Privilege Destroy Democracy.* Washington, D.C.: Regnery.

Robinson, Harlow. 1994. *The Last Impresario: The Life, Times, and Legacy of Sol Hurok.* New York: Viking.

Rodgers, Harrell R. Jr. 1975. "Prelude to Conflict: The Evolution of Censorship Campaigns." 18 *Pacific Sociological Review* 194.

Rodgerson, Gillian, and Elizabeth Wilson, eds. 1991. *Pornography and Feminism: The Case against Censorship.* London: Lawrence & Wishart.

Rodriguez-Salgado, M. J. 1992. "Columbus's Fall from Grace." 29 (5) *Society* 48.

Roeder, George H. Jr. 1993. *The Censored War: American Visual Experience during World War II.* New Haven: Yale University Press.

Rohde, Stephen F. 1991. "Campus Speech Codes: Politically Correct, Constitutionally Wrong." *Los Angeles Lawyer* 23 (December).

Roiphe, Katie. 1994. *The Morning After: Sex, Fear, and Feminism.* Boston: Little, Brown.

Rollins, Ed, with Tom DeFrank. 1996. *Bare Knuckles and Back Rooms: My Life in American Politics.* New York: Broadway Books.

Rose, Douglas D., ed. 1992. *The Emergence of David Duke and the Politics of Race.* Chapel Hill: University of North Carolina Press.

Rose, Mark. 1993. *Authors and Owners: The Invention of Copyright.* Cambridge: Harvard University Press.

Rosen, Jeffrey. 1995. "Cheap Speech." *New Yorker* 75 (August 7).

Rosenblatt, Roger. 1994. "Their Finest Minute." *New York Times Magazine* 22 (July 3).

Roth, Philip. 1959. *Goodbye, Columbus.* New York: Random House.

Rubin, Gayle. 1984. "Thinking Sex: Notes for a Radical Theory of the Politics of Sexuality." In Carole S. Vance, ed., *Pleasure and Danger: Exploring Female Sexuality.* Boston: Routledge & Kegan Paul.

Rubin, William, Hélène Seckel, and Judith Cousins. 1995. *Les Demoiselles d'Avignon.* New York: Museum of Modern Art and Harry N. Abrams.

Rush, Gary B. 1967. "Status Consistency and Right-Wing Extremism." 32 *American Sociological Review* 86.

Rushdie, Salman. 1988. *The Satanic Verses.* New York: Viking.

———. 1991. "1,000 Days in a Balloon." *New York Times* B8 (December 12).

———. 1992. *Imaginary Homelands: Essays and Criticism, 1981–1991.* London: Granta Books.

———. 1993. "Reply." In Steve MacDonogh in association with Article 19, eds., *The Rushdie Letters: Freedom to Speak, Freedom to Write.* Lincoln: University of Nebraska Press; Dingle, County Kerry, Ireland: Brandon Book Publishers.

———. 1996. *The Moor's Last Sigh.* New York: Pantheon.

Rushton, J. Philippe. 1994. *Race, Evolution, and Behavior: A Life History Perspective.* New Brunswick, N.J.: Transaction Publishers.

Ruskkoff, Douglas. 1994. *Media Virus! Hidden Agendas in Popular Culture.* New York: Ballantine Books.

Russell, Diana E. H., with Laura J. Lederer. 1980. "Questions We Get Asked Most Often." In Laura J. Lederer, ed., *Take Back the Night: Women on Pornography.* New York: William Morrow.

Rutherford, Jonathan. 1990. "A Place Called Home: Identity and the Cultural Politics of Difference." In Jonathan Rutherford, ed., *Identity: Community, Culture, Difference.* London: Lawrence & Wishart.

Ruthven, Malise. 1990. *A Satanic Affair: Salman Rushdie and the Rage of Islam.* London: Chatto & Windus.

Ryan, Joan. 1995. *Little Girls in Pretty Boxes.* New York: Doubleday.

Ryan, Michael. 1995. *Secret Life: An Autobiography.* New York: Pantheon.

Saadi, Nourredine. 1994. "The Hole Left by God." In *For Rushdie: Essays by Arab and Muslim Writers in Defense of Free Speech.* New York: George Braziller.

Sabato, Larry, and Glenn R. Simpson. 1996. *Dirty Little Secrets: The Persistence of Corruption in American Politics.* New York: Times Books.

Sacks, David O., and Peter A. Thiel. 1995. *The Diversity Myth: "Multiculturalism" and the Politics of Intolerance at Stanford.* Oakland, Calif.: Independent Institute.

Sacks, Oliver. 1989. *Seeing Voices: A Journey into the World of the Deaf.* Berkeley: University of California Press.

———. 1995. *An Anthropologist on Mars.* New York: Knopf.

Safire, William. 1991. "Linguistically Correct." *New York Times Magazine* 18 (May 5).

Santiago, Danny. 1983. *Famous All over Town.* New York: Simon & Schuster.

Saunders, David. 1992. *Authorship and Copyright.* New York: Routledge.

Schauer, Frederick. 1987. "Causation Theory and the Causes of Sexual Violence." 1987 *American Bar Foundation Research Journal* 737.

Schechter, Harold. 1994. *Depraved: The Shocking True Story of America's First Serial Killer.* New York: Pocket Books.

Scheerer, Sebastian. 1978. "The New Dutch and German Drug Laws: Social and Political Conditions for Criminalization and Decriminalization." 12 *Law & Society Review* 585.

Scheler, Max. 1961. *Ressentiment.* Glencoe, Ill.: Free Press.

Schell, Orville. 1994. *Mandate of Heaven: A New Generation of Entrepreneurs, Dissidents, Bohemians, and Technocrats Lays Claim to China's Future.* New York: Simon & Schuster.

Schlenker, Barry R., and Bruce W. Darby. 1981. "The Use of Apologies in Social Predicaments." 44 *Social Psychological Quarterly* 271.

Schlesinger, Arthur M. Jr. 1992. *The Disuniting of America.* New York: W. W. Norton.

Schmidt, Leigh Eric. 1995. *Consumer Rites: The Buying and Selling of American Holidays.* Princeton: Princeton University Press.

Schuck, Peter H. 1987. *Agent Orange on Trial: Mass Toxic Disasters in the Courts.* Cambridge: Harvard University Press.

Schur, Edwin. 1980. *The Politics of Deviance: Stigma Contests and the Uses of Power.* Englewood Cliffs, N.J.: Prentice Hall.

Schwartz, Marilyn, and the Task Force on Bias-Free Language of the Association of American University Presses. 1995. *Guidelines for Bias-Free Writing.* Bloomington: Indiana University Press.

Scott, Joan Wallach. 1992. "The Campaign against Political Correctness: What's Really at Stake." 54 *Radical History Review* 59.

Scott, Marvin B., and Stanford M. Lyman. 1968. "Accounts." 33 *American Sociological Review* 46.

Seabrook, John. 1994. "My First Flame." *New Yorker* 70 (June 6).

Sennett, Richard, and Jonathan Cobb. 1972. *The Hidden Injuries of Class.* New York: Random House.

Shapiro, Allan E. 1976. "Law in the Kibbutz: A Reappraisal." 10 *Law & Society Review* 587.

Shea, Virginia. 1994. *Netiquette.* San Francisco: Albion Books.

Sheehan, Thomas. 1993. "A Normal Nazi." 40 (1–2) *New York Review of Books* 30 (January 14).

Sheff, David. 1993. *Game Over: How Nintendo Zapped an American Industry, Captured Your Dollars, and Enslaved Your Children.* New York: Random House.

Sheldon, Michael. 1994. *Graham Greene: The Enemy Within.* New York: Random House.

Shell, Marc. 1993. "Babel in America; or, The Politics of Language Diversity in the United States." 20 *Critical Inquiry* 103.

Shepard, Richard F. 1996. *The Paper's Papers: A Reporter's Journey through the Archives of the New York Times.* New York: Times Books.

Sherry, Norman. 1989. *The Life of Graham Greene*. Vol. 1, 1939–1955. New York: Viking.

Signorile, Michelangelo. 1993. *Queer in America: Sex, the Media, and the Closets of Power*. New York: Random House.

Silberman, Neal. 1993. *"A Prophet from Amongst You": The Life of Yigael Yadin: Soldier, Scholar, and Mythmaker of Modern Israel*. New York: Addison-Wesley.

Simon, Jonathan. 1994. "In the Place of the Parent: Risk Management and the Government of Campus Life." 3 *Social and Legal Studies* 15.

Singer, Mark. 1992. "The Prisoner and the Politician." *New Yorker* 108 (October 5).

Slatalla, Michelle, and Joshua Quittner. 1994. *Masters of Deception: The Gang That Ruled Cyberspace*. New York: HarperCollins.

Smith, Dinitia. 1994. "R. Emmett Tyrell Jr." *New York Times Magazine* 14 (July 3).

Smolla, Rodney A. 1992. *Free Speech in an Open Society*. New York: Knopf.

Sontag, Susan. 1982. "The Pornographic Imagination." In *A Susan Sontag Reader*. New York: Farrar Straus & Giroux.

Sowell, Thomas. 1993. *Inside American Education: The Decline, the Deception, the Dogmas*. New York: Free Press.

Spector, Malcolm, and John Kitsuse. 1977. *Constructing Social Problems*. Menlo Park, Calif.: Cummings.

Spender, Stephen. 1994. *World within World*. Rev. ed. New York: St. Martin's Press.

———. 1997. *Spender's Poetry*. New York: Viking.

Spivak, Gayatri Chakravorty. 1989. "Reading *The Satanic Verses*." 2 *Public Culture* 79.

———. 1990. "Reading *The Satanic Verses*." 11 *Third Text* 41.

Squires, James D. 1993. *Read All about It! The Corporate Takeover of America's Newspapers*. New York: Times Books.

Stan, Adele M., ed. 1995. *Debating Sexual Correctness: Pornography, Sexual Harassment, Date Rape, and the Politics of Sexual Equality*. New York: Delta.

Steele, Lisa. 1985. "A Capital Idea: Gendering in the Mass Media." In Varda Burstyn, ed., *Women against Censorship*. Vancouver: Douglas & McIntyre.

Steele, Valerie. 1995. *Fetish: Fashion, Sex, and Power*. New York: Oxford University Press.

Steinem, Gloria. 1980. "Erotica and Pornography: A Clear and Present Difference." In Laura J. Lederer, ed., *Take Back the Night: Women on Pornography*. New York: William Morrow.

Steiner, Wendy. 1995. *The Scandal of Pleasure: Art in an Age of Fundamentalism*. Chicago: University of Chicago Press.

Stempel, Tom. 1993. *Storytellers to the Nation: A History of American Television Writing*. New York: Continuum.

Stenbuck, Jack, ed. 1995. *Typewriter Battalion: Dramatic Front-Line Dispatches from World War II*. New York: William Morrow.

Sterling, Bruce. 1992. *The Hacker Crackdown: Law and Disorder on the Electronic Frontier*. New York: Bantam Books.

Stern, Gerald M. 1977. *The Buffalo Creek Disaster.* New York: Vintage.

Stern, Howard. 1993. *Private Parts.* New York: Simon & Schuster.

Sternhell, Zeev. 1986. *Neither Right nor Left: Fascist Ideology in France.* Trans. David Maisel. Berkeley: University of California Press.

Stewart, Susan. 1991. *Crimes of Writing: Problems in the Containment of Representation.* New York: Oxford University Press.

Stockdale, Jan. 1995. "How Do Children View TV?" 7 (1) *LSE Magazine* 13 (summer).

Stoller, Robert J. 1991. *Porn: Myths for the Twentieth Century.* New Haven: Yale University Press.

Stone, Allucquère Rosanne. 1995. *The War of Desire and Technology at the Close of the Mechanical Age.* Cambridge: MIT Press.

Stone, Gregory, and William H. Form. 1953. "Instabilities in Status: The Problem of Hierarchy in the Community Study of Status Arrangements." 18 *American Sociological Review* 149.

Strossen, Nadine. 1995. *Defending Pornography: Free Speech, Sex, and the Fight for Women's Rights.* New York: Scribner's.

Styron, William. 1967. *The Confessions of Nat Turner.* New York: Random House.

Sunstein, Cass R. 1993. *Democracy and the Problem of Free Speech.* New York: Free Press.

Sweetman, David. 1993. *Mary Renault: A Biography.* New York: Harcourt Brace.

Sykes, Charles. 1988. *ProfScam: Professors and the Demise of Higher Education.* Washington, D.C.: Regnery Gateway.

———. 1990. *The Hollow Men: Politics and Corruption in Higher Education.* Washington, D.C.: Regnery Gateway.

———. 1992. *A Nation of Victims: The Decay of American Character.* New York: St. Martin's Press.

Tannen, Deborah. 1986. *That's Not What I Meant! How Conversational Styles Make or Break Your Relations with Others.* New York: William Morrow.

———. 1990. *You Just Don't Understand! Women and Men in Conversation.* New York: William Morrow.

———. 1994. *Talking from 9 to 5.* New York: William Morrow.

Tanner, Laura E. 1994. *Intimate Violence: Reading Rape and Torture in Twentieth Century Fiction.* Bloomington: Indiana University Press.

Tatalovich, Raymond. 1995. *Nativism Reborn? The Official English Language Movement and the American States.* Lexington: University of Kentucky Press.

Tatar, Maria. 1992. *Off with Their Heads! Fairy Tales and the Culture of Childhood.* Princeton: Princeton University Press.

Tavuchis, Nicholas. 1991. *Mea Culpa: A Sociology of Apology and Reconciliation.* Stanford, Calif.: Stanford University Press.

Teff, Harvey, and Colin Munro. 1976. *Thalidomide: The Legal Aftermath.* Westmead, England: Saxon House.

Thomas, Benjamin P. 1952. *Abraham Lincoln: A Biography.* New York: Knopf.

Thwaite, Anthony, ed. 1993. *Selected Letters of Philip Larkin, 1940–1985.* London: Faber & Faber.

Tierney, Kathleen. 1982. "The Battered Women's Movement and the Creation of the Wife Beating Problem." 29 *Social Problems* 207.

Timberlake, James H. 1966. *Prohibition and the Progressive Movement, 1900–1920.* Cambridge: Harvard University Press.

Tisdale, Sallie. 1994. *Talk Dirty to Me: An Intimate Philosophy of Sex.* New York: Doubleday.

Titmuss, Richard M. 1972. *The Gift Relationship.* New York: Vintage.

Toobin, Jeffrey. 1994. "X-Rated." *New Yorker* 70 (October 3).

Tracey, Michael, and David E. Morrison. 1979. *Whitehouse.* London: Macmillan.

Treacy, Michael, and Fred Wiersema. 1995. *The Discipline of Market Leaders.* Reading, Mass.: Addison-Wesley.

Trillin, Calvin. 1994. "Drawing the Line." *New Yorker* 50 (December 12).

Trow, Martin. 1958. "Small Businessmen, Political Tolerance, and Support for McCarthy." 64 *American Journal of Sociology* 270.

Troyer, Ronald J. 1989. "The Surprising Resurgence of the Smoking Problem." In Joel Best, ed., *Images of Issues: Typifying Contemporary Social Problems.* New York: Aldine de Gruyter.

Trump, Ivana. 1994. *For Love Alone.* New York: Paper Books.

Turkle, Sherry. 1995. *Life on the Screen: Identity in the Age of the Internet.* New York: Simon & Schuster.

Turner, Patricia A. 1994. *Ceramic Uncles and Celluloid Mammies: Black Images and Their Influence on Culture.* New York: Archer Books.

Tyrell, R. Emmett Jr. 1992. *The Conservative Crack-Up.* New York: Simon & Schuster.

Underwood, Doug. 1995. *When MBAs Rule the Newsroom: How the Marketers and Managers Are Reshaping Today's Media.* New York: Columbia University Press.

United Church of Christ. 1995. *The New Century Hymnal.* Cleveland: Pilgrim Press.

Updike, John. 1994. *Brazil.* New York: Knopf.

Upham, Frank K. 1987. *Law and Social Change in Postwar Japan.* Cambridge: Harvard University Press.

Vallicrev, Pierre. 1971. *White Niggers of America.* Trans. Joan Pinkham. Toronto: McClelland & Stewart.

Vance, Carole S., ed. 1984. *Pleasure and Danger: Exploring Female Sexuality.* Proceedings of the Scholar and Feminist Conference IX, "Toward a Politics of Sexuality," Barnard College, April 1982. Boston: Routledge & Kegan Paul.

van Dijk, Teun A. 1987. *Communicating Racism: Ethnic Prejudice in Thought and Talk.* Newbury Park, Calif.: Sage.

Veblen, Thorstein. 1979. *The Theory of the Leisure Class.* New York: Penguin.

Vidal, Gore. 1992. *Live from Golgotha.* New York: Random House.

Vidal-Naquet, Pierre. 1993. *Assassins of Memory: Essays on the Denial of the Holocaust.* Trans. Jeffrey Mehlman. New York: Columbia University Press.

Viereck, Peter. 1955. "The Revolt against the Elite." In Daniel Bell, ed., *The New American Right.* New York: Criterion.

Vizzard, Jack. 1970. *See No Evil: Life inside a Hollywood Censor.* New York: Simon & Schuster.

Vlad, John Michael. 1993. *Back of the Big House: The Architecture of Plantation Slavery.* Chapel Hill: University of North Carolina Press.

Volokh, Eugene. 1992. "Freedom of Speech and Workplace Harassment." 39 *UCLA Law Review* 1791.

Wade, Nicholas. 1972. "Creationists and Evolutionists: Confrontation in California." 178 *Science* 724.

Wagatsuma, Hiroshi, and Arthur Rosett. 1986. "The Implications of Apology: Law and Culture in Japan and the United States." 20 *Law & Society Review* 461.

Walker, Alice. 1996. *The Same River Twice: Honoring the Difficult: A Meditation on Life, Spirit, Art, and the Making of the Film* The Color Purple *Ten Years Later.* New York: Scribner.

Walker, Samuel. 1994. *Hate Speech: The History of an American Controversy.* Lincoln: University of Nebraska Press.

Wallace, Anthony F. C. 1956. "Revitalization Movements." 58 *American Anthropologist* 264.

Wallis, Roy. 1976. "Moral Indignation and the Media: An Analysis of NVALA." 10 *Sociology* 271.

———. 1977. "A Critique of the Theory of Moral Crusades as Status Defence." 1 *Scottish Journal of Sociology* 195.

———. 1979. *Salvation and Protest: Studies of Social and Religious Movements.* New York: St. Martin's Press.

Wallis, Roy, and Richard Bland. 1979. "Purity in Danger: A Survey of Participants in a Moral-Crusade Rally." 30 *British Journal of Sociology* 188.

Walsh, Frank. 1996. *Sin and Censorship: The Catholic Church and the Motion Picture Industry.* New Haven: Yale University Press.

Waltman, Jerold. 1991. "Communities in Conflict: The School Prayer in West Germany, the United States, and Canada." 6 *Canadian Journal of Law and Society* 27.

Warner, Kenneth E., Linda M. Goldenhar, and Catherine G. McLaughlin. 1992. "Cigarette Advertising and Magazine Coverage of the Hazards of Smoking: A Statistical Analysis." 326 *New England Journal of Medicine* 305.

Warner, Marina. 1995. *Six Myths of Our Time: Little Angels, Little Monsters, Beautiful Beasts, and More.* New York: Vintage Books.

Watkins, Mel. 1994. *On the Real Side: Laughing, Lying, and Signifying: The Underground Tradition of African-American Humor That Transformed American Culture, from Slavery to Richard Pryor.* New York: Simon & Schuster.

Wattenberg, Ben J. 1995. *Values Matter Most: How Republicans or Democrats or a Third Party Can Win and Renew the American Way of Life.* New York: Free Press.

Weaver, Mary Anne. 1994. "A Fugitive from Injustice." *New Yorker* 48 (September 12).

Webb, George E. 1995. *The Evolution Controversy in America.* Lexington: University of Kentucky Press.

Weber, Max. 1978. *Economy and Society.* 2 vols. Ed. Guenther Ross and Clauss Wittich. Berkeley: University of California Press.

Webster, Richard. 1990. *A Brief History of Blasphemy.* Southwold, England: Orwell Press.

Weldon, Fay. 1992. *Life Force.* New York: Viking.

Wellesley College Center for Research on Women. 1992. *How Schools Shortchange Girls: The A.A.U.W. Report.* Washington, D.C.: AAUW Education Foundation and National Education Association.

Wertham, Fredric. 1954. *Seduction of the Innocent.* New York: Rinehart.

Westby, David L., and Richard G. Braungart. 1970. "The Alienation of Generations and Status Politics: Alternative Explanations of Student Political Activism." In Robert S. Siegel, ed., *Learning about Politics.* New York: Random House.

Whitehouse, Mary. 1993. *Quite Contrary: An Autobiography.* London: Sidgwick & Jackson.

Whiteside, Thomas. 1979. *The Pendulum and the Toxic Cloud.* New Haven: Yale University Press.

Whittle, J., J. Conigliaro, C. B. Good, and R. P. Lofgren. 1993. "Racial Differences in the Use of Invasive Cardiovascular Procedures in the Department of Veterans Affairs Medical System." 329 *New England Journal of Medicine* 621.

Wiener, Jon. 1996. "The Cigarette Papers." *Nation* 11 (January 1).

Wilkes, Michael S., Bruce Doblin, and Martin Shapiro. 1992. "Pharmaceutical Advertisements in Leading Medical Journals: Experts' Assessments." 116 *Annals of Internal Medicine* 912.

Williams, Jeffrey. 1994. *PC Wars: Politics and Correctness in the Academy.* New York: Routledge.

Williams, Linda. 1989. *Hard Core.* Berkeley: University of California Press.

Williams, Patricia J. 1987. "Spirit-Murdering the Messenger: The Discourse of Fingerpointing as the Law's Response to Racism." 42 *University of Miami Law Review* 2128.

Wilson, A. N. 1992. *Jesus.* New York: W. W. Norton.

Wilson, John K. 1995. *The Myth of Political Correctness: The Conservative Attack on Higher Education.* Durham, N.C.: Duke University Press.

Wilson, Kenneth L., and Louis A. Zurcher Jr. 1976. "Status Inconsistency and Participation in Social Movements: An Application of Goodman's Hierarchical Modeling." 17 *Sociological Quarterly* 520.

Wilson-Bareau, Juliet, with John House and Douglas Johnson. 1993. *Manet: The Execution of Maximilian, Paintings, Politics, and Censorship.* London: National Gallery Productions; Princeton: Princeton University Press.

Winn, Marie. 1985. *The Plug-in Drug: Television, Children, and the Family.* Baltimore: Penguin.

Wolf, Naomi. 1991. *The Beauty Myth.* New York: Morrow.

Wolin, Richard, ed. 1991. *The Heidegger Controversy: A Critical Reader.* Cambridge: MIT Press.

Wolinsky, Marc, and Kenneth Sherrill, eds. 1993. *Gays and the Military: Joseph Steffan versus the United States.* Princeton: Princeton University Press.

Wood, Michael, and Michael Hughes. 1984. "The Moral Basis of Moral Reform: Status Discontent vs. Culture and Socialization as Explanations of Anti-pornography Social Movement Adherence," 49 *American Sociological Review* 86.

Woodward, C. Vann. 1991. "Freedom and the Universities." *New York Review of Books* 32 (July 18).

Woog, Dan. 1995. *School's Out: The Impact of Gay and Lesbian Issues on America's Schools.* Boston: Alyson Publications.

Yaffe, Maurice, and Edward C. Nelson, eds. 1982. *The Influence of Pornography on Behaviour.* London: Academic Press.

Yngvesson, Barbara. 1988. "Making Law at the Doorway: The Clerk, the Court, and the Construction of Community in a New England Town." 22 *Law & Society Review* 409.

——. 1993. *Virtuous Citizens, Disruptive Subjects: Order and Complaint in a New England Court.* New York: Routledge.

Young, James B. 1993. *The Texture of Memory: Holocaust Memorials and Meaning.* New Haven: Yale University Press.

Young, Marion Iris. 1990. *Justice and the Politics of Difference.* Princeton: Princeton University Press.

Zablocki, Benjamin. 1971. *The Joyful Community.* Baltimore: Penguin.

Zhou, Jian-ning, Michel A. Hofman, Louis J. G. Gooren, and Dick F. Swaab. 1995. "A Sex Difference in the Human Brain and Its Relation to Transsexuality." 378 *Nature* 68 (November 2).

Zillmann, Dolf, and Bryant Jennings. 1989. *Pornography: Research Advances and Policy Considerations.* Hillsdale, N.J.: Lawrence Erlbaum Associates.

Zurcher, Louis A. Jr., and R. George Kirkpatrick. 1976. *Citizens for Decency: Antipornography Crusades as Status Defense.* Austin: University of Texas Press.

Zurcher, Louis A. Jr., R. George Kirkpatrick, Robert G. Cushing, and Charles K. Bowman. 1971. "The Anti-pornography Campaign: A Symbolic Crusade." 19 *Social Problems* 217. Reprinted in Charles M. ViVona, ed., *The Meanings of Deviance.* New York: MSS Information, 1973.

——. 1973. "Ad Hoc Antipornography Organizations and Their Active Members: A Research Summary." 29 *Journal of Social Issues* 69.

INDEX

●●